Reading *Pomegranate Gospel* is a bit like being told that a specific Rorschach ink blot is a prophet juggling an hour glass: once the book's inspired ideas are implanted, you'll have trouble seeing the Bible any other way; in fact, you'll wonder how religious establishments got away with their interpretations for so long, considering *Pomegranate* is a hell of a lot more fun and ultimately more satisfying.

~ *Leigh Ann Weatherford*
Professor of English, Orange Coast College

Pomegranate Gospel is a gift to those of us who open the Bible every week to prepare a sermon or get ready for a Bible Study class. His unfiltered insights into the literary dimensions of the biblical stories and characters bring them to life with such energy, wit, and passion that we find ourselves challenged to discover anew what it means to seek "peace, love, and understanding."

~ *Rev. Michael H. Carrier, Pastor,*
Congregational Christian Church of Franklin, New Hampshire

Other books by Gary Hoffman:

Writeful

Adios, Strunk & White: A Handbook for the New Academic Essay
Glynis Hoffman co-author

Pomegranate Gospel

BIBLE REVIVALS FOR SECULAR TASTES

By Gary Hoffman

VERVE PRESS

Pomegranate Gospel: Bible Revivals for Secular Tastes by Gary Hoffman

ISBN-10: 0-937363-08-1   ISBN-13: 978-0-937363-08-9
Library of Congress Catalogue Number: 2015957529
Printed in the United State of America
Published by Verve Press Since 1984
     PO Box 1997, Huntington Beach, CA 92647

Cover Concept: Gary Hoffman
Cover Graphics: Karen Corriente
Page Layout: Karen Corriente

Library of Congress Cataloguing-in-Publication
Hoffman, Gary
     Pomegranate Gospel: Bible Revivals for Secular Tastes/
     Gary Hoffman p.346

ISBN-10: 0-937363-08-1   ISBN-13: 978-0-937363-08-9
1. Bible—Criticism, interpretation, etc.
2. Bible as Literature
3. Bible as Literature—Study & teaching

I. Hoffman Gary II Title
BS 511 .H644 2016   LC 2015957529
220.6 HOFFMAN

Dedicated to Bill Maher, comedic host of HBO's *Real Time*, who sees the Bible used to justify evil but now will perceive that the Bible informs a secular life.

We may pretend that we're basically moral people who make mistakes, but the whole of history proves otherwise.
    —Terry Hands

If I speak in the tongues of men and of angels, but have not love, I am a noisy gong or a clanging cymbal.
    —Paul, First Corinthians

CONTENTS

The book begins with a discussion of the hindrances that prevent reading the Bible as secular literature and offers a sketch of the various audiences for whom this book is intended. It then considers how our limited view of the Bible throughout history has inspired ideologies, events, and attitudes that range from beautiful to annoying to horrifying—yet many of which are only loosely grounded in the text. The chapter concludes with an enticing list of some of the strange, beautiful, and confounding things revealed by a close reading of the secular Bible and suggests the extent to which understanding the Bible as literature might offer true enlightenment.

A short description of the evolution of the Bible addresses the common misconception that the Bible is a non-evolving, uniform text. It segues into an explanation of two opposite versions of God and of creation in the Book of Genesis that are usually conflated into one version by other retellings: the seven-day version, placed first (but actually written around 600 years later) to "correct" the earlier Adam-and-Eve version, which appears second. One version represents God as composed, the other as temperamental. They place different emphases on morality, and offer conflicting ideas about the relationship between men and women, about humans' respect for the environment, and about the nature of fate.

A second-person point of view pays homage to Eve's innocent and then noble spirit, and traces this spirit through Ruth and Esther in their respective Biblical books. The chapter debunks the myth of the serpent as Satan and the partaking of the tree of knowledge as evil. It demonstrates the ways Ruth, a Moabite, who puts love before religion, is an extension of Eve's spirit, which will birth David's lineage. It reveals the ways Eve's spirit is further manifested in Esther, a Jewess turned

Persian queen by marrying king Ahasuerus, one of the most powerful leaders in the ancient world, giving Esther a position that allows her to use her shrewd wit to overcome evil.

4:39 "In a World of Patriarchal Power . . ." (A Trailer for Satire?)

Freed from traditional religious and cultural myths, a "Martian" observer discovers that much of the Book of Genesis is a satire on power rather than a glorification of Israel's patriarchs. The chapter's outsider point of view reveals darkly humorous scenarios about those whom God stands behind despite their immoral or violent natures: Noah, Abraham and Sarah, Isaac and Rebekah, Jacob with his sons Simeon and Levi in their handling of the rape of their sister Dinah, and Jacob's son Judah, who has sex with his own daughter-in-law Tamar. In this satiric context, the ritual of circumcision takes on a different throb than in modern religious settings.

5:49 The Straight Man and Abraham: Inaugural Humor

God is put in a new light by viewing Him in the role of a straight man as a foil to Abraham, whose overblown reactions and interruptions to God's miracles and the upcoming destruction of Sodom and Gomorrah become increasingly comedic. Genesis is packed with dark humor, as in the story of Lot and his daughters. The chapter includes a fresh interpretation of the Abraham and Isaac sacrifice story, which turns out to be more about blindness than blind faith. It also includes analysis of many artworks such as Hansellar's depiction of Lot and his daughters, and Caravaggio's, Brunelleschi's, and Ghiberti's depictions of Abraham and Isaac.

6:57 Sibling Sizzle: Child Psychology Busted

A stroke of genius in the Book of Genesis is its suggestion that the primary energizer of the human condition is a battle between rejection and jealousy—a battle dramatized in stories of parental favoritism and sibling rivalry. This chapter explores a contemporary clinical psychologist's advice on how to minimize the rejection, angst, and aggression created by sibling dynamics and demonstrates how Genesis makes such advice look optimistic, even unrealistic, next to the stories of Cain and Abel, Jacob and Esau, Rachael and Leah, and Laban and Rebekah. The chapter also considers how the use of piety weakens the initial raw depiction of sibling sizzle in the story of Joseph and his brothers.

10:143 REALLY, JESUS: SCENES FROM ACADEMIA

Four surprising, rarely considered aspects of Mark's gospel are illuminated, made more vivid by being cast as anecdotes set in modern academic settings. A professor uses one of Jesus's quotes about family to explain his commitment to studying *Moby Dick*; another professor defends her use of an offensive scene in an Ingmar Bergman film by recalling the metaphoric definition of the Holy Spirit in Mark and Luke; an art class studies a performance art piece performed by Jesus on the subject of defilement and then mimics it; and an art history professor jettisons her art history book to discuss the ways paintings of the crucifixion add to and distract from the gospel's descriptions of the event.

11:161 EPISTLE TO LUKE: CRINGES AND CHEERS

A startled writer pens a personal letter to Luke celebrating his momentous additions of parables to Mark's gospel. The writer also highlights details that make him wince: manipulative birth scenes of John the Baptist and Jesus, depictions of Jesus's youth that undermine his courage in the book of Mark. The epistle touches on Jesus's confrontation with Satan (including its later use by Dostoevsky); the complex parables of the sinful woman at Simon the Pharisee's home and the good Samaritan; Jesus's surprising, Zen-like response to ambition; stunning responses on the hypocrisy of lawyers; and ideas about wasted potential in the parable of the prodigal son and the parable of the talents. The letter notes some strong additions Luke made to Mark's tragic ending, but also recounts the ways he flubbed it.

12:179 HUMMUS IN EPHESUS: A PAGAN CONVERSATION

A dialogue between two lovers visiting Ephesus, who banter about their sexuality and identification with pagan art while discussing highlights of the books of Matthew, 1 Corinthians, and Revelation. The dialogue reveals how the Artemis of Ephesus statue ironically appears to be the prototype for the bizarre depiction of Jesus in Revelation, and underscores the fine line between idols and church sculpture. It also touches on Paul's stances on sexuality and his definitions of love, leading to speculation of Jesus's sexuality and a discussion of early church councils on Jesus's humanity. Includes the relevance of Emerson's "Divinity School Address," Flannery O'Connor, and Miguel de Unamuno to Paul.

13:211 EXISTENTIAL MENU: ECCLESIASTES, JONAH, JOB

An existentialist considers three different recipes of Biblical dread, all of which are startling in a canon where one expects a meaningful universe. The writer of Ecclesiastes poetically dismantles everything civilization holds dear—wisdom, wealth, strength, skill, being human rather than animal—showing how each is undone by irony, vanity, subterfuge, and chance, but then offers a subtle solution to this void. In the Book of Jonah, the Lord plays the "Other," scaring the hell out of Jonah, who cannot get in sync with Him, and leaving Jonah with comic angst in a more complex story than the legendary Jonah-and-the-whale myth. The Book of Job, finally, shocks readers with a deal made between God and an affable Satan. God, with the attitude of a show-off coach, is tempted into a bet with Satan and tosses him an innocent Job, as if Job's mere purpose is to come off the bench to take existential blows from Satan, the ultimate saboteur of truth.

of the House of Saul. There are glimpses into David's heart as it flips between spring fever and winter frost: his love-hate relationship with Joab; a murderous affair with Bathsheba; grief over his daughter's rape by his son, whose shame turns love to hatred; sadness over Absalom's revenge for the rape; Ahithophel's sleazy advice for Absalom to have public sex with David's concubines on a roof; and uncertainty as David relinquishes command to his son Solomon, as brutish as he is wise.

17:285 EPISTLE TO GRAPHINK: THE ILLUSTRATED JUDGES

A letter from a consultant to a graphic novel publisher advises avoiding graphic novel conventions for an edition of the Book of Judges. Because the tales in Judges employ surrealistic elements—panoramic actions zooming onto nightmarish details; leaders with quirky traits; plots with large time jumps; dream reoccurrences linking the mini-plots— the consultant suggests a series of surreal illustrations modeled on Rene Magritte's non-action, still-life paintings, ironic counterpoints to the frenetic, bloody horrors of Judges. The epistle provides an analysis of six contexts in Judges: the refrain ("And the people of Israel did what was evil in the sight of the Lord"); the gutting of Eglon by Ehud; the "heroine" Jael's staking of Sisera's brain to the ground; the defeat of the Midianites by the comically weak Gideon and insecure Lord; Jephthah's unwitting sacrifice of his daughter; and Samson, who tells the Philistines, "If you had not plowed with my heifer, you would not have found out my riddle," before going on a surreal rampage.

18:301 BRAINS-AND-BREASTS POETRY:
PROVERBS, PSALMS, SONG OF SOLOMON

This is an analysis that covers the strengths and limitations of the poetic verses in Proverbs, which work like wisdom pills; Psalms, which bounce between the sentimental and the furiously angry; and Song of Solomon, which drip with wet-dream sexuality. To clarify the value of each of these books, the analysis considers the whirlwinds of poetic activity that build on the Bible's poetry themes centuries later: William Blake adding new fire to Proverbs; Emily Dickinson infusing air into Psalms; John Donne using dark humor and wit to pop open the sexuality of Song of Solomon.

AFTERWORD

INDEX

ART REFERENCES

PREFACE
WITH ACKNOWLEDGEMENTS

Pomegranate Gospel is the result of key moments and people in my life, and considering their contributions to the book's genesis necessitates my dropping far back in time. Most immediately the contributors include my loving wife and colleague Glynis, who, as we joke, does not let me leave the house with anything, clothes or metaphors, until she has made suggestions. Big thanks to my colleague and friend Andy Stuart, who carefully verified Biblical quotes and made very helpful editorial suggestions and corrections, including adding his musical knowledge to the Brains-and-Breasts Poetry chapter. My son, Jesse, PhD., made important suggestions for that same chapter, and my daughter Casey, PhD., child psychologist, contributed greatly to the Sizzling Sibling chapter. I cannot give enough credit to freelance editor Keely Boeving, formerly of Oxford University Press. She made abundant style suggestions and tested every inch of my logic, always respectful of my voice and purpose but pushing me to press more weight and swim extra laps. This book became stronger because she was the editor.

Stepping back further in time, this book is the result of my years of teaching literature, especially the Bible as literature, and using various books of the Bible in my Critical Thinking and Writing about Literature courses, exposing the Bible to hundreds of students who in turn forced me to consider and reconsider myriad details and implications. I am proud of so many of them for being willing to put aside their faith-based or atheistic-based assumptions to look at the Bible with a fresh eye, "as if we just found the scrolls in a desert cave today," a phrase I always use to set the classroom stage.

I would be derelict not to jump back decades further to the 1970s and '80s to give credit, because I would never have read the Bible, nor had the confidence to allow myself to read it free of decades of others' assumptions, if not for my best friend and colleague over those decades teaching at Orange Coast College, Gary Freeman. (Yes, people would mix our names up all the time as we coolly accepted comments meant for the other.) Gary had become a college English professor after a long ministry and time as a national columnist for the Church of Christ. As I followed along with his Bible as Literature class, he affirmed my reading of the Bible and my fresh look at details he felt "he had looked at for too long." This book would not exist without all those years of friendship and mutual intellectual engagement.

The development of my friendship with Gary and the interests that emerged from it stemmed from even earlier experiences. Becoming the reader and writer that led to this book is the result of studying as an undergraduate and graduate student at UCLA and USC. Those universities taught me the importance of impartiality when reading disparate texts from different time periods and with diverse aesthetics. This became crucial training for later being able to read the Bible outside of cultural and religious biases. During those years I credit my mother, a comparative literature professor, for giving me Erich Auerbach's *Mimesis*, a book that convincingly argued that a writer's perspective can be revealed through only a small blood sample of the writer's style and content, an essential belief and skill that allowed for my detecting the myriad voices and points of view in the Bible.

However, it would be unjust to suggest only the English major prepared me for this book. Before English studies there was my groundbreaking freshman year UC Berkeley, where first of all as an architecture student, I learned that creation does not come from fantasies or clichés but from solving problems, and that forms follow function, finally manifest in this book in the use of different writing strategies for different chapters depending on which more effectively clarifies a Biblical storytelling technique or theme. In studying architecture, I also learned the importance of interdisciplinary tools, likewise evidenced in this book in the belief that visual artists contribute to Biblical arguments. These realizations dovetailed with the intellectual ferment at UC Berkeley in the mid-1960s, strengthening my personal resolve that everything is always open to new consideration and questioning: design, politics, education, relationships, religion, the Bible.

And of course, I did not enter the university as a blank slate. My formative teenage years prepared me not only for college studies in art, architecture, and literature, but also developed my religious and secular ideas. At Pasadena High School, my friend Michael Carrier and I would make Kiwanis Key Club-sponsored visits to different houses of worship every weekend—Buddhist and Jewish temples, a Mormon and Catholic Church, Christian Science and other Protestant churches (mosques in Istanbul and Morocco would come much later in life)—these experiences nurturing our religious tolerance. I noticed worshippers were no more happy or unhappy in one house of worship than another. Religious affiliation seemed arbitrary. To get out of our home on school nights, Michael and I and girlfriends also went to Young Life for Christ sing-alongs, where follow-up sermons centered on Jesus as a magic man who bumped our egos (represented by a stick figure of a person) out of psychic thrones (represented by a stick-figure chair). The simplistic explanations provoked us to pull the facilitator's leg with what later became Bart-Simpson questions: "If your leg is amputated, later, when you die and go to heaven, is the leg there waiting for you?" We were skeptical teenagers and I was disturbed by attempts to use the name "Jesus" as a password that allowed easy access into mindless conformity. After high school and Princeton Theological Seminary, Michael became a Presbyterian minister. We took different routes to finally arrive at more thoughtful views of the Bible.

However, what prepares us for all our future paths more than our childhood experiences? I am obliged to slide back into my childhood in El Paso, Texas, a city that exposed me to many different religions and cultures and contributed to my strong belief in individual religious thought and a gradual rejection of any one group's interpretation of God. El Paso was over 50 percent Mexican, where Reform Jews also picked godparents—traditional sponsors of Christian baptism—for future guardians. El Paso was where my live-in Mexican nanny amused my brother and me with mystical Catholic morality manifest in 1950s horror comic books, trying to scare us into being good by showing us that if we lied, we would end up like the woman whose tongue turned into a snake. It was a home where Christmas tree bubblers competed with Menorah candles. It was a city where a magical choir transformed harsh-sounding Hebrew prayers into operatic scores at a Jewish temple one day and the next could be found singing at the Episcopal Church, a church where on yet another day I went for cotillion. To live a Texan childhood was to live a life dominated by the ritual of footfall, especially GRA-Y, YMCA, hard-hitting tackle starting at eight years old, coached by young dads decked in trench coats and cowboy hats who unknowingly competed with (and pretty much won out against) a college professor rabbi decked out in silky black robes on Saturday morning, football game day. Then, on Sundays, many of my friends' church day, I was left breathless, taken in by the brutal ballet conducted by the toreros of Juarez in their *trajas de luces*. As a child, El Paso was a swimming, tennis, baseball, boxing, art-class world where all my friends from different ethnic backgrounds and religions—Arabs, Armenians, Catholics, Episcopalians, Jews, Methodists, Mexicans, cowboys and cowgirls—all smiling in Levi jeans, shuffled from event to event in the haze of El Paso heat. It was a time of laughter where there was no space for strict catechism.

There was a god, though, always prodding me. It was the god of the West Texas Chihuahua Desert, a harsh plateau where I could see a dirt storm coming from miles away, finally catching me and packing my ears and nose with whirlwinds of sand and demonstrating how much of life was anticipation followed by dramatic impact. The wind talked all the time, especially when, from the age of five to fifteen, my weekly ritual was loping and then galloping across that desert, my dad chasing after me as we headed down dry riverbeds. The desert was a natural place to give loose reins to both a horse and to the imagination, where tales from anywhere had credibility. Blink back then and I would see Poncho Villa's *villistas* riding along the Rio Grande, their saddle *latigos* worn to a frazzle, their *conchos* gleaming in the Texan sun; blink later and I saw David's sword-swinging soldiers ride hard to collect enemy foreskins to appease Saul or David scampering across the barren Desert of Ziph to escape Saul's tortured discontentment. The desert became the proper stage for human drama, a place where the human psyche finds little shade for protection, where ideas about God really do speak out of the whirlwind and where the dust does not just coat the disciples' sandals but settles on everything everywhere.

Pomegranate
Gospel

1:17

JUST PITH
AN INTRODUCTION

Most contemporary readers in the Western world, let alone the whole world, would be shocked to find how much of the Bible is cleverly written to be humorous, satirical, psychologically insightful, and morally complex, while at the same time, within the same cover, other esteemed parts lack these elements and are poorly written or improperly executed. For a variety of reasons, most readers have never been encouraged to consider the Bible as anything other than an inflexible religious text, with little to offer in the way of literary merit, and as a result, it finds little readership outside of explicitly religious Judeo-Christian circles. Yet the Bible is an extraordinarily rich text, with much to yield for secular and spiritual readers alike.

Pomegranate Gospel: Bible Revivals for Secular Tastes seeks to revitalize the Bible for all readers by revealing and interpreting the book's humor and satire, pointing out its various philosophies on God and humans, and revealing its psychological, aesthetic, and literary relevance to a modern secular world. The book combines close reading with sped-up retellings to bring out both controversial weaknesses (such as the callowness found in the Gospel of John) and unexpected strengths (like the powerful, dark satire in the Book of Genesis). Many readers intuit these Biblical truths could be true, but have not been encouraged to pursue or articulate this awareness.

It is easy to understand why. In fact, a host of factors limit readers from understanding the Bible as secular literature: preconceived, simplified stories created by Sunday school coloring books and Hollywood films that shape our understanding of the Bible from an early age; beliefs that sacred texts exclude humor, wit, and psychological insight; assumptions that the Bible was written by one author (usually God or Moses), rendering readers tone deaf to changes in point of view; centuries of details inserted into various stories to correct or legitimize objectionable or ambiguous ideas; mash-ups of different versions of the same story that blur the strength of the primary story; the need for many to take miracles as literal, not affording them the metaphorical validity that would otherwise be given to them in a Greek or Zuni myth.

Pomegranate Gospel is an attempt to buff out these obstacles to release the brilliance of the Bible, a process similar to an archaeologist chiseling and brushing off an ancient Byzantine wall, covered by plaster and clumsy restorations, to reveal stunning, forgotten mosaics. This book offers a unique discussion on the Bible as a work of literature, both fantastic and flawed. While innumerable books have attempted to plumb the depths of this sacred text, few have approached it as a literary work; more common are books devoted to establishing historical Biblical accuracy (focused on archaeological excavations rather than literary elements), academic textbooks and guides (reference books committed to a neutered committee voice that flat-lines the Bible's strengths and weaknesses), scholarly articles (obligated to touch on previous studies, nodding to past insights and assuming previous Biblical knowledge), or self-help religious books (heart-felt but based on cherry-picked, positive, loosely read passages).

Pomegranate Gospel, in contrast, sparks an unexpected and new discussion on the Bible that will be of interest to laypeople, atheists, writers, artists, rabbis and preachers, Bible studies, and literature classes. This book is not only for those wanting to understand Biblical references, but also for readers desiring inroads for enjoying the Bible as secular literature. It is not only for spiritual souls shunning institutionalized religion, but also for those looking to freshen Bible study classes. It not only offers material for ministers, pastors, and rabbis seeking stimulation for sermons, but for atheists underestimating the secular richness of the Bible. And in the classroom, it is not only for Biblical scholars introducing the Bible to their non-scholarly students, but also for literature teachers tired of textbook-based approaches to the Bible. We are all in need of new ways to approach the Bible, and secular and religious people alike can benefit from understanding this text as more than a staid, dusty book of religious rules and outdated stories.

An old Jewish tradition uses a pomegranate's seeds as symbols for the 613 commandments of "dos" and "don'ts" found in the Bible, mostly in four books in the Torah: Exodus, Leviticus, Numbers, and Deuteronomy. This book is a fresh bite of the pomegranate in order to taste the seeds not as symbols of finite rules, but as infinite storytelling details that variously shock, delight, and in essence, enlighten us through a re-bite of the tree of knowledge. As a means of further engaging with these ideas, this book will also touch on the work of visual artists who have taken similar bites and whose visual "commentaries" help illuminate the Bible's many layers and continuing relevance.

To give homage to the Bible's various styles and structures, every chapter of this book is a surprise, a different gift box. Some are big boxes with compressed narrations of entire Biblical books and full analysis of their subtleties; some are small jewel boxes with surprising incidents and startling insights. More importantly, writing about the Bible with one style or voice does not serve the various purposes and techniques used in the Bible itself; using chapters written from unique perspectives and styles allows *Pomegranate Gospel* to better serve the Bible's diverse authors, stories, and insights. Similarly, as a reminder that the order of the Bible's books were arranged by religious councils over centuries and that there is no sacrosanct order, the chapters here are arranged so that the Old and New Testaments get equal importance, with chapters on one testament interrupted by chapters on the other. Such an arrangement helps to show the contrast between the two, and also encourages the reader to skip around to read different chapters, mirroring the typical process most take in reading the Bible's books themselves.

The Bible has, of course, fertilized Judeo-Christian religions, with these faiths often taking the details from the Bible to create or reinforce their own rituals and legends. Such a process has, over centuries, minimized any understanding of the Bible as secular literature describing the human condition. Today, many Christians and Jews do not read the Bible, and are only familiar with passages isolated in sermons or appropriated in commercial art or film. Isolated from their literary contexts, one often swears on these misconceptions, instead of the actual details of the Bible; people name children after Biblical characters, for instance, without ever understanding those characters' often troubling, unattractive qualities.

Such a limited view of the Bible has inspired ideologies, events, and attitudes that range from beautiful to annoying to horrifying; yet many are only loosely grounded in the text, if grounded in it at all. Some such outcomes have been undeniably negative: Protestants bashing Catholic sculptures in Rouen in 1562; men practicing Leviticus's laws by marking chairs "unclean" that women sit on within seven days of their menstruation; Catholics in 1480 breaking the tracheas of Jews and Muslims from Andalusia when they didn't convert; the 785 CE mosque of Cordoba with its forest of horse-shoe arches later clogged by a Catholic chapel; knights to Nazis claiming that Jesus was not a Jew but killed by outsiders called Jews; the 2010 Virginia House of Delegates passing a law against requiring chip implants in pets by denouncing the chips as the Biblical "mark of the beast." Some of what the Bible has inspired, of course, has been beautiful: the sun streaking though Chartres Cathedral's glass depicting an apostle baptizing a new follower, both surrounded by brilliantly lit indigo-blue puzzle-pieces of glass; the celestial sounds of Handel's "Messiah" or the mystical rhythms of the Kaddish performed by a cantor. Yet most are either annoying or ambiguous: determining whether one is an orthodox Jew or a strict Lutheran based on whose vaginal canal one slides through; a preteen Jew, illiterate in Hebrew, enunciating Hebrew letters during a Bar Mitzvah; the decision to confess or not confess to a cleric hidden behind a screen; a gold necklace with a cross made out of diamonds worn by a teenager for a mega-church confirmation; Michelangelo's eighteen-year-old virgin with a thirty-three-year-old Jesus stretched over her lap in the Vatican; deciding divine intervention in a Navajo tale is mythical, but in a Biblical tale, factual; the belief that if one does not accept supernatural events as literally true, one does not have the right to talk about Biblical ideas.

On the other hand, if we were to actually establish a broad-minded, less limited view of the Bible that delved into its secular core, what we would find would undoubtedly surprise most people. This delving, too, reveals aspects of the Bible that are variously pleasing;

annoying, beautiful, and horrifying, but they also lead to what is enlightening. We find, for instance, two views of the world based on two Gods, one calmly ordered, the other furiously jealous; a spoof on legacy through progeny when a patriarch's daughters replace their charbroiled suitors with their drunken dad's erection; a strike at kingly privilege when a lustful David kills a woman's husband by placing him on the frontline of a bloody battle; gospels that seduce with the sentimentality of Jesus's infancy and one that avoids it to strengthen his teachings; a probably bisexual David's relationship with Jonathan as the embodiment of political expediency; God punishing a Pharaoh for adultery even though a disingenuous Sarah tricked him to "go into" her, all to Abraham's benefit; a Jewish queen's combination of ego and principle giving her wits to control her powerful Persian-king husband, starting with a command to kill enemy eunuchs and ending with saving Jewish Persians; Jonah's existential crisis when the Lord asks him to deliver a message that he could care less about; a parody of ritual when the God of Exodus concocts obsessive-compulsive-like schemes; Jesus pulling the leg of those who hate him; a spoof on ritual hospitality when Lot offers a crowd of rapists his virgin daughters to protect handsome angel houseguests from being sodomized; caveman-like, jaw-bone-swinging killer Samson surprising the reader with a clever sexual innuendo about his wife; a sisterly baby-cook-off competition (who can get the most, the fastest) between Leah and Rachel; God giving a bored Satan license to ruin the faith of a "blameless and upright man" who then suffers not only from Satan's stings but his friends' negative assumptions; a judge of Israel not foreseeing he is giving up his daughter's life to have God always make him a winner; Saul endangering David by demanding a wedding present of one hundred enemy foreskins, and a hidden David snipping a piece of Saul's robe while he craps in a cave; Moses getting his jollies by raising and lowering his magic staff in rapid-fire succession to stop-start, start-stop hectic battle movements; Jesus forcing a rethinking of morality through classical rhetoric—"He who is faithful in a very little is faithful also in much; and he who is dishonest in very little is dishonest also in much."

They are surprising, shocking, appalling, hilarious—completely unlike the stories of the Bible we thought we knew. Moral priorities and ethical confrontations, satires and spoofs, psychological insight and tragedy. Enlightenment. This, ultimately, is what we find when we crack into the Bible's secular pith. The seeds are there. Bite.

2:23

PICK YOUR GOD
CONTENT OR BENT

We pick up the Bible (either Hebrew or Christian) and assume it is an eternally fixed text. One Bible. One God. We forget that oral storytellers and reporters have made millennia worth of changes to the Bible—sometimes borrowing from older stories such as the Babylonian epic of Gilgamesh, or retelling their own stories such as in the gospels, whereby some stories were lost, degraded, or improved. We also forget that when it comes to the early stories of the Old Testament, it was not until much later that storytellers began to record those oral accounts on papyrus, once again improving and embellishing some, weakening others—a complex evolution. We forget that once they were written, these stories met with many different fates: some were destroyed, others still hidden in caves, some finalized in Aramaic, many in ancient Hebrew, others in Greek, and then into Latin.

Throughout history, groups have been understandably nervous about taking out older versions of Bible stories as they discovered or wrote new versions; so sometimes, as we will see in chapters that follow, they included both. Sometimes religious groups decided to leave whole chunks out, such as the various Apocrypha—legends, didactic tracts, "historical" accounts, additions to existing stories—bounced in and out of the Bible since 450 CE (Common Era, a substitute for AD, Anno Domini, the year Christ is born) until the present. Nothing in the present text reminds us that the Gospel of Thomas—a list of sayings and parables by Jesus with no narrative, no mention of the crucifixion or resurrection—was thrown out of the canon, perhaps by the Bishop of Athanasius who considered the Thomas gospel heresy, as it presented Jesus too much as a human prophet, not a god. The bishop's critic, Arius, had argued at the Council of Nicaea in 325 CE that because there was a time when Jesus, not yet born, did not yet exist, he could not be co-eternal with God—that is to say, that he could not have existed before the Genesis of the world. It was a controversial claim that would have completely altered the shape of Christianity. Arius lost out on a vote. The other bishops wanted Jesus to be clearly perceived as an eternal god, not so much a mortal.

However, over a thousand years later, the Gospel of Thomas had its spirit resurrected by Thomas Jefferson in his revision of the gospels, in which Jefferson cut out all the miracles and resurrections. He read this edited version, *The Life and Morals of Jesus of Nazareth*, every morning and night for his own comfort and shared it with a few friends; it was never widely published but a copy exists at the Smithsonian Library. And it is not just Thomas who lost out; there are other books, only just discovered in 1945 from the Nag Hammadi manuscripts, thirteen ancient codices found in Egypt, all pertinent to the New Testament, perhaps intentionally destroyed to simplify discussions about the canon. Later the Gospel of Mary Magdalena and Gospel of Judas were discovered in Egypt. Should they be included? The gospels were written at least fifty years after his death. Does it matter? Today we read the Bible based on choices made at councils long ago that some day might be unmade.

As we read and discuss the Bible, we are seldom reminded that William Tyndale created the first English translation (published in pieces and at various points between 1526 and 1537), and that Tyndale, like most translators, took much poetic license that most of us accept today under the heading of The English Bible. Unless we know Hebrew or Greek, we cannot know what belongs to Tyndale. He gave the Bible its majestic tone, highlighted later in the King James Bible. According to a *New York Times* editorial on the showing of Tyndale's Bible at the New York Public Library, it was Tyndale who first used the words "Jehovah," "scapegoat," "Am I my brother's keeper?" and "Let my people go."[1] Perhaps some translators might have thought these additions to be presumptuous, but in 1526, these choices did not create the most anger; the blasphemy was his changing the Bible from Latin, the language of priests, to English, thereby making the Bible accessible to common folks. This evolutionary step was enough to see Tyndale burnt at the stake.

At divinity school, we would find that the Greek and Hebrew

versions of the Bible have much to offer, but most of us pick up a Bible based on Tyndale's version and later revised as the King James version of 1611 (a committee project headed by Lancelot Andrewes, who is also credited with much of the writing). The King James Bible, in turn, has been modernized into newer versions that maintain the original flavor but with a more modern vernacular. The one I will quote from is the Revised Standard Bible, which claims to have been "translated from the original tongues being the version set forth A.D.1611 revised A.D. 1881–1885 and A.D. 1901 compared with the most ancient authorities and revised A.D. 1946–1952."

Many would rather not think of the Bible as a result of literary evolution and wish there was a definitive original version, but even if such a text could exist, would it give us a more enlightened collection of literature than what we have now, or would much of it be merely a good rough draft? Just as we are all part of a centuries-old biological and cultural genealogy, one that at different points might include criminals, at other points, saints, so too are the parts of the Bible. Every part has had its own evolution and when we open the Bible, we find parts that are memorably crafted and other parts insanely boring, some parts insightful and some shallow, some folksy, some historical, some primarily metaphorical.

And yet it is not merely the Bible's different styles that defy expectation, but our most basic expectations of the contents in the Bible are upset in the first pages. We think that when we open the Bible we will see one version of God. All our lives we have been told there is only one; our Sunday school coloring books referred to only one; Jewish and Christian prayers mention only one (not including the son or holy ghost). However, no matter what translation we pick up, within the first few pages of any Bible there is a substantial, philosophical choice staring us in the face. There are two versions of God. These two Gods have two extremely different personalities, different abilities, different relationships with the environment, and they create humans in two entirely different spirits. Around 350 BCE (Before the Common, Current, or Christian Era, a substitute for BC, Before Christ) a group of scribes that scholars call the "P" writer (priestly writer), grew dissatisfied with the God created by someone who scholars refer to as the "J" writer (Jahwist writer, who uses the Hebrew YHWH for God). The J writer, of 600 BCE or earlier, had described the God who creates in the garden of Eden as more emotional and less orderly than the P writer imagined. Now, maybe 400 years later, the P writer has a different version that he or his group like better, and they stick their story with their calmer, orderly God—the one who creates the universe in seven days—in front of the older J writer's version to start Chapter 1:1 of Genesis. The J writer's God and creation story is unceremoniously pushed out of the way to a later start at Chapter 2:4. Reading the Bible as literature, we now have two different accounts of the same character, and we have a choice: which God creates a beginning that speaks more accurately to the human condition?

As we start to read the two versions, we must ask ourselves, is the world an orderly place, where humans are at the top of that order, not so concerned with moral issues, but believe their destiny is to have dominion over all other living things on earth? If we answer yes, then, as demonstrated below, we will feel that the P writer's God and creation story is correctly inserted first. Or, on the other hand, do we believe that the human condition is essentially one of straining under the dilemma of whether or not to protect our innocence at the expense of having wisdom? That it is only through the painful loss of innocence that we gain knowledge, especially of what is good and evil? That, in fact, it is our curiosity that leads us to disobey the security of the status quo as we stumble into a life that proves to be tricky, erratic, and unpredictable? If that's the case, then, as we shall see, we will wish the J writer's God and creation story had been left as the first version and that the P writer had stayed out of the way.

As we read the two stories, we may recall that our Sunday school teachers—indeed, that Western culture in general—conflate the two Gods and two stories into one. But that cannot be. In the first place, the P writer's God creates "man in our image" (Gen 1:26). (No one really knows who "our" refers to; many Christians believe it is the Trinity, but of course that is a concept in a story that comes centuries later, so more likely "us" and "our" refer to God's cherubim or are even a leftover from previous stories where there were more gods.) The P writer reinforces, "in the image of God he created him; male and female he created them" (Gen 1:26-27). But the J writer's earlier God, in contrast, "formed man of dust from the ground, and breathed into his nostrils the breath of life" (Gen 2:7). In teaching a creation myth, a story of our spiritual formation, should our children hear that they are in God's image or that they are from the dust of the earth? Do we want to foster a sense of heightened self-worth, or one of humility?

Before we make a definitive decision, we grapple with the idea that the God of the P writer, who created the earth and all living things in seven days, is not necessarily a good or bad entity, as He has no interest in creating moral dilemmas. He uses the word "good" in the way a potter says the pot he has thrown is good, or the way one says the house one built or the dinner one made is good: after creating light, God "saw that the light was good" (Gen 1:4); after gathering the land and seas "God called the dry land Earth, and the waters that were gathered together he called Seas. And God saw that it was good" (Gen 1:10); afterwards the earth brings forth trees that bear fruit and seed and "God saw that it was good" (Gen 1:12). And while He may not be good or bad, the P writer's God *is* extremely powerful, creating big-ticket items such as the sun and moon and animal species, "each according to their kind," implying an orderly variety of species and phyla. Do we want our children to see this almost Darwinian progression as the most important aspect of the human existence? Or do we want our children to know they are of humble origin, dust—the same dust we become when our lives are over? Which God should come first for our children?

And there are still more serious choices. There are two different ways man and woman is each created, each with different inferences. As described above, the P writer has God make man and woman at the same time, implying they are equal, while the J writer's God seems to give man primacy because man is made first; then God sees man is alone and needs "a helper fit for him" (Gen 2:18). Here the J writer pulls our leg, displaying a sense of humor absent in the P writer: we anticipate it will be a woman as companion, but God first thinks animals, and "formed every beast of the field and every bird of the air, and brought them to the man to see what he would call them; and whatever the man called every living creature, that was its name" (Gen 2:19). Is this a joke about the importance of husbandry to men, satire that would be missed by a child, or is this an appeal to children and their love of animals' innocence? Unlike with the P writer, the J writer's God asks man to help decide what to call the animals, like a parent involving a child in a shared project, establishing God's relationship with man as being somewhere between parental and patronizing, perhaps a set-up for being overly protective. The P writer will have nothing to do with such ambiguous parent-adult-child-animal drama and instead inserts a serious line of order, creating the animals before man, and then reduces all his creations to products for human consumption, devoid of their own spirit so common in other creation myths, as God tells the man and woman to "Be fruitful and multiply, and fill the earth and subdue it; and have dominion over the fish of the sea and over the birds of the air and over every living thing that moves upon the earth" (Gen 1:28), a final benediction that helps satisfy His sixth day of creation before resting. The P writer's God does not promote any of the reverence or sense of stewardship of nature we associate with nomadic tribes or our modern awareness that the world is getting used up at an alarming rate. Should we pick this God whose celebrates humans as dominators?

While the P writer emphasizes male-female tag-team dominance, instead the J writer senses that the relationship between men and women is more complicated. In the J version, after the animals, when a helper more "fit" for man is finally created as a woman, she is birthed from the man's rib (Gen 2:21-22), a reversal of one of women's biggest creative acts. The inference appears to be that a woman, this "flesh of [man's] flesh" (Gen 2:23) is secondary to man. That is, until the next verses. There, the J writer reveals the power the rib-birth offers women: "Therefore a man leaves his father and his mother and cleaves to his wife, and they become one flesh" (Gen 2:24), the woman trumping a man's parents, physically and spiritually. At the most primal level, which God gets it right—the one created by the P writer who shows men and women equal but without identity or passion, and with a mandate to subdue the world, or the J writer's God, who implies a more ambiguous, humorous, changing power dynamic between the sexes? We can pick our God.

This is where the P and J writers' overlapping interests with creation end, but the J writer's story continues to surprise us by introducing a world of moral dilemmas. In this regard, our expectations are busted again when, in the J writer's garden-of-Eden creation story, we find that, contrary to everything we have been told, there is no mention of a tree that is evil, or an apple, or Satan. There is a tree of the knowledge of good and evil—the two come only as a bundle; and it is a "delight to the eyes" (Gen 3:6) (if one pictures a tree with bright fruit, then perhaps it is a pomegranate since apples were probably not cultivated in the Middle East in ancient times); and there is a "subtle" (Gen 3:1) serpent, who (despite the writer of Revelation centuries later saying Satan is "the serpent of old") is not developed as a disguised Satan until a retelling of the story over 2,000 years later, most popularly retold by John Milton in *Paradise Lost*, who in addition makes him a jealous angel commanding his own armies. An entirely different production.

In the Bible, the serpent (no gender given) is never referred to as "evil"; instead, he is called "subtle," maybe because the serpent understands God's threat that Adam will die if he eats from the tree of good and evil is itself a threat based on a subtle deceit. Adam does not literally die with the first bite. One might argue that death has a more metaphorical meaning, the death of innocence (innocence does die, a result of Adam and Eve becoming wise), but God's reference to death is not nuanced at all. It is literal and threatening: "You may freely eat of every tree of the garden; but of the tree of the knowledge of good and evil you shall not eat, for in the day that you eat of it you shall die" (Gen 2:16-17). The serpent is certainly wily, opening the discussion with Eve by asking what could be a disingenuous question in order to have a pretext for talking about God's threat: "Did God say, 'You shall not eat of any tree of the garden'?" (Gen 3:1) However, contrary to popular belief, the serpent is not a liar. In fact, the serpent is brutally frank and understands the underlying psychological context: the serpent knows that the basis for God's threat is His jealousy, and informs Adam and Eve that God will be angry because "your eyes will be opened, and you will be like God, knowing good and evil" (Gen 3:5). The J writer dramatizes the idea that one cannot understand good without knowing evil, and gives us a jealous God to explain the pain that comes from knowing both and the inevitable disobedience that comes from exercising curiosity to obtain both. This is an amazing decision by the writer in depicting the ultimate basis of the human condition, a choice that emphasizes not a lesson about the obedience to patriarchy but one that highlights the most defining quality of the human spirit—our thirst for knowledge, to be spiritually and morally mature, not always understanding that the result can bring both pleasure and pain.

God's demand that Adam and Eve not eat from the tree of knowledge sounds parental, revealing a need to keep His creations innocent, but the serpent adds another motive: losing innocence brings a god-like knowledge. Having one's eyes opened, making one like God, implies that morality, knowing good and evil, is one of the most celestial forms of knowledge (and again, one that always comes with a price). Only ignorance is bliss: ignorance that our bodies are merely water bags drying up over decades, ignorance that the brain cells that fill our skull cup will turn to mush, ignorance that we have animal impulses that run out of control or sublimate into unexpected actions or thoughts, ignorance that we are discoverers who invent amazing devices that help us one moment and then kill us the next, ignorance that we are do-gooders in one breath who can turn into self-interested politicians the next. More to the point, bliss comes from our ignorance that we cannot know what good is without having been the victim, the perpetrator, or the witness of evil. When we are no longer ignorant, our naïve bliss dies.

God's punishments for Adam and Eve after they eat the fruit symbolize this death of bliss: pain in childbirth, female subservience to males, constant toil and subservience to the soil, and return to dust from which they were made (Gen 3:16-19), albeit part of a natural cycle implied when they were made. Humorously, adding to the serpent's argument that the disobedience will not result immediately in physical death, it is only when the list of punishments is over that the J writer has God remember any discussion involving death in terms of immortality. Almost as an afterthought, God has an important, nervous last-minute remembrance of death, quickly turning His attention to a second plant, the tree of life (Gen 2:9) that births immortality. This brings an urgent, protective response from God, evidenced by His panicked hustling of the curious humans out of the garden: "Then the LORD God said, 'Behold, the man has become like one of us, knowing good and evil; and now, lest he put forth his hand and take also of the tree of life, and eat, and live for ever'— therefore the LORD God sent him forth from the garden of Eden" (Gen: 3:22-23). Again, "us" could refer to God's "cherubim" (Gen 3:24) or a past pantheon of gods, or perhaps the trinity, although it was not really something on a writer's mind in 900 BCE. A surrealist would not be too far afield to think that the other entity in "us" is the "flaming sword which turned every way, to guard the way to the tree of life" (Gen 3:24), spinning as if it has a life of its own.

God's stymieing of humans from obtaining something else He has exclusive rights to—immortality—echoes the serpent's explanation of God's demand to keep humans' eyes closed to the knowledge of good and evil. This suggests that God does not block immortality so much as a punishment but as a consequence for threatening His exclusive rights. The J writer amazingly writes a creation story that focuses on the connection of moral growth, the loss of innocence, the pain that follows, and parental reactions from a God who seems protective but embodies darker impulses in the cosmos, based on the jealous nature of power that is focused on control. Because God is humanized, given base human impulses like jealousy, we are left with the idea that we are all struggling in a world dominated by the human impulse to be overprotective, controlling, and driven ultimately by envy or jealousy; left with the idea that these qualities are so powerful they are embodied in a solo god, not tempered by other gods as in the Greek pantheon; and left thinking that our nobility comes from rebellion that demands a high price. Can a resilient child absorb this story? It is surely one that can shock our inner child the rest of our lives.

3:33

WONDER WOMEN
EVE, RUTH, ESTHER

You are Eve, birthed from Adam's rib, a creation that appears to imply indebtedness to man, but there is more to the story. Adam says you are bone of his bones and flesh of his flesh, "Therefore a man leaves his father and his mother and cleaves to his wife, and they become one flesh" (Gen 2:24), so you, and those women who follow you, will trump a man's parents, pulling him away from those who birthed him, and he will come to you naked, exposed physically and emotionally, "not ashamed" (Gen 2:25). What comforting power your presence has—and not because you are different, but because in the secret past you and man are the same flesh.

In the beginning, Eve, you are innocent. Why should you doubt a serpent that says the only reason God tells you not to disobey is that "your eyes will be opened, and you will be like God, knowing good and evil" (Gen 3:5)? You would be mindless and heartless if you were not enticed by a tree that "was good for food, and that it was a delight to the eyes, and . . . was to be desired to make one wise" (Gen 3:6). Eve, are not nourishment, beauty, and wisdom reasons to live? You would be an empty shell if you did not desire these. You have no understanding that disobedience is evil, nor is it possible for you to imagine what spiritual death floods the brain when obedience trumps curiosity. You, symbolic of all women, will come to realize a life-long double bind, because your obedience—appealing to controlling men like the God who put you here; and your curiosity—appealing to free-spirited men like the god Apollo who, as the god of intellectual inquiry, music, poetry, dance, and protector of herds, was thought of as a creative force before your God was created.

And now you do something else that you'll be blamed for: you share nourishment, beauty, and knowledge with your husband. You would be selfish not to. Moments before tasting the fruit, you two were both innocent and could not have known that wisdom is the awareness of good and evil and its components: the pain of moral dilemmas, self-consciousness, self-protection, the need to cover genitals with fig leaves. And man will add the burden of shame, followed by blame (he will not take responsibility for eating from the tree of good and evil, but blame you—did not Adam say "The woman whom thou gavest to be with me, she gave me fruit of the tree, and I ate" [Gen 3:12]), and you will falter too and blame the serpent who told you the truth about your eyes opening to moral dilemma. God put you and the tree of good and evil here. Maybe He got His way. Was He a trickster?

Then hundreds of years later we meet you again, embodied in the spirit of Ruth in the Book of Ruth, she of the Moabites who did not worship Israel's God and who were often enemies of Israel. That ancient conflict does not matter because the writer of Ruth will disappear Eve's parental Hebrew God. That God will not walk in your tale's fields as he did in the garden of Eden. In place of God's commands and decisions, you and your sister Orpah will set aside Moabite culture to marry Naomi's Israeli sons, who die (Naomi telling both you and Orpah that you may return to your people since she has no husbands to offer), but since love is at your centers, Orpah with great sadness will return to her people and you will put love of a person above love of gods, telling Naomi "where you go I will go, and where you lodge I will lodge; your people shall be my people, and your God will be my God" (Ruth 1:16).

Today, Ruth, you are the Israeli woman who leaves her people to go with a Palestinian mother-in-law, the Catholic woman who walks away from her church to be with her Islamic mother-in-law, the Islamic woman who leaves her village to be with her Hindi mother-in-law. You are rare. You put love before obedience to the gods of your birth. Ruth, you are a free spirit but not a rebel, grinding away your religious bones to fertilize your new life, fluid with the sand the way the sand and water and woman merge to create a Zen wholeness centuries later in Teshigahara film *Woman of the Dunes*. Like a woman of the dunes, you know instinctively that home is a fluid notion. You will owe no allegiance to a jealous god, your entering an Israeli culture where the author of the Book of Ruth has peopled the fields with those who go about their business with no references to God, seemingly forgetting that your trickster, punishing God in the garden of Eden ever existed.

You will meet an Israeli man, Boaz, who sees your sacrifice, your humility, your satisfaction with what is gleaned, your willingness (with Naomi's cultural advice) to lie at his feet and not be tempted away by more youthful men, and so he protects you as a foreigner. Next Boaz, in your same spirit of humility, is willing to give you away to a next of kin as part of your dead husband's land, but the next of kin knows it would be unfair to take you, "lest [he] impair [his] own inheritance" (Ruth 4:6). Fate (with no trickster God to interrupt) then will allow you to stay with Boaz who "went in to" (Ruth 4:13) you, rewarding you with a baby, Obed, starting the most important lineage in Israel that will lead to David and, according to two gospels, to Jesus; however, you, keeping the spirit of gratefulness, will reward your baby to Naomi to nurse because you know you mean more "than seven sons" (Ruth 4:15) to Naomi who loves you. Love rules your story. Where is jealousy? Where are strict boundaries? Where is blame? Where are jealous gods? All were a vision of the J writer in Genesis. They find no place here.

Into the world you bring a mixed-tribe baby, a male who will be the father of Jesse who will be the father of David. Your book's writer does not know that the writers of Samuel and Kings will reveal complex secrets about David, making him less heroic and more tragic than assumed here. It does not matter. For now this is the David who unifies Israel and whose star will be a symbol of people, many of whom will forget that David derives from your ecumenical spirit, the same fire that centuries later will bring Jews and Muslims together for cross-cultural collaborations in the art and science of Moorish Spain, and will later bring an Israeli into a marriage with a Palestinian, a Catholic with a Buddhist. You do not know that religion will invent versions of God to prevent this. Ruth, you will only make rare appearances in small stories that only a few ever hear.

Then, Eve, your spirit and passion are embodied in the Book of Esther, as the soul of Esther, a Jew who lives in Persia, a foreign land watched over by Zoroastrian gods sometime between 538–333 BCE. One of the most powerful rulers of world history, the Persian king Ahasuerus (probably Xerxes), commanding an empire that expands from India to Ethiopia, is turned inside-out by your beauty, and so he will eventually cleave to you. Like the God in Eden, obedience is his power game, and on the seventh day of a banquet-binge, the king, "merry with wine" (Esther 1:10), asks his wife Vashti to join him. When she refuses his eunuch-delivered request (who knows why? Is she sick of his demands or is she just a bitch?), the king becomes irrational, believing her refusal will create a slippery slope wherein all the princes' wives will become willful, independent and bitchy (Esther 1:17); so, in every language of the empire, the king sends out couriers on weeklong journeys, to command all women to be obedient to their husband's rule. Then, you guessed it: bye-bye Vashti.

Your uncle Mordecai, who adopted you when your parents died (making you an uncle-niece team that defies traditional families), puts you forth as a replacement for Vashti, but charges you not to reveal you are Jewish. Your beauty soothes the madness of the king who immediately loves you more than all the other women, crowns you his queen, and is tamed by this emotion sweeping over him: he grants remission from taxes throughout all his lands (he can only think big) and liberally gives gifts. Like Ruth and Naomi, your presence in a strange empire breeds goodwill. You are a woman who finds "favor in the eyes of all" (Esther 2:15).

You have been crowned queen, but you don't sit idly by: Mordecai reveals enemy eunuchs to you and you reveal them to your husband, who hangs them quickly without much said. At the same time, the king's need for obedience transfers to a chosen minister or vizier, Haman, who relishes his gifted power but does not gain respect from your uncle Mordecai: he must sense that Haman is all pretense and station, demanding blind worship. Learning Mordecai is a disobedient Jew, Haman's anger spreads like a disease, spewing an empire-wide dictum (that parallels the kings' before his transformation), demanding all Jews from Ethiopia to India be destroyed, "young and old, women and children" (Esther 3:13), reminding king Ahasuerus that Jews "do not keep the king's laws, so that it is not for [his] profit to tolerate them" (Esther 3:8). Your king-husband, blind to the fact that you are a Jew, entertains Haman's plan.

On this news, Mordecai and the Jews rip their clothes, covering their bodies with ashes and sackcloth—a symbolic protest of predicted misery. But you, in silk gowns and jewels, your eyes not completely open regarding good and evil, ignore the ashes and only think to send fresh clothes to Mordecai so that he may enter the city of Susa. Mordecai's eyes, however, are wide open, and he rejects your offer, instead sending words to pierce your regal complacency: you have been resting on your successful softening of the king but are forgetting your Jewish identity, which could usurp your Persian crown. Mordecai, who previously had you hide your Jewish identity (he can mourn in the ash-sackcloth parade but does not let his grief fog his shrewdness), reminds you that you will not escape the fate of other Jews (he knows that fear gets attention), but that you are in a position to save the Jews (appeals to heroism can work), and that if you keep silent someone else will rise to save the Jews (you like being number one) while you and your lineage will perish (more fear), but finally, he says, "who knows whether you have not come to the kingdom for such a time as this?" (Esther 4:14) (now you can be a savior). Something works. Something he says makes you a woman with your eyes wide open.

Again you find favor in Ahasuerus's eyes and are given the golden scepter that allows you to approach him with a blend of social grace and manipulation: you make a request to have Haman come to a royal dinner, an hors d'oeuvre for Haman's self-important soul, your invitation making Haman "joyful and glad of heart" (Esther 5:9). This time restraining his wrath on seeing Mordecai, puffed up by his newly bestowed honors, Haman brags to his family that you invited him alone to have dinner with the king. Yet his wife Zeresh, sensing Mordecai's irreverent reverence, chews at her husband's optimistic heart, ordering him to have gallows ready to choke Mordecai by requesting the king give Haman an early-morning killing for a wake-up call.

But you could never have predicted that during a sleepless night before the dinner, the king's subconscious will flow on an unexpected river, sensing that somehow righteous deeds have gone unrewarded. In the morn he anxiously rips through the record of memorable deeds, finding one breezed over earlier in the narrative that he (and readers of the story) have forgotten: it's the warning of assassin eunuchs ready to slice the king, but blocked by Mordecai who was never honored (Esther 6:2-3). You could not ask for a better situation. As the king closes the record book, Haman walks in, his request for Mordecai's neck ready to slip from his lip, when the king asks, "What shall be done to the man whom the king delights to honor?" (Esther 6:6). Pride and presumption swelling, Haman assumes the king is referring to him, the vizier's selfishness choking him as his demands tumble forth: the king should give away his royal robes, his royal horse, and royal crown, and the rewarded person should parade through the streets to glean all attention. Are you surprised when the king acts at once? He orders Haman to make this overblown distribution—but to Mordecai, the unrewarded. (Now the manipulative wife Zeresh foresees Haman's ruin and gets ready to run.)

Then, Esther, you commence your banquet. First you offer a platter of humility, agreeing you would hold your tongue if the Jews and yourself were to be sold as slaves to spare your king's affliction, but otherwise you desire that you and your people not be sold for destruction. When your husband-king asks who would desire such a massacre, modesty falls away and you stridently assert, "A foe and enemy! The wicked Haman!" (Esther 7:6). Later, sloshed with wine, Haman asks for forgiveness and, just as the king pops in from the garden, accidentally falls on your couch (do his pants bunch up as with an erection?), seemingly positioned for someone to flop on top. That does it for your emotionally baked king, who hangs Haman on the gallows built for Mordecai. The king's anger then abates like a giant burp. You and Mordecai are awarded with the loot of the House of Haman; a reprieve is sent out from Ethiopia to India to spare the Jews, who are encouraged to arm and slay any who might attack them, a flip of fortune so great that the Jews gain power and recognition to the point that now even non-Jews "declared themselves Jews, for the fear of the Jews had fallen upon them" (Esther 8:17). Esther, you get more than you need. Another writer seems to enter your story at this point in the text and has the Jews run amuck with their newly found power, but your story ends more poetically with Mordacai, who "spoke peace to all his people" (Esther 10:3).

Eve, your curiosity morphs from Ruthian humility to Estherian expediency. You are of three moral minds.

4:39

"IN A WORLD OF PATRIARCHAL POWER . . ."
(A TRAILER FOR SATIRE?)

In a world where the patriarchs of the tribes of Israel are held in high esteem, if not worshipped, by three of the world's great religions, one would expect to find loving, caring rulers who exemplified a moral code for generations to follow. One would expect their biographers to create a tone of reverence for their geneses, papyrus-filled sacred texts devoid of a satire or details that undermine a patriarch's moral rectitude. Instead, when it comes to the text of Genesis, the reader finds something shocking. Early in this sacred report, one finds the Lord already disappointed, "sorry that he had made man on the earth, and it grieved him to his heart" (Gen 6:6), for man had become corrupted and filled the earth with violence. Startling enough, but at least after the Lord decides to redo His genesis, beginning with wiping out all his creations by flooding the lungs of every living thing on earth (not only people but, except for a measly two of each kind, innocent animals too), and picks only one man to make a covenant with, named Noah (along with his descendants), one would hope that this patriarch would be of sound mind. Instead, after the flood has washed away the rest of humanity, Noah leaves the ark, tills the ground for grapes, becomes so drunk that he lays naked in his tent (Gen 9:20-21), and is found by his son Ham, who requires his brothers Shem and Japheth to avoid looking at their dad's sorry body by walking backwards and tossing a cover over the old man. At this point Noah revives from his stupor and, in irrational shame, curses Ham by demanding his son Canaan become a life-long slave to Ham's brothers (Gen 9:22-27). Not exactly father of the year material.

In a post-flood world, one would predict the Lord to be refreshed from cleansing the earth of violence, satisfied by the pleasant sniff of a smoky blend from "every clean animal and . . . every clean bird" (Gen

8:20) grilled by Noah's burnt offering, but instead the writer describes a Lord *still* disappointed. He suggests the worldwide drowning achieved nothing, with God exclaiming that He will never do anything like this again because "the imagination of man's heart is evil from his youth" (Gen 8:21). With the Lord in this kind of funk, one would hope He would at least be pleased to find that humanity—knowing only one language—wishes to unify, to continue with a solo, shared language (that might prevent misunderstandings), to live together by building "a city, and a tower with its top in the heavens [and a desire] to make a name for [themselves] lest [they] be scattered abroad upon the face of the whole earth" (Gen 11:4). Instead the writer shows us a Lord, threatened by the strength of humanity's unity, claiming "this is only the beginning of what they will do; and nothing that they propose to do will now be impossible for them" (Gen 11:6). After knowing that both man's pre-flood and post-flood imagination can quickly turn to violence, one would hope the Lord would welcome such common purpose and ease of communication, but instead He commands a group referred to as "us" (perhaps a reference to earlier gods of mythology) to "go down, and there confuse their language, that they may not understand one another's speech" (Gen 11:7). The people are thus forced to abandon their project of unification, now called Babel, because it was where the Lord confused their language and "scattered them abroad from there over the face of all the earth" (Gen 11:8). This depressed God is not looking so good.

But now, in a world of genesis, a patriarch arises that the Lord has even more faith in, one He will make a great nation for and will bless, and make his name great so that he will be a blessing to the world. His name is Abram, later to be sanctioned Abraham. One would anticipate the writer of the life of the patriarchs would highlight the moral character of such a person, but instead we find Abram choosing deception as the best modus operandi, starting in the land of Egypt. Here he tells his wife Sarai (later to be named Sarah) to pretend she is his sister, fearing the Egyptians will kill him to obtain Sarai who is "beautiful to behold" (Gen 12:11), but thinking that as his sister "it may go well" (Gen 11:13) with him—and indeed it does. For his pretend sister's sake, probably with marriage on his mind, the Pharaoh gives

Abram plentiful animals and servants. In a world where future leaders are shaped for generations to follow, the reader guesses that Abram will pay a price for his deceit and his lack of courage, but instead something incredible happens. The Lord inflicts the deceived Pharaoh with great plagues. Now, ironically because so often he is depicted as an ancient enemy, the Pharaoh has to give Abram a lecture on morality: "Why did you not tell me that she was your wife? Why did you say, 'She is my sister,' so that I took her for my wife? Now then, here is your wife, take her, and be gone" (Gen 12:18-19). And so Abram leaves with "all that he had" (Gen 12:20) and is "very rich in cattle, in silver, and in gold" (Gen 13:2), with no regret nor apology to either the Pharaoh or Sarai, but instead a focus on his and his brother Lot's wealth and their need to expand in different directions. In a world new to political dealings, there appears to be expansive room to make fun of those who often benefit despite their poor ethical values. Morality through satire? Let's hope so.

In a world where God now seems anxious to populate the land with new patriarchs, one would not expect Sarai to be infertile, and then, with no room for patience, claim her Egyptian maid Hagar's vagina and womb to be a substitute for her own (Gen 16:1-2), giving the maid to Abram to "embrace" (Gen 16:5)—but this is exactly what happens. Once the act of using a lowly maid for procreating a line of patriarchs takes place, one might think that a writer of a sacred text would consider this as an opportunity for a lowly maid to accept her role with humility, the start of a spiritual attribute to continue for generations, but instead after conceiving, Hagar "looked with contempt on her mistress" (Gen 16:4), birthing pride and allowing vanity to trump loyalty to God-covenanted clans. The borrowed-womb deal collapses. Instead of dealing directly with her surrogate-mom Hagar, Sarai (of course ignoring her own part in the plan), turns in anger to Abram: "May the wrong done to me be on you!" (Gen 16:5). And now that it is on him, one would look forward to great wisdom from the Lord's anointed patriarch, a rising to the occasion for the benefit of his child, but instead Abram ducks any responsibility and tells Sarai "your maid is in your power; do to her as you please" (Gen 16:6). Unsurprisingly Sarai deals "harshly" (Gen 16:6) with her, and Hagar flees. So much for peace, love, and understanding. Whether Hagar is compensated by a great multitude of descendants, or cursed by submitting to her mistress and by birthing Ishmael—"a wild ass of a man, his hand against every man and every man's hand against him" (Gen 16:12)—is never settled in a world where the Lord has a penchant for moral lightweights. Morality through satire? Let's hope so.

In a world where a reader would imagine it likely that after so many morally challenging events a major tribal patriarch would have his consciousness raised, one is surprised to find much later in Genesis, after the raining of brimstone and fire on Sodom and Gomorrah by the Lord, Abraham still using Sarah to pull his "she-is-my-sister" trick on other rulers, now in Gerar. This time, however, before King Abimelech sleeps with Sarah, believing she is Abraham's sister, the king's subconscious hears the voice of God: "Behold, you are a dead man, because of the woman whom you have taken; for she is a man's wife" (Gen 20:3). Immediately Abimelech brings forth his moral curricula vitae for God to consider, how Abraham said Sarah was his sister and Sarah said Abraham was her brother and how "in the integrity of [his] heart and the innocence of [his] hands" (Gen 20:5) he had taken Sarah into his home. In this world of moral choice, one wishes to believe the Lord would foster strong moral self-esteem by giving the king credit for listening to his unconscious, but instead God makes sure, in another dream, that He himself gets the credit, saying He knows the king acted out of the integrity of his heart but it was "I who kept you from sinning against me; therefore I did not let you touch her" (20:6). He then tells the king to restore Sarah to Abraham because he is a prophet, and again refrains from commenting on Abraham's deceit. But the moral issue is not lost on Abimelech, who, like the Pharaoh before him, scolds Abraham for bringing sin upon him and his kingdom (Gen 20:9-10).

This time Abraham has excuses. (Or should they be seen as the excuses of a new writer—the writer of this section himself duplicitous—working with the character of Abraham to correct this and the earlier story?) First Abraham says he had to be deceitful because he thought, "There is no fear of God at all in this place" (Gen 20:11), when in fact it is his own deceit that the king needed to fear. Secondly, he pulls out a technicality: Sarah "is indeed my sister, the daughter of my father but not the daughter of my mother; and she became my wife" (Gen 20:12). Abraham is trying to have it both ways: Sarah is his sister when the result is gaining favors from a king; his wife for purposes of catching a foreign king in a sin by sleeping with her. (Not to mention that women are traditionally identified more by who their mother is than their father, particularly in the Jewish tradition, making Sarah primarily a wife in this case.) Just to make sure Abimelech is the one left with shame, falling all over himself in making amends to Abraham by having him take a host of riches as he leaves with Sarah (Gen 20:14), Abraham adds this bit to clear Sarah of deceit: That when "God caused [Abraham] to wander from [his] father's house, [Abraham] said to her, 'This is the kindness you must do me: at every place to which we come, say of me, He is my brother'" (Gen 20:13). Morality through satire? Could be.

In a world where satirical notes undermine power, circumcision in Genesis seems like another cruel joke, not a sacred ritual (that comes later in the pious context of Leviticus 12:2). Here, in a fresh new world where any new ideas for primal rituals are on the table, when this writer has God first come up with the idea of raw penal cuts for patriarchs of dubious morality, where every male, whether of one's household or a foreigner bought with one's money, gets snipped so God's "covenant be in your flesh" (Gen 17:13), one has to wonder if this is a spoof on religious identification. This is a writer who creates a God who doesn't ask allegiance by an oath, or a tattoo on the thigh, or a scar on a cheek, but asks for all males to drop their pants and snip the foreskins of their penises, tossing away the most sensitive part of a man's genitals, parts that later David will consider to be collectibles, spoils reaped when killing the armies of Philistines (1Sam 18:27).

This is a world where two of the patriarchs of Israel, Simeon and Levi, Abraham's great-grandsons, will use the soreness of this snipping as a perverse punishment when their sister Dinah is "seized" and "humbled" (Gen 34:2), raped by Shechem of a different tribe. When Shechem unexpectedly finds his soul "drawn to Dinah" (Gen 34:3) and he loves her, Shechem's dad, Hamor the Hivite, proposes to Judah (Abraham's grandson and Dinah's dad) unification through marriage of families and opening of land. Jacob listens quietly until Dinah's brothers return from the field so that he can turn the proposal over to them (brothers do so well with sisters dating other guys, right?). Simeon and Levi, seeking revenge, answer "deceitfully" (Gen 34:13) that they will allow this unification of tribes and marriage of Dinah and Shechem only on this condition: "that you will become as we are and every male of you be circumcised" (Gen 34:15), and thus every man in Hamor's tribe, Shechem being the first, complies immediately. "On the third day, when they were sore," Dinah's brothers, "took their swords and came upon the city unawares, and killed all the males. They slew Hamor and his son Shechem with the sword, and took Dinah out" (Gen 34:25-26), and stole all the Hivites' animals, houses, small children, and women. So much for peace, love, and understanding. And then, in a world of warrior-crazy clans, where Jacob anticipates his sons will run amuck, one would think he would rejoice in his murderous sons for doing the family's bloody work, but being more a politician than clan dad, Jacob distances himself from his own sons: "You have brought trouble on me by making me odious to the inhabitants of the land, the Canaanites and the Per'izzites" (Gen 34:30), who he fears could destroy him and his household. So much for family values. Is this morality through satire? It better be.

In a world where a reader expects moral knowledge to be passed on from one generation to another, one might think that Abraham's son Isaac would embody a fresh sense of morality absent from his dad's youthful deceits, but instead, when Isaac finds himself in the land of Philistines, out come the same old insecurities and lack of courage that Abraham displayed. Isaac fears for his life because he thinks a ruler might desire his wife Rebekah, who was "fair to look upon" (Gen 26:7), so he has Rebekah pretend to be his sister, just as his father had done with Sarah. But Abimelech, king of the Philistines, will not be fooled again; he discovers the lie in time when he looks out a window and catches Isaac "fondling" (Gen 26:8) Rebekah's tit, and scolds Isaac: "One of the people might easily have lain with your wife, and you would have brought guilt upon us" (Gen 26:10). Then, in total panic over merely the potential of adultery being committed that could trigger God's wrath, Abimelech proclaims, "Whoever touches this man or his wife shall be put to death" (Gen 26:11). But in a world peppered by irrational reactions devoid of moral sensibility, no one can anticipate if the Lord will support what is fair. And indeed, the Lord immediately blesses Isaac, who grows so wealthy that Abimelech sends him away (Gen 26:12-16), as if not knowing what to expect from a manipulator who gains favors from God. Morality through satire? A writer making fun of his or her leaders? It gets more difficult not to think so.

In a world where a reader might think that the immoral foibles of Abraham's progeny, represented by Isaac and his own missteps, would finally be studied by the third generation, which would begin to reverse the sins of the grandfathers and fathers, one is instead startled to see primal instincts swamp moral concerns yet again. The third generation's failings become apparent when Isaac's son Jacob, with the support tactics of his mother Rebekah, steals a blessing from his brother Esau, leading to a host of vicious sibling sizzles (discussed in Chapter 6 of this book).

Well surely, by the fourth generation, when Jacob's sons become fathers, one might find high moral standards; after all, Jacob has been blessed and his name is now Israel—"God said to him, 'Your name is Jacob; no longer shall your name be called Jacob, but Israel shall be your name'" (Gen 35:10)—so he is the patriarch of a huge future contingent of people. In a world exhausted by sibling rivalries, we must hope that Israel's son Judah, who in his youth ganged up with other brothers to sell their sibling Joseph into slavery because he was favored by their father, Israel, will have learned from these foolish ways when he himself becomes father of the fifth generation.

Instead, Judah turns in a different direction. First he goes into his wife Shua's vagina three times to conceive three sons, Er, Onan, and Shelah. Er marries a woman named Tamar. In the world of the patriarchs who have birthed so many generations of moral failures, surely this one will represent a new start. But instead, the reader finds that no specifics are necessary for Er to be found "wicked in the sight of the LORD; and the LORD slew him" (Gen 38:7) just like that. The reader then takes heart to see that Judah offers Tamar to Onan, Judah urging him to quickly get into Tamar's vagina to "perform the duty of a brother-in-law to her, and raise up offspring for your brother" (Gen 38:8), but we are quickly caught off guard when Onan, knowing the child will not be his own (technically his brother's) pulls out of her vagina and "spilled the semen on the ground" (Gen 38:9). This displeases the Lord, who zaps Onan to the ground. In a world of the patriarchs, one is stunned that a missed-shot wad can equal a whack from God because ritual trumps emotions, but nevertheless it does. Judah now asks Tamar to wait for his youngest son Shelah to grow up, but by the time he does, Judah's offer to Tamar is forgotten.

In a world of patriarchs, one would expect the leaders of future generations to be the ones who display moral rectitude, so it is surprising to find it is a woman who, disappointed at having watched two husbands fail moral standards, feels forced to take the future in her own hands. Tamar sheds her widow's garments, dressing instead like a harlot with a veil covering her face, and heads out on the main road, where she encounters Judah. Not recognizing his dolled-up daughter-in-law, Judah wishes to go into her vagina, so she asks for his signet, cord, and staff until he can pay her with a kid from his flock (Gen 38:13-20). He goes into her vagina and she conceives by him and re-dresses in her widow garb. Judah's friend hopes to recover his identifying signet, cord and staff, but cannot find the harlot he went into, so Judah tells him, "Let her keep the things as her own, lest we be laughed at" (Gen 38:23).

A few months later, Judah hears his daughter-in-law is pregnant through harlotry. In a world of moral standards, one would expect a leader to search her out, perhaps imagine what disappointments led to harlotry, and display a let-him-who-has-not-sinned-cast-the-first-stone empathy. This is not to happen. Instead, Judah orders her to be burned. However, Tamar won't go down so easily; she arrives and produces Judah's three signature items, announcing, "By the man to whom these belong, I am with child" (Gen 38:25). Judah immediately reverses, acknowledging the items, and claims, "She is more righteous than I, inasmuch as I did not give her my son Shelah" (Gen 38:26). One would expect a morally outstanding leader to now admit to his role in the pregnancy and ask forgiveness, especially for his own commands to turn Tamar into tinder before knowing she was carrying his son.

Not in this world of the patriarchs; instead, Judah faults himself only for not following through on the brother-husband ritual (which diverts from the ridicule he was earlier so concerned about), and satisfies himself with never going into Tamar's vagina again.

Is this yet another example of what patriarchs should *not* look like, or a realistic portrayal of what they often are? Are these Genesis folktales in fact spoofs on moral leadership, on the bumbling of God-given power? Pray to the Lord that they are.

5:49

THE STRAIGHT MAN AND ABRAHAM
Inaugural Humor

Requirements for a "straight man": With two comic partners, the straight man stays completely serious while his partner acts strange or eccentric, the seriousness of the straight man making the partner look all the more ridiculous. The graveness of the straight man can take the form of poise, patience, shocked outrage, or restrained frustration. This straight man's solemnity provides a foil, or contrast, to the comic partner.

In Genesis, when the Lord is stern or very serious, He sometimes becomes just such a foil when He is stuck with the quirky, eccentric behavior of those with whom He makes a covenant. For instance, after vacillating between anger and disappointment in the early chapters of the book, the Lord gets down to serious business, especially when He appears to ninety-nine-year-old Abram (isn't a special birthday party coming up for the old man?) and says "I am God Almighty; walk before me, and be blameless. And I will make my covenant between me and you, and will multiply you exceedingly. No longer shall your name be Abram [exalted father], but your name shall be Abraham [father of a multitude]" (Gen 17:1-5). After discussing the use of circumcision to identify his people (Abraham gets snipped at ninety-nine—some birthday present!), God explains that Sarah, no longer Sarai, will start the birthing of the multitudes. The Lord's serious proposal does not elicit a serious response: Abraham falls "on his face and laughed, and said to himself, 'Shall a child be born to a man who is hundred years old? Shall Sarah, who is ninety years old, bear a child'?" (Gen 17:17). Abraham even wonders if God could be talking about Ishmael, who is thirteen, birthed from Sarah's maid

Hagar (Gen 17:18). The writer does not have God react to Abraham's incredulity with a sarcastic reprimand, or off-putting surprise, or grinning understanding, or comeback humor, but instead, straight as an arrow, He proceeds with details such as the first son with Sarah will be called Isaac who will be blessed and who will multiply, fathering twelve princes for a great nation. (Perhaps there is a little understated humor since in Hebrew Isaac means "he laughs," but the Lord's serious tone does not waver.)

Lest the reader doubt that the patriarch's skepticism about God's magic has dissipated, that the scoffing hee-haws have dried up, when the Lord returns in the spring, Sarah, who no longer has periods—"ceased to be . . . after the manner of women" (Gen 18:11)—continues the disbelief and "laughed to herself," wondering, "After I have grown old, and my husband is old, shall I have pleasure?" (Gen 18:12). She humorously wonders about orgasm, not birthing, despite the seriousness of the multiplying project that the Lord has made top priority. The resolute Lord ignores her remark, quickly getting back to the birthing issue at hand, and without cracking a smile, asks, "Why did Sarah laugh, and say, 'Shall I indeed bear a child, now that I am old?' Is anything too hard for the LORD?" (Gen 18:13-14). Seeing she touched one of God's serious nerves, Sarah's smart talk quickly dries up, and, out of fear, she immediately tries to reverse with an "I-did-not-laugh" defense, only to be rebuffed by the Lord: "No, but you did laugh" (Gen 18:15). As straight man, God gives Abraham and Sarah a comic tint.

Soon thereafter, when the Lord knows something evil is going on in Sodom and Gomorrah, he decides not to share it with Abraham because the Lord knows "all the nations of the earth shall bless themselves by him" (Gen 18:18), suggesting the Lord wants to keep Abraham's associations with God's necessary dirty work at a distance and keep Abraham's moral consciousness squeaky clean, since other nations are going to look to Abraham for ultimate blessings. Abraham has other plans. Instead of disappearing as per the Lord's desire, he gets in the Lord's face, launching into a line of endless questions, again putting the Lord in the role of a straight man who can only answer with straightforward, simple responses while Abraham frantically bounces around Him:

Abraham: "Wilt thou indeed destroy the righteous with the wicked? Suppose there are fifty righteous within the city; wilt thou then destroy the place and not spare it for the fifty righteous who are in it?" (Gen 18:23-2)

The Lord: (No immediate response.)

Abraham: (Realizing he might be looking a bit philosophically overwrought and presumptuous regarding the Lord's decision to zap humans, calls the questioning back a bit.) "Far be it from thee to do such a thing, to slay the righteous with the wicked, so that the righteous fare as the wicked!" (Still not convinced he has overstepped, further points to the outrageousness of his questioning God's violence.) "Far be that from thee!" (Gen 18:25)

The Lord: (Answers straightforwardly without explanation.) "If I find at Sodom fifty righteous in the city, I will spare the whole place for their sake" (Gen 18:26).

Abraham: (Giddy from receiving an answer without the Lord's scorn, cannot help himself, so ups the ante but still slathers his question with humility.) "I have taken upon myself to speak to the Lord, I who am but dust and ashes. Suppose five of the fifty righteous are lacking? Wilt though destroy the whole city for lack of five?" (Gen 18:27-28)

The Lord: (Ignores Abraham's verbal skirting around, avoiding mentioning a total number by instead offering to subtract five.) "I will not destroy it if I find forty-five there" (Gen 18:28).

Abraham asks about forty; the Lord responds positively. Begging the Lord not to be angry, Abraham asks about thirty and gets another positive answer. Then twenty. Then ten. The Lord answers all in the affirmative and finally seems to have had enough of Abraham's angst and "went his way" (Gen 18:23). Humans have always been tormented by the fact that in wars and natural disaster the innocent die along with those who are evil. In the moment these things happen, our questions are especially anguished, but in this Biblical moment, the writer cleverly gives us the relief of seeing our anxieties looking foolish and neurotic, manifest in Abraham, played out comically against the Lord as a straight man.

However, nothing can prepare the reader for the dark humor of Chapter 19 when, instead of the Lord, two angels appear at the gates of Sodom and are met by Abraham's brother Lot who offers them shelter at his home. After first refusing, saying they will sleep in the street, they acquiesce and return with Lot to his home, but before they can lie down for the night, "the men of Sodom, both young and old, all the people to the last man, surrounded the house; and they called to Lot, 'Where are the men who came to you tonight? Bring them out to us, that we may know them'" (Gen 19:4-5). By presuming they are sexually appealing mortals, not angels, the whole town's collective male desire to have sex with the men ("know them" being a euphemism for sex in the Bible) is hyperbolic and grotesque, but their collective desire is nothing compared to Lot's response.

Lot goes out to the men and begs his "brothers [not to] act so wickedly" (Gen 19:7), offering instead his "two daughters who have not known man; let me bring them out to you, and do to them as you please; only do nothing to these men, for they have come under the shelter of my roof" (Gen 19:8). Is this a spoof on hospitality run amuck? Or a satire on those who would curry favor with the Lord's messengers at the expense of their love for their children? In either case, Lot's allowing his daughters to be raped is especially grotesque, given he will be supported by a Lord who also keeps Abraham away from any family violence so that nations can bless themselves through him. As the town crushes into Lot's house, the angels blind them; instead of groping the angels, the men have to grope for the door (Gen 19:11). Despite suffering an attempted attack in the Lot home, the angels are nevertheless willing to collect any of Lot's family and save them from the Lord's destruction of the city. Unfortunately, Lot's future sons-in-law do not to take Lot seriously (who could?) and, thinking his warnings that the city will be destroyed are more manipulation than actual threat, do not leave (Gen 19:14). Even Lot, his wife, and his daughters dodder and have to be dragged out of town by the angels (Gen 19:16). Lot's wife looks back (a symbol of nostalgia, an inability to move on?) and becomes a pillar of salt, reminiscent of Orpheus looking back at Eurydice too soon before she can join life again, and losing his wife forever.

Lot's family is not a swift group. Its spastic actions and those of their male neighborhood find their straight man not in God but His angelic messengers, whose coolness play throughout the scene until Lot's family is out of the fire. Then the writer gives us an even darker surprise. The image of weak, virgin daughters just barely having escaped from their father's offering of them to the rapists of the town now reverses; with their prospective husbands burnt to a crisp, they take turns, on separate nights, getting their pa drunk, and then somehow get him sexually aroused while he sleeps, one erection per night per daughter, so that he is able to go into them that they "may preserve offspring through [their] father" (Gen 19:32), one of their sons later heading up the Moabites, the other, the Ammonites. The Lord and His angels are no longer physically present as straight men in these scenes of Lot sleeping with his daughters, but the Lord's and the angels' silence provides a straight man in absentia that is easily imagined by the reader against the frenetic behavior of the scene.

Dark humor is not to everyone's taste, and many of the early painters of Lot and his daughters make Lot look more alert and participatory, undermining the humor and switching the emphasis to erotic, perverse voyeurism for those who get off on an older man having sex with a much younger woman while striking dark Freudian Electra chords. Other painters make Lot look numb and the girls more gentle, sometimes the firstborn daughter, who cooked up the whole idea, looking more engaged than the younger daughter. The best depiction of the scene is by the modern Dutch painter Marcelle Hanselaar, *Lot and His Daughters 2*, showing the daughters both stoking sex embers, one demented and, like a desperate animal, crazily mounting her dad's erection, the other comforting Lot's head but with a slightly anticipatory look that suggests she is thinking of her go at him the following night. However, Lot's expression is the main focus. It is shrill, as if his nerves have been jolted simultaneously by an orgasm and an electric wire, not knowing if he is being shocked or ejaculating, his head almost decapitated by the experience, comically capturing his irreversible loss of moral control.

After these scenes, the idea of the Lord as straight man in Genesis gets grimmer and even subtler. Chapter 22 interrupts with an Abraham story so different in tone from the other episodes about him, so solemn, that one might imagine a new writer stepping into Genesis; it is the story that is often thought of before all the others because of its piety: God tests Abraham by asking him to kill his son Isaac. First, we need to address some crucial prior details most do not consider when they remember the story. In Chapter 21, Abraham sees Isaac playing with Ishmael, his son from Hagar, and is displeased when Sarah, seeing it too, lets her resentment of Hagar flare up again and tells Abraham to cast out Hagar and Ishmael. God steps in and tells Abraham to move on, to simply do as Sarah wishes and not to worry, compensating by promising to make a nation for Hagar and Ishmael. In Chapter 22, God speaks in a sonorous tone with a less casual attitude about sons: "Take your son, your only son Isaac, whom you love, and go to the land of Mori'ah, and offer him there as a burnt offering" (Gen 22:2).

However, as we know, Isaac is not his only son. Is this a new writer, oblivious to the fact that Abraham has just had a bitter exchange with Sarah regarding his other son, Ishmael? Or is the writer presenting a God who has canceled Ishmael out and now, arbitrarily or technically, decides only Isaac counts? In either case, God seems pinched, focused on a task with no regard for Abraham's history with his sons. That staunchness makes Him a different straight man, a foil to Abraham mechanically carrying out a murder as a proof of devotion. The world's great religions see the story as a test of faith and few readers question the nature of God's character in this episode because the cool, straight man role of the earlier scenes is gone. The horror of the situation makes it easy for a reader to forget God's straight face because now He is asking for what many would consider a pagan sacrifice, and not even of an enemy but of a loved one, with all the hurt and betrayal involved in such a sacrifice. Would Buddha, Jesus, or Mohamed ask for this as a test of loyalty? It is hard to imagine.

More importantly, in contrast to Abraham's previous questioning of God on how many innocent people it would take to save a wicked city, here, upon being asked to kill his own son, Abraham does not argue at all but blindly stumbles along, tricking Isaac to continue to the altar of sacrifice with the expectation that "God will provide himself the lamb for a burnt offering" (Gen 22:8). (He cannot really have faith this will happen or the test would be off.) Nor does Abraham cry out in anguish. Is it because he is so blind with faith that he is zonked? Or has he been put through so many tests of dubious nature and always been rewarded with the Lord's blessing and the promise of a multitude of descendants that he has grown numb? Even readers who want to see Abraham's blind faith as noble grow uncertain with the following line: "Then Abraham put forth his hand, and took the knife to slay his son" (Gen 22:10), along with the next lines when the angel of God interrupts him, telling him the test is over. If Abraham is depicted as far enough into the kill act that only an angel grabbing his knife arm with force can stop him, the reader gets queasy and is only a slight step away from rejecting the story as a metaphor for faith. In fact, for a contest in the early 1400s, the scene was depicted in bas relief for the doors of the Baptistery of Battistero d'San Giovanni in Florence, by both Ghiberti (who depicts Abraham pointing his knife at Isaac but leaning away from his son, and with the angel having plenty of space and so time to stop Abraham's kill with a word) and Brunelleschi (who depicts Abraham with his arm thrust strongly forward with a hand starting to choke off Isaac's air, knife pulled back at a powerful angle, and the angel having to grab his arm lest the kill take place). The judges praised both artists' interpretations; however, obviously not able to accept the violence of the scene, asked both artists to work together and reconcile the images. Brunelleschi, unwilling to compromise his more violent vision, ultimately conceded to Ghiberti. (Brunelleschi did go on to design the great Duomo next to the baptistery.)

The following century, Caravaggio made the absurdity of the test even more poignant. At first in 1598 he (or maybe someone else, as this painting, hanging at Princeton University, is of disputed origin) approached the scene more in Ghiberti's spirit, depicting Abraham with his hand placed calmly on Isaac's bushy head in exact parallel to the angel's hand placed on the sacrificial ram's bushy head, as if both are being blessed and comforted. Abraham's face is turned towards the background, so there can be no judgment of his state of mind, and his knife arm has been relaxed by the angel's hand, whose sympathetic expression catches the full light. Isaac's body is calmly stretched, his upper body raised on his elbows, as if getting up from a nap to awaken the day. The entire emphasis is on peaceful resolution, not on violence.

But in 1603, Caravaggio created a different scene (hanging in the Uffizi Gallery in Florence) with an emphasis squarely on the angel's stiff arm, desperately, strongly blocking Abraham from following through on his throat slicing, the angel's other hand pointing towards the ram with explanation and perhaps a tinge of admonishment suggested by the tautness of the angel's fingers. Isaac is screaming in terror. Caravaggio puts a heavy spotlight with shadows on Abraham's furrowed brow, making him look especially confused, underscoring his general mindlessness, or the lack of internal struggle with this perverse test of faith. Abraham comes off as a nuisance, playing out frenetic behavior that God's angel needs to watch over for a Lord who, for this painting, now stands back, away from the scene. The Biblical writer did not make the humor of this scene definitive or sharp, but there are enough elements in the story to justify Caravaggio's bringing out details that help us remember that the scene is the result of a God who is a straight man and that Abraham is once again the fall guy. This time the humor is unbearably bleak.

SIBLING SIZZLE
CHILD PSYCHOLOGY BUSTED

The writer of Genesis would have chuckled to see the list of rational responses and sound advice to parents, recommended by psychologists at the Mayo Clinic web site,[1] for dealing with sibling conflict. The suggestions include: avoid comparisons (praise for different accomplishments); stay out of battles (allow kids to resolve conflicts without taking sides or shaming in public); listen to complaints (share one's own childhood stories); show special love (have private time with each sibling). The list assumes the adult grew up in a rational environment; has no preconceived ideas as to what makes a child a joy or someone to run from and no preferences as to which sibling is easier to spend time with; has no personal investment in what a child should become as a productive adult; and has faith that nurturing will overcome flaws of nature or that adult intellect can pin down a child's primal passions. In short, it assumes that the parent is not perpetrating problems based on his or her own parent having failed to practice these recommendations.

After a good giggle the writer of Genesis might put an arm around that adult's shoulder and whisper "Good try," and then argue that the world turns on the irrationality of both parent and child; that in fact, erratic emotions are what drive the human experience. The Book of Genesis does not delay in making this point. Once pushed out of the garden of Eden, despite earlier fig-leaf shame, the first Adam-and-Eve act is the conception of Cain. Interestingly, Eve refers to her son as a man, not a baby or child: "I have gotten a man with the help of the LORD" (Gen 4:1). This throws the reader immediately into the world of seriousness and purpose, turning quickly away from indulgence in innocent play. Soon she conceives Abel, time further collapsing in the narrative so that in the next sentence he is already a keeper of sheep while Cain is a tiller of the ground (Gen 4:2). Folk tales typically shrink time to get to the essential in life: This is a story of the first children, therefore a story about the essence of all parent-child relationships, where what goes on in childhood, no matter how dreadful or wonderful, fades. In this story, the cosmic father God, the parent of all parents, steps into the scene to represent the force that bottom-lines life: arbitrary decisions often determine one's fate.

The paradigm shown in the Cain-Abel-God-the-Father story is one we recognize, a dynamic starting early in childhood and never finishing: an authority figure choosing between two people, whether children or adults. Like two children bringing drawings to a parent to post on the refrigerator, "Cain brought to the LORD an offering of the fruit of the ground, and Abel brought of the firstlings of his flock and of their fat portions. And the LORD had regard for Abel and his offering, but for Cain and his offering he had no regard" (Gen 4:3-5). With our strong desire for cosmic fairness, we desperately look for a reason why the Lord would pick one over the other, but there is nothing in the story's context that makes meat more desirable than fruit. The meat will later be used to offer God a flavorful, favorable smoky sacrifice; the fruit of the vine will later be associated with the Jewish Passover, Shabbat, and other occasions as well as with the Christian sacrament of the Eucharist, but none of these ideas are in place here. And even if one believes the Lord has a preference, it is irrational for a parental figure, the parent of all parents, to show preference for one's offering over another. Your drawing of sheep goes on the fridge; your drawing of grapes goes in the trash.

In her essay, "Supporting Sibling Relationships,"[2] Dr. Laurie Kramer lists nine "competencies" that should be "promoted to enhance prosocial sibling relations," including number four, "Social and emotional understanding (e.g., perspective taking, decentering, learning to assess and respect siblings' unique views, needs, goals, and interests as legitimate in their own right)" and number nine, "Evaluating parental differential treatment practices (e.g., openly discussing the impact of parental differential treatment perceived as unfair, and adjusting parental behaviors so that children's unique needs are met)" (Kramer 53). Jesus, someone who recognizes everyone's potential to practice peace, love, and understanding, would be a big Dr. Kramer fan, and any worthy parent, teacher, or psychologist would want to sign on with her. But the writer of Genesis senses that responsible adults (let alone irresponsible ones) have their own strengths and weaknesses, have suffered their own rejections and rejoiced in their own acceptances; so despite good intentions, these past experiences result in biases not so easily disguised.

The Lord, here a symbol of cosmic unfairness, is also the parent of all parents who unexpectedly favors one gift over another, a cosmic version of parental weakness. As a symbol of cosmic unfairness, the Lord's attitude suggests that sometimes even the gift of one's beauty, or creativity, or intelligence, or patience, or in Cain's case, productivity, will not offer a reprieve from rejection. We are not chosen for good reasons and not chosen for biased reasons. The result of rejection is hurt, and hurt can quickly turn to anger, especially when the choice is not fair; hence, "Cain was very angry, and his countenance fell" (Gen 4:5). Cain's anger, since he is one of two primal, mythical siblings, represents the anger of all our rejections, not only as individuals, but rejections of social, religious, and political groups. The world is beset by angry nations.

The Lord, as a symbol of parental weakness, violates several of Dr. Kramer's suggestions for prosocial sibling relationships, in particular the aforementioned numbers four (respect of siblings unique views and needs) and nine (openly discussing the impact of parental differential treatment perceived as unfair). In fact, after making what appears to be an arbitrary choice that causes much pain and anger, God takes on a righteous tone, asking Cain, "Why are you angry, and why has your countenance fallen? If you do well, will you not be accepted?" (Gen 4:6-7). The Lord's question is maddening, since He gives no hint as to what Cain should have done, or should do now to "do well," especially after his brother has just been arbitrarily accepted. It is almost inconceivable that a parent would accept one child's sheep drawing and then wonder why the other child, artist of the trashed grape drawing, would have his or her countenance fall and anger ensue, and that the parent would then proceed to blow that rejection off with a do-well-next-time attitude. Would it be far-fetched for modern psychologists to claim God has a personality disorder, rejecting Cain's offering in order to build a sense of insecurity in Cain, and then reorganizing reality by asking the unfairly treated child, "Why are you so upset?" as if Cain's reaction is unnatural? This insecurity is sure to set Cain up for a never-ending quest for approval. Dr. Kramer would not approve of the Lord pouring the salt of righteousness into a sibling's wound. The writer of Genesis seems disturbed too.

The Lord, however, goes on, seemingly unaware of the damage He is inflicting upon the rejected child. "And if you do not do well, sin is couching [some Bibles write "crouching"] at the door; its desire is for you, but you must master it" (Gen 4:7), He tells Cain, making one wonder if the Lord has created rejection as a test, suggesting that the inability to rebound continues one's descent into a misery that begets destruction. Manufactured rejection is not a test on Dr. Kramer's list of competences to "enhance prosocial sibling relations," but more a test one can imagine given only by a perverse parent, and at best, a test created by fateful circumstances, not a rational human. However, insofar as the Lord does represent the parent of all parents, because of the innate desire for parental approval, Cain does not retaliate against his cosmic father, but instead transfers his anger onto his sibling. Indeed he lashes out violently against his brother Abel, killing him (Gen 4:8). Then, in another brilliant stroke, the writer dramatizes Cain's resultant despair, cynicism, and bitterness, all with one smart-ass response to the Lord when He asks after Abel's whereabouts: "I do not know; am I my brother's keeper?" (Gen 4:9). The Lord, though, is an earth-seer who tells Cain He hears the "voice of your brother's blood . . . crying to me from the ground. And now you are cursed from the ground, which has opened its mouth to receive your brother's blood from your hand" (Gen 4:10-11). Being cursed from the ground now soaked with the blood of a sibling who died because he was favored and his brother was rejected makes the crime seem immutable, beyond expiation.

This first, primal sin then is *not* the innocent, non-violent act of Adam and Eve, too innocent to know sin or disobeying God to gain wisdom. The first sin is envy: hatred that results from the one-two punch of rejection while knowing someone else is accepted. Sin can be couching at the door, but when fueled by envy born from rejection, the passion behind the sin is beyond even the Lord's control or warnings to Cain. In the novella *Billy Budd, Sailor*,[3] Herman Melville points to

60

envy as a passion "irreconcilable in reason," a passion no one seriously confesses to because there is something "in it universally felt to be more shameful than even felonious crime," and "not only does everybody disown it, but the better sort are inclined to incredulity when it is in earnest imputed to an intelligent man. But since its lodgment is in the heart not in the brain, no degree of intellect supplies a guarantee against it" (Melville 327).

Envy as it appears in Genesis tests two more of Kramer's "competencies" for sibling relationships—number eight, "Conflict management and problem solving (e.g., learning to consider conflicts as social problems and then using collaborative methods to solve these problems)" and number five, "Emotion regulation (e.g., identifying and managing emotions and behaviors in emotionally challenging and frustrating situations)" (Kramer 53). According to child psychologist Dr. Casey Hoffman,[4] part of this managing is an attempt to give the sense that the world is safe and predictable so that good behavior begets good outcomes. When a child's negative emotions become overwhelming, the parent helps the child deescalate them back to a manageable base line. In essence God has destabilized Cain's sense of security so that there is a complete reversal of emotional regulation, allowing envy to run amuck. Again, we see that the Lord represents the unfairness of parents (and others) too weak to practice Dr. Kramer's guidelines.

Then the Lord, oblivious to His own responsibility in the chain of events (but then again, fate is mindless), punishes Cain: "When you till the ground, it shall no longer yield to you its strength; you shall be a fugitive and a wanderer on the earth" (Gen 4:12). This is ironic, considering that his fruits of the earth had already not counted for anything, and had set off his rejection, misery, and hatred in the first place. Now all Cain's smart talk dries up, and he begins to plead to the Lord, "My punishment is greater than I can bear. Behold, thou has driven me this day away from the ground; and from thy face I shall be hidden; and I shall be a fugitive and a wanderer on the earth, and whoever finds me will slay me" (Gen 4:13-14). Even though he had not won the Lord's approval, the Lord's parental involvement (which offered the hope of approval though it never came) and the soil that gave Cain his purpose are now both gone, replaced with the threat of others wanting retribution for Cain murdering his brother.

The writer then complicates the story, however, when the Lord responds to Cain's concern about being whacked by offering him protection: "'Not so! If anyone slays Cain, vengeance shall be taken on him sevenfold.' And the LORD put a mark on Cain, lest any who came upon him should kill him" (Gen 4:15). Perhaps the Lord's desire to keep him alive but continually rejected and unfulfilled is a greater punishment than death itself. Or perhaps the writer is suggesting that the hurt, rejection, and destruction of envy, now embodied by Cain, will never disappear from the human condition. In any case, Cain's sin is not visited upon his son and the intensity of the story dissipates. When Cain moves "east of Eden" (Gen 4:16), his family members thrive and his wife conceives Enoch, whose name is given to one of the first cities built by Cain (Gen 4:17). Could the writer be suggesting that the desperate need to find approval, brought on through rejection, also drives people to create, to find renewed purpose after disappointments? Or more comically, could the writer be suggesting children find happiness by getting away from personality-disordered parents?

Cain's progeny go on to be the fathers of those who "dwell in tents and have cattle" (Gen 4:20), "who play the lyre and pipe" (Gen 4:21), and who forge "instruments of bronze and iron" (Gen 4:22)—in other words, those who turn chaos or wilderness into civilization. There are grave dangers with ambition, though, and in this early chapter of Genesis that danger is represented by the arrogance of Lamech, from Cain's fourth generation, who kills a man for wounding him and kills a young man for "striking" (Gen 4:23) him, and then desecrates the historical protection for Cain by using it as an excuse for his committing murder because of insults, claiming, "If Cain is avenged sevenfold, truly Lamech [can be avenged] seventy-sevenfold" (Gen 4:24). However we are left without any notion of whether or not this violence comes from rejection or envy, causing the reader to wonder if Lamech's story could be a later addition.

Several chapters later into Genesis, after "the LORD was sorry that he had made man on the earth, and it grieved him to his heart"

(Gen 6:6) and wipes out the world—with the exception of Noah and his family—with a flood, He finally starts over with a new nation of greatness by making a covenant with Abram, later to become Abraham. More sibling sizzle soon follows. Isaac and his wife Rebekah conceive their two children, Jacob and Esau (Gen 25:25-26). The writer again centers on sibling fire as central to the human condition, preordaining it through both Rebekah's knowing the "children struggled together within her" (Gen 25:22) and the Lord's prophesy that "Two nations are in your womb, and two peoples, born of you, shall be divided; the one shall be stronger than the other, the elder shall serve the younger" (Gen 25:23), thereby extending the acceptance-rejection, hurt-anger cycle between siblings to large groups of people. The writer also continues to bust any expectation that the oldest automatically becomes the privileged child.

Immediately, the younger twin, Jacob, instinctively takes advantage of the older, Esau, grabbing his heel, using Esau's physical strength to pull out of their mother's womb and into the world (Gen 25:26). Jacob's name, meaning "holder of the heel," implies his passivity. The activity of Esau and passivity of Jacob is further emphasized by Esau becoming "a skillful hunter, a man of the field, while Jacob was a quiet man, dwelling in tents" (Gen 25:27), this last, ominous phrase, "dwelling in tents," not implying an introspective philosophizer, but correlating more with an inactive, protective, secretive person. The arbitrariness of a parent preferring one child's personality (reminiscent of the Lord's choice of Abel over Cain) is highlighted by the abruptness of the next line: "Isaac loved Esau, because he ate of his game; but Rebekah loved Jacob" (Gen 25:28). No reason is given for Rebekah's love. The quick, terse compound sentence underscores there is no space for her reasons. They are irrelevant. She seems like a parent who would be uninterested in Dr. Kramer's guidelines for prosocial behavior. Isaac's love, meanwhile, is based on dietary needs, and coupled with the fact that Isaac does not hunt with his son, puts his affection on a shallower, more primitive basis. Also, whereas Abel and Cain's gifts were more equal, both having to do with producing sustenance, here only Esau provides food. Jacob's "gift," it seems, is his ability to take advantage of someone else's position or, soon to be made evident, someone else's desperation (gifts that might serve unscrupulous lawyers or politicians).

Soon after the parents declare their allegiances, Jacob again takes advantage of his brother, who comes in from the fields "famished" (Gen 25:29), smells Jacob's "boiling pottage" (Gen 25:29), and begs to be fed. Like his dad Isaac, Esau has gut-filling priorities, and Jacob will eventually snake both his brother and father using food as a distraction. First he demands Esau, in order to fill his gut, sell him his birthright (his rights and privileges for being born first). Jacob makes his brother swear to it, and Esau, who does not have the smarts to think long-term, rationalizes away the worth of his birthright, convincing himself he will die if he does not promptly slurp pottage (Gen 25:31-33). (We have all known the feeling.) Jacob feeds him; Esau walks away (Gen 25:34). With great psychological insight, the writer captures Esau's self-loathing for his short-term decision and inability to evaluate his own desperation or to perceive his brother's selfish disrespect for his sibling; instead Esau projects all blame and misery on the stolen birthright itself: "Thus Esau despised his birthright" (Gen 25:34).

Some years later, when Esau turns forty, he takes two Hittite wives who "made life bitter for Isaac and Rebekah" (Gen 26:35). No reason is given, but considering upcoming events, one can imagine the wives' troublemaking is a reaction to Esau's poor judgment, Isaac's senility, and Rebekah's manipulative personality, something that daughters-in-law would be quick to sniff out. Rebekah's pinnacle move comes at the end of Isaac's life: "When Isaac was old and his eyes were dim so that he could not see, he called Esau his older son" (Gen 27:1) and asks Esau to hunt and "prepare for me savory food, such as I love, and bring it to me that I may eat; that I may bless you before I die" (Gen 27:4). Food continues to be everything to the old man. Rebekah, listening to the conversation, relays it to Jacob. Hoping to secure Isaac's blessing for her favorite son, she tells Jacob to get two substitute goats for the savory meal so they can preempt Esau's wild game and secure the blessing from blind Isaac before he knows he is not giving it to Esau (Gen 27:5-10).

Jacob, always thinking ahead, always concerned about what could put him at a disadvantage, worries that Isaac will feel his smooth body instead of Esau's hairy mantle: "Perhaps my father will feel me, and I shall seem to be mocking him, and bring a curse upon myself and not a blessing" (Gen 27:12). Rebekah, never unsure of herself, incites, "Upon me be your curse, my son; only obey my word" (Gen 27:13), and, putting into play a trick reminiscent of Odysseus's hiding under wooly sheep to escape the blinded Cyclops, outfits Jacob in Esau's best garments and puts "the skins of the kids" on "his hands and upon the smooth part of his neck" (Gen 27:16).

Now Rebekah's early, intuitive affinity for Jacob is clear: they are kindred connivers. These parent-child affinities parallel the third Dr. Kramer competency that enhances prosocial sibling relationships: "Shared experiences that build support (e.g., appreciating siblings' unique knowledge of one another and of their family to strengthen bonds)" (Kramer 53), but the guideline does not take into account how a shared parent-child bond can undermine a sibling bond. These "shared experiences" between siblings sag to bread pudding when there is kindred umbilical cording between one of the parents and one of the siblings, a connection that starves out the second sibling and often the second parent. These unexpected unions stifle sibling bonds and instead stoke sibling sizzle.

Jacob, pretending to be Esau, goes to his father and serves up game, positioning himself to steal his brother's blessing. Isaac, however, wonders how the hunt-and-bake could have happened so quickly (Gen 27:18-20). Devoid of principle, Jacob's contrived explanation takes the Lord's name in vain: "Because the LORD your God granted me success" (Gen 27:20). Isaac hears Jacob's voice but feels the hairiness of Esau, so he asks Jacob again if he is his son Esau, only to have Jacob continue to lie (Gen 27:22-24). Ultimately, Isaac can smell the field of Esau's garments (Gen 27:27), and so he gives Jacob the magical blessing: "May God give you of the dew of heaven, and of the fatness of the earth, and plenty of grain and wine. Let peoples serve you, and nations bow down to you. Be lord over your brothers, and may your mother's sons bow down to you. Cursed be every one who curses you, and blessed be every one who blesses you!" (Gen 27:28-29). As Jacob leaves, Esau enters. The startled Isaac wonders who he has just blessed, and when he finds out it is not Esau, "Isaac trembled violently" (Gen 27:33), realizing he "ate it all before [Esau] came" (Gen 27:33)—both Jacob's food and his lies—but despite the dissemblance used to steal the blessing, feels he cannot redo it—"yes, and he shall be blessed" (Gen 27:33). When Esau hears this, his brain clears, becoming more aware of his loss and thus more anguished than before, crying "out with an exceedingly great and bitter cry, and [saying] to his father, 'Bless me, even me also, O my father!' But [Isaac] said, 'Your brother came with guile, and he has taken away your blessing'" (Gen 27:34-35).

By his agony, Esau intimates that it is not power he wants from the blessing, unlike Rebekah and Jacob, but love and acceptance. This hidden need is reinforced both by his mentioning that since childhood he has now been snaked twice by Jacob, and by his asking only for leftovers: "Is he not rightly named Jacob? For he has supplanted me these two times. . . . Have you not reserved a blessing for me?" (Gen 27:36). After Isaac admits that he has given Jacob total power over Esau, servants, and produce, Isaac cannot imagine what else Esau could want: "What then can I do for you, my son?" (Gen 27:37). So Esau requests again, now for only a crumb, "Have you but one blessing, my father? Bless me, even me also, O my father" (Gen 27:38), the anguished request for just a small blessing and the repetition of the word "father," a reference Jacob never used when he conned his father, further reinforcing that Esau's request is for love and recognition, not power. But Isaac is a blind fool who can only conceive a blessing as a right to power and has no ear for what Esau is asking for, so his only response is to reiterate the political consequences of a ritual he has no notion of how to modify or mollify: "Behold, away from the fatness of the earth shall your dwelling be, and away from the dew of heaven on high" (Gen 27:39). Then, with an eye on Esau's future change in political status, he adds, "By your sword you shall live, and you shall serve your brother; but when you break loose you shall break his yoke from your neck" (Gen 27:40).

In her essay "Supportive Sibling Relationships," Dr. Kramer points out that "siblings provide daily practice in understanding the minds of others—a skill that comes in quite handy for negotiating complex social interactions beyond the confines of family," and refers to a study by Pernoff, Ruffman and Leekam[5] which demonstrates that young children with an older sibling were more able to detect a false belief than those without siblings. Kramer points out that such a skill can set the groundwork for the development of empathy and being supportive, but also "evil," probably meaning anything anti-social and destructive (Kramer 44). However, as the story of Jacob and Esau dramatizes, a child can have a genetic disposition to plot success, including taking advantage of others (reinforced by a cheerleading parent), before social encounters between siblings—devoid of parental interference—have a chance to modify negative dispositions. In the story of Jacob and Esau, rejection of Esau—intentional on Rebekah's part and unintentional and blind on Isaac's part—leads to anger and hate, the Cain-and-Abel primal cycle. Furthermore, where acceptance of Abel and rejection of Cain was enough to set off anger and hate, now the accepted sibling, Jacob, is a scoundrel who can oil the rejection of the other sibling. The end result is a sizzling grease fire, with Esau fuming, "The days of mourning for my father are approaching; then I will kill my brother Jacob" (Gen 27:41).

Esau's words are reported to Rebekah, who relays them to Jacob but muffles Esau's fury by casting his threat as more psychologically self-serving than dangerous: "Behold, your brother Esau comforts himself by planning to kill you" (Gen 27:42). Then she deprecates Esau's hurt and anger, telling Jacob to flee to her brother Laban's land "until your brother's fury turns away; until your brother's anger turns away, and he forgets what you have done to him" (Gen 27:44-45) and, unless she fears they might kill one another, given that only Jacob's life is threatened, disingenuously worries, "Why should I be bereft of you both in one day?" (Gen 28:45). As Jacob prepares to follow her advice and leave town, Isaac blesses Jacob again, hoping he will be "fruitful and multiply" (Gen 28:3). Jacob takes off and before long, presumably wary from his life on the lam, falls asleep and dreams of a ladder connecting earth with heaven in which angels travel back and forth, with the Lord above promising Jacob great lands, descendants, and support (Gen 28:12-15). Given Jacob's morally weak character, it is hard not to believe that the dream is either a delusion of grandeur or a satiric comment by the book's author on who ends up having a ladder to the top of the power world; otherwise one has to consider the intercession of a different writer, a literalist who takes blessings of power as sacrosanct and is thus compelled to upgrade Jacob's status despite his unethical actions.

After the ladder scene, the story quickly recovers its earlier, less pious tone. Jacob journeys on and runs into Rachel, Laban's beautiful daughter, who is attending sheep (Gen 29:6). He assists her by rolling back a rock that opens a gush of spring water (sexual innuendo for her readiness?) (Gen 29:10), kisses her, and weeps at having found the daughter of Rebekah's brother Laban (Gen 29:11). Laban in turn takes Jacob into his household and offers Jacob one of his daughters in exchange for seven years of hard work (Gen 29:13-17)—either Rachel, the younger daughter, or Leah, the oldest, whose "eyes were weak" (Gen 29:17), a flaw in what appears to be a bucolic home-away-from-home, and a hint that Jacob may be in for more surprises. Initially things go smoothly: he works seven years to earn Rachel in marriage, years that "seemed to him but a few days because of the love he had for her" (Gen 29:20). Laban gives him a wedding feast (Gen 29:22), but in the dark of the night, concerned about the fate of his older daughter, he puts the less desirable, weak-eyed Leah in Jacob's bed so that he attaches his penis to her instead of Rachel (Gen 29:23). When Jacob finds out and is shocked by what Laban has done, Laban gives an oops-I-gave-the-wrong-wedding excuse, explaining that in his country the oldest daughter must wed before the youngest and adding that if Jacob agrees to bust his ass for another seven years, he can have Rachel too. Jacob agrees to this arrangement and quickly gets into Rachel's vagina (Gen 29:25-28), but Laban now has Jacob by his short and curlies for a total of fourteen years. Jacob finally suffers some comeuppance for his past trickery.

The story now shifts to the two female siblings' sizzle. Leah emerges as the rejected sibling, initially passed over and now perceiving that Jacob has more love for Rachel. Fate steps in to give the less beautiful Leah a different advantage: "When the LORD saw that Leah was hated, he opened her womb; but Rachel was barren. And Leah conceived and bore a son, and she called his name Reuben; for she said, 'Because the LORD has looked upon my affliction; surely now my husband will love me'" (Gen 29:31-32). She continues to pop out three more sons, including Judah, each time becoming more convinced she will be loved for her production line (Gen 29:33-35). However, Jacob does not respond to his wife's fertile productivity, and the writer instead keeps the focus on the sister tug-of-war: "When Rachel saw that she bore Jacob no children, she envied her sister; and she said to Jacob, 'Give me children, or I shall die!'" (Gen 30:1). This is a desperate, hyperbolic claim that puts misplaced pressure on a guy who seems to have already spent more time shooting sperm into Rachel than into Leah. The writer understands that birthing is a woman's most creative act, but Rachel's envy is a reminder that birthing can also be an extremely vain and prideful act, leading to the fierce sibling competition that drives women into baby cook-offs. The misplaced pressure sickens Jacob (more willing to get into vaginas than worry about babies), whose "anger was kindled against Rachel, and he said, 'Am I in the place of God, who has withheld from you the fruit of the womb?'" (Gen 30:2).

Rachel can no longer wait for her womb to open. Instead she drags her maid Bilhah into the assembly line, having Jacob go into Bilhah so she "may bear upon my knees, and even I may have children through her" (Gen 30:3), and indeed Bilhah does bear Jacob's child. Rachel then cinches the concept that Bilhah's womb is synonymous with her own, claiming that Bilhah's infant is in fact hers: "God has judged me, and has also heard my voice and given me a son" (Gen 30:6). (In each case of conception, the resulting children are named by the essence of the action or mother's interpretation of the birth— here it is Dan, which means, "He judged"—so they become everlasting embodiments of the competitive events.) Having secured one child for herself, Rachel has Jacob go into Bilhah's vagina again (Gen 30:7); she births; and Rachel feels she is finally a competitor, designing her metaphor to pin down the significance of the baby game: "With mighty wrestlings I have wrestled with my sister, and have prevailed" (Gen 30:8). Although egg-dried, Leah refuses to stop taking her sister to the mat, accepts Rachel's new going-below-the-maid's-belt rule, and drags the womb of her own maid, Zilpah, into the action (Gen 30:9), now having Jacob fertilize Zilpah for Leah's benefit and then claiming

Zilpah's two sons as her own to neutralize Rachel's maid-birthed extensions (Gen 30:10-13).

The episode escapes many of the social circumstances that might lend themselves to Dr. Linda Kramer's seventh competency to enhance prosocial sibling relationships: "Forming neutral or positive attributions regarding the sibling's intent (e.g., learning to check or correct faulty attributions that may falsely impute negative or hostile intent)" (Kramer 53). In Rachel and Leah we watch siblings participating in a cycle of bad intentions that are coaxed by primal instincts to compete outside of parental regulation. There are no faulty attributions; there is no false imputation of hostile intent for a parent to influence. Perhaps having competitive Laban as a father influences the sisters. We do not watch his parenting, but we see how he operates, specifically as someone who took advantage of Jacob. In any case, the sisters' hostility is spot on. Their actions are hostile yet so overwrought as to be comical. The sizzle makes one wonder how much of the world's progeny is not the result of the desire to turn one's life over to loving a child, but rather originated out of vanity and competition.

And the cycle in this story is by no means over. Leah's son Reuben finds mandrakes (a herbaceous plant that produces delirium and folkloric fertility) and brings them to Leah, but Rachel, suffering from infertility, demands them from her nephew (Gen 30:14). Leah slugs back with, "Is it a small matter that you have taken away my husband? Would you take away my son's mandrakes also?" (Gen 30:15). For these women, having the gift of pregnancy or having the gift of an adoring husband is a wash. Rachel concedes the mandrakes to Leah, who corrals Jacob for another round with her vagina and womb (Gen 30:16), conceives another baby, rationalizes that the infant is God's way of gifting her for ingenuously using her maid's womb as her own (lest anyone think it was absurd), believes that her husband will honor her because she has popped six sons, and now bears the first daughter, Dinah (Gen 30:19-21). Then, the reader (and God) almost forgetting Rachel, "God remember[s] Rachel" (Gen 30:22) who bears Joseph (Gen 30:24). All the births set the stage for a future generation of sibling strife.

Jacob is ready to pull up stakes. He asks Laban for back-wages in the form of spotted and speckled sheep and goats and black lambs, and claims his honesty in taking only the animals Laban has promised him will be verified when Laban checks on his herds (Gen 30:25-33). Laban tries to alter the breeding patterns of the herds to prevent Jacob from having large flocks, but Jacob counters by using peeled, wooden, phallic poles, with their tips seemingly circumcised to reveal their rawness (ejaculation stimulators that only a conniver and indiscriminate penis-poker like Jacob could conceive), so only the goats and sheep Jacob "specked-out" are encouraged to multiply (Gen 30:35-39). Laban's flocks weaken, so he looks with disfavor on Jacob (Gen 31:1-2). For his part, Jacob tells his wives their dad has cheated him and so God has given him a method of getting fair compensation (Gen 31:5-13). A lie.

The women could not care less how Jacob sticks it to their dad; in fact, they are only interested in doing a choral bitch about what is owed to them: "Is there any portion or inheritance left to us in our father's house? Are we not regarded by him as foreigners? For he has sold us, and he has been using up the money given for us. All the property which God has taken away from our father belongs to us and to our children; now then, whatever God has said to you, do" (Gen 31:14-16). The episode offers a comic twist on Dr. Kramer's first helpful suggestion to promote prosocial sibling relationships: "Positive engagement (e.g. play, conversation, the promotion of mutual interests among siblings)" (Kramer 53). Perhaps Rachael and Leah were encouraged to have interactions that developed mutual interests, but it never occurs to parents that their children, normally locked in competition between themselves that is fueled by envy, would use those "mutual interests" to undo their parents.

And here the siblings' actions are replete with lies. Jacob's entourage takes off without telling Laban, Rachel even going so far as to steal "her father's household gods" (Gen 31:19), stuffing them into her camel bags on the way out the door. Laban then pursues the group, guided by a dream whereby God tells him not to say "either good or bad" (Gen 31:24) as he approaches Jacob's party, so that when he catches up to the gang of thieves, he asks Jacob why he has secretly stolen away without having been given a proper send-off

(Gen 31:26-27). His words paint the daughters as mere captive booty, an ironic suggestion since they had bitched about being captives in order to cheerlead Jacob's manipulations of their dad. Laban turns reasonable, however, mentioning that God has mitigated his right to harm Jacob for scheming and that he understands why Jacob would want to return to his father's land; however, he is disappointed that Jacob would steal his household gods (Gen 31:29-30).

Jacob explains that he was afraid Laban would not let his daughters go (a dubious claim, considering that they are Jacob's own wives). He gives Laban permission to look through his baggage to find stolen goods, and claims that "Any one with whom you find your gods shall not live" (Gen 31:32), not realizing that it is his wife Rachel who has hidden them in the camel's saddle on which she sits (Gen 31:32). Laban searches everywhere except under Rachel's butt because she claims she cannot rise before her father, "for the way of women is upon me" (Gen 31:35), knowing that most men run from a woman's period. Laban's accusations of thievery now anger Jacob, who spews a list of complaints about Laban's taking advantage of him (Gen 31:36-42); Laban fires back with his rights to his daughters and grandkids, finally calming the spitfire by asking Jacob to make a covenant with him (Gen 31:43-44). They do, but ever weary of Jacob, Laban warns about taking advantage of his daughters or taking other wives, then kisses and blesses them and returns home (Gen 31:50), still having no idea of his sizzling siblings' disregard for him. It is a typical case of parental delusion.

Another writer who addresses the potential of siblings to join together in ways most might take for granted is Dr. Jonathan Caspi, editor of *Sibling Development: Implications for Mental Health Practitioners*.[6] He points to another benefit siblings enjoy: "Because of their familiarity and accessibility, children may view siblings as relatively 'safe' individuals to confide in, seek advice, or ask informational questions that may be embarrassing to ask of peers or teachers. . . . A trusting relationship between siblings can help prevent behaviors linked with long-term negative impacts" (Caspi 45). Again, as rational optimists, we assume siblings would be working out healthy concerns, questioning each other and giving each other advice for having healthy sexual, emotional, or social relationships. We forget that the exchanges can just as likely be unhealthy, including conspiring against parents, and the price of embarrassment would be worth it if more sound, earlier advice came from a non-sibling. The "trusting relationships" can have either positive or negative results, and can have lifelong impact. Like many siblings, Rachael and Leah have their times of contention and times of collusion that grow out of their past shared experiences.

The writer of Genesis continues to dramatize these unexpected sibling dichotomies as the story turns again to Jacob and Esau, now much further into adulthood. Caravanning further into his father's territory, Jacob knows he will collide with Esau, who he has not seen for decades, so he anxiously sends out messengers to scout out his brother. The messengers discover that Esau commands a large military, a report that scares the hell out of Jacob, who knows that he had snaked Esau when they were younger (Gen 32:3-6). Jacob quickly divides his group up into two contingents, figuring that if Esau attacks one, the other can escape (Gen 32:7-8), and then whines to God about His having sent him home given his past, while also questioning his own worthiness (Gen 32:9-12). His cowardice and self-doubt serve as reminders that he has always been a man of the tent. Then, deciding to preempt Esau with a gift of hundreds of animals, he divides them, sending them ahead in test groups to see if Esau can be appeased (Gen 32:13-20).

While the gifts move on ahead of him, Jacob moves his family across a stream ahead of himself. Finally alone, Jacob finds himself wrestling with a man "until the breaking of the day." The unknown wrestler, failing to prevail over Jacob, then "touched the hollow of his thigh; and Jacob's thigh was put out of joint as he wrestled with him. Then he said, 'Let me go, for the day is breaking.' But Jacob said, 'I will not let you go, unless you bless me'" (Gen 32:24-26). Grabbing a male's thigh and putting it out of joint could be a euphemism for grabbing and twisting his testicles, but despite the man exerting such pain, Jacob is cheeky enough to say he will not let the man go until he is blessed, and lo and behold, he is blessed and in a big way, his name changing from Jacob to Israel (Gen 32:28), reaffirming Jacob as a major patriarch of Israel despite his past immorality. A satire on power? A commentary on the mystery of God's selections? Or again, is this a different writer, desperate to turn the story away from sizzling siblings, recreating Jacob as deserving all the power bestowed by Isaac's blessing? (This name change also occurs later in Chapter 35, further suggesting there were later story insertions.)

Getting back to more earthy endeavors, Jacob meets Esau's huge constituency, but Esau is his bear-hugging self, running to meet and embrace Jacob, both now weeping (Gen 33:4). Jacob's large family in tow startles Esau, and Jacob explains that they are "the children whom God has graciously given your servant" (Gen 33:5)—completely ignoring the competitive sisterly sizzle with borrowed wombs in tow and instead pretending the big fam is the result of his own righteousness. Jacob lays it on, telling Esau that "truly to see your face is like seeing the face of God" (Gen 33:10). Esau first politely refuses Jacob's gifts but finally acquiesces (Gen 33:9-11). When all the brothers' soul butter is finished, Esau asks Jacob to journey with his group. Jacob, however, says he needs to move more slowly, and points to the exhaustion of his people and animals, which will need to saunter even further behind, disconnecting them from Esau's lead (Gen 33:12-14). These rationales make for amusing, polite interchanges that nonetheless hint at the siblings' distrust and need to disconnect. The issue is resolved by them each trekking in different directions (Gen 33:16-17).

Although the story of Shechem was discussed in "In a World of Patriarchal Power . . . ," it is worth considering it from the angle of sibling relationships. When Jacob bivouacs outside the city of Shechem in the land of Canaan, his daughter Dinah is raped by Hamor the Hivite's son Shechem (Gen 34:2), whose "soul was drawn to Dinah" (Gen 34:3). Dinah's feelings are never revealed, but this unusual situation calls for a complex resolution. Instead of Jacob, the man of the tent, stepping up and taking things into his own hands, he waits for his sons to come in from the fields (Gen 34:7). One prototypical way to bring male siblings into "mutual interest" is by having them protect a sister against outside male interest, let alone against a male who raped their sister. The writer knows that sister-brother protection kicks in regardless of unexpected positive outcomes between their sister and an outside male. In this case there is an unexpected wish for unity, the father Hamor requesting peace, love, and understanding from Jacob for the union of his son with Dinah: "The soul of my son Shechem longs for your daughter; I pray you, give her to him in marriage. Make marriages with us; give your daughters to us, and take our daughters for yourselves. You shall dwell with us; and the land shall be open to you; dwell and trade in it, and get property in it" (Gen 34:8-10).

While the man of the tent sits back and watches, his sons, because of Shechem's delight in Dinah, willingly go along with the deal as long as Hamor's whole tribe, both young and old, are circumcised (Gen 34:14-17), which every male agrees to, having their penises cut regardless of their ages. Then, "On the third day, when they were sore, two of the sons of Jacob, Simeon and Levi, Dinah's brothers, took their swords and came upon the city unawares, and killed all the males. They slew Hamor and his son Shechem with the sword, and took Dinah out of Shechem's house, and went away" (Gen 34:25-26), then stole all their wealth, livestock, small children, and wives (Gen 34:28-29). Jacob's affinity for thievery is born into his sons, and thievery, coupled with premeditated violence and hypocrisy, spills out of the sons. Greed in, greed out. One of the first examples of siblings working together towards a common goal is for malicious, vengeful reasons. Jacob's reaction to the wickedness is just as shocking: he distances himself from his sons' deed, even though he had turned the matter over to the primitive fire inherent in a brother's connection with a sister, and now he is more obsessed with his political standing than with morality: "You have brought trouble on me by making me odious to the inhabitants of the land, the Canaanites and the Per'izzites; my numbers are few, and if they gather themselves against me and attack me, I shall be destroyed, both I and my household" (Gen 34:30). The vicious sons are nonplussed.

The teaming up of Leah and Rachel against their father, despite their previous resentment of each other that led to the fierce baby competition, and the teaming up of Simeon and Levi in the Shechem-Dinah affair, are a misuse the skills of the second principle offered by Dr. Linda Kramer, "Cohesion (e.g., recognizing and valuing instances of help, support, protectiveness, cooperation, loyalty, trust, and pride)"

(Kramer 53). When parents, teachers, and psychologists promote such a competency, they never consider that sizzling siblings might instinctively form cohesions not only for positive purposes but also for selfish or treacherous purposes. Sometimes parents benefit from these tribal dynamics, and indeed Jacob's entourage gets a full benefit package from God; Jacob and Esau have plenty of land between themselves, and most of Chapter 36 is devoted to listing their descendants. All of this gain and glamorization of lineage makes one wonder again if a new writer has tried to desperately correct the wicked, often darkly satiric, consequences of all the sibling sizzle.

Interrupted only by the Judah-Tamar story discussed in "In a World of Patriarchal Power . . . ," the last story in Genesis then gets back to siblings, this time focusing on Jacob's son Joseph. It starts off with a good dose of sibling fury; then, however, the narrative not only loses the folktale power-punch of the earlier stories by being stretched over thirteen chapters, but becomes an attempt by the writer (perhaps a different writer?) to damper the sizzle, pummeling reality through unrealistic characterizations and a fantastical plot. When there is sizzle in the Joseph story, instead of being created by an arbitrary parental figure's preference for one sibling over the other (the Cain-Abel story), or the resentment created by a trickster sibling (the Jacob-Esau story), or the primitive competition between sisters (the Rachel-Leah story), here it is primarily precipitated by Joseph's piety and self-righteousness and the fact that such attributes serve him well. The promotion of such traits makes one wonder again if a writer is trying to correct the earlier darkness associated with sibling rivalries.

At seventeen, Joseph is the favorite son of Jacob (often referred to as Israel at this point), because he is born in Jacob's old age (Gen 37:1-3). Joseph, a bit of a snitch, brings Jacob a nebulous, ill report of the brothers born of Rachel and Leah's maids (Gen 37:2). Probably this snitching, in addition to Jacob having a special long robe made for Joseph, and of course the brothers knowing Joseph is the most loved, boils the brothers' hatred of Joseph into such a thick, primal stock that they "could not speak peaceably to him" (Gen 37:4). Further compounding the situation, Joseph has a dream about bound sheaves in the field where his "sheaf arose and stood upright; and behold, [the brothers'] sheaves gathered round it, and bowed down to [Joseph's] sheaf" (Gen 37:7). When he (foolishly) relays the dream to his brothers, they quickly interpret it to mean that Joseph will reign over them (Gen 37:8) (although one cannot help but wonder if the subliminal erect-versus-limp-penis imagery insults them as well).

Joseph then has a second narcissistic dream in which "the sun, the moon, and eleven stars were bowing down" to Joseph (Gen 37:9), which his father Jacob interprets as not only brothers bowing down to Joseph, but also Jacob himself and his wife bowing down (Gen 37:10). Despite the increasing resentment of the brothers, Jacob "kept the saying in mind" (Gen 37:11), thereby keeping the dynamic alive. The bros are sickened by Joseph's dreams of self-aggrandizement, so they conspire to "kill him and throw him into one of the pits" (Gen 37:20) for wild animals to eat, and then sarcastically wonder, "what will become of his dreams" (Gen 37:20). Their plan is sinful but their sarcasm seems appropriate. Joseph's dreams are sizzle-lighting punks. Complete with interpretations, these dreams undermine a psychologist's or parent's attempt to encourage Dr. Kramer's seventh competency that promotes prosocial sibling relationships: "Behavioral control (e.g., refraining from undesirable sibling-directed behaviors such as bossiness, teasing, and failing to respect personal boundaries and space)" (Kramer 53). Joseph and Jacob accept the mysticism of the dreams and do not see they are attacks; but in fact they are bossing, teasing, and disrespecting the personal space of Joseph's brothers.

One brother, Reuben, feels too guilty about the plan to murder Joseph, so instead the group throws Joseph in the pit without killing him (Gen 37:21-24). While they snack, brother Judah assuages his own guilt by recommending they sell Joseph to passing Ishmaelites instead of killing him, reminding the bros that, after all, "he is our brother, our own flesh" (Gen 37:27). When later we learn about the Tamar-Judah incident, in retrospect one is not surprised that Judah comes up with an off-brand, self-serving version of brotherly love. While the brothers debate amongst themselves, Midianite traders, seeing Joseph in the pit, get the same money idea, pull him out, and sell him to the Ishmaelites, who take him to the Egyptians (Gen 37:28). Reuben finds the pit empty and "ren[ds] his clothes" (Gen 37:29), but the brothers collect their wits, ruin Joseph's robe with goat blood and show it to their father, who decides Joseph has been shredded by a wild animal. He mourns his son for several days, refuses comfort from the siblings, and threatens going to Sheol, the land of the dead, to see his son (Gen 37:31-35). The conniving Jacob has become more sentimental, especially about the sons he has had in his old age.

Meanwhile, the Egyptian "Pot'i-phar, an officer of Pharaoh" (Gen 39:1), buys Joseph and puts him in charge of his possessions. Everything Joseph oversees prospers, the Lord blessing the Egyptian's house for Joseph's sake (Gen 39:2-3). Yet things seem just a bit too cozy for this brother, now removed from angry siblings; it is as if the storyteller is desperate to finally create a sibling who escapes the consequences of his faults, separated from the other bros' sizzle by both geography and power status. Then, however, because Joseph is handsome, Potiphar's wife tries to drag him into her bed (Gen 39:7). Joseph refuses, telling her that her husband has entrusted him with everything, "nor has he kept back anything from [him] except yourself, because you are his wife" (Gen 39:9). Joseph's need to give voice that she is an exception to what he has been given comes off as presumptive, an unintentional hint that he assumes everything comes to him, despite his quickly protesting that his lying with her would be a "great wickedness, and sin against God" (Gen 39:9). Many days later (causing one to wonder why Joseph has delayed in asking Potiphar to let him leave), Potiphar's wife grabs hold of him, Joseph slipping his garments (running naked?) as he flees, and she proceeds to use the clothing as proof that he has insulted and assaulted her (Gen 39:12-18). This accusation naturally inflames Potiphar, who throws Joseph in jail, where the Lord makes sure Joseph's charisma charms the prison keeper who in turn allows Joseph the run of the place (Gen 39:20-23). His special privileges include befriending and taking charge of the Pharaoh's butler and baker, both of whom have been thrown in jail for incurring the Pharaoh's anger (Gen 40:1-2).

When the butler and baker express trouble over their dreams and the fact that there is no one to interpret them (Gen 40:6-8), Joseph steps up and chimes in, "Do not interpretations belong to God? Tell them to me, I pray you" (Gen 40:8), again Joseph proving an unctuous mix of piety and bravura. Ironically, he exhibits little imagination in deciphering their dreams. The butler's dream is of a grape vine with three branches quickly ripened with grapes that are pressed into the Pharaoh's cup (Gen 40:9-11). Joseph easily assigns a positive outlook to such a productive image: in three days the butler will be restored to his office and, befitting his role as a butler, he will place a cup in the Pharaoh's hand (Gen 40:12-13). Joseph immediately takes personal advantage of his interpretation, telling the butler to remember Joseph's help and use it to get him out of prison (Gen 40:14-15). The baker sees the interpretation is favorable and wants Joseph to interpret his dream, where he has "three cake baskets on [his] head" (Gen 40:16), birds snacking out of the top one that has an assortment of food (Gen 40:17). Joseph quickly interprets the food loss as foretelling a negative outcome for the baker: his head will be lifted up in a hangman's noose and the birds will eat his flesh (Gen 40:18-19). Both prophecies come true (Gen 40:20-22). Joseph is storing up successes that will be used to put him above his siblings in the next scenes.

The Pharaoh, in turn, has his own dreams of thin cattle eating fat cattle and thin ears of corn swallowing up plump ears (Gen 41:1-4), but his magicians cannot interpret them. Then the butler remembers Joseph, who is brought out of prison to the Pharaoh to interpret the dreams. He does so, explaining that they are about years of plenty chased by years of famine, leading the Pharaoh to decree that food be stored for the unproductive years (Gen 41:35-36). It's a commonsense solution, but Joseph is nonetheless rewarded with jewelry, wives, and status, his jail sentence presumably commuted (Gen 41:40-45). When the famine hits, the Pharaoh steers all his people to Joseph, who sells grain to them and indeed to the whole famished earth (Gen 41:54). Joseph does not open a wilderness soup kitchen, however; instead, he becomes entrepreneurial, gearing up storehouses with money to be made (Gen 41:56-57).

The famine extends to Canaan, where Joseph's father and brothers still live. Jacob, hearing that grain has been saved in Egypt, sends all the brothers there except for the youngest, Benjamin, whom Jacob protects as one of his favorites because he is youngest (Gen 42:1-4). The brothers arrive in Egypt not knowing that Joseph is now governor, nor recognizing him when they arrive, bowing "their faces to the ground" (Gen 42:6), partly because Joseph assumes an officious role, whereby "he treated them like strangers and spoke roughly to them" (Gen 42:7).

An erratic series of events ensues. First Joseph remembers dreams that reveal his brothers (whom he fully recognizes, even if they don't know him) are spies trying to assess the weakness of the land (even though they are clearly on a food mission) (Gen 42:9), so he tests his bros by demanding they bring their youngest brother back with them while committing one brother to Egyptian prison as collateral until that return, then sending all the others back to Canaan with bags of grain, threatening death if they falter in any of the plan (Gen 42:15-16). The bring-back-leave-one-take-some plan reveals Joseph as an overwrought thinker and schemer. Despite the brothers still not recognizing the governor is Joseph, the death threat immediately plays on the their past guilt, all of them remembering when they "saw the distress of [Joseph's] soul, when he besought us and we would not listen" (Gen 42:21), and Reuben interpreting the governor's threat as a "reckoning" (Gen 42:22). As the brothers journey back with the grain, having left Simeon in prison as collateral, they do not realize that Joseph has returned their grain money to them, and when they discover the money in their grain sacks, "their hearts failed them, and they turned trembling to one another, saying, 'What is this that God has done to us?'" (Gen 42:28). They are emotionally jolted. Only those with a deeply guilty conscience would read any good fortune and generosity as being a moral trap. The event gives them sibling sin jitters.

Back home, Jacob is also dismayed about the money, but his primary concern is that the siblings are down by two, Joseph and Simeon, and that they now wish to put Benjamin in jeopardy (Gen 42:36). Reuben makes an outlandish offer: if he does not return with Benjamin, he will slay two of his own sons (Gen 42:37). Jacob still fumes about their having told this governor, Joseph *in cognito*, that there was a twelfth son, but the brothers rightly plea that there was no way they could have known the consequences (Gen 43:6-7). Judah offers to take the blame if anything goes amiss but insists that they all get on the road before his and the other brothers' families starve, amusingly suggesting, "if we had not delayed, we would now have returned twice" (Gen 43:10). To guarantee success with their return, Jacob demands they take food delicacies as gifts (evidently the famine has left them only short on staples) and return the money that appears to have been given to them as an oversight (Gen 43:11-12). Without hesitation, the brothers jump on Jacob's plan. The writer continues to soften any archetypal sibling tensions, using Joseph's masquerades to prevent any open confrontation with his brothers' past, and further erasing tensions with the brothers' willingness to carry their sacks of guilt with sacks of redemptive gifts.

The brothers' confusion continues when they return to Joseph, who calls them inside for a feast, the brothers wondering whether they are being trapped because they hauled away all the unasked-for money (Gen 43:16-18), a minor infraction that results in unrealistic fear given this is a group that once easily allowed their jealousy to scheme towards murdering or slave trafficking a brother. On the other hand, Joseph, still in disguise, uses his money-doping trick for some more self-righteous preaching: "Rest assured, do not be afraid; your God and the God of your father must have put treasure in your sacks for you; I received your money" (Gen 43:23). If Joseph were testing his brothers' integrity, would they have been less ethical keeping the money, telling Joseph about the wonderful thing that happened on their way home? Joseph's setting up the money prize to now claim it was an act of God, plus now getting the charitable money back as per Judah's idea of guaranteeing success, has the whiff of a charlatan casting himself in the role of divine spokesperson in order to sell snake oil to the peons. This "generosity"—giving money away and having it brought back—does not cost Joseph a shekel.

Joseph, still not letting on as to his identity, then inquires about the health of his father (Gen 43:27), goes to pieces on seeing his brother Benjamin (Gen 43:29-30), finally sits down to dinner with "the first-born according to his birthright and the youngest according to his youth; and the men looked at one another in amazement" (Gen 43:33). The reader does, too. Where is the moral conflict? Everything has been so safely absorbed. The flipping back and forth between

Joseph's arrogance and the piling on sentimentality for the youngest brother (extra food is piled on Benjamin's plate, too), gives one the impression that a writer is strong-arming the plot to keep the sibling sizzle doused, not allowing it to flare as in the beginning of the Joseph story or any of the earlier Genesis stories. The brothers' bags are loaded up again with food and money, and now a silver cup is included in Benjamin's pack (Gen 44:1-2). Yet again, when the brothers have traveled but a short distance, Joseph pulls a quick switch and has his steward intercept the bros to claim the cup is stolen (Gen 44:4-6). Another test or another false alarm?

Aghast, the brothers are anxiety-laden once again, wondering why they would be accused of stealing when they had just returned money they did not even ask for, and again go crazily out of their way to prove their innocence, offering, "With whomever of your servants it be found, let him die, and we also will be my lord's slaves" (Gen 44:9). The steward who has intercepted them, presumably speaking for Joseph, says that the thief will "be [Joseph's] slave, and the rest . . . shall be blameless" (Gen 44:10). When the cup is found in Benjamin's pack, the brothers rend their clothes realizing that he is the "guilty" one (Gen 44:13). The significance of the test remains a mystery, no more cleared up when they return to Joseph, bowing down and giving themselves over as slaves (Gen 44:14-16), which simply serves as another opportunity for Joseph to play the righteous and magnanimous leader: "Far be it from me that I should do so! Only the man in whose hand the cup was found shall be my slave" (Gen 44:17). Judah humbly recounts the whole reason for bringing Benjamin on the trip in the first place, retells Joseph, still in disguise as governor, that Joseph himself had demanded they bring Benjamin (Gen 44:18-21); reminds Joseph of Benjamin's importance to their father Jacob, especially given the loss of his other in-old-age son, Joseph (Gen 44:27-28); cautions that not bringing Benjamin back would have a crippling effect on Jacob (Gen 44:31); and makes himself culpable for these misfortunes, asking to stay as ransom for Benjamin (Gen 44:33).

The sacrificial Judah (unlike his self-serving character in the earlier Tamar story) causes Joseph to go all to smash, crying uncontrollably, and to finally reveal himself to his brothers, the distraught Joseph immediately asking about their father (Gen 45:1). The brothers are too "dismayed" (Gen 45:3) to answer. Joseph reassures the brothers, "now do not be distressed, or angry with yourselves, because you sold me here" (Gen 45:5)—not because they have acted humbly and respectfully during all Joseph's reward-demand-reversal plots, not because they have displayed impeccable respect and loyalty to each other (incredulous for that many siblings, whether they be righteous or guilt-ridden)—but because God planned all the treachery and success, from pit to piety (Gen 45:5), from brother to governor: "God sent me before you to preserve for you a remnant on earth, and to keep alive for you many survivors. So it was not you who sent me here, but God" (Gen 45:7-8). Joseph's *deus-ex-machina* explanation, coupled with the writer going out of the way to create eleven newly righteous siblings, defuses much of the sibling tensions of the earlier Genesis stories.

In fact, sibling sizzle seems wiped off the face of the earth when Joseph promises great prosperity for all the brothers and all their families, as well as all their future generations (despite the interruption of famines [Gen 45:9-11]). Joseph asks that their father leave his homeland in order to experience the splendor of Egypt, and falls to pieces shedding more tears over Benjamin, who returns the gratitude with his own sobbing (Gen 45:14). Joseph asks his brothers to return again to Egypt so he can give them "the best of the land of Egypt, and [they] shall eat the fat of the land" (Gen 45:18). With loads of gifts and herds, he sends all the brothers to get Jacob, warning them to "not quarrel on the way" (Gen 45:24)—a strange, patronizing remark for a group that has been unified and responsible to a fault. Of course, there are times when all families, all siblings, come together without resentments or jealousies, but at best these conflict-free times last nanoseconds, and Joseph's guarantees of indulgences for his bros in Egypt shows a lack of humility that might have given the reunion in Egypt a spiritual or moral presence.

Back in Canaan, Jacob's emotional revival on hearing about Joseph's wellbeing results in reviving references to Jacob being called Israel (a reference that had dissipated in the narrative), as well as God coming forth to tell him, "do not be afraid to go down to Egypt; for I will there make of you a great nation" (Gen 46:3), and that there

"Joseph's hand shall close [Jacob's] eyes" (Gen 46:4), and that twenty lines of descendants will follow (Gen 46:8-25). Afterwards, even though "every shepherd is an abomination to the Egyptians" (Gen 46:34), probably because of nomadic intrusions and over-grazing, true to the fanciful story line, the Pharaoh amazingly sees no threat to Israel and his family moving into his land of Goshen, mostly as shepherds, telling Joseph, "The land of Egypt is before you; settle your father and your brothers in the best of the land" (Gen 47:6), and then putting them "in charge of [his] cattle" (Gen 47:6). Jacob in turn blesses the Pharaoh (Gen 47:7). Jacob's family and the Egyptian Pharaoh's family are all one big happy nation. No sibling sizzle here, on either the micro-bro or macro-nation level.

Not everything is smooth sailing, though, as the famine in both Canaan and Egypt persists. The Egyptians beg Joseph for food, which he gives them in exchange for horses and other herds (Gen 47:13-16); then the next year, since they have depleted their money, the Egyptians sell themselves and their land to Joseph, who gives them seed to plant and demands that a fifth of their produce be handed over to the Pharaoh (Gen 47:18-21). Joseph is a corporate businessman, making mergers to stay on the side of power, capitalizing on the desperation of the peasant Egyptians while his family profits and "were fruitful and multiplied exceedingly" (Gen 47:27). With Jacob-Israel dying, Egypt is evidently only a place to exploit, as Israel wants to be returned to the land of his fathers (Gen 47:29-31).

Before he dies—ironically with dim sight, reminiscent of his father Isaac's blindness of which Jacob took advantage to steal the blessing from Esau—Jacob, or Israel, blesses Joseph's children, this time with his own son Joseph trying to manipulate the blessing: "Israel stretched out his right hand and laid it upon the head of E'phraim, who was the younger, and his left hand upon the head of Manas'seh, crossing his hands, for Manas'seh was the first-born" (Gen 48:14). But Joseph is "displeased" (Gen 48:17) that the right hand, evidently the one that counts the most, is not on Manasseh's head as the firstborn, so he flips Israel's hands (Gen 48:17). Not for long. Jacob/Israel refuses the switch, adamantly correcting Joseph: "I know, my son, I know; he also shall become a people, and he also shall be great; nevertheless his younger brother shall be greater than he, and his descendants shall become a multitude of nations" (Gen 48:19). Jacob's primal essence, the younger brother who stole his father's blessing from his older brother, flares up in his final moments as he picks the younger son over the older, an homage to younger-son-as-trickster, spotlighting Jacob's craftiness that mostly has faded into old-age sentimentality. But this time, the benefactor is also a grandfather who is conscious of what he is doing, so no sibling thievery comes into play. The writer has a sharp ability in this scene to bring up past ironies while still tamping down sibling sizzle.

In his preface to *Sibling Development: Implications for Mental Health Practitioners*, Dr. Caspi points out that "interestingly, siblings may be different because of each other. That is, siblings (or the lack of them) make us who we are. If an individual had a different or no sibling, his or her personality, identity, and behaviors would be different. For example, the daughter who is introduced by her parents as the 'outgoing one' only carries this identity if her sibling is more reserved. Should she instead have a sibling who is more extroverted, she would not have this designation, nor would it becomes part of identity" (Caspi xiv). This is true in the earlier Genesis stories, where siblings receive equal time and depth and, through contrasts, their characters became more strongly defined; but since the writer in Genesis treats Joseph as a privileged character, separate from his eleven brothers, who in turn are mostly treated as one entity, Caspi's personality definition through contrast of characters is here neutered. In place of these contrasts, the writer has Jacob bless all twelve sons, the twelve tribes of Israel, with personal descriptions, some less flattering—Reuben, "Unstable as water" (Gen 49:4), Simeon and Levi, "Cursed be their anger, for it is fierce; and their wrath, for it is cruel!" (Gen 49:7)—some more so—Judah, "couched as a lion, and as a lioness; who dares rouse him up?" (Gen 49:9) and especially Joseph, "a fruitful bough" (Gen 49:22), "with blessings of heaven above" (Gen 49:25).

When Jacob dies, he is not only mourned by Joseph, who again goes all to smash, but also the Egyptians, who weep for seventy days (Gen 50:1-3). Joseph therefore merges the Pharaoh's servants and elders, in their full regalia and chariots, with his own household into

85

one large funeral possession out of Goshen and back into Canaan. Nations come together and then, after the funeral, return together back to Egypt, not only in a physical journey, but in a spiritual union, as if the story of Exodus were run in reverse (Gen 50:7-13).

But insecurities creep back. Joseph's brothers, seeing their father is now dead, say, "It may be that Joseph will hate us and pay us back for all the evil which we did to him" (Gen 50:15). Could they be serious? After all the soul butter and slosh between themselves and Joseph? They send a message to Joseph that at first glance seems like a direct admission of their past sin (despite Joseph already making it clear their actions were not their own but God's): "Your father gave this command before he died, 'Say to Joseph, Forgive, I pray you, the transgression of your brothers and their sin, because they did evil to you'" (Gen 50:16-17). However, by claiming that their father commanded Joseph to forgive (who knows if it is true or not), the brothers avoid taking responsibility for asking forgiveness on their own behalf, fearful of making themselves vulnerable, a requisite in asking forgiveness. They show no spiritual strength.

And yet, once again, Joseph assures them that everything was part of God's plan (Gen 50:19-21)—an easy way for the writer to defuse any sibling conflict. Such ease has a downside. The writer unravels any genuine sibling bonding that could only come through Joseph accepting his brothers' suffering or love, and their taking responsibility for their own transgressions. Instead, their bonds remain superficial and a little too convenient. Soon Joseph dies, but first he prophesizes that his sons will lead his people back to the land of Abraham (Gen 50:24). However, Joseph, in some ways more a brother to the power of the Pharaoh than to his own biological bros, is "put in a coffin in Egypt" (Gen 50:26). The Book of Genesis closes on that phrase, and despite some faltering in this last story, the book as a whole is a testament to sibling sizzle as the underestimated tinder that fuels the heat of the human condition.

EPISTLE TO HOLLYWOOD
THE REAL STORY OF MOSES

Dear Hollywood,

I hope, by the grace of God, that I will be helpful in assisting you with my consultation on your desire to remake a film version of the Book of Exodus, or the "Second Book of Moses," covering Moses's beginnings, his rise to power, the Passover, and the Ten Commandments. You state that your version will stick very closely to the text, unlike earlier films, but I warn you, the writers of this text are not among the Bible's strongest and as a narrative, Exodus presents serious problems. As per your request, I brief you on these issues below.

Costumes and Setting: The story is about the ancient Egyptians, which in itself affords the opportunity for the most dramatic settings and costumes in ancient history. In this regard, you may want to trade historical authenticity for visual flash, because many scholars believe the stories are more realistically based on the Babylonian exiles of the 6th Century BCE, and that they were then revised again during an even later exile of the Jewish people by the Persian king Cyrus the Great around 538 BCE. Egypt was only remotely involved, and even then not at home; instead it was with expeditions as far northeast as the Euphrates, as a way to keep back Assyrian threats. Many Jews returned to the Kingdom of Judah after the deportation to Babylonia, but just as many stayed in Egypt, Syria, and Persia, rather than leaving en masse.

If you really want to surprise audiences by depicting historical reality instead of the Biblical myth, you would have to change the whole setting and circumstances of the story. I advise instead respecting the initial writers' creative license—now "authentic" to Exodus—and worrying about other, more important narrative and character issues discussed below. Sticking with the creative license in the Bible you can also avoid the negative reaction received in 2001 by Rabbi David

Wolpe when his Los Angeles congregation came unglued because he told them most archaeologists had disproven the Bible's version of an exodus out of Egypt. The *Jewish Journal of Greater Los Angeles* called the reaction "a hurricane" and several wondered, "Did he have to say it on Passover?"[1]

The character of the Lord: This presents a real problem. In books such as Genesis, Job, and Samuel, the Lord as a character is much more interesting and unpredictable, often vacillating between being quirky, cranky, and creative, and is often portrayed entering into complex, sometimes morally questionable, relationships with the leaders with whom He makes covenants. Unfortunately, this is not the case in Exodus. Putting aside, for a moment, the Lord's obsessive-compulsive disorder in this book (explained below), His relationship with Moses is very predictable, in that the Lord never plays games with him, never creates dilemmas, and instead offers Moses a slew of miracles to use for his own, and the Lord's own, aggrandizement. For the first twenty chapters until Moses receives the Ten Commandments, the Lord doles these miracles out one after another to the point of tedium, depicting the Lord as a magician with an endless number of tricks in lieu of anything philosophical to offer Moses.

The first question is one of identity and appearance. In Exodus, the Lord sometimes appears as a cloud column and once as a flaming bush (both offer good animation possibilities), but usually with an often-repeated, tedious résumé that He tells Moses to recant for his doubters: "I am the LORD. I appeared to Abraham, to Isaac, and to Jacob, as God Almighty. . . . I also established my covenant with them, to give them the land of Canaan, the land in which they dwelt as sojourners" (Ex 6:2-4). Then the résumé continues with other accomplishments—the Lord seems to be a real curricula vitae stuffer. I recommend you ditch these intros or risk making Him appear insecure. And then there is the curious case of His name. When Moses, perhaps trying to move past the lengthy resume recitation, tells the Lord that His people want to know His name, the Lord tells Moses to present Him as "I AM WHO I AM" (Ex 3:14), something that sounds rich in philosophical implications (implying that a simple label does not replace His reality, His presence, His name), but it is unclear if the Lord has faith that the people will understand this complexity, requesting Moses to use only part of the name and tell the people of Israel, "I AM has sent me to you" (Ex 3:14).

Another big problem is that I hear a different voice enter Exodus partway through the book—someone today we might describe as an "engineer-head" or perhaps as being on the autism spectrum, obsessed with instructions. This author enters the text at key points in an attempt to create the Lord in the writer's own image. For instance, when the Lord decides He will kill every Egyptian first-born but not the first-born of Israelites (by the way, an authentic detail you may wish to forego given contemporary, precarious attempts to promote global good-will), the Lord needs to create a way to pass over those not to be killed. (Yes, that is where the high holy day Passover comes from, a term for deciding the killing of innocents.) You would think that nailing a piece of jewelry, or a mezuzah, on the door would be enough to indicate to the Lord that these houses should be spared His killing spree. Not with this writer. Here's what his obsessive-compulsive disorder requires:

> Tell all the congregation of Israel that on the tenth day of this month they shall take every man a lamb according to their fathers' houses, a lamb for a household; and if the household is too small for a lamb, then a man and his neighbor next to his house shall take according to the number of persons; according to what each can eat you shall make your count for the lamb. Your lamb shall be without blemish, a male a year old; you shall take it from the sheep or from the goats; and you shall keep it until the fourteenth day of this month, when the whole assembly of the congregation of Israel shall kill their lambs in the evening. Then they shall take some of the blood, and put it on the two doorposts and the lintel of the houses in which they eat them. They shall eat the flesh that night, roasted; with unleavened bread and bitter herbs they shall eat it. Do not eat any of it raw or boiled with water, but roasted, its head with its legs and its inner parts. And you shall let none of it remain until

the morning, anything that remains until the morning you shall burn. In this manner you shall eat it: your loins girded, your sandals on your feet, and your staff in your hand, and you shall eat it in haste. It is the LORD's Passover. For I will pass through the land of Egypt that night, and I will smite all the first-born in the land of Egypt, both man and beast; and on all the gods of Egypt I will execute judgments: I am the LORD. The blood shall be a sign for you, upon the houses where you are; and when I see the blood, I will pass over you, and no plague shall fall upon you to destroy you, when I smite the land of Egypt (Ex 12:3-13).

I hate to break it to you, because I know how much you want to keep the authenticity of the story, but these instructions are not even the most wearisome of Exodus, and actually take on the flavor of an astounding lost art of lamb-cooking. They are downright dramatic compared to the directions for building the ark and its lamps, the tabernacle and its curtains, the altar and the priests' garments, and other associated rituals that take up all of Chapters 25 to 32 and then, believe it or not, are repeated by Moses *again* from Chapters 35 to 40. Either the writer is franchising tabernacles, making sure there is no room for duplication errors, or wishes to appeal to construction-kit lovers (dress patterns, catalogue instructions, model clipper ships) or those who love watching others piece things together, like viewers of reality television. While we could easily montage some lamb-slaughter footage with a rich orchestral score, the ark will take more initiative. You could interrupt the narrative and switch to a documentary how-to format for these chapters. Otherwise, again, I suggested you modify your commitment to authenticity.

If you are still not daunted by the task, here's a stronger taste of what would have to go in such a documentary tract: "You shall make poles of acacia wood, and overlay them with gold. And you shall put the poles into the rings on the sides of the ark, to carry the ark by them. The poles shall remain in the rings of the ark; they shall not be taken from it. And you shall put into the ark the testimony, which I shall give you. Then you shall make a mercy seat [cover] of pure gold; two cubits and a half shall be its length, and a cubit and a half its breadth. And you shall make two cherubim of gold; of hammered work shall you make them, on the two ends of the mercy seat. Make one cherub on the one end, and one cherub on the other end; of one piece with the mercy seat shall you make the cherubim on its two ends" (Ex 25:13-19).

By the way, you might spot a side issue here (and another reason I wonder if this could be a different writer from the main narrative): a violation of the commandment against "graven images" of anything from heaven and above (golden cherubs) (Ex 20:4). Also, the emphasis on gold connected with religious items, something symbolized later in Exodus by the golden calf, seems inappropriate because gold is associated with idols and earthy opulence, not the spiritual. If you wish to avoid this discrepancy, you might again consider passing over some of the book's authentic details.

At the risk of overwhelming you—but hopefully strengthening my point—here's an even stronger taste of the writer's neurosis: "You shall also make curtains of goats' hair for a tent over the tabernacle; eleven curtains shall you make. The length of each curtain shall be thirty cubits, and the breadth of each curtain four cubits; the eleven curtains shall have the same measure. And you shall couple five curtains by themselves, and six curtains by themselves, and the sixth curtain you shall double over at the front of the tent. And you shall make fifty loops on the edge of the curtain that is outmost in one set, and fifty loops on the edge of the curtain which is outmost in the second set" (Ex 26:7-10). It is hard to read this as a parody on religious ritual because a satirist would have known to quit with the instructo-philia earlier in the narrative or risk overkill.

This kind of obsessive, detail-oriented mentality is evident in modern-day Matzah, a duplicate of the unleavened bread, as a symbol of remembrance. Much of your audience will know that Matzah is a symbol of redemption and freedom, the bread not having had time to rise when the Israelites left Egypt in haste. I think most people believe Matzah is something decided on by ancient Jews to remember the exodus, but really the Lord gives the Israelites no choice about eating this dry cracker. He requires the unleavened bread as "the ordinance of the passover," and then uses the opportunity to start in with the rules:

"no foreigner shall eat of it; but every slave that is bought for money may eat of it after you have circumcised him. No sojourner or hired servant may eat of it. In one house shall it be eaten; you shall not carry forth any of the flesh outside the house; and you shall not break a bone of it. All the congregation of Israel shall keep it. And when a stranger shall sojourn with you and would keep the passover to the LORD, let all his males be circumcised, then he may come near and keep it; he shall be as a native of the land. But no uncircumcised person shall eat of it" (Ex 12:43-48). So much for High Holy Day hospitality! And Matzah is just a small part of an even bigger plan of remembrance that includes sacrificing the first of the male cattle, then "every firstling of an ass you shall redeem with lamb, or if you will not redeem it you shall break its neck" (Ex 13:13). To remember the "strength of hand" (Ex 13:14) the Lord used to deliver the people out of Egypt, the first-born of man shall also be redeemed with a mark on the hand or between the eyes, the writer's OCD mentality leaving nothing unlabeled, let alone leaving one's life consumed with ritual.

I realize that I may be becoming monotonous myself, but I should also point out that, after the deliverance of the Ten Commandments, the Lord brings up many rules, some sensible, and some that will really make you wonder whether the writer is sociopathic. For instance, "if you make me an altar of stone, you shall not build it of hewn stones; for if you wield your tool upon it you profane it. And you shall not go up by steps to my altar, that your nakedness be not exposed on it" (Ex 20:25-26). Now, I can understand chiseling a stone for a river god could be profane because water "chisels" stones, rendering them beautiful to behold and special only in a way nature can determine, not man. But for this moral-giving God, looking for a temple, not a river, the "not chiseling" reads almost like "not touching," a kind of haphephobia (fear of invasion of space). God also could be diagnosed with genophobia (fear of sexual relations), here expressed through His obsessing about the altar steps having a view under the robes of one's nakedness. I am not sure there is a strategy for depicting such a comically absurd concern for an altar's stones.

Are you really up to the challenge of depicting a God with these kinds of psychological issues? Good luck. I will spare you all the rules regarding what should happen when an out-of-control ox kills someone—whether it should be stoned to death, be eaten or have its meat thrown out. You might want to focus instead on the Lord's few, more reasonable and empathetic commands, such as the one Moses brings to the people: "You shall not oppress a stranger; you know the heart of a stranger, for you were strangers in the land of Egypt" (Ex 23:9)—but that means ignoring his demand that a sojourner cannot break Matzah unless he gets his penis's foreskin snipped (Ex 12:43-59).

The character of Moses: Contrary to popular belief, the Israelites start off having a big rep with the Egyptians. For instance, "the Egyptians were in dread of the people of Israel. So they made the people of Israel serve with rigor" (Ex 1:12-13); the Egyptian midwives cannot kill Hebrew infants as they are birthed because "the Hebrew women are not like the Egyptian women; for they are vigorous and are delivered before the midwife comes to them" (Ex 1:19); and immediately after Moses is rescued as an infant by the pharaoh's daughter, the text shows him grown-up and tough—seeing an Egyptian beating a Hebrew, "he looked this way and that, and seeing no one he killed the Egyptian and hid him in the sand" (Ex 2:12). There is something sneaky, but nothing wimpy, about the Hebrews.

Then things change: God shows up as a flame and Moses crumbles, first afraid to look at God's face (despite all the chatter between the two) and then doubting his ability to represent a God who can deliver the Hebrews from Israel. Moses thinks of himself as having "uncircumcised lips" (Ex 6:30), a phrase that I think goes beyond humility, even poor self-esteem, to self-degradation, suggesting that unlike his circumcised penis, which marks a covenant with God, Moses's ability to give lip on the Lord's behalf lacks potency. Indeed, earlier in Chapter 4, Moses shuns his responsibility to speak for God and asks the Lord to find someone else, the Lord quickly picking his brother Aaron. This father-brother team has no Genesis-type conflict or psychological depth, so it is easy for Aaron, with his circumcised lips, to be "a mouth" (Ex 4:16) for Moses.

Narrative arc: At this point Moses's character goes flat as he becomes obsessively preoccupied with whether he has any credibility with his people. Performing miracles replaces character development. The gimmicks God offers Moses to establish trust in himself and the Lord—"If they will not believe you . . . or heed the first sign, they may believe the latter sign" (Ex 4:8)—end up creating a tiresome plot formed by a tiresome series of miracles (albeit ripe for special effects): a rod turns into a serpent (Ex 4:3); a hand slid into his bosom is pulled out as leprous and then, shoved back in and out, is restored (Ex 4:8); Aaron's rod swallows up Egyptian serpent-making rods (Ex 7:12); striking the water turns the Nile into blood, fouling it for drinking (Ex 7:17); a plague of frogs swamps beds, ovens, and mixing bowls (Ex 8:2); a plague of gnats covers every speck of dust (Ex 8:16); a plague of flies ruins the Egyptian's lands and then suddenly is removed down to the last fly (Ex 8:21); thrown dust becomes skin boils and sores (Ex 9:9); a hail storm chased by fire comes and goes (Ex 9:23); a plague of locusts chews grain stubs down to the ground (Ex 10:14); darkness floods the land so that only the people of Israel have light (Ex 10:23); and there is a bizarre teaser-jealousy-plague where the Lord guarantees that hopefully the Pharaoh "'will drive [Moses and the Hebrews] away completely. Speak now in the hearing of the people, that they ask, every man of his neighbor and every woman of her neighbor, jewelry of silver and of gold.' And the LORD gave the people favor in the sight of the Egyptians" (Ex 11:1-2). The "favor" they receive is all the Egyptians' jewelry, not an escape from Egypt, and when they do leave, the people of Israel are not so focused on their unleavened dough in their kneading bowls as on this Egyptian jewelry and "thus they despoiled the Egyptians" (Ex 12:36), an ironic obsession with opulent booty from a God who later commands, "You shall not steal" (Ex 20:15).

The miracles' effects never stick for long, so the plot becomes an interminable cycle of failures and start-overs, the Lord undoing each miracle by making sure that, instead of being intimidated, the Pharaoh's heart is hardened to the point of oppressing the Hebrews even more! Sometimes the Pharaoh's heart is hardened because his magicians can duplicate the Lord's miracles, sometimes because they cannot duplicate them, and sometimes the Pharaoh is just pissed that the miracle happened at all. Even when God claims, "this time

I will send all my plagues upon [the Pharaoh's] heart, and upon your servants and your people, that you may know that there is none like me in all the earth" (Ex 9:14), while the Pharaoh admits that he has sinned, that the Lord is right, and that he and his people are wrong, thus stopping the deluge of hail and thunder, the Pharaoh still "sinned yet again, and hardened his heart" (Ex 11:34), and so the cycle of plagues and hardening of heart continues just when the reader thinks it is over. In your attempt to produce an authentic depiction of this book, despite an audience's love affair with special effects, how much of this spinning-out-and-winding-in plot do you think an audience can take? You are also fighting against an audience's expectation that the plot moves urgently forward to a land-flowing-with-milk-and-honey climax (Ex 3:8).

When the Pharaoh finally allows Moses's group to leave, the Lord avoids sending them by the fastest route, in order to circumvent an encounter with the Philistines because the Lord doubts the Israelites' courage: "Lest the people repent when they see war, and return to Egypt" (Ex 13:17). Also, just as they travel on the belief that the Pharaoh approved their release, the Lord appears to grow uneasy with the deal because He hardens the Pharaoh's heart again, requiring the Egyptians to pursue Moses (Ex 14:4). The Lord is in a rut. If you stay honest to the narrative, it is going to be difficult to portray a warrior Pharaoh that is jerked back and forth *ad infinitum* and *ad nausea*, leaving an audience to wonder if the Pharaoh's stressed and hardened-not-hardened heart will lead to acute coronary thrombosis. In the meantime, in contrast to the opening chapters, the Hebrews are cranky, complaining about Moses leading them into the wilderness and crying that "it would have been better for us to serve the Egyptians than to die in the wilderness" (Ex 14:12). Moses even treats them like whiny kids, shushing them up by promising, "The LORD will fight for you, and you have only to be still" (Ex 14:14).

Of course any script will have the task of keeping Moses's working of that magical rod from becoming stick shtick. He lifts it to open the sea, allowing the Hebrews to cross, but then uses it to command the sea to drown the Egyptians. Seeing the dead Egyptians on the seashore puts fear in the Hebrews, turning them into believers, not out of physical or moral courage but from shock. When Moses's people grow tired and start complaining again, the Lord—knowing not to serve another gagging round of Matzah—rains bread from heaven. (Side note: the "murmurings" from the Israelites keep coming fast and furious with regrets for leaving Egypt. Staying honest to the narrative, you will have a challenge depicting a group that should be thankful for its escape yet cannot stop complaining and wanting to go "home" to Egypt.) In what is probably the funniest scene in the narrative, Moses discovers that by raising his hand, his people prevail over the Amalekites; lowering his hands, the Amalekites prevail, so— with a case of fickle-God fever (or like a kid that cannot refrain from turning a light switch on and off)—Moses keeps lowering and raising his hand to the point of growing so weary that "they took a stone and put it under him" (Ex 17:12) in order to give him relief from impending carpal tunnel syndrome. How can you stay honest to the story and depict a hero who becomes so mindless with his rod-power? Can this kind of comedy really work in a story focused on finding the promised homeland?

When Moses gets the Ten Commandments, it takes a while for God to write on stones "with the finger of God" (Ex 31:18) and the people get restless and desperate to worship something, anything, so Aaron helps them melt their jewelry (perhaps what they tricked out of the Egyptians?) to fashion a gold calf to worship. The Lord is of course furious and calls them "a stiff-necked people" (Ex 32:9), implying they are arrogantly obtuse, and threatens to wipe them out and start over with a new nation for Moses. Here Moses displays his greatest insight, knowing he is dealing with a vain God continuously concerned about his rep: he appeals to the Lord's fear by playing the this-exodus-would-look-absurd-if-you-killed-the-ones-you-freed card. Moses asks, "Why should the Egyptians say, 'With evil intent did he bring them forth, to slay them in the mountains, and to consume them from the face of the earth'?" (Ex 32:12) It works, but when some of the people still insist on more visible gods, they get sliced and diced, the Lord insisting he is a merciful God "slow to anger" (Ex 34:6) but "who will by no means clear the guilty" (Ex 34:7), and Moses, again admitting that many of the Hebrews are stiff-necked people, asks the Lord to "pardon our iniquity and our sin and take us for thy inheritance" (Ex 34:9). Finally God makes his covenant with Moses and his group, and this is where, for the second time, the story tumbles over chapters with obsessive rules the Israelites are to follow, which continue until the conclusion of the book.

The Ten Commandments as Scenarios: In Chapter 19, only Moses and Aaron are allowed by the Lord to come up Mount Sinai, and Moses then delivers the Ten Commandments to the people below. In fact, the Lord cautions, "whoever touches the mountain shall be put to death" (Ex 19:12). These commandments call out for explanations that require much more development than their usual listing in a sonorous voice. The American patriot Thomas Paine, one of the key instigators of the American Revolution, in his pamphlet *The Age of Reason; Being an Investigation of True and Fabulous Theology*, argued against miracles and was skeptical of anyone claiming to literally seeing God as Moses does. He also wrote that most of the commandments were sensible laws that any reasonable legislator would come up with and did not need to be handed down by God. Fair enough. But that does not distract from the creative possibilities when it comes to depicting the commandments.

The issues are complicated: How does one reconcile "Thou Shalt not kill" with the Lord killing plenty of people, including innocent Egyptian babies, in this story? Does honoring one's father and mother include turning them in if they are abusive or addicts? And how does a true believer reconcile sitting in a theater and watching the film you are going to make with "You shall not make for yourself a graven image, or any likeness of anything that is in heaven above, or that is in the earth beneath" (Ex 20:4)? Does that include special effects of the flaming bush? Early Christian art created ingenious ways to get around this commandment when it came to depicting Jesus: using mosaics made from stones, shells, and glass that, in the dark Byzantine churches and caves, flickered in candlelight, too transient and fleeting to be labeled "graven." Tougher to do with film, but see what your special effects team might think up. Maybe the whole film has to be done in a really creative, Byzantine-animation style? Just a thought.

Regarding the idea of Ten Commandment scenarios, I know this would be difficult to do and would take a very contemporary structure that would demand intercutting to different times in history, but exploring the implications of the Ten Commandments during the film has infinite possibilities and perhaps should be thought about as a separate film production. If you are interested, please view the miniseries called *The Decalogue*[2] by the Polish director Krzysztof Kielslowski, a series of ten episodes (called "decalogues"), set in a Polish city with each episode exploring the implications of a different commandment. The details of the episode's story give each commandment complex and wide-ranging inferences. For instance, Decalogue One, "I am the LORD thy God. Thou shalt have no other Gods before me," is about a loving relationship between a college math professor and his very young son who is excited about math and computers and the new ice skates he is getting for Christmas. Father and son share the computer to calculate the safety of a pond's ice, but their faith in logic, coupled with a freak ice thaw, ends with tragic consequences. Or Decalogue Six, "Thou shalt not commit adultery" which is about a young, sexually inexperienced male voyeur who watches a promiscuous woman's affair, falls in love with her, and out of jealousy tries to disrupt her life. When she learns who he is, she punishes him back, with scarring results for both characters, not because of an adulterated marriage but the adulteration of love. I think if you see *The Decalogue*, you may think of a project that not only establishes the Ten Commandments as the centerpiece of the Book of Exodus, but also pulls them out of Exodus and away from all the problems of the narrative I have described for you above. Something else to think about.

After you have time to think through the considerations I outline for you here, please get in touch and we can try to work out some solutions. I want to thank you again for your generous stipend and I hope we can work together on future projects. In the meantime, the grace of God be with you, and

with all sincerity,
Gary Hoffman

8:99

DISCIPLE LOWLIGHTS
TRUST AND DISGUST

In the Gospel of Mark, the dynamic between teacher Jesus and his disciple-students, his "fishers of men" (Mk 1:17) drives much of the book's narrative tension. Their relationship inspires Jesus to flare with creative light, but that flame often lowers to a flicker in the minds of the disciples, who are dampened by their spiritual impotence. Mark's depiction of Jesus's growing impatience with his disciples' inability to "get it" humanizes Jesus, yet Mark also humanizes the disciples: they are not saints, but rather often spiritual weak links, representing the part of humanity that frustrates the few like Jesus who try to offer their creative energy to reach beyond our boundaries.

The distance between Jesus and his disciples is first evidenced during Jesus's parable of the seed, an earthy metaphor with rich layers: one seed falling in shallow soil, quickly springing up but without deep roots, dying quickly in the sun; another seed falling among thorns that also grow up and choke out the seed so it does not yield grain; the third falling in good soil and yielding exponential amounts of grain (Mk 4:1-8). Alone with his disciples, Jesus makes a declaration regarding the importance of metaphor, a case for understanding connotation, reading between the lines. Indeed, this anti-literalist teacher implies that those who cannot look beyond appearances, who fail to analyze, will not enjoy the secret Kingdom of God. He tells the group, "To you has been given the secret of the kingdom of God, but for those outside everything is in parables; so that they may indeed see but not perceive, and may indeed hear but not understand; lest they should turn again, and be forgiven" (Mk 4:11-12). (Jesus always believes forgiveness grants humanity an opportunity for correction of its fallibilities.) Jesus, perhaps noting the blank looks on disciples' faces, registers his frustration with the group: "Do you not understand this parable? How then will you understand all the parables?" (Mk 4:13) But we are all analytically anemic to some extent and the writer of Mark hits on a forgiving device: he has Jesus interpret the parable lest we the reader become weak links to the Kingdom of God ourselves. He explains that the seeds are the word (his teachings, principles) that he sows and that when these words are sown in people, Satan comes and takes the word away (Mk 4:13-20).

Jesus explains that the first seed that quickly springs up in shallow soil represents the word joyfully received by people who "have no root in themselves, but endure for a while; then, when tribulation or persecution arises on account of the word, immediately they fall away" (Mk 4:17). Jesus seems to be addressing the tendency of humanity to give allegiance to a moral or ethical principle and espouse it to others, but then quickly abandon the idea when they see they will be punished for it, sometimes even abandoning a principle for feeble or less noble reasons such as wanting approval from a certain group—academia, government, business associates, social circles— that undervalues that principle. The seed that grows among thorns and is choked, meanwhile, represents "those who hear the word, but the cares of the world, and the delight in riches, and the desire for other things, enter in and choke the word" (Mk 4:18-19). Jesus symbolically poses the question: How many times have people turned away from moral or ethical ideals because of material gain, higher office, or immoral actions to obtain that gain? Of course the one who hears the word (the person who believes in ideals such as peace, love, and understanding, without bending under rejection or persecution, or without being distracted by material delights) gains the satisfaction of being loving, courageous, forgiving, helpful, moral.

Jesus brings the whole matter of understanding parables back to the ability to learn not by having truths handed over but by deciphering truths that are meant to be discovered: the idea that one needs to bring "a lamp" to everything—"For there is nothing hid, except to be made manifest; nor is anything secret, except to come to light" (Mk 4:21-22)—and the amount of light one brings to understanding the word are measures of what is to be gained. In fact, not bringing light results not only in loss of insight but the diminishing of what was once understood: "Take heed what you hear; the measure you give will be the measure you get, and still more will be given you. For to him who has will more be given; and from him who has not, even what he has will be taken away" (Mk 4:24-25). Either the soul hydrates or dries up.

In fact, hydration is key in the parable of the mustard seed, which Jesus uses to answer the question, "With what shall we compare to the kingdom of God, or what parable shall we use for it?" (Mk 4:30). He points out that the mustard seed "is the smallest of all the seeds on earth; yet when it is sown it grows up and becomes the greatest of all shrubs, and puts forth large branches, so that the birds of the air can make nests in its shade" (Mk 4:31-32). Jesus is referring to an especially large variety of mustard plant, but anyone who has seen a hopelessly scorched field of summer knows that just a small amount of water turns the field lush with green mustards, a dynamic symbol for anything that appears insignificant, almost nonexistent, having the potential to bring forth renewed productivity, nourishment, or joy. Accepting this concept, not sitting in an idealized city in the clouds, is the kingdom of God, an idea lost on the dim-witted listeners who are preemptively blocked by the deceptively simple parable. Jesus continues to use parables, but lest the disciples' souls dry up, "privately to his own disciples he explained everything" (Mk 4:33-34). He knows they are spirits with special needs.

But the disciples' lights continue to dim. In the second half of Chapter 6, Jesus tries to take the disciples to a "lonely" place (Mk 6:31) so that they may rest after a long sojourn of teaching, but the crowds, which Jesus is constantly trying to avoid in the Gospel of Mark—a device that demonstrates Jesus's humility while at the same time enabling the reader to witness his teachings—keep tracking him down and so follow to this lonely place. Jesus does not withhold but teaches them many things, and as the hour grows late, everyone's stomachs are gurgling. The disciples are ready to disperse the group to look for food, but Jesus has them keep everyone there to share five loaves of bread and two fish, and, by looking "up to heaven" (Mk 6:41) and breaking the bread and fish into pieces, the food multiplies and is dispersed to thousands, making the point that no matter what one has, one can always share.

The disciples depart by boat and Jesus remains alone on land, but he soon sees the disciples are stressed in rowing because the wind is against them (a symbol of their continuous spiritual struggle). Jesus easily walks out on the water to them (a symbol of his ease in the world and the miracle of his existence), but the most important aspect of his astonishing water-walk is that he "meant to pass by them" (Mk 6:48), an indication of his coolness, his not wanting the miracle of his walking on water to distract from his helpfulness. When his guys accidentally see "him walking on the sea they thought it was a ghost, and cried out; for they all saw him, and were terrified" (Mk 6:48-50). Jesus calms them, explaining it is actually himself in the flesh, and that they should have no fear.

And then something incredibly upsetting and yet simultaneously comically ludicrous happens. In order to really appreciate this scene in Mark, however, first consider how the other gospels change the story: In Matthew, Jesus has Peter walk to him on the water, Peter sinking as he fears the wind so that he must be caught and scolded by Jesus, "O man of little faith, why did you doubt?" (Mt 14:31); in Luke, while Jesus sleeps in the boat, all cry out as the boat fills with water, and instead of scolding any of them, Jesus rebukes the waves which immediately calm, putting the emphasis on the disciples' sense of wondering who this person could be that "commands even wind and water, and they obey him?" (Lk 8:25).

But in Mark, there is no such scolding about doubt, and the emphasis on miracle diminishes. The disciples in Mark "thought it was a ghost, and cried out; for they all saw him and were terrified" (Mk 6:49-50), astounded just as they are in the other gospels, but not because Jesus walks on water. Not even because Jesus controls the weather. No, the reason for their astonishment, incredibly, is that "they did not understand about the loaves" (Mk 6:52). That's right. Despite Jesus having just walked on water, these guys are still trying to figure out what-the-sweet-mother-of-Jesus happened last time their teacher conducted his drama on sharing loaves of bread and fish. They are still in a stupor, slow to interpret that moment's significance: there is no light coming from them that endorses the importance of sharing. But Mark also implies that there is a dangerous side to puzzlement, in this case the grappling with the gleam of generosity, which is not immediately apparent. Not understanding the significance of symbol makes people feel insecure, leading to frustration and often to anger in proportion to that frustration, and indeed Mark adds, right after describing the disciples still mulling over the bread-loaves-fish event, that "their hearts were hardened" (Mk 6:52), because they are baffled by the significance of the metaphorical miracles they have witnessed.

In Chapter 8, the disciples' light almost blinks out. Jesus "began to teach them that the Son of man"—in Mark, Jesus always describes himself as the Son of man and not of God, underscoring his humility—"must suffer many things, and be rejected by the elders and the chief priest and the scribes, and be killed, and after three days rise again. And he said this plainly" (Mk 8:31-32), not figuratively or hyperbolically. He is dead serious. There are different ways "to arise" after death, but Jesus knows there is always a price to be paid for countering authority; the price, in his case, will be death. The reader has witnessed previous examples of Jesus ignoring the authority of tradition, such as when, despite Jesus explaining to the Pharisees that the "Sabbath was made for man, not man for the sabbath" (Mk 2:27), in the synagogue they nevertheless "watched him, to see whether he would heal [a man with a withered hand] on the Sabbath, so that they might accuse him" (Mk 3:2). Their hatred is not hidden from Jesus, who is "grieved at their hardness of heart" (Mk 3:5), but he does indeed heal the man, and the Pharisees immediately hold "counsel with the Hero'di-ans against him, how to destroy him"(Mk 3:6).

The disciples prefer darkness in Chapter 8, denying the inevitability of the consequences for any action or principle that goes against authority, tradition, and protocol. Peter even "rebuke[s]" (Mk 8:32) Jesus for describing this deadly price, but Jesus is disgusted by Peter's weakness, which he seems to read in all the disciples' expressions: "turning and seeing his disciples, he rebuked Peter, and said, 'Get behind me, Satan! For you are not on the side of God, but of men'" (Mk 8:33). Helping someone when it is necessary—Sabbath or no Sabbath, the law or not the law—is on the side of God. Jesus adds, "For whoever would save his life will lose it; and whoever loses his life for my sake and the gospel's will save it. For what does it profit a man, to gain the whole world and forfeit his life?" (Mk 8:35-36). This paradox confounds the disciples. The question the disciples do not understand is what kind of life is saved and what aspects of another life are lost saving it. From a metaphorical point of view, a life "saved" from a worldly standpoint might be devoted to following mindless religious rules at the expense of helping others, or worse, lives devoted to attaining power or material assets. These covetous, mindless lives can only exist by losing lives that uphold principles through sacrifices.

A bit later in Chapter 9, talking to the disciples, Jesus adds to the dynamics of the sacrifice, noting that it will trigger a betrayal—"The Son of man will be delivered into the hands of men, and they will kill him" (Mk 9:31)—but again the disciples "did not understand the saying, and they were afraid to ask him" (Mk 9:32). They either do not want to know the answer, do not want to look stupid, or worse, already sense that their insecurity will betray Jesus's light in the end. Creating this divide between the disciples and Jesus, Mark puts emphasis on the importance of courage, highlighting the danger of spiritually weak people supporting ideals until courage is required, and then in the face of rejection or persecution, quickly tossing those ideals away. Fully knowing the outcome, Jesus goes on to demonstrate true courage and sacrifice.

The disciples' light continues to diffuse. John tells Jesus they "saw a man casting out demons in your name, and we forbade him, because he was not following us" (Mk 9:38). The disciples are vain enough to think their group has a patent on what Jesus has been teaching. Mark here anticipates all future Jesus fans who want to believe that only Jesus can validate his principles and practices—not other poets, prophets, philosophers, teachers—an assumption reeking of self-righteousness. The disciples are also simple enough to think there has to be a special pay-off for following their main man around in the desert, when really Jesus has made it clear from early in the narration that the light he stands for must stand alone. Over and over Jesus has begged people he heals to take the credit themselves and to "say nothing" (Mk 1:44) to anyone about his role (totally the opposite of much of the character of Jesus in the Gospel of John, who is constantly reminding everyone he is the Son of God, and wants full credit for it.)

At this point, James' and John's desperation flares up: "Teacher, we want you to do for us whatever we ask of you" (Mk 10:35), they tell him, and what they want is throne status: "Grant us to sit, one at your right hand and one at your left, in your glory" (Mk 10:37). Jesus tells them this is not for him to grant, that it is "for those whom it has been prepared" (Mk 10:40) and, while the other disciples are pissed that the two were trying to power-grab positions they themselves covet, Jesus turns everything upside down, mocking their lording-over-others attitudes, redefining the whole dynamic as "whoever would be great among you must be your servant, and whoever would be first among you must be slave of all. For the Son of man also came not to be served but to serve, and to give his life as a ransom for many" (Mk 10:43-45). Jesus of course serves many with forgiveness, with poetic teaching, with healing, and ultimately with his life. He also serves by not giving up on his disciples who in the narrative more and more represent our callow selves. This helps shift some of the focus onto Jesus's faith in transformation, not solely his leadership.

"Serving others" in Jerusalem's temple means something different than in Jesus's teachings: it is based on self-gain and commercial ventures rather than spiritual meditation. Jesus tosses over the tables of the moneylenders, infuriating the chief priests and scribes so they "sought a way to destroy him; for they feared him, because all the multitude was astonished at his teaching" (Mk 11:18). Chapters 11, 12, and 13 leading up to the Passover in Jerusalem are especially fruitful, describing both Jesus's wit and insights, which take on a sharp edge as he knows he moves closer to his death. One example of this wit comes at a point in Jerusalem when Jesus argues with the Sad'ducees, a Jewish sect of high social and economic status in the temple, about their stunted hypothetical concerns: a concern about which of seven brothers, who died consecutively, each in turn taking on the same woman as a wife and each failing to impregnate her, will end up after the resurrection with that woman as their wife (Mk 12:19-23). A different scribe overhears and admires Jesus showing the men their ignorance, including their failure to see the absurdity of marriage concerns after rising from the dead. He begins to talk to Jesus, and in the exchange the scribe remembers, "to love one's neighbor as oneself, is much more than all whole burnt offerings and sacrifices" (Mk 12:33). Jesus commends the scribe as being "not far from the kingdom of God" (Mk 12:34), a complement he has never been able to grant to the disciples. The fact that an outsider can understand Jesus further highlights how difficult it is to find a flicker of understanding with the disciples.

Meanwhile the disciples are goo-goo over the "wonderful stones and . . . wonderful buildings" (Mk 13:1) of the temple, praising grandeur despite Jesus's warnings of what counts as majesty inside the temple: "Beware of the scribes, who like to go about in long robes, and to have salutations in the market places and the best seats in the synagogues" (Mk 12:38-39)—timeless narcissists who care more about status, privilege, and being noticed than meditation and introspection; "who devour widows' houses" (Mk 12:40)—timeless predators on the lookout for vulnerable women and their possessions; "and for a pretense make long prayers" (Mk 12:40)—timeless pontiffs who concoct long-winded, attention-seeking, insincere prayers. These are the realities behind the "wonderful stones." Jesus warns of institutional horrors behind the wondrous walls: that if his "fishermen of souls" hold to his ideals, and are able to interpret through careful critical thinking and present his lessons figuratively, they will be beaten in the synagogue, and that they will need to reach into their inner-most selves, avoiding anxiety about polished presentation so that the Holy Spirit will speak through them, but still they "will be hated by all for my name's sake" (Mk 13:13). Jesus is desperately trying to appeal one last time to their courage, but these weak links still seem more confused than faithful. Indeed one disciple, Judas Iscariot, already conspires to betray Jesus for money, and when Jesus announces that one of the disciples at the Passover table will betray him, they all feel implicated, saying "to him one after another, 'Is it I?'" (Mk 14:19), not one of them secure enough in their love or beliefs to avoid feeling indicted.

Jesus sees the disciples' lights will snuff out. He turns to a proverb that reminds him that he is alone and the disciples, like so many people, will not maintain their strength of conviction: "You will all fall away; for it is written, 'I will strike the shepherd, and the sheep will be scattered'" (Mark 14:27). Peter denies he will fall away but Jesus knows "this very night before the cock crows twice, [Peter] will deny [him] three times" (Mk 14:30). When Jesus goes to Gethsemane, a secluded place to contemplate the fate of his actions, knowing his life will end, he asks Peter, James, and John to keep watch, an act of support and comfort, but while Jesus goes through painful meditation, doubt, and rediscovery of purpose—"Abba, Father, all things are possible to thee; remove this cup from me; yet not what I will, but what thou wilt" (Mk 14:36)—to Jesus's astonishment the disciples nap. Even after admonishing them for sleeping one hour, he forgivingly offers them another chance: "Watch and pray that you may not enter into temptation; the spirit indeed is willing, but the flesh is weak" (Mk 14:38). They still sleep. And then they sleep a third time—a trinity of discomfort, fallibility, and insensitivity.

Although Judas commits the climactic betrayal by kissing Jesus, he is a dramatic embodiment of the other disciples. All are devoid of light. In Chapter 14, using a kiss to give Jesus away to the crowd of scribes and elders who come with swords and clubs seems especially grotesque because nowhere in Mark's narrative are any of the disciples close to Jesus, none depicted as kindred spirits despite Jesus's continuous attempts to teach and trust them. While the chief priests and whole council seek testimony against Jesus so they may put him to death, Peter, who had followed the crowd to the courtyard of the high priest, is spotted warming himself (a symbol of self-preservation) by one of the high priest's maids, who recognizes him as one of Jesus's disciples. "But he denied it, saying, 'I neither know nor understand what you mean'" (Mk 14:68). She insists. He denies again, and then a third time "he began to invoke a curse on himself and to swear, 'I do not know this man of whom you speak'" (Mk 14:71). The cock crows a second time. Peter remembers Jesus's prediction of his denial, and weeps.

Over the course of history, insightful artists have clarified the significance of these betrayals. The kiss of Judas provides a dramatic moment, but whether Judas's betrayal is unique to him or hints at being indicative of all the disciples' betrayals can be handled in subtle ways by painters. In the most dimwitted depictions, such as *Betrayal of Christ* by Caspar Isenmann, painted between 1462-1465, Judas is singled out, disassociated from the other disciples, the only person with a crooked Semitic nose, red hair, and droopy eyes, while Jesus has a disappointed pout, turning away from Judas as if confused by the situation.

In contrast, Giotto, painting between 1304-1306 on his mural of the Scrovegni (Arena) Chapel in Padua, captures the spirit of Mark's gospel: Jesus is calm, his face inches from Judas's, Jesus's eyes centered, open, alert, fully aware of the betrayal's significance and with deep understanding of the disciples' weakness. Since his look contains neither hatred nor disappointment, it is a look appropriately directed at any of the disciples. Jesus is a person of stature, taller than Judas, so that his gaze is cast downward as if staring at a mindless, guilty child. Judas's eyes do not make contact, drifting up into his ape-like, receded brow as if he is not quite sure why he is here, a familiar mindset of the disciples we witness throughout Mark's story. The baboon, squat shape of his head contrasts with Jesus's noble proportions, underscoring the spiritual and intellectual difference between the two men.

One of the main focuses in Giotto's painting is Judas's golden cloak, upward-sweeping folds enclosing the two men as if to enshrine the event while simultaneously covering up the disciple's despicable act. Judas's cloak draws towards another metallic-colored one made shameful by the hooded person turning his back to the viewer, and made further ignoble by the official, with the staunch stance of a short figure, who grabs a rose cloak of a third person probably fleeing—perhaps John the Evangelist, who is often depicted as fleeing in Christian iconography—but since the grabbed person is out of the frame, it could be anyone, a reminder that all the disciples, like spooked sheep, will scatter. An extension of Judas's betrayal is fixed by the figure who looms above the short, hooded person's fist, reaching towards Jesus with a dagger, his face in line with Judas's and all the others, his hairstyle, outreached arm, and squat face mirroring Judas's, his hand recklessly cutting off the priest's servant's ear in the narrative. Mark keeps this person anonymous, devoid of name or description, representing every man; Matthew makes the person "one of those who were with Jesus" (Mt 26:51); John makes him Peter (here with his nimbus), all versions extending Judas's betrayal, but Giotto uses John's account of Peter to eliminate any doubt that there is collective shame and panic among the disciples.

In his *Taking of Christ*, painted in 1602, Caravaggio intensifies some of the elements in Giotto's work. The person fleeing is more easily identified in Christian iconography as the beardless disciple John the Evangelist, here fleeing to the left in terror, his hand desperately flailing into dark space, his existence not a mirror of Judas as in Giotto's painting, but one of fear, another side of betrayal. Judas's furrowed brow, reminiscent of Abraham's in Caravaggio's painting of Isaac's sacrifice, indicates confusion but also, with his eyes focused on Jesus, indicates a misplaced hatred seeping out of that anger. The look is reminiscent of the hard-hearted frustration the disciples experience throughout Mark's narrative. Jesus's relaxed mouth suggests acceptance but his slightly furrowed forehead and cast-down eyes, coupled with his darkened sockets, show overwhelming disappointment—nothing new in his relationship with all the disciples, only now with intense sadness. Judas's stunted arm, merged with the mailed armor of the soldier's hand on Jesus's neck, adds to the grotesque violation, forcing Jesus's prayer-clasped hands downward into a painful twist. John's cloak canopies the three heads together, with Jesus trapped between the two linked versions of betrayal.

The hand of the person in the right corner, holding up the lamp, is sometimes thought to be Caravaggio's, but his inquisitive face could also be that of any viewer of the painting, straining to witness the scene. His hand deftly lifts the lantern up above the scene (symbolic of observational distance); however, most of the lantern is buried from our sight with only its top bobbing in the sea of darkness. The partial illumination represents all of our struggles to understand why the world betrays the Son of man who teaches so much and who sacrifices his life to uphold his values, not to save us from sin, but to show us what courage it takes to hold onto our inner light that he has come to represent. Perhaps, like the disciples, we all want to be strong while in the sphere of a courageous person, but revert to our weaker selves when we lose faith in that person's presence.

9:111

FROM HALLOW TO CALLOW
MARK TO JOHN

One of my friends is excited about the Gospel of John, but another one says it is juvenile and encourages me to only read the Gospel of Mark. What makes one of the gospels of Jesus Christ callow instead of hallow?

The Gospel of John replaces Jesus's humility, analytical thinking, humor, and creativity, all so essential in the Gospel of Mark, with a Jesus centered on witless glory. It also inserts a confused depiction of the Jewish community and Jesus's role in it; dehumanizes the disciples, especially in the case of a mechanized Judas; slops up Pontius Pilate's character while turning Mark's solemn crucifixion into a manifesto of insecurity; and replaces a story of universal significance with a meaningless plot littered with careless dialogue. That is how a hallow story becomes callow.

Isn't Jesus's humility a constant in all the gospels?

No. In Mark, Jesus has abundant humility, but not so in John. For instance, Mark has Jesus constantly designate himself as "the Son of man," rather than referring to himself as "the Son of God." Mark's Jesus never insists that everyone knows he represents the Father in heaven, which would be a quick, facile way to make him a spiritual hero. Similarly, when he heals someone, Mark's Jesus usually does everything he can to empower others: when healing a group of unclean spirits who cry out, "You are the Son of God" (Mk 3:11), Jesus "strictly ordered them not to make him known" (Mk 3:12); when curing a man with leprosy "he sternly charged him, and sent him away at once, and said to him, 'See that you say nothing to any one'" (Mk 1:43-44); when a woman, who has been hemorrhaging for twelve years, knows to touch his garments to heal but then is ashamed for having done so after being questioned, she elicits Jesus's response, "Daughter, your faith has made you well; go in peace, and be healed of your disease" (Mk 5:34). In Mark, crowds track Jesus down, but he is the embodiment of modesty, constantly trying to avoid a spotlight from heaven.

In contrast, the Jesus we meet in the Gospel of John never displays such humility or modesty. He does the opposite. John's Jesus constantly replays versions of the same announcements of aggrandizement, namely that he is the Son of God, and furthermore, threatens dire consequences for those who deny his status: "he who comes from heaven is above all. . . . he whom God has sent utters the words of God, for it is not by measure that he gives the Spirit; the Father loves the Son, and has given all things into his hand. He who believes in the Son has eternal life; he who does not obey the Son shall not see life, but the wrath of God rests upon him" (Jn 3:31-36). "Not by measure"—in other words, without variance in what one receives regardless of one's limited understanding of the parables—is a slap at the patience required to decipher the careful revealing of spirit through parables, which are never used by John's Jesus, either because John was himself threatened by them, because he lacked the faith in mankind's energy to decipher the truth through poetic inference, or because he perceived them to be a threat to blind faith.

No, John's Jesus never couches his identity with modesty. When a woman tells Jesus that the Messiah is coming who will show all things, he quickly lets her know, "I who speak to you am he" (Jn 4:26). The abruptness of his response, coupled with the seizing of power in other lines, makes John's Jesus appear insecure, instinctively putting mankind in a double bind about his authority versus God's: "The Father judges no one, but has given all judgment to the Son, that all may honor the Son, even as they honor the Father. He who does not honor the Son does not honor the Father who sent him." (Jn 5:22-23). John's Jesus goes out of his way to let all know that he has been given God's power to judge (Mark's Jesus never asserts such power), but more menacingly, that he has been given this power not primarily for the purpose of bringing mercy or forgiveness into the world, rather to immodestly bring honor on himself ("that all may honor the Son even as they honor the Father"). He tops this announcement off with a threat: if one does not care for Jesus's judgments, one automatically rejects the Lord and loses out on "eternal life" (5:24). This judgment does not represent the dove one associates with Mark's peace, love, and understanding, but rather points the way to totalitarianism.

How else is insecurity manifested in John or Mark's depictions of Jesus?

In many instances, when John's Jesus claims his power, John immediately undercuts the claim lest Jesus look subversive, or as if he's acting on his own, thereby diminishing Jesus's ability to make judgments based on his own secular experiences: "I can do nothing on my own authority; as I hear, I judge; and my judgment is just, because I seek not my own will but the will of him who sent me" (Jn 5:30), completely dissipating any hope of a more merciful judgment than the harshness of the Old Testament God. John's Jesus tries to temper these statements with self-serving modesty by downplaying his role: "my judgment is just, because I seek not my own will but the will of him who sent me" (Jn 5:30), but the idea that Jesus acts merely as God's mouthpiece, not modifying God's judgments based on his own earthly encounters and wisdom, does little to inspire faith in John's Jesus as a lover of mankind.

Furthermore, a lot of space in the Gospel of John is devoted to Jesus insisting he is the Son of God. Pulling rank is never a maneuver for those who are secure. When he raises Lazarus from the dead, "Jesus lifted up his eyes [to heaven] and said, 'Father, I thank thee that thou hast heard me. I knew that thou hearest me always, but I have said this on account for the people standing by, that they may believe that thou didst send me'" (Jn 11:41-42), focusing more on the raising of Lazarus as a sign or proof of his supernatural abilities than on the fact that his good friend is now not dead after all. These unearthly abilities are downplayed by Mark's Jesus, who never calls in requests from the Father for miracles to prove his greatness to anyone. In fact, the Gospel of Mark (and much of Luke and Matthew) suggests that the necessity to perform miracles to prove one's worth is a temptation that does not enable humanity to find its own moral strength. Mark, unlike John, shuns shrill ego claims. Even when Mark's Jesus is crucified, he stays silent when "the chief priests mocked him to one another with the scribes, saying, 'He saved others; he cannot save himself. Let the

Christ, the King of Israel, come down now from the cross, that we may see and believe" (Mk 15:31-32).

Luke goes further. When Jesus is tempted by the devil in the wilderness, one of the temptations is the demand for miracles: "'If you are the Son of God, command this stone to become bread.' And Jesus answered him, 'It is written, "Man shall not live by bread alone""' (Lk 4:3-4). The Jesus in Mark and Luke not only turns down miracles to prove his worth, but Luke uses the devil's imagery to make a new point concerning the importance of spiritual wellbeing versus the physical wellbeing represented by the bread. John's Jesus typically does not display the security necessary for this kind of restraint: he would never forego the chance to answer a demand for a miracle. He cannot wait to glory in it.

Are there any qualities of Mark's Jesus that show up in the Jesus of John's gospel?

In the Gospel of John there are a few reminders of the earlier Gospel of Mark, remnants of a more secure Jesus. The testing of Jesus by the scribes and Pharisees, when they bring a woman to him who has committed adultery and demand that according to the law of Moses she be stoned to death, is reminiscent of their tests in Mark. So is Jesus's response, staring them off, unraveling their bravura, and pushing them away with, "Let him who is without sin among you be the first to throw a stone at her" (Jn 8:7). Also with a Markesque tone, John's Jesus says, "This is my commandment, that you love one another as I have loved you. Greater love has no man than this, that a man lay down his life for his friends" (Jn 15:12-13); however, immediately qualifiers neutralize such lines—"You are my friends if you do what I command you. No longer do I call you servants, for the servant does not know what his master is doing; but I have called you friends, for all that I have heard from my Father I have made known to you" (Jn 15:14-15). Right away friendship is based on doing what is commanded, and commands must have the authority of God and must be delivered through Jesus's connection with Him; this is not love for its own sake arising from Jesus's grappling with the human condition, through which he might in fact become an example of a spiritually secure and mature spiritual leader. When Mark's Jesus proclaims values, they carry their own weight, without God's certificate of approval; similarly, Mark's Jesus does not suggest that only grandiose proclamations, delivered from God's shoulders, have worth. The reader can count on Jesus in his own right.

Do both Mark and John focus on moral values?

Mark focuses on a much wider array of moral values needed in this life than John does. For instance, Mark covers the forgiving of sins, even those sanctioned by religion (Mk 2:7-10); helping those in need before the righteous (Mk 2:15-17); practicing moral actions before fulfilling religious dogma (Mk 2:27-3:6); forgiving blasphemies, but not the blasphemy of peace, love, and understanding represented by the Holy Spirit (Mk 3:28-31); placing morality and good works over family ties (Mk 3:32-35); understanding metaphor as a means of participating in the spiritual, a process antithetical to literalism and parochialism (Mk 4:10-14); perceiving immorality as spiritual uncleanliness instead of physical unsightliness (Mk 7:1-23); sacrificing for a cause as a reason to live (Mk 8:31-38); diminishing ones' greatness and unique abilities for a larger good (Mk 9:33-41); promoting glee and wonder over intellect (Mk 10:13-16); warning that riches corrupt or distract from a moral life (Mk 10:23-26); serving with ability and insight as more important than serving with credentials (Mk 11:27-33); caring about others as more important than ritual sacrifices to God (Mk 12:31-33); shunning status, pretentiousness, and hierarchy in places of worship (Mk 12:38-40).

John's Jesus avoids virtually all of these secular moral issues and instead focuses on the reward of faith-based eternal life; John's concept that our spirits can exist forever constantly distracts from the importance of living a moral life in the present. For instance, large gobs of text insist on Jesus's unearthly connections to his Father as an end-all: "I do nothing on my own authority but speak thus as the Father taught me. And he who sent me is with me; he has not left me alone, for I always do what is pleasing to him" (Jn 8:28-29); however, there is no immediate follow-up teaching regarding what might be pleasing to the Father, neither burnt meat nor moral living. Like a playground kid competing for attention by bragging about what his father does, John's Jesus uses such proclamations of greatness to easily win followers—"As he spoke thus, many believed in him" (Jn 8:30)—reminding the reader that having faith in a non-secular hierarchy is attractive, and easier than grappling with moral parables. In the next passage John's Jesus says, "If you continue in my word, you are truly my disciples, and you will know the truth, and the truth will make you free" (Jn 8:31-32), a noble sentiment, but again, John offers no specific dynamic that reveals the truth about anything in human terms, neither directly nor metaphorically. Nothing. The reader might have ideas about the ways that truth in relationships works, or how morality sets one free, but not because John's Jesus gives the reader any new insight.

The reader's only option is to believe that Jesus represents an absolute truth by his mere existence and connection to the Father. Belief in a person as an icon, alive or represented by a statue, to represent the absolute truth, is dangerously akin to idolatry, because it is far removed from philosophy or spiritual contemplation. John's Jesus continues, "I say to you, every one who commits sin is a slave to sin. The slave does not continue in the house for ever; the son continues for ever" (Jn 8:34-35). That sin enslaves is also a meaningful idea but, as with the reference to "truth," sin is not defined, forcing the reader to miraculously conceive how a sin can be enslaving, concepts that Jesus in Mark and the other synoptic gospels never leaves undeveloped, exemplifying such concepts with parables. John asks the reader to have faith in the permanence of an unearthly God and cares little about explaining what those earthly values might look like.

How are metaphors used differently in the Gospel of John and the Gospel of Mark?

John's Jesus uses metaphors for self-aggrandizement; Mark's Jesus uses metaphors to test and teach his listener. The Gospel of John begins with a stunning, full-choral metaphor: "In the beginning was the Word, and the Word was with God, and the Word was God" (Jn 1:1). In this first sentence the "Word," capitalized, holds a sky of possibility. The Greek word used in the text is "logos" which can refer to the controlling principle of the universe. In English "Word" could be read as praise of language as the essence of all we know, or of the symbolic language that sanctifies God. This metaphor is full of potential until we hit this line: "He was in the beginning with God; all things were made through him, and without him was not anything made that was made" (Jn 1:2-3). Now "the Word" is replaced by "He," so praise of language fades, now limited to "He" who is the powerful maker of everything, duplicating God's efforts, and if this is presumably Jesus, the metaphor subverts him as a philosophical force, pointing to him as a maker of the world, an unnecessary throwback to Genesis. The "Word" dissipates and with it the metaphorical possibilities.

To depict Jesus as a co-maker of "all things" redirects his role away from political, spiritual, and religious leadership; instead, he becomes a character in a child's *pourquoi* tale: "How the World Was Made." The next sentence does correct this: "In him was life, and the life was the light of men. The light shines in the darkness, and the darkness has not overcome it" (Jn 1:4-5). The beauty of that line cannot be denied; like other lines such as, "I am the bread of life; he who comes to me shall not hunger, and he who believes in me shall never thirst" (Jn 6:35), it captures the imagination in terms of knowing we are in the presence of someone special. However, the metaphors are nevertheless vague about what the light and fulfillment of nourishment represent in any moral terms.

Parables, on the other hand, as complex, extended metaphors, comment on moral conditions and force the reader to struggle with interpretive moral dilemmas. They do not glamorize Jesus, such as a phrase like "I am the light of the world" (Jn 9:5). In the Gospel of Mark, Jesus tells the disciples, "To you has been given the secret of the kingdom of God, but for those outside everything is in parables; so that they may indeed see but not perceive, and may indeed hear but not understand; lest they should turn again, and be forgiven" (Mk 4:11-12). The parable of the seed (explained in Chapter 8, "Disciple Low Lights"), forces the reader to actively participate in deciphering the inferences of the different levels of spiritual weakness represented by each condition of the seed. Mark suggests that unless someone is able to interpret—in other words, to contemplate the significance of language—the person is not adept at understanding the spiritual and moral implications of life's dilemmas. This contemplation demands a level of maturity and patience to work through a poetic expression foreign to the adolescent mind that instead prefers to be given "the Word."

In fact, John seems anxious to find a way to dispense with the parables or the wit he knows exists in the earlier synoptic gospels, recasting such use of intelligence and creativity by Jesus into a temporary necessity that should be tossed to find spiritual enlightenment: "I have said this to you in figures; the hour is coming when I shall no longer speak to you in figures but tell you plainly of the Father" (Jn 16:25), as if this is a change when in fact it is what John's Jesus has been doing throughout his gospel. To drive this point home, John has Jesus's disciples give a gigantic sigh of relief that they no longer need to decipher meaning, no longer need to participate in the demanding process of deciphering parable: "Ah, now you are speaking plainly, not in any figure! Now we know that you know all things, and need none to question you; by this we believe that you came from God" (16:29-30). No more critical thinking; school is out; shallowness is rewarded; the true God is revealed. For John, parables are obsolete.

What other differences exist between Jesus's mentality in Mark and John?

An important difference between the two gospels is that Mark's Jesus not only shows wit in creating and interpreting parables but also employs satiric social wit to confound adversaries. John's Jesus does not. This makes for two very different spiritual aptitudes. The writer of John either misunderstood how crucial the parables are for obtaining moral enlightenment or lacked the maturity to engage in parables when he read the earlier synoptic gospels (Mark was written between 55-70 CE, Luke and Matthew between 65-80 CE, John between 80-90 CE). John creates a Jesus who insists the listener either believes in his superiority or not, and this results in an irritable, impatient persona who appeals to an adolescent mentality that feels more secure around declarations of truth than around teasing and irony.

For instance, when John's Jesus is confronted by nonbelievers, who ask, "How long will you keep us in suspense? If you are the

Christ, tell us plainly" (Jn 10:24), instead of coming back with wit that pushes them away from simple answers and forces them to question their own values, Jesus petulantly scolds them with an overwrought metaphor: "I told you, and you do not believe. The works that I do in my Father's name, they bear witness to me; but you do not believe, because you do not belong to my sheep. My sheep hear my voice, and I know them, and they follow me; and I give them eternal life, and they shall never perish, and no one shall snatch them out of my hand. My Father, who has given them to me, is greater than all, and no one is able to snatch them out of the Father's hand. I and the Father are one" (10:25-30). My sheep get me; you do not; you get nothing; too bad for you because I am like God.

Given a similar situation, when Mark's Jesus is confronted by the authorities and scribes of the temple for being an outsider, not paying his dues, and not being properly credentialed—"By what authority are you doing these things, or who gave you this authority to do them?" (Mk 11:28)—Jesus does not pull rank that he is his Father's messenger and the Son of God, but instead immediately displays a dispassionate, mature coolness by offering a conundrum that they must answer if he is to answer. "I will ask you a question; answer me, and I will tell you by what authority I do these things. Was the baptism of John [the Baptist] from heaven or from men?" (Mk 11:29). Without John's listen-only-to-me, I-said-I-am-the-son-of-God shrillness that pulls Jesus away from nonbelievers, separating him from humanity, Mark's Jesus makes himself more accessible, momentarily positioning himself close to those out to destroy him. By requiring them to answer an equally loaded question, he calmly shifts the ball to the "credentialed" group. They realize they cannot say John's baptism was "by heaven" or Jesus will ask why then did they not believe in John the Baptist's proclamations of a coming messiah and the Holy Spirit descending on Jesus; but if they say "from men," they are afraid of further empowering followers of John the Baptist, who the people saw as a prophet. Jesus has shifted the argument away from himself, momentarily redirecting the rancor to set off bickering inside the "credentialed" group's circle that yields no comfortable or clever comeback because they are politically tongue-tied. When they respond "We do not know" (Mk 11:33), the

119

group's impotency and lack of wit gives Jesus his response: "Neither will I tell you by what authority I do these things" (Mk 11:33). John's Jesus would not be able to control himself, and, as an insecure literalist, would immediately shout out an answer: "By God's authority!"

Coolness and thoughtfulness in the face of treachery is the mark of maturity, making Jesus someone worthy of following. The writer of Mark is not asking us to accept Jesus based on his claims of importance, but on his intelligence, courage, and spiritual strength. Mark's Jesus displays the same wit when he is confronted by the Herodians, who see Jesus as a threat to King Herod's rule, particularly when Jesus tells the parable of the vineyard. In the parable, a man builds a vineyard and lets it out to tenants, but when the man sends a servant to collect some of the produce, the tenants beat him and leave him empty handed, an event that recurs with a succession of sent servants. The man figures that if he sends his son they will show more respect, but instead they find even more reason for violence, thinking they will automatically gain the son's inheritance by killing him. Jesus explains that instead, the end result is that the man came out and killed the tenants and gave the vineyard to others, a lesson not so much about quid pro quo justice but about the arrogance of small-minded assumptions. Mark's Jesus underscores this point, making an unexpected reference to Psalm 118:22-23: "Have you not read this scripture: 'The very stone which the builders rejected has become the head of the corner; this was the Lord's doing, and it is marvelous in our eyes'?" (Mk 12:10-11), a metaphor that captures the human arrogance of rejecting people or ideas as inferior or unworthy (represented by the rejected rock), that often become the basis (or "the head of the corner") for wondrous, unexpected realities. Making such an unexpected connection between the parable and the line in Psalm 118 is a special kind of wit.

The Herodians feel indicted by the parable, probably sensing it is an attack on Herod's traditional temple, so instead of embracing Jesus's claim that spurned ideas can have wondrous potential, they get together with the Pharisees, who feel Jesus has interpreted the Torah too lightly, to trap Jesus into insulting the Roman tribunal and giving them reason to destroy him. They start by trying to set Jesus up with false flattery: "Teacher, we know that you are true, and care for no man;

for you do not regard the position of men, but truly teach the way of God. Is it lawful to pay taxes to Caesar, or not?" (Mk 12:14-15) A religious fanatic, which they assume Jesus to be, might rant against the falseness of the Roman gods or the tyranny of Caesar who occupies the land, or about how maintaining spiritual values requires the shunning of taxes, but again, knowing their hypocrisy, Jesus stays cool. He plays along, thereby entering their social group and grabbing control of the social interaction, by having them bring him a Roman coin. When he asks them, "Whose likeness and inscription is this?" (Mk 12:16), they answer "Caesar's" (Mk 12:16), to which he responds, "Render to Caesar the things that are Caesar's, and to God the things that are God's," (Mk 12:17), leaving them "amazed" (Mk 12:17) because he uses his wit to avoid an either-or situation, deflating the tension between the earthly and spiritual, the oppressor and the oppressed, the Roman gods and the Hebrew God, allowing all dualities to exist without conflict, an option the group does not expect nor one with which an immature John would be comfortable.

How is Jewish culture, and Jesus's role in it, depicted in Mark? Is that culture responsible for Jesus's death?

Mark limits the culpability for Jesus's death to very specific elements of his Jewish culture. Jesus is a Jew hemmed in by groups of Jewish officials who represent different interests in the Jewish community, sometimes at odds with each other, but since they are strong believers of traditional rules, they come together to portray universal orthodoxy that chokes on innovation. Mark has them unified in their resentment of Jesus's lack of credentials and creative interpretation of Judaism. The groups include the Pharisees, who believe in the traditions of their fathers as much as Mosaic law; the scribes, village lawyers who strictly follow the laws of the Torah in drafting documents; Sadducees, who normally are at odds with the Pharisees, especially not believing in spirits such as resurrections and angels, and who also reject Old Testament scriptures except for the Torah (the first five books) and who are aristocratic supporters of the tenuous armistice the Jews have with Rome; and the Herodians, a political party who thought it expedient to support Herod Antipas, ruler of the Galilee territory under the Roman prefect, Pontius Pilot. The Sanhedrin, or higher counsel, was a group of seventy Jewish leaders (many from the above groups) who served as a type of Supreme Court. Jewish leaders who descend from Aaron (Moses's brother, and the Israelite's first High Priest) and work in the temple are called priests, in contrast to rabbis who are not necessarily paid, have no special lineage, and are primarily teachers working out of local synagogues.

Early in Mark, Jesus startles watchful scribes who are buried in tradition. When Jesus forgives a paralytic for his sins, the scribes respond by "questioning in their hearts, 'Why does this man speak thus? It is blasphemy! Who can forgive sins but God alone?'" (Mk 2:6-7). They are oblivious to the restorative potential for both the forgiver and the forgiven when it comes to forgiving those indicted by their inflictions. The scribes are insensitive to the psychological or spiritual release that comes from the immediacy of forgiveness, especially from a person of Jesus's confidence and stature, as opposed to perfunctory prayers to God. Mark's Jesus, especially intuitive and savvy, flushes the scribes out even though they have not spoken: "Why do you question thus in your hearts? Which is easier, to say to the paralytic, 'Your sins are forgiven,' or to say, 'Rise, take up your pallet [makeshift bedding] and walk'?" (Mk 2:8-9). Then, to undermine the scribes' assumptions, Jesus, to the amazement of everyone present, connects forgiveness to the physical empowerment of leaving, now in a positive context, by having the paralytic walk off on his own. Whether a reader wants to see this as divine miracle or mythic storytelling, Mark's message is the same: orthodoxies, of any religious faith, are pinched and limited, especially those that thwart forgiveness.

The Pharisees and scribes are equally disturbed when they see Jesus eating with tax collectors (only the lowest of the low willing to do this job) and with a general group of sinners, but Jesus explains, "Those who are well have no need of a physician, but those who are sick; I came not to call the righteous, but sinners" (Mk 2:17), implying that those who are well-off, spiritually or psychologically or sometimes even physically, are not those who need immediate attention; those without these strengths are the ones in need. This attitude disrupts traditional group dynamics that assume people who are doing everything "right" should be rewarded, and those who are not should be scorned. Jesus in Mark pulls the rug out from under righteousness and ambition, a threat to any group's belief in a privileged hierarchy.

On the Sabbath, the Pharisees catch Jesus and his disciples plucking ears of grain, and later they watch to see if Jesus will heal a man with a withered hand "so that they might accuse him" (Mk 3:2) for doing activities that violate the Sabbath. In response, Mark's Jesus states that "The sabbath was made for man, not man for the sabbath; so the Son of man is lord even of the sabbath" (Mk 2:27-28) and follows with, "Is it lawful on the sabbath to do good or to do harm, to save life or to kill?" (Mk 3:4), reevaluating Sabbath rituals and rules as trumped by necessity and help, reminding the power structure that humans create religious rituals, not God. Of course, the thought that rituals are not sacrosanct is a threat to any leadership whose power and self-importance depends on providing, partaking in, and officiating at rituals. (Luke later has Jesus add, "'Which of you, having a son or an ox that has fallen into a well, will not immediately pull him out on a sabbath day?' And they could not reply to this" (Lk 14:5-6), showing their hypocrisy.) In Mark, Jesus notices the silence of the Pharisees, again senses their anger, and "grieve[s] at their hardness of heart" (Mk 3:5) as the Pharisees "went out, and immediately held counsel with the Hero'di-ans against him, how to destroy him" (Mk 3:6), stoking the hatred that will build towards desiring his death.

Why is it important that Mark depicts the Jewish officials as so hostile to Jesus?

Mark dramatizes the tragedy of Jesus by having Jews condemn a fellow Jew. Jesus's tragedy is far more painful when based on the resentment and envy of his authority by the Jewish culture that he belongs to than if the betrayal had been committed by the Romans or any other people of different cultures or faiths, because in a treacherous world we usually count on people of our culture, faith, family, and our inner circle to support us, not turn on us. When Judas finally leads the chief priests and scribes to Jesus to take him and condemn him, he does so as a Jew of Jesus's inner circle. Judas is linked with the Sanhedrin's members who seek testimony against

123

Jesus. They bear false witness against him, especially literalists who hear Jesus say "I will destroy this temple that is made with hands, and in three days I will build another, not made with hands" (Mk 14:58), a metaphor that mocks the idea that religion is primarily based on the physicality of places of worship as opposed to religion primarily built on renewed spirit and rediscovered morality. The accusers are either too shallow to understand metaphor or cynical enough to know others do not, scaffolding on the misconception that Jesus is proposing a physical attack. The false testimonies clash (Mk 14:59), but when the high priests ask Jesus about the claims, he modestly stays silent (Mk 14:61), realizing that people who hate him will not hear reason or will purposely misinterpret metaphor. However, when asked if he is the Christ, he finally affirms, and this is the blasphemy the officials have been waiting to use to condemn him to death.

Does John limit culpability for Jesus's death to very specific elements of his Jewish culture?

No. John starts to move responsibility from Jewish authorities to Jews as a group. He subverts all of the above in Mark that goes into making the story of Jesus a tragedy, to a large degree because he is the only gospel writer to continuously use the term "Jews" instead "crowds," and often refers to those hostile to Jesus as "Jews" rather than by their official leadership terms, such as scribes and priests. Even though at the time of writing (although not the time of the story) there was a group identified as "Christians" who were separate from Jews, creating distance between the Jews and Jesus is a dangerous storytelling mistake, hinting at a hateful desire to see Jews as separate from Jesus and the disciples when they are not. The simple-minded narrative decision suggests an adolescent attitude about the nature of evil—assuming it comes from outsiders, non-believers, rather than from insiders threatened by freethinking individuals or from power sources acting out of political expediency.

There are a few, atypical times where John's gospel shows Jesus referred to as a Jew, such as by a Samaritan woman who wants to know how Jesus could ask her for a drink knowing the Jews have no dealings with Samaritans. Of course, typical of other parts of John, his

Jesus blows the opportunity to make the point about the ways caring neighbors trump group identity that Luke will make with the parable of the good Samaritan, instead having Jesus center on himself: "If you knew the gift of God, and who it is that is saying to you, 'Give me a drink,' you would have asked him, and he would have given you living water" (Jn 4:10). More typical of the Gospel of John, when Jesus drives the commercial enterprises out of the temple on the first Passover, John writes "The Jews then said to him, 'What sign have you to show us for doing this?'" (Jn 2:18) and later "a discussion arose between [John the Baptist's] disciples and a Jew over purifying" (Jn 3:25), again hinting at a difference between the Baptist's disciples and this single Jew when, in fact, they are all Jews.

Likewise, Jesus is distanced from his Jewish heritage in the following passage: "The man went away and told the Jews that it was Jesus who had healed him. And this was why the Jews persecuted Jesus, because he did this on the sabbath. But Jesus answered them, 'My Father is working still, and I am working.' This was why the Jews sought all the more to kill him, because he not only broke the sabbath but also called God his Father, making himself equal with God" (Jn 5:15-18). John's Jesus, once again identifying himself as being equal to God and suggesting that Jews, not officials, seek to kill him, subtly infers that he and God are outside the Jewish world, thereby pushing the Jews away as a murderous group. John again seems unaware of the importance of portraying betrayal from within, opting only for obvious betrayals from outsiders. In this sense, John's mentality is more aligned with the Jewish officials who see Jesus as an outsider. Every time John seems to nod to Mark and the synoptic gospels, such as when the Jews (again not necessarily the Jewish power group) marveled at his teaching despite lack of credentials—"How is it that this man has learning, when he has never studied? (Jn 7:15)—John quickly shifts away from Jesus being a person of innovation and courage who takes on traditions, a holy man with principle, and instead makes him a God relay switch: "So Jesus answered them, 'My teaching is not mine, but his who sent me'" (Jn 7:16).

Once in a while the Pharisees are seen attacking Jesus, but instantly the attackers refer to themselves only as the Jews, and this provides an opportunity for John's Jesus to distance himself from common ancestry: "I know that you are descendants of Abraham; yet you seek to kill me, because my word finds no place in you. I speak of what I have seen with my Father, and you do what you have heard from your father" (Jn 8:37-38). John's Jesus makes scant attempt to suggest his descendants and Abraham's are the same. A few passages later John catches himself and has Jesus scold his detractors for not doing what Abraham would do, but then tells them their father is the devil, declines to identify himself with Abraham, and in fact, implies God glorifies him more than Abraham: "The Jews said to him . . . 'Are you greater than our father Abraham, who died? And the prophets died! Who do you claim to be?' Jesus answered, 'If I glorify myself, my glory is nothing; it is my Father who glorifies me, of whom you say that he is your God. But you have not known him; I know him'" (Jn 8:52-55), and then adds that Abraham rejoiced to see his day of his arrival and that "before Abraham was, I am" (Jn 8:58), elevating himself as a god existing from eternity, not a prophet who shares humans' universal fates. Other Jews have those.

In Mark, how culpable are Pilate and the Romans in Jesus's prosecution?

The Romans are culpable for political, not religious or personal, reasons. In Mark, when the elders and scribes join the high priests in taking Jesus to the Roman governor Pontius Pilate, Pilate asks Jesus about the charges. "But Jesus made no further answer, so that Pilate wondered" (Mk 15:5), the verb "wondered" hinting at Pilate's skepticism of the Jewish leadership's purpose. Pilate, knowing that there was a feast where he could release one Jewish prisoner, and knowing that one was Barabbas, a Jewish rebel accused of murder, thinks to first ask, "Do you want me to release for you the King of the Jews? For he perceived that it was out of envy that the chief priests had delivered him up" (Mk 15:9-10). Only in the Gospel of Mark does Pilate intuit that the frantic responses of the priests, coupled with the quiet responses of Jesus, imply the officials are threatened by the popularity of Jesus's thinking outside of the status quo. Jesus's only response comes when Pilate asks him if he is king of the Jews, to which he responds, "You have said so" (Mk 15:2), turning the question back on Pilate, refusing to confirm a label of authority. When the chief priests stir up the crowd to have Barabbas freed instead of Jesus, Pilate asks what he should do with Jesus, and the crowd yells to crucify him, leading to "Pilate [asking] them, 'Why, what evil has he done?' But they shouted all the more, 'Crucify him.' So Pilate, wishing to satisfy the crowd, released for them Barab'bas; and having scourged Jesus, he delivered him to be crucified" (Mk 15:14-15). Mark draws a complex portrait of Pilate, a person with sharp psychological insight but also a politician who puts morality aside for expediency.

There is nothing complicated about the Jewish leadership; they want Jesus dead. However, again it is important to remember that Jesus and his followers are Jewish as well. Christians ignored this second component for centuries when making ethno-religious slurs, calling the Jews "Christ killers." Even when the Second Vatican Council (1962-1965) under Pope Paul VI declared there was no collective guilt to be put on all Jews for Jesus's death, the Church did not articulate that the Jews who pushed Jesus to his death were part of an envious authority, killing a fellow Jew, not a Christian. It is also a mistake to blame the Romans alone for killing Jesus when Mark makes it clear that the death is the result of a political collusion and, as a story about the human condition, a collusion that plays itself out over and over again in history, one that occurs within any country, any religion, any profession, any family when its established authority is threatened by confident, successful new thinkers, who address the needs of everyone, especially those without power.

In John, how culpable are Pilate and the Romans in Jesus's prosecution?

In the Gospel of John, Pilate and the Roman's culpability is more a matter of filling a preordained script, causing the narrative of Jesus's conviction to be unrealistic and misdirected, displaying none of the political savvy found in Mark. After the resurrection of Lazarus and other miracles, "many of the Jews" (Jn 11:45) run to the Pharisees, who get together with chief priests and center their concerns on a numbers game: "If we let him go on thus, every one will believe in him, and the Romans will come and destroy both our holy place and our nation" (Jn 11:48), but Caiaphas, one of the high priests, shakes off their reasoning, explaining it is practical to kill Jesus, not because of his new teaching, but as a scapegoat to save the country: "You know nothing at all; you do not understand that it is expedient for you that one man should die for the people, and that the whole nation should not perish" (Jn 11:49-50). John adds the escape-responsibility qualifier found throughout his gospel, usually spoken by John's Jesus—"He did not say this of his own accord" (Jn 11:51)—turning Caiaphas into another prophet-fulfillment puppet in John's script.

Caiaphas goes on to explain "that Jesus should die for the nation, and not for the nation only, but to gather into one the children of God who are scattered abroad. So from that day on they took counsel how to put him to death" (Jn 11:51-53). The thrust then is on Jesus's death so the Romans have someone to kill, avoiding the mass killings it would take to destroy the nation, and also to unite people around a shared icon who would bring together believers throughout the world, but unified only under an icon of God, not under worthy philosophical ideals that one would stake his or her life on. They will not be unified for tolerance of diverse ways of praying, for instance, or for tolerance of neighbors from other cultures, or for allowing love to trump religious differences and hate itself.

In John, when Jesus is finally taken to Pilate, Pilate first tries to send him back to the Jews to judge him, but they respond that it is unlawful for them to kill him. Yet then John nixes the morality inherent in this statement by implying that the Jews are acting out a small part of a bigger script and so their laying off of Jesus is only "to fulfill the word which Jesus had spoken to show by what death he was to die" (Jn 18:32), and that the Romans are already programmed to handle the literal killing. Preordained script is the excuse for everything in John. When Jesus is brought back to Pilate, John mangles the whole discourse from Mark, starting with Jesus's response to Pilate's question, "Are you the King of the Jews?" (Jn 18:33). Instead of trying to deflect the question as Mark has Jesus do, John's Jesus gets snotty: "Do you say this of your own accord, or did others say it to you about me?" (Jn 18:34), an adolescent's worry of the source of one's reputation, an unimaginable concern in Mark. Pilate snips back, "Am I a Jew?" (Jn 18:35), not displaying the insight of Mark's Pilate, but presented instead as a crank annoyed for being expected to know the ins-and-outs of Jewish gossip.

John, reminiscent of a pagan hero worshiper who is worried about wimp factor, gives Jesus excuses for not physically battling people rather than depicting a modest, tragic hero: "if my kingship were of this world, my servants would fight, that I might not be handed over to the Jews; but my kingship is not from the world" (Jn 18:36). Of course, the Jews are again portrayed as the outsiders, not Jesus. When Pilate then hears Jesus admitting he is a king (forget the modesty depicted in Mark), John tortures Mark's dialogue, having Jesus respond to Pilate's "So you are a king?" (Jn 18:37) by doling out more glory talk, not humility: "You say that I am a king. For this I was born, and for this I have come into the world, to bear witness to the truth" (Jn 18:37). Pilate's response is unintentionally humorous: "What is truth?" (Jn 18:38). It's a good question.

As in Mark, Pontius Pilate in John finds no crime, so when the chief priests yell to crucify Jesus, Pilate tells them to crucify him themselves, and "the Jews" yell back they have a law that he must die for claiming he is the Son of God (Jn 19:4-7). Pilate, who should be bolstered by his own belief in the Roman gods, rather than separating himself from such religious concerns, suddenly grows fearful (why?) and asks Jesus where he comes from (why?), a mental crack-up that would only be given to a caricature of a bad guy (Jn 19:8-9). When Jesus does not answer, Pilate pulls rank and lets Jesus know he is at his mercy; as he does throughout John's gospel, Jesus lets Pilate know that he, as Roman prelate, is part of a script and will have no power to make decisions on his own "unless it ha[s] been given you from above" (Jn 19:11). John's Jesus tells Pilate that the Jews, who delivered him, have "the greater sin" (Jn 19:11), John presuming that unlike Pilate, they are so sinful that he cannot offer them the excuse of merely playing a part in his Jesus-exits-to-heaven script.

When Pilate says he will release Jesus, John has the Jews threaten Pilate by suggesting that his actions will ruin his friendship with Caesar (Jn 19:12), John going out of his way to make the Jews pernicious by voicing a Roman issue, one obviously already on the mind of a Roman governor whose job is to squash Jewish rebellions. John does not display any of the political savvy that Mark depicted in Pilate and instead bounces his character around from smartass, to thoughtful, to fearful, to reasonable, to manic, as he now hands Jesus over to the scribes to be crucified (what happened to the Roman soldiers?), writes up a sign for the cross in Hebrew, Latin, and Greek that says "Jesus of Nazareth, King of the Jews" (Jn 19:19), which the scribes want corrected to say "This man said, I am King of the Jews" (Jn 19:21), to which Pilate basically says "too bad"—"what I have written I have written" (Jn 19:22)—lots of frenetic behavior that not only destroys Mark's more consistent, nuanced version of Pilate but also replaces the solemnity and seriousness of the miscarriage of justice in Mark with a confused narrative that says more about John's adolescent judgments than a meaningful Jesus.

What is the difference in how personal betrayal, namely perpetrated by Judas, is portrayed in the two gospels?

As discussed above, Mark portrays the intimacy of inner-circle betrayal as more painful than those abuses from outside-the-circle enemies; John does not. We know that pain from betrayals by, say, a lover, family member, co-worker, or friend are especially hurtful because they come from someone with whom we have shared our innermost thoughts, who knows us well, and this in turn creates a deeper wound because it obliterates our belief in trust and the emotional strength that comes from feeling secure. Mark dramatizes the betrayal of Jesus as growing from someone's secret resentment, fueled by envy the betrayer probably cannot articulate. In Mark, the betrayal comes from Judas, but he is presented as someone who, to some degree, represents all the disciples, and indeed they all do betray Jesus's ideals throughout the story; some like Peter even betray him at the end of the narrative. Mark's Jesus experiences a profound sorrow of betrayal when, at Gethsemane—where his "soul is very sorrowful, even to death" (Mk 14:34)—he asks his disciples to keep watch and instead they sleep. He sees them asleep again and asks Peter a second time if he could not "watch and pray that you may not enter into temptation; the spirit indeed is willing, but the flesh is weak" (Mk 14:39), and a third time he finds them sleeping, this time when he senses he "is betrayed into the hands of sinners," which links their apathy to Judas's betrayal.

Although John does not mention it, Mark emphasizes that Judas betrays Jesus with a kiss, a symbolic act that intensifies his violation of intimacy. Furthermore, the feeling of betrayal in Mark is made especially potent by Jesus's doubts about the sacrifice he is making in the name of God the Father. At Gethsemane he anguishes, "Abba, Father, all things are possible to thee; remove this cup from me; yet not what I will, but what thou wilt" (Mark 14:36), momentarily feeling that although God can do anything, he, Jesus, cannot, and he is tempted to give up the cup that represents his purpose; however, he understands God has given him a higher purpose, higher than his own desire for wellbeing. Then again later, Mark's Jesus on the cross, now broken and suffering, has more doubts and yells out to God, "My God, my God, why hast thou forsaken me?" (Mk 15:34), again Mark flesh-and-blooding Jesus as human—animating both his strengths and weaknesses, presenting a wise spiritual leader, who we can only hope to aspire to be like, as we identify our own doubt in Jesus's anguish of being left alone and in pain by God.

John seems oblivious to the dynamics and pain of betrayal, and his gospel lacks Mark's complex conception of such inner doubt, such humanity in the Son of Man. By removing any sense of tragedy in his gospel and instead substituting a preordained, mechanical kill process, the crucifixion in John is tantamount to a win-win hostage exchange whereby Jesus, who really is invincible and merely returning to his Father, leaves this world as a substitute for others not having to pay any kind of emotional, intellectual, or moral pain involved in having to watch a tragedy. It turns out that only having faith that Jesus is the son of God and glorifying him ensures eternal life: "For God so loved the world that he gave his only Son, that whoever believes in him should not perish but have eternal life. For God sent the Son into the world, not to condemn the world, but that the world might be saved through him" (Jn 3:16-17), and again, despite the talk of saving and not condemning, as in much of John, there is a threat that not accepting such a fantastic exchange for eternal life carries punishment: "He who believes in him is not condemned; he who does not believe is condemned already, because he has not believed in the name of the only Son of God" (Jn 3:18).

This threat would be unthinkable in Mark, whose emphasis is on forgiving. One might argue that being "condemned already" is a metaphor for a meaningless existence, one without faith in anything, but the issue still remains: what does John's Jesus offer to make secular life meaningful? The passage continues with John avoiding the sorrow and pain of betrayal fueled by envy, instead choosing to make evil an abstract concept, removing it from the secular world of immorality, and only defining it as disbelief: "men loved darkness rather than light, because their deeds were evil. For every one who does evil hates the light, and does not come to the light, lest his deeds should be exposed" (Jn 3:19-20). However, as throughout John, those deeds are never defined or developed except as disbelief of any son-of-God claims.

But perhaps the biggest way the betrayal is treated differently in the two gospels is that when John gets to the last scenes where Judas betrays Jesus, instead of focusing on the anguish of personal betrayal, John has Judas commit the betrayal through a *diabolus ex machina*, the devil as a sudden outside force who turns Judas into a mere stagehand, gutted of human insecurity and folly or envious resentment or even self-interest for blood money. John also deadens any sorrow Jesus feels about the betrayal, portraying Jesus as only centered on getting back home to heaven: "And during supper, when the devil had already put it into the heart of Judas Iscariot, Simon's son, to betray him, Jesus, knowing that the Father had given all things into his hands, and that he had come from God and was going to God, rose" (Jn 13:2-3). When Jesus announces one of the disciples will betray him, instead of, as in Mark, all disciples feeling implicated—"They began to feel sorrowful, and say to him one after another, 'Is it I?'" (Mk 14:19)—and Judas quickly sneaking into the darkness, John relieves the disciples of any sense of guilt by having his Jesus orchestrate everything, announcing the betrayer is the one he gives a dipped morsel to, and immediately giving it to Judas: "Then after the morsel, Satan entered into him. Jesus said to him, 'What you are going to do, do quickly'" (Jn 13:27-28). John's Jesus is in control, impatiently pushing everything to the next station in a killing production to release him to heaven.

John's Jesus even goes further to deflate any idea of betrayal, clarifying for everyone that his death is part of a plan he has total control of and needs to get finished up: "I tell you the truth: it is to your advantage that I go away, for if I do not go away, the Counselor will not come to you; but if I go, I will send him to you" (Jn 16:7). This counselor, later identified in John as the Holy Spirit, is apparently going to bring vague ideas of sin, righteousness, and judgment, all centered on disbelief of Jesus's glory, and furthermore, the Holy Spirit "will teach you all things, and bring to your remembrance all that I have said" (Jn 14:26), again spoken without specifics. John's idea is to get Jesus out of the world, the icing on top of a prophesy cake recipe, so that the reader can get to all the magic of the resurrection: all Jesus has to say as he dies on the cross is "It is finished" (Jn 19:30). Unlike Mark's Jesus, John's Jesus is a god who cannot wait to leave the world of human strife, a god who believes in a transfer ticket to the Holy Spirit or Counselor, a god who cannot wait to prove his divinity with a resurrection. His earthly kingdom is not the kingdom of heaven.

Does the Holy Spirit or Counselor represent the same concept in Mark and John?

No. In Mark the Holy Spirit is mentioned by John the Baptist, as the spirit Jesus will baptize with instead of water, but the only clue as to what the spirit signifies comes in the next lines when Jesus is baptized: "the heavens opened and the Spirit descend[ed] upon him like a dove" (Mk 1:10). The dove is a vulnerable bird (exposed prey for predators), a symbol of peace, not power or aggression. Because doves mate for life, they are also a symbol of fidelity. The Holy Spirit is mentioned again later in Mark, when Jesus says it will speak for the disciples in times of tribulation when followers will be beaten for his sake, an intuitive response they will have in times of horrendous injustice: "And the gospel must first be preached to all nations. And when they bring you to trial and deliver you up, do not be anxious beforehand what you are to say; but say whatever is given you in that hour, for it is not you who speak, but the Holy Spirit" (Mk 13:10-11). The Holy Spirit in Mark is an eternal force of peace, love, and understanding that endures despite persecution.

As mentioned above, in John the Holy Spirit is also referred to as the "Counselor." By being a substitute for all Jesus has taught, an actual teacher, the spirit is personified, turned into a phantom, and loses the metaphorical dove aspects of peace and fidelity. John further degrades Mark's abstract concept after the crucifixion, when Jesus appears and has his disciples look at his wounds as proof of his appearance. During this encounter, Jesus wishes peace be with the disciples, and then breathes on them and tells them to receive the Holy Spirit. He goes on to explain the significance of having the Holy Spirit: "If you forgive the sins of any, they are forgiven; if you retain the sins of any, they are retained" (Jn 20:23). This qualified forgiveness, whereby essentially Jesus gives the disciples the right to forgive some and not forgive others, with no rubric on what qualifies for forgiveness, further deflates the spirit of Mark's Holy Spirit, as a clear and consistent symbol, a dove of peace, love, and understanding.

How does Mark make the crucifixion meaningful?

In the Gospel of Mark, the reader's encounter with the living Jesus followed by the experience of his death is especially devastating because Jesus is an unusual hero, not like anyone else in the Bible or many others in world literatures. Jesus represents many ideals civilization holds dear—that reason should trump empty traditions, that forgiveness can heal, that our intolerances should be squelched— but ideals we realize are easily compromised by ambition, selfishness, self-righteousness, and fear of reprisals. Mark's Jesus embodies an amazing array of positive traits to defend these ideals—creativity, wit, selflessness, intuition, rationality, forgiveness, humility, morality, charisma, courage, and an acceptance that when all these attributes undermine simple-minded truths, empty rituals, egotistical authority, those who are undermined do not convert, but instead are threatened by them.

In Mark, Jesus's pain is not only physical, but also spiritual, beginning with his faltering on the cross, asking God why he has been forsaken. Hoping for miracles, the first witnesses are in denial of this pain and instead insist that Jesus's muttering of doubt is only him asking for Elijah to take him down; to keep him ready for this, they hold up a reed with vinegar to drink, only to be shocked when "Jesus uttered a loud cry, and breathed his last" (Mk 15:37). A centurion, significant because he is an outside observer not politically invested, watches Jesus take his last breath and exclaims, "Truly this man was the Son of God!" (Mk 15:39), not because he is a man of miracles who can save himself by coming off the cross, as "those who passed by derided him to do" (Mk 15:30-31), but because the Roman centurion senses he is watching the death of someone both innocent and wondrous. In a sense, Jesus's worth is being resurrected in the mind of an outsider who is transformed by the event.

After Jesus's death, a respected member of the Sanhedrin, Joseph of Arimathea, obtains permission from Pilate to take Jesus's body down from the cross and (a reminder that human decency can exist even within such an officious group), then "wrapped him in a linen shroud, and laid him in a tomb which had been hewn out of the rock" (Mk 15:43-46) and rolls a rock over the entry. This man-made cave is too earthy to be considered a mausoleum, a place that venerates the dead by denying the worm or pretending to prevent the return to dust, but it is also airy, not totally under the earth, so does not imply a direct return to dust and the feast of worms. Instead the cave is a place in between, a womb for the dead that is reminiscent of a womb for the living, an ideal symbol of the potential for death as a catalyst for rebirth. In this case, since there is no literal resurrection in Mark, the rebirth is the remembrance of Jesus, his characteristics, ideals, and the courage one needs to maintain those ideals.

How do the women in Mark's gospel enhance the significance of Jesus's crucifixion?

In his depiction of the women who witness the crucifixion, Mark takes the focus off family nostalgia and idealized views of motherhood. Instead, these women symbolize a non-sentimental love and acceptance of Jesus. Mary Magdalene (mentioned for the first time in Mark), Mary the mother of James the younger and of Joses (Jesus's family), and Salome (we learn for the first time was a follower who had ministered to Jesus; she is not to be confused with Herodias's daughter who brings Herod John the Baptists' head), and many other women who come up from Jerusalem witness the crucifixion from afar (Mk 16:1). Later, the two Marys see where Jesus is laid to rest, and then enter the tomb. Mark's major, positive focus on women for the first time in his gospel is understood best by considering how his depiction of women differs from their use in the other gospels. Mark never uses women to focus on sentimentality, nor motherhood, nor familial loyalty. The nativity scene and virgin birth are absent in Mark; Mark's narrative starts off with Jesus in his prime with no connection to an innocent baby boy with adoring animals crowding around his manger.

Any sentimentality about motherhood and family is further collapsed when Mary, along with Jesus's brothers and sisters, are shunned earlier in Mark's gospel (perhaps metaphorically, but still surprisingly) when looking for Jesus. Jesus uses the occasion to make a point that principles are more important than family bonds: "And he replied, 'Who are my mother and brothers?' And looking around on those who sat about him, he said, 'Here are my mother and my brothers! Whoever does the will of God is my brother, and sister, and mother'" (Mk 3:33-35). Mark also downplays not only the biological family, but also community pride and sentimentality in the legacy of its youth. For instance, Jesus teaches in his home town synagogue, shocking and offending much of the congregation, who wonder, "Where did this man get all this? What is the wisdom given to him? . . . Is not this the carpenter, the son of Mary and brother of James and Joses and Judas and Simon, and are not his sisters here with us?" (Mk 6:2-3). Jesus replies, "'A prophet is not without honor, except in his own country, and among his own kin, and in his own house' . . . And he marveled because of their unbelief" (Mk 6:4). Mark shows Jesus speaking to the notion that when we are growing up, our home town distorts who we are by picture-framing our youth, innocence, or immaturity, and never completely reconciles that sentimental perception with who we are when we return home mature as doctors, politicians, teachers, or the son of man. In some ways, only strangers in our adult worlds, who did not know us in our youth, appreciate us for what we have become.

Because Mark has taken the focus off of sentimentality and family nostalgia, the women begin to signify something else, not motherhood or stereotypic domesticity, but rather sensitivity, deep feeling, mourners who understand the significance of losing Jesus. They replace men and thereby shift the focus to the women representing our feminine selves that exist in both men and women—love, forgiveness, and acceptance of change—as opposed to our male selves that exist in all men and women of skepticism, competitiveness, anger, and tenacity. Salome is an unexpected representative of these attributes, being the only person in Mark we are told to have ministered to Jesus (Mk 15:41). At the crucifixion, the women are the only mourners, the first ones to suffer the sting of Jesus's loss. When the sun arises, the symbol of the resurrection of the new day, the two Marys and Salome go to anoint Jesus and find the boulder of the tomb has been rolled away. They enter and find a young man in a white robe, and are amazed because they have found life inside the cave's "womb," in the form of a youthful sentinel who conjures feelings of hope. The youth tells them not to be amazed, that he knows they are seeking Jesus, that Jesus has risen, and to tell the disciples and Peter (who had denied him) that he will be in Galilee as he had said (Mk 16:6-7). Mark keeps the young man incognito, and along with his sudden appearance, the man's testimony is hopeful, but is read as more of a mythological symbol of rebirth than a definitive promise that Jesus has physically reappeared.

Then the women "went out and fled from the tomb; for trembling and astonishment had come upon them; and they said nothing to any one, for they were afraid" (Mk 16:8). This is the end of Mark's narrative, at least as far as the oldest and most reliable manuscripts are concerned. There is no resurrection but the promise of one. The pain associated with Jesus's death is not diminished, but the rush of possibility is upon the women, leaving them amazed, trembling, conflicted. They are at a threshold and their lives are intensified by this loss and the potential of renewal through remembrance and hope and love. Mark's ending leaves the women and the reader searching, rethinking the legacy Jesus has left, and considering how to keep that alive, wondering if it is up to us to keep his spirit viable. Loss is a change that intensifies our lives, often leading to a new understanding of priorities. The reader's spirit of discovery, ministered by the women, is the resurrection. (To appease readers who cannot stand the ambiguity of Mark, a later apologist added lines [Mk 16:9-20] to the end of some texts of Mark's gospel, often denoted by a different color or a footnote, that present a literal resurrected Jesus, diminishing Mark's powerful ending.)

Does John defuse or enhance the significance of Mark's crucifixion?

Instead of enhancing Mark's meaningful ending to his gospel, John satisfies readers who would rather not experience the pain, loss, rethinking, and inner discovery connected with Mark's ambiguous resurrection by creating an icon that is eternal, indestructible, and beyond human vulnerability. A Jesus who can supernaturally reappear, something Mark carefully modulates, excites such readers. They want the Son of God, not Mark's son of man. However, John's retelling goes even further, starting with the replacement of Jesus's doubt on the cross expressed to his Father, with a hurry-up, get-back-to-heaven, I'm-out-of-here one-liner, "It is finished" (Jn 19:30).

Interestingly, John has a slightly different lineup of women who view the crucifixion: Jesus's mother Mary (the siblings are not mentioned in John's gospel, perhaps because they raise questions about Mary having normal sexual relations with non-virgin births), Mary wife of Clopas (Mary's sister), and Mary Magdalene. Noticeably left out is Salome who, as we know from Mark, ministered to Jesus; John once again opts against details that might have made Jesus more human, a person with emotional needs that are never specified but could easily have included anguish and disappointment with those who did not understand his ideas and even hated him for them. Also diverging from Mark, the women in John witness not from a distance, but close up to the cross, so they are made part of a single visual icon, physically interwoven with Jesus, not symbolic of a renewed outside perspective: "When Jesus saw his mother, and the disciple whom he loved standing near, he said to his mother, 'Woman, behold, your son!' Then he said to the disciple, 'Behold, your mother!' And from that hour the disciple took her to his own home" (Jn 19:26-27). Presumably the disciple is John, a narrator who draws attention to his new importance to Mary, distracting from Mark's focus on the women. Mary herself is characterized only as serving the function of a mother to validate her son Jesus ("Look at me, Mom!"). She is pulled outside of Mark's group of women who together embodied a larger feminine principle than woman-as-a-mom icon.

John also removes Mark's centurion, and instead has the Jews ask Pilate to provide Roman soldiers to break the legs of those crucified so they can be removed from their crosses (the removal of the crucified being a rule of the Sabbath), but when they find Jesus already dead and breaking his legs superfluous, one soldier pierces his side, water running out instead of blood, fulfilling prophesies and initiating the transforming of Jesus into a supernatural icon (Jn 19:31-37). Joseph of Arimathea (who Mark had made part of the Jewish Sanhedrin, a reminder there can be empathy within this powerful Jewish group) is, in John's gospel, made into a disciple of Jesus who needs to secretly take Jesus down "for fear of the Jews" (Jn 19:38), but then, in the conflicted spirit of much of John's gospel, works with Nicodemus to provide Jewish burial customs for Jesus. This all makes for tortured storytelling.

In John's version of the resurrection, only Mary Magdalene finds the stone removed from the tomb (not a cave, so inferences of the cave-as-womb are lost), and she runs to tell Peter and "the other disciple, the one whom Jesus loved" (Jn 20:2). Again John scraps Mark's humility, instead working himself into a major role as part of Jesus's inner circle, and even outruns Peter to get to the tomb as if in a playground race (Jn 20:4), while all the other disciples, who never made it to this scene in Mark (perhaps too ashamed to see the man they had betrayed), come running behind. Looking into the tomb, Mary weeps at her loss but then, rather than Mark's mysterious figure, she sees two angels, who are now concerned for her, thus raising the scene's sentimental temperature (Jn 20:11-12). Then John turns up the magic more: Jesus is actually there incognito as a gardener (no reason given) and responds to Mary by her first name, implying an intimacy between the two, a surprise since she never appears in the narration until the crucifixion. Now recognizing him, Mary addresses Jesus "Rab-bo'ni" (Jn 20:16)—John parenthetically adding this is Hebrew. (Why Hebrew all of a sudden? One wonders if John picks an arbitrary occasion to use a non-Greek word to compensate for leaving out Mark's Jesus using Aramaic to question God for forsaking him.) Calling Jesus "Teacher" rather than "Lord," also emphasizes Mary and

Jesus's spiritual, even emotional, closeness. However, John quickly ices any earthly warmth, Jesus telling Mary not to "hold" him because he has "not yet ascended to the Father" (Jn 20:17). John gives no details to suggest a spiritually symbolic ascension: Jesus is ready to launch straight up and being with Mary is preventing take off. John replaces emotional and spiritual complexity with a magical action that shreds not only Mark's profound atmosphere, but also Jesus's potentially close bond with Mary Magdalene.

What are the implications of John's more definitive resurrection compared to Mark's?

Surprisingly, John's resurrection is without end. After hearing of the resurrection, in the evening the disciples shut the doors "for fear of the Jews" (Jn 20:19), John slipping into a misconception of Jesus's own religion again, implying the disciples are somehow beyond their Jewishness. Jesus appears, wishes them peace, shows them his hands and side (a childish assumption that phantoms are real if they still have bloody holes), breathes the Holy Spirit on them, and lets them know if they forgive the sins of anyone, they will indeed be forgiven, but if they retain the sins of anyone they will be suddenly retained, leaving the reader wondering what qualifies for forgiveness. The disciple Thomas shows up late and says unless he can stick his fingers in Jesus's bloody wounds, he will not believe, an opportunity he gets eight days later; but John wants it both ways, both the proof of the resurrection through blood in a ghost and the claim that one should not need proof of blood, as Jesus tells Thomas, "Blessed are those who have not seen and yet believe" (Jn 20:29). John has no concept that less is more and so keeps tossing detail on top of detail of resurrected Jesus in action, a desperate attempt to establish the physical, literal reality of resurrection. Breaking any notion that a writer needs to show and not tell, John shovels out a hyperbolic pile of vagueness on top of the existing business: "Now Jesus did many other signs in the presence of the disciples, which are not written in this book" (Jn 20:30). This short-cut writing testifies to John's anxiousness about not having enough proof for Jesus as phantom. He leaves the reader in a hyperbolic hole, a long way from the delicate themes of rebirth in Mark.

John actually seems fearful of ever ending the resurrection scenes, almost as if he senses that if the miracles do not keep coming, he will lose Jesus's worth. He extends the time after Jesus's death on the cross far past Mark's. Even now, resurrected, he has Jesus perform more miracles with fish nets, (fish multiplying in what appears to be a tired version of the earlier multiplication of bread and fish to feed multitudes); invite everyone for breakfast, then ask the disciples if they love him and as they answer in the positive, assign each of them a clichéd metaphor (then feed my lambs, then tend to my sheep, then feed my sheep); and finally he has a strange encounter with Peter about being carried to where he does not wish to go, but then asking Peter to follow him. In this scene Peter turns to glimpse "the disciple whom Jesus loved, who had lain close to his breast at the supper and had said, 'Lord, who is it that is going to betray you?'" (Jn 21:20), John again aggrandizing himself as being the closest to Jesus and removing himself from any possibility of guilt, unlike Mark's disciples who all feel indicted, representatives of human vulnerability. Peter questions Jesus about John's special fate because the word is spreading that John "was not to die" (Jn 21:23). Jesus clarifies that this is not what he said but John clearly channels his privilege in Jesus's response to Peter, "If it is my will that he remain until I come, what is that to you?" Jn 21:22).

John comes forth now to let the reader know that he "is the disciple who is bearing witness to these things, and who has written these things; and we know that his testimony is true" (Jn 21:24). John insists on making himself a special authority, and so disappears any omniscient narrator. Still not knowing how to end a story and still concerned that the reader has not read enough to ensure Jesus as the Son of God, or ensure the literalness of the resurrection, John ends his gospel with a super-hero-comic-book, bed-time-story-that-promises-more-to-come ending: "But there are also many other things which Jesus did; were every one of them to be written, I suppose that the world itself could not contain the books that would be written" (Jn 21:25). This is the end of John's gospel. While Mark's ending leaves the reader trembling, wondering about his or her responsibility for resurrecting the values and memory of Jesus, in John, Jesus is left on an eternal miracle treadmill, spinning the reader further away from the pains and hopes of secular life.

REALLY, JESUS
SCENES FROM ACADEMIA

Scene 1

Sammy, an instructor in his early thirties, stands in front of a college class discussing the last lines of "Cetology" in Moby Dick, *the word "draught" archaic for "draft"*: "God keep me from ever completing anything. This whole book is but draught—nay, but the draught of a draught." *He has asked the secretary to interrupt his class and let him know when his family from out of town shows up to visit the campus. Suddenly the department secretary sticks her head through the doorway.*

~ Your mother and brothers are outside asking for you.

~ "Who are my mother and my brothers? Here are my mother and my brothers! Whoever does the will of God is my brother, and sister, and mother." Mark 3:33-35. Or I should say the will of Melville?

~ *Really?* You want me to tell them that? *Really?*

~ Some situations call for the same kind of spirit. Hyperbole to make a point? Maybe. Could Jesus have been literal? Why not? Anyway, thanks Betty. You can go tell them I will be out soon. So, what questions do you all have?

~ Don't you like your family?

~ Most of the time. But how important is family when set against one's philosophical ideals or passions? Remember that line is from Jesus in the Gospel of Mark.

~ But he loved his family.

~ Jesus used every situation to prioritize values. After all, none of Jesus's family, including Mary, is mentioned until the third chapter in the Gospel of Mark, the oldest gospel.

~ Really? No Christmas material?

~ No nativity scene. No letters home. The nativity scene waits until later versions of Jesus's story by Matthew and Luke. Readers bond to babies, but stories that start with experienced teachers or healers usually diminish the biological family's worth. Idealists are usually people who are not really into family portraits. Anyway, my family can wait until after class.

~ Well, that seems pretty weird. I thought Jesus was into "family values."

~ They aren't at the top of his priorities. In fact, Luke makes Jesus's reaction to family priorities even more dramatic than Mark does. Part of Luke's set-up is to have Jesus first preach a complicated parable, so before we get back to Jesus on family values, it is important to see just how rich this parable is. It is about an "unclean spirit" that "has gone out of a man" (Lk 11:24), the unclean spirit seeking rest but finding only "waterless places," and then returning to the man's soul, "my house from which I came" (Lk 11:24). But when the evil spirit returns, he finds his host's house "swept and put in order" (Lk 11:25)—perhaps a metaphor for the host's antiseptic mentality. I sometimes wonder whether this is an attack on those who think righteousness has to do with fanatic orderliness and rigidity. What do you think?

~ Like when people say Godliness is next to cleanliness or something like that? But what about family values?

~ Hold on. I'm getting there. But first, yes, an attack on that cleanliness-next-to-Godliness mentality because the empty host's soul ironically becomes even more vulnerable to the evil spirit, in fact seven times more vulnerable, since the evil spirit brings "seven other spirits more evil than himself, and they enter and dwell there; and the last state of that man becomes worse than the first" (Lk 11:26). Perhaps this is a commentary on one's vulnerability to sin when willfully sweeping away remembrances of past moral trespasses rather than continuously contemplating their consequences?

~ Yeah, like when you ask someone questions about their past and they kind of just go numb.

~ Yeah, that's what I was thinking too—but where is the family stuff again?

~ So here's what's funny. A woman in the crowd, beside herself as Jesus is developing this complex metaphor, obviously taken by the brilliance of the parable (hilarious, because as we just did, most of us have to read the passage three times to believe that the parable could be devaluing righteousness that depends on cleaning up the soul), raised her voice and said to him, "Blessed is the womb that bore you, and the breasts that you sucked!" (Luke: 11:27). Unimpressed by the sentimental slurpiness of motherhood, Jesus snaps back, "Blessed rather are those who hear the word of God and keep it!" (Lk 11:28). The story cuts to the increasing crowds, but the reader's mind cannot move from an image of a chagrined woman glancing around at the crowd, feeling a little foolish that her flattery and celebration of motherhood, albeit exuberant, had been ignored.

~ Then Jesus is kind of a smartass.

~ Just enough to shock, to keep an audience on its toes. But whoever looks for this Jesus on Sundays? How often does a church find a place for a witty, slightly smart-alecky spiritual leader? You guys let me know when you find one and I'll visit that church with you, but now I better see my visiting family. Class dismissed and I'll see you Wednesday.

Scene 2

Clara, a college instructor, has just shown her class Ingmar Bergman's film Cries and Whispers. *A student, who is distraught over having had to see the film, runs to see if the Dean of Humanities is available to file a complaint.*

~ Can I see you a moment?

~ Sure. What's the problem?

~ My literature professor showed a film in class that really upset me because of what I'm going through right now. I don't think we should have to watch films like that.

~ What film did you see?

~ It's by Ingmar Bergman called *Cries and Whispers*, about two sisters and a maid reacting to a third sister's dying of cancer.

~ Oh yes. I saw that film years ago. I remember the images make heavy use of reds and whites. Traditional church ceremonial colors, right? I remember being very moved by that film. It was a very spiritual experience for me.

~ Well, I wasn't so spiritually moved when I had to watch as one of the sisters inserts a broken piece of a wine glass into her vagina, cuts herself, bleeds onto her legs and bed sheets, declares that life is "a tissue of lies," and smears blood on her face!

~ Jesus! Oops, sorry. I forgot about that scene.

~ It really triggered some upsetting thoughts and is causing me a lot of anxiety. I don't think I should have to write on this film either.

~ Okay. Let me talk to your professor and get back to you.

The student leaves. Later, the professor meets with the dean, who recounts the student's complaint.

~ Sure. It's an important scene where the wife is making a dramatic statement to her cold and loveless husband who is struck with horror. Look, this is a literary work of art and there is no way to know if a student is going to be offended by this or that because of his or her own issues and anxieties and sense of propriety about love, sex, and death. Any work of literature has that potential.

~ But Clara, this is a scene that is bound to upset a lot of students for different reasons. Maybe you should be more sensitive about the kinds of films you show.

~ Look. The film is about a dying woman, about the emotional blocks that prevent her sisters from comforting her, and the loveless men who have reinforced the women's cynicism. It is also about a servant who is able to comfort with peace, love, and understanding. The terrible cutting scene is meant to offend because it symbolically dramatizes one sister's emotional impotence and her hatred and rage that come from her rejection and cynicism. I think Jesus would defend showing this film. He might even say, "You can degrade me, but whosoever blasphemes Bergman's film, a testament to love and the impulses that destroy it, blasphemes the Holy Spirit."

~ Isn't that a little dramatic? You sound like a religious freak.

~ Maybe a little hyperbolic. But so was Jesus. You would be more sympathetic to the reference after reading the Gospel of Mark and thinking about how the Holy Spirit is defined. Remember, John the Baptist preaches repentance for the forgiveness of sins and foresees a person coming, "mightier than I" (Mk 1:7), who will baptize not with water but with the Holy Spirit. When Jesus is baptized by John, a Spirit appears, defined by only one metaphor: "he saw the heavens opened and the Spirit descending upon him like a dove" (Mk 1:10); then a voice comes from heaven validating Jesus as His beloved son. Matthew adds that Jesus "saw the Spirit of God descending like a dove, and alighting on him" (Mt 3:16). A dove is not a bird of prey, but rather preyed upon, so it is a symbol of peace and vulnerability, a trait reinforced by the fact that doves make insecure nests.

~ Jesus, Clara! Now Audubon?

~ No, listen. I am going somewhere with all this. Doves mate for life, so they can also be symbols of fidelity. As an allusion to the Noah story, the dove becomes a symbol of hope because the dove finally comes back in the evening and "lo, in her mouth a freshly plucked olive leaf; so Noah knew that the waters had subsided from the earth" (Gen 8:11), a signal of the end of God's wrath and killings. Artists have often made the dove white, a symbol of purity, but out of the hundreds of doves that are indigenous to the Middle East, none are white. Artists who render the dove white, a color that represents purity, draw away from its actual qualities and therefore what the dove really represents.

~ Man. I knew you were into birding, but this is ridiculous.

~ Let me finish. You're into symbols, right? Vulnerability, fidelity, hope, and forgiveness (values expressed by John the Baptist) are all components of love. There is no other attempt in Mark to define the Holy Spirit. Later in Mark, Jesus tells the disciples that they will be hated for holding to his teachings, but instructs that when they are delivered up, they should "not be anxious beforehand what you are to say; but say whatever is given you in that hour, for it is not you who speak, but the Holy Spirit" (Mk 13:11). Jesus knows that in the end (especially when one faces persecution from an insecure, authoritative power), if one truly believes in notions of peace, love and understanding, that spirit will give humanity hope and trump the cynicism and violence of power.

~ So you claim this film is about the Holy Spirit, and the woman in the vagina-cutting scene is cynical and violent, so therefore a violation of it.

~ Yes, exactly. And by the way, the servant in the film is the embodiment of the Holy Spirit; her whispers are in the spirit of the peace, love, and understanding that the two sisters cannot give to their dying sister.

~ But should you be talking about religion in class? "Holy Spirit" sounds so religious.

~ People have a hard time defining the "spirit" in "Holy Spirit." The human imagination sometimes cartoons the word into "ghost" (a word never mentioned in the Bible), and then turns "ghost" into an object that looks like floating, translucent ectoplasm, something otherworldly. After Mark, there are myriad attempts to redefine the concept of Holy Spirit: Matthew identifies Mary's conception of Jesus to be by the work of the Holy Spirit (Mt 1:18); theologians point to the Old Testament word for "breath" being the same word for "spirit"; the apostle John uses the Greek word "paraclete," which means advocate or protector, in connection with spirit; Paul in Corinthians uses "spirit" as the essence within (1 Cor 6:19); theologians for centuries have debated whether "spirit" refers to an angelic sprite. But Mark, the oldest gospel in the English Bible, uses "dove" to define the spirit. Not a hawk. Not a ghost. Not special light beams for spiritually assisted conception.

~ Okay, okay. I get it. It's a symbol—but we're still talking about a film with vagina cuts, right?

~ No, you don't get that the Holy Spirit is not just a theme in the film but important to what kinds of films to select as part of a literary culture. Holy Spirit is so important in Mark that Jesus says, "all sins will be forgiven the sons of men, and whatever blasphemies they utter;

but whoever blasphemes against the Holy Spirit never has forgiveness" (Mk 3:28-29). Luke's Jesus ups the Holy Spirit's value, making the concept even more sacred than Jesus himself: "And every one who speaks a word against the Son of man will be forgiven; but he who blasphemes against the Holy Spirit will not be forgiven" (Lk 12:10). In quote number 44 of the Gospel of Thomas—a gospel not included in the Bible, but perhaps written even earlier than the gospels in the Bible, and maybe more closely linked to the Q source (a still-missing list of Jesus's sayings from which, many scholars claim, all the gospels borrow)—Thomas allows forgiveness for even blaspheming the Father: "Whoever blasphemes against the Father will be forgiven, and whoever blasphemes against the Son will be forgiven, but whoever blasphemes against the Holy Spirit will not be forgiven, either on earth or in heaven."

~ Shit, Clara. I give up. Blessed is the professor who defends the Holy Spirit manifest in *Cries and Whispers*. Is that what you want me to say? Blessed is the professor who puts the film before political correctness and I guess before the student who blasphemes the spirit of the film.

~ Yes. Really. This is not bullshit. Say it. And blessed is the preacher who is tolerant of blasphemy of religious hierarchy and authority and instead directs his or her passion against those who blaspheme the peace, love, and understanding promoted by Ingmar Bergman. I think Bergman is more in tune with the Holy Spirit than the disciples. At the end of Matthew's gospel, when Jesus commissions the disciples to "make disciples of all nations, baptizing them in the name of the Father and of the Son and of the Holy Spirit, teaching them to observe all that I have commanded you" (Mat 28:19-20), I wonder if they ever comprehended the dove symbolism that defines it.

~ I wonder if Mark's reader even remembers the dove of the first chapter. Do you really have time to explain all this symbolism to complaining students? I don't.

~ For Christ's sake, we are literature teachers! We all need to pay more attention to metaphor: In the name of the Father, and the Son, and the Spirit of the Dove.

Scene 3

Simone has been teaching an introductory studio art class that explores the advantages of different media. Today will be a radical departure.

~ Good morning, class. Today I want to tell you about performance art of the mid-to-late twentieth century, a semi-theatrical, anti-commercial, provocative art that blurs boundaries: interacting with audiences instead of a stage, using the actual artist in the art work.

~ Can we go see one?

~ Performance pieces usually surprise an audience by not being publicly announced and are usually without repeat performances. Realize these are not collectible, physical pieces of art. One of the first performance artists was Chris Burden, whose work *Trans-fixed* involved nails being driven through his palms, crucifying him to the back of a Volkswagen that was then pushed out of a garage on a major avenue, the engines "screaming" for him for two minutes before the VW was pushed back into the garage and the doors were closed.

~ Why did he do that? What was that supposed to mean?

~ Maybe a metaphor for how others only get a glimpse of our personal anguish, or a metaphor for our sacrifice to technology, or the shocking ways we hide our pain.

~ Do they always involve physical violence like that?

~ No, they are all very different and surprising. Francis Alÿs created **When Faith Moves Mountains**, which included five hundred volunteers changing the earth's surface by all shoveling to move a giant sand dune over a few inches, a metaphor for how hundreds of small acts result in new mythic realities. His other work, *The Green Line*, used a leaky can of green paint that Alÿs dripped for two days past Jews, Arabs, check points, and key buildings in Israel to retrace the line of the green crayon Moshe Dayan drew on a map of Jerusalem to divide the city in 1948, dividing Israeli territory from Jordanian territory and creating a no man's land. That boundary was altered over the decades, with horrendous results for Israelis and Palestinians, and the assumptions of this boundary are questioned by the drips of Alÿs' new, unexpected line.

~ These seem like a lot of physical work, like putting on a play but more unpredictable.

~ Absolutely. And one of the only ways to appreciate performance art, which not only demands prep but the ability to immediately absorb unexpected reactions from an audience, is to do one.

~ You're shitting me!

~ No, let's do one!

~ Well, first we have to decide: who do you want to be the audience or target of this performing art piece? We have a diverse student body.

~ I think we should direct our artwork at students who are complacent.

~ Get more specific.

~ Yeah. What about those who practice really shallow versions of religion? Like, they are into Hallmark cards with pastel, flower-bordered gushy texts full of prayers.

~ So you want to make fun of religious groups on campus?

~ Not all; just those students who think prayers are only for making self-righteous wish-fulfillments, all based on a belief in a God who is always protective and on the right side, *their* side.

~ Okay. Where are you going to find this group? They could be mixed in with lots of different kinds of students.

~ I know some students, and faculty too, who are a good sample of this group and eat in the cafeteria adjacent to the experimental restaurant. They aren't really religious. But they are always wearing expensive clothes and many of them believe that they are virtuous because they work out. Like that's their religion. Some others who sit with them are vegans but not cool about it. They kind of think the rest of us are barbarians.

~ Well, okay. Maybe you need to do something that will affect all kinds of students. Maybe you want something that will mostly shock students who, in one way or another, probably think too well of themselves. Let's see if you can come up with something that might give them all pause, make them rethink their righteous assumptions no matter what they believe in.

~ Hey, we have been reading the Gospel of Mark in my literature class and there is a scene where the disciples get really dirty and shock everyone. We could do something like that.

~ If you want to get dirty, you guys should come to the horticulture club. Next week we are planting a bunch of herbs for the culinary department. We could leave off the usual protective gear. Believe me, your nails will get packed with mud; small mulch clogs will cling to your forearms; mud will cake on your knees; and dust will mat your sweaty hair.

~ Then what?

~ We'll reenact the defilement scene in the cafeteria.

The next week the students work in the soil, stay dirty, and walk into the cafeteria, reeking with body odor (most remembered not to use deodorant), catching the attention of many students. They head to the food order lines. Many students and much of the cafeteria staff are stunned, even sickened, and after the art students bring their food back to the table and take a seat among their shiny classmates, whose eyes begin to roll back into their heads in disapproval. The art students use their defiled hands to pick up their taco specials, dripping with guacamole salad, and chomp them down, forcing many students to move to other tables. Finally, one art student stands up after the other.

~ Listen up! In the Gospel of Mark, Pharisees and scribes come from Jerusalem to see Jesus, but those in the Jewish tradition "do not eat unless they wash their hands, observing the tradition of the elders; and when they come from the market place, they do not eat unless they purify themselves" (Mk 7:3-4).

~ The ritual cleaning before eating is a tradition created by humans, maybe for health reasons, but not by God. Rules can be broken. For instance, a group decides not to use funds it earmarked for a new synagogue, church, or mosque and use them instead to help people who suffered from buildings crumbling in an earthquake. Traditions, like any endeavor, are never sacrosanct; they are created by humans and can be changed by humans. Remember, "The sabbath was made for man, not man for the sabbath" (Mk 2:27).

~ "Hear me, all of you, and understand: there is nothing outside a man which by going into him can defile him; but the things which come out of a man are what defile him" (Mk 7:14-15).

~ "Do you not see that whatever goes into a man from outside cannot defile him, since it enters, not his heart but his stomach, and so passes on?" (Mk 7:18-19). Therefore, I declare all foods clean.

~ "What comes out of a man is what defiles a man. For from within, out of the heart of man, come evil thoughts, fornication, theft, murder, adultery, coveting, wickedness, deceit, licentiousness, envy, slander, pride, foolishness . . . they defile a man" (Mk 7:20-23). Also texting answers to friends while taking exams, plagiarizing papers, having friends write your term paper, padding your college applications with involvement in organizations you do not really care about, flattering professors, fabricating reasons for absence, relying on cliché responses in class discussions, obtaining an education for disingenuous reasons—these defile a student, not earthy mulch and animal manure.

After eating, the art students file out, to some looks of astonishment and some light-hearted chatter, and regroup to evaluate the performance piece.

~ I think we sounded like idiots who missed out on the unit in the health science text on dangerous bacteria.

~ Maybe quoting Jesus made us appear to be insane or religious freaks.

~ Maybe. But maybe Jesus's performance looked just as crazy as ours did. I mean he went crazily out of his way to make a point about orthodoxy and intolerant religious purists.

~ I know, but I just worry we sounded arrogant.

~ Fuck it. I liked that we might have shocked anyone who was at all self-righteous about anything, or even just in a rut with a lunch routine.

~ I saw a few students laughing at us, but some were just smiling as if they were pleased with themselves for recognizing the performance's allusion to Mark. Don't you agree, Professor?

~ Yes. So do you guys think Jesus was one of the earliest performance artists? Do you think he orchestrated his disciples' lack of cleanliness into artistic drama, or was he more spontaneous, quickly spotting hypocrisy and ready to improvise on whatever the social situation would bring to express his moral outrage?

~ I think he had to know ahead of time, because he kept his disciples from washing—just like you guys had us get dirty first. Unless those guys were dirty all the time.

~ Well, do you all think the reactions and concerns you are talking about might be the same ones Jesus and the disciples walked away with? Do you think they even saw the same kinds of reactions you did?

~ What else could they have seen? It makes me wonder though, did Jesus anguish over the different reactions, or did he expect them?

~ Right, and that should also make us all ask, does art have to be pragmatic, or is the process of art an end in itself, a way to clarify one's own values, even when it confuses others? The Gospel of Mark never says. It leaves that for us to decide. Maybe it's something only an artist would even think about.

Scene 4

A team-taught humanities class has just finished a study of the Gospels. Getting ready over the weekend, Fiona, an art history professor, decides to remove art history labels and general definitions of time periods from her lecture so she can talk about Jesus and not art history styles. Now she addresses the students of the humanities class.

~ Look, whether you see Jesus as the divine Son of God, or as a philosopher-prophet who was punished for his ideas that threatened authority and orthodoxy, his death is a tragic event. Let's start by looking at the gospels you read. What kinds of visual details did you come away with reading about the different crucifixion scenes?

~ It's like a murder, but not described with too many visual details. In John, water, instead of only blood, squirts out of Jesus. Sort of turning him into a symbol of the essence of all life.

~ Yeah. Mostly only the people present and their actions are mentioned.

~ That's true. Really, visual descriptions of Jesus are absent throughout the story, in keeping with the Bible as a whole, especially compared to many other ancient texts. How do you think that is an advantage?

~ You can make up your own descriptions.

~ When there is nothing to look at, it makes everything more psychological. You think more about the meanings of what people are saying and doing.

~ I agree. Both of you make good points. In fact, that might be why there are so many crucifixion paintings—unlimited attempts to visualize this one event, and each one, by visualizing so much that is not in the Bible, allows every artist to merge their own vision with the written gospel. This adds new inferences, allowing the artist to give new commentary to the crucifixion's meaning. For instance, I am going to show you Grünewald's crucifixion for the Isenheim Altarpiece painted some time after 1510. Notice how in this painting Jesus looms upward like a broken eagle—his shoulder is dislocated, his fingers curled into the black sky like spiked claws—but his feet are hammered close to the ground, dispelling any notion that his spirit can ascend, implying that he is more a prophet of the earth than God's angel. He is tethered to a makeshift cross, half-milled, half-chiseled. I don't think you can accurately say he wears his crown of thorns. Why?

~ Because it's enmeshed into his hair like barbwire.

~ What difference does that make to who he is?

~ He's less in control or more trapped. The Gospel of John makes it seem like he is in total control—but not here.

~ Good. Also notice, it is not just nighttime, but the world is a night. Stars are dead. Golgotha is not a mere Jerusalem hillside but a mountaintop beyond all cities. All that makes the crucifixion less hopeful and more desperate.

~ Why do blisters and sores break out all over his body?

~ Those are associated with rye ergot fungus, which can give one Saint Anthony's fire, something many people living in the Colmar area where this was painted suffered from at the time. Grünewald is giving the viewer yet another way of identifying with Jesus's suffering. On the other hand, notice that his alienation is increased by having Semitic features, while the mourners surrounding him, the two Marys and two Johns, all have Northern European facial characteristics. John the Apostle comforts Mary, and John the Baptist, already beheaded but brought back here, holds the Bible and points at Jesus as the fulfillment of the Bible's word. Their red clothes make them like two red flames in the night, somewhat brightening the scene along with the delicate white lamb with a cross in his hoof.

~ It's a symbol of Jesus as the innocent lamb, even though Jesus does not look as fresh and innocent as the lamb.

~ Good point. What does such an overt symbol of gentleness in this harshly realistic scene do for the painting?

~ I think it makes Jesus's sacrifice for his values even more symbolic.

~ Yes, and therefore in this case more universal and timeless because the lamb with the cross is not only an add-on to this specific scene, but outside of the painting's realistic, harsh style. Do any of you have a problem with using a sacrificial lamb as a symbol of the sacrifice of Jesus?

~ I do. When we studied the gospels we noticed how witty and insightful Jesus is. He can perceive the Pharisees' and scribes' hardness of hearts. He's not into the soft innocence that I associate with a lamb.

~ I agree. Well put. I think Jesus shows a love and patience that is not sweet but has deep understanding, and other times is not patient at all, like when he throws over the moneylenders' tables in the temple in Mark Chapter 11 and Matthew Chapter 21. It is okay to disagree with all or part of an artist's interpretation, and if you wrote about the differences we are talking about, you would need to support yourself with the kinds of details from the gospels you just mentioned. Let me show you a painting by Pieter Bruegel the Elder, finished about fifty years later, referred to as *The Procession to Calvary*. In this painting, instead of Jesus being forefront and overly large on the crucifixion as in the Grünewald, he is shrunk out of sight on his way to the place of his murder, a killing field depicted far in the distance. What do these two visual elements add to the Biblical story?

~ Is that Jesus in blue clothing in the very middle carrying a cross? I can't tell for sure, because there are so many people you have to look past and so many are clustered around him.

~ Yes, that is Jesus. Let me zoom up on him. Notice the criminals he is to be crucified with are in the wagon in front of him, being worked over by judgmental, squinty-faced priests. There are several characters trying to pull on the cross for Jesus, and one sadist with his foot on the cross, stymying his movement.

~ His face looks fairly calm and his size and features make him seem like he could be anyone, no one special. I guess the killing field is far away to show that everyone gets there before Jesus because they flock there to witness killings all the time. All these things make Jesus's crucifixion more everyday-ish.

~ Lots of good points. We saw that Grünewald had blended the harshness of reality with the importance of Jesus, but not here. Almost as if Bruegel is suggesting that you never know who could be a Jesus. By the way, usually Simon of Cyrene is depicted as pressed into helping Jesus carry the cross, but Bruegel shows him in a crowd down in the lower left of the painting—let me zoom up onto this crowd. Notice the soldiers, one with a spear, herding him out of the crowd, and perhaps it is his wife, her rosary beads pinned to her skirt, who tries to hold him back while he splays his spread feet and legs to create resistance. Bruegel is adding physical and psychological drama to Simon's involvement that is absent from the Biblical scene, a way of suggesting that everyone present has their own particular insecurities that separate them from Jesus's own anguish.

~That's so weird. This makes me visualize the scene entirely differently than when I read it. And why does his wife have rosary beads and why are there priests? The Catholic Church did not exist yet.

~ Doesn't this also say the crucifixion does not just exist as a single event of one special time, but something that will happen over and over again, a murder committed by any group that insists that its own ideas cannot be questioned?

~ Yes, very good point. Notice that the clothing, which is contemporary of 1564 in the Netherlands, also reinforces this idea. Imagine the viewer's shock looking at a painting of the scene today, taking place in the main quad of our campus where everyone is dressed as you all are! Think about how much that would update the crucifixion the way Bruegel does at his time. Also, the red-clothed soldiers are Spanish soldiers who occupied the Netherlands at the time, reminding us that there can always be an occupying military presence in cahoots with the current religious or political leaders; that wasn't limited to the Romans. What about the fact that Jesus is obscured but right in the center of the composition?

~ It is more like a tease, not an honor.

~ Why?

~ Because all these hundreds of other people get just as much importance, always drawing my eye away from Jesus.

~ That's true. But he's still in the center, still of utmost importance, even though we are blinded from recognizing his importance. Who are some of the people that do get your attention?

~ In the upper center I notice a drunk falling off his horse; well to the right of him, an enemy soldier giving alms; in the back left here, kids playing games; groups of gossipers everywhere; here maybe a person who is running after stealing grain.

~ Good. Also notice in the foreground we see a traditional mourning group with Mary and the Apostle John comforting her, but their antiquated clothing and position pushed way forward away from the distant crucifixion scene make them especially dislocated, a play within a play from another time period, almost an afterthought, not part of a world that can give homage or comfort to Jesus anymore. Explain the significance of this "tease," as you refer to it, that sends the viewer's thoughts in so many directions?

~ That people have lost the importance of the crucifixion.

~ No, I think that Bruegel implies that not too many people understood or felt the loss of Jesus at this time or any time.

~ I think lots of times people are not paying attention when great thinkers in philosophy, religion, science, or anything else die. Even if they are murdered.

~ Those are all good ideas. I also think that sacrifices of people of peace, love, and understanding go on all the time all around us, simultaneously with all these other solemn, ignoble, innocent, or even poetic activities. Notice the person further back but just above Mary with his hooded face turned away and hands forward with what appears to be loaves in the water in front of him. It's an allusion to Ecclesiastes, "Cast your bread upon the waters, for you will find it after many days" (Eccles 11:1), the idea that what we have the courage to cast out to see if it is well received or shared might return to us as reward and growth, another private but more positive connection with the significance of Jesus's life and death.

~ That windmill on the cliff really sticks out. What's that all about?

~ Sometimes I wonder if the windmill perched on the hill reminds us that the productivity of the world never stops, but that the world is also a precarious place, the windmill almost looking as if it could teeter over. And notice it is in a world where stormy skies remind us that the tragic world is ready to descend, regardless of how little attention we are paying to it. Bruegel brings out and adds so much to the gospel's crucifixion. Now I want to show you another one for you to take notes on and then write up to turn in for a grade.

The screen fills with an image of Marc Chagall's White Crucifixion, *painted in 1938; silence fills the room as students notice different details from the other paintings, ones inferring new meanings about Jesus's death. A few students start writing down their responses.*

EPISTLE TO LUKE
CRINGES AND CHEERS

Dear Luke,

After receiving your gospel three days ago, I am startled by the momentous parables you have added in your rewrite of the Gospel of Mark, which was probably written ten to twenty years before you wrote yours. I also respect your acknowledging that, aside from Mark, you have borrowed from the *quelle* (Q) source of Jesus's sayings that was never discovered, also admired by your colleague, Matthew. But first I need to clear the air regarding some details in the beginning of your account that made me wince. Really, some parts made me so uneasy that I almost stopped reading.

You almost lost me when, in the opening lines, you insisted your reason for writing your gospel was so that the reader "may know the truth concerning the things of which you have been informed" (Lk 1:4), setting yourself up as a more viable source for knowing Jesus than several other narratives. Does that include Mark, to whom you are clearly indebted? I was also disturbed that you added a big infancy scene for John the Baptist, distracting from his eating-locust-and-honey, wild-man-in-the-desert profile that kick-starts Mark's narrative. Mark circumvents using family and babyhood (symbols of tradition and status quo) to infantilize the Baptist, instead starting his narrative with the Baptist's sudden, forceful adult appearance and his stunning announcement that after him will come one "mightier" whose sandal thong he will "not [be] worthy to stoop down and untie . . . [and who] will baptize you with the Holy Spirit" (Mk 1:7-8).

On the other hand, before even getting to John the Baptist's rituals, you magic-up his mom and dad, Zechariah and Elizabeth, borrowing from Old Testament clichés about otherworldly abilities to produce a baby despite old age, opening up "barren" (Lk 1:7) Elizabeth for birthing. You also really tested my patience with twenty-six verses spinning out John the Baptist's family dynamics. Then, for God's sake, you start up another miracle-birth sequence with the Virgin Mary's birth of baby Jesus, another seductively sentimental family-with-baby ploy that makes caring about Jesus, like John the Baptist, a mushy affair. Your buddy Matthew does the same thing with Jesus's birth; I really wish you both had respected Mark for avoiding this and putting faith in both prophets as mature adults. Luke, let's face it. One's babyhood ultimately does not matter: even parents of criminals and enemies once loved their babes as newly born gods and goddesses. Besides, do any of us, especially a writer-philosopher as you, want ourselves judged by our baby-story albums?

In connection with adding moms and babes, I was let down by your misunderstanding of Mark's concept of the Holy Spirit. Whereas Mark ties it to a dove (Mk 1:10) that represents peace, fidelity, and vulnerability in times of persecution, you grab the ambiguous nature of the word "spirit" to serve more magical purposes, here as a substitute for Mary not having sex with Joseph, with Gabriel letting Mary know, "The Holy Spirit will come upon you, and the power of the Most High will overshadow you; therefore the child to be born will be called holy, the Son of God" (Lk 1:35). Your Holy Spirit thus becomes a reproductive concoction and the term "overshadow" becomes a substitute for sexual gratification, a fantasy for women more interested in a finished child than the sexual or personal relationship that produces one. You further abuse Mark's Holy Spirit in this sentimental line: "And when Elizabeth heard the greeting of Mary, the babe leaped in her womb; and Elizabeth was filled with the Holy Spirit" (Lk 1:41). Not only does a leaping baby have a high gush factor, you are going out of your way to conflate the Holy Spirit with one of the joys of motherhood every expectant mother experiences. I got queasy reading this section. I wonder if Mark's Jesus, who spurns his family (and defines it more figuratively), would find your sentimentality off-message, or even claim that you are blaspheming the Holy Spirit, using it as an emotional force to win mom converts.

Then I noticed you tried to balance the exclusiveness of these births with Mary speaking to her lowly position in life: "My soul magnifies the Lord, and my spirit rejoices in God my Savior, for he has regarded the low estate of his handmaiden . . . he has filled the hungry with good things, and the rich he has sent away empty" (1:46-53), but this humility is undermined by your many references to the lineage of David. At the time of Jesus, David was held in high esteem, a unifier of the tribes of Israel, but Luke, I suggest you reread 1 Samuel and 2 Samuel and see if the flimsiness of David's moral weight is really something you want to attach to Jesus. Also, I wondered why you foreshadowed your whole gospel story, first sung out by Zechariah (Lk 1:67-80), and then by righteous, devout Simeon (Lk 2:25-35) and then by the prophetess Anna (Lk 2:36-40): their proclamations generalize themes of Jesus's story without the reader experiencing any of it. At this point, my faith in you as a "show-don't-tell" author began to falter.

Then you gave me hope. One of your strong narrative additions to Mark includes insightful details about John the Baptist's personality when he starts sermonizing. Aside from preaching the forgiveness of sins as in Mark's gospel, you give him heat addressing the multitudes: "You brood of vipers! Who warned you to flee from the wrath to come? Bear fruits that befit repentance, and do not begin to say to yourselves, 'We have Abraham as our father'; for I tell you, God is able from these stones to raise up children to Abraham. Even now the axe is laid to the root of the trees; every tree therefore that does not bear good fruit is cut down and thrown into the fire" (Lk 3:7-9). I enjoyed the dark humor when the multitudes come to him for what they thought would be a spiritually refreshing baptismal dunk, and instead John spit-fires metaphors at them, challenging old traditions represented by Abraham, throwing people's dead spiritual wood into the fire. Catching the multitudes off balance, knocking the wind out of them, you have them quickly ask what they should do and, their guards down, John lists what Jesus would command: share one's clothes and food, collect no more taxes than are due, and to soldiers, "Rob no one by violence or by false accusation, and be content with your wages" (Lk 3:14), actions that do not negate one's gains in life but stress sharing and stymying greed. And when asked if he is the Christ, John the Baptist embellishes on Mark's idea that one mightier than him will baptize with the Holy Spirit (Mark's dove finally shows up) but adds also "with fire" (Lk 3:16), which foreshadows Jesus's passion and anger for those who betray his ideals.

But then I stumbled again. Contrary to this passionate rhetoric you have created for John, when it comes to the character of Jesus, you soften Mark's rebel-outsider figure by depicting him as a twelve-year-old youth with a traditional Jewish upbringing. Sure, you try to demonstrate his independence through his spending three days in the temple "sitting among the teachers, listening to them and asking them questions" (Lk 2:46), while his parents search for him, but you undermine his independence by making it the result of Joseph and Mary running off with all their kids, not realizing one is missing (which has humorous possibilities you seem oblivious to). When they return and find him in the temple, you mention that "all who heard him were amazed at his understanding and his answers" (Lk 2:47); however, you completely soften Jesus by not giving specifics as to what he says in the temple that might challenge the worshippers, and by replacing the adult Jesus in Mark who dismissed his family—"they said to him, 'Your mother and your brothers are outside, asking for you.' And he replied, 'Who are my mother and my brothers?' And looking around on those who sat about him, he said, 'Here are my mother and my brothers! Whoever does the will of God is my brother, and sister, and mother'" (Mk 3:32-35)—with a preteen Jesus who relies on this mild, cliché response: "How is it that you sought me? Did you not know that I must be in my Father's house?" (Lk 2:49). True, his parents are confused by the pun on father with "Father's house" to represent God's temple rather than Joseph's abode. It is one thing to put people doing God's will before family but much less controversial to put God the Father himself, whom believers already feel trumps everything on earth, before family. (I do see some pluck later—six chapters later in 8:19-21, you offer a watered-down version of Mark's rejection-of-family passage; however, you leave out Mark's momentous, shocking line, "Who are my mother and my brothers?") You also weaken young Jesus by going out of your way to point out that he finally leaves with his parents, and "was obedient to them; and his mother kept all these things in her heart" (Lk 2:51), sapping Jesus of the integrity he has in Mark, where he truly put spirit and ideals before family. Come on, Luke. If you are going to write about Jesus, you need more courage.

Midway through Chapter 3 you finally get to Jesus's ministry at thirty years of age, but by spending fifteen verses to validate Jesus's lineage back through David, to Noah's sons, all the way to Adam, you are not only tedious, but again put too much importance on tradition, which diminishes Jesus's value as an outsider and original force, and furthermore you show a lack of close reading of the Old Testament, given that many of the patriarchs you want to connect to Jesus have questionable morality. At this point I got discouraged, but luckily thought to skip to Chapter 4, Jesus's confrontation of the devil in the wilderness, a dramatic, strong addition to Mark's quick reference to this event. Indeed, what you write has daring implications. When the devil tempts Jesus, hungry from wandering forty days without eating, by asking him to prove himself as the Son of God by turning stone into bread, you ingeniously have Jesus respond by editing the lines from Deuteronomy—"And he humbled you and let you hunger and fed you with manna, which you did not know, nor did your fathers know; that he might make you know that man does not live by bread alone, but man lives by everything that proceeds out of the mouth of the LORD" (Deut 8:3)—to simply read, "It is written, 'Man shall not live by bread alone'" (Lk 4:4). The original lines from Deuteronomy put the emphasis on God's power and authority, where he offers food not tasted before, perhaps a metaphor for new commitments, and then qualifies that He has or will have new commands that are more important than sustenance. However, by leaving the Lord's actions and commands out of the quote, you require the reader to focus on Jesus's faith that humans are capable of holding any spiritual ideals as more dear than their daily bread—that spirit can trump physical need.

You then have the devil show Jesus all the kingdoms of the world, saying, "To you I will give all this authority and their glory; for it has been delivered to me, and I give it to whom I will. If you, then, will worship me, it shall all be yours" (Lk 4:6-7), but Jesus rejects secular power, quoting the commandment that one shall worship only the Lord. In your version, Jesus also rejects authority because he has come to challenge it, putting ideals, values, and morality above political power and the various fixed doctrines, prices, and oppressions that come with authority. In what reads like a dream, you have the devil take Jesus to "the pinnacle of the temple" in Jerusalem, and say to

Jesus, "If you are the Son of God, throw yourself down from here; for it is written, 'He will give his angels charge of you, to guard you'" (Lk 4:9-10), to which Jesus responds "You shall not tempt the Lord your God" (Lk 4:12), rejecting the temptations to offer miracles to prove himself. The story thus keeps the reader focused on Jesus's teachings, not always an easy task for you or for other gospel writers, who are tempted to offer miracles to ensure Jesus's divine power.

Fyodor Dostoevsky, a writer who has reviewed your work, was inspired by this exchange between the devil and Jesus and used it as a central core to his chapter "The Grand Inquisitor" in his novel *The Brothers Karamazov*. In one of the character's dreams, the Church's Inquisitor, who torches all non-believers at the stake, sees that Jesus has returned to medieval Spain, and after arresting him for fear of his interfering with the mass killings, scolds Jesus for believing that "man shall not live by bread alone," something the Inquisitor says very few have the strength to practice. He adds that, because more naturally humanity does live by bread alone—prioritizing a filled stomach before morality—human nature feels comfortable turning over freedom to an authority, and even believing in the superstitions that empower it. Therefore the Grand Inquisitor reveals to Jesus that the Church has made a secret pact with your devil, supporting and agreeing to miracle, mystery, and authority that allow humanity a comfortable ignorance, an illusion of a happy life. The Grand Inquisitor argues that Jesus's placing the heart's intuition and the willingness to questioning of doctrine over authority puts dangerous value on the "exceptional, vague, and enigmatic," all reflected in Jesus's use of parable and wit. Luke, with your single rendition of the wilderness scene, you have a fan.

After this powerful scene with Jesus and Satan, I began to worry that one of your protégés started riffing with your narrative before sending it off to publication, as the storyline becomes absurd, with Jesus's character breaking from the one you are developing. All of a sudden Jesus starts following tradition: he politely reads traditional passages in the synagogue; all speak well of him, wonder where his "gracious words which proceeded out of his mouth" (Lk 4:22) come from, and are amazed he could be Joseph's son. But then, in an unexpected burst, the people are infuriated by his reference to a time in Israel when only a Syrian leper was cleansed (it's not clear if the cleansing was done by Jesus or not, or why this happens among several lepers in Israel), and they lead Jesus to a place outside the city "that they might throw him down headlong. But passing through the midst of them he went away" (Lk 4:29-30). The unclear reference to the Syrian, coupled with the audience being pleased with Jesus's eloquence, but without any reference to Jesus challenging traditions as in Mark, followed by an unexplained emotional explosion from the audience to want to kill Jesus, and topped off with his immediate use of a magical escape route, all baffled me. I decided to ignore this section because the previous scene with Satan gave me faith that your voice could return.

And praise the Lord, it did return. I was struck by the enigmatic story you include that tells of the sinful woman who approaches Jesus at the home of Simon the Pharisee, who is himself stumped as to why Jesus would accept her preciously kept gift of alabaster-vased oil anointment, knowing she is a sinner. (Having Jesus encounter a Pharisee, who usually would be threatened by Jesus's teachings, in his home, adds an intimacy with the Pharisees absent in Mark.) To answer Simon, Jesus tells the parable of two debtors, one owing more than the other, and the creditor forgiving both. When Jesus asks Simon who would love the creditor the most, Simon correctly answers that it is the one who owes the most; Jesus quickly uses this answer to segue back to the sinful woman who gave Jesus more than Simon did when she came to Simon's home: "Do you see this woman? I entered your house, you gave me no water for my feet, but she has wet my feet with her tears and wiped them with her hair. You gave me no kiss, but from the time I came in she has not ceased to kiss my feet. You did not anoint my head with oil, but she has anointed my feet with ointment" (Lk 7:44-46).

Mark's ever-humble Jesus may not have allowed the woman to offer him so much and would be quick to get her back on her feet, but you have Jesus focus on the meaning of her desperation for forgiveness: "Therefore I tell you, her sins, which are many, are forgiven, for she loved much; but he who is forgiven little, loves little" (Lk 7:47). Jesus connects her being especially loving with her sinning, suggesting that with a more tenuous existence comes more struggle, something foreign to a person like Simon the Pharisee who has led a protected, controlled lifestyle that results in less suffering, less need for forgiveness, but also in a proportional lack of peace, love, and understanding. This leaves Simon less impassioned to give the love that the sinful woman wants so desperately to offer. Because the souls of the sinful have struggled on their journey, they become tinder that easily sparks into love; those souls that are protected often keep that light at a low flicker.

Although you make such meaningful use of Jesus's relationship with a Pharisee here, you never present Jesus's relationship with the disciples as interestingly as Mark, who uses them as a foil, depicting them as never quite catching on to what Jesus is doing. Your disciples are flatter characters, portrayed as missionary drones: "And he called the twelve together and gave them power and authority over all demons and to cure diseases, and he sent them out to preach the kingdom of God and to heal" (Lk 9:1-2), humbly taking nothing with them, staff or food or money. However, you are at your best when you pleasantly catch the reader off guard by this addition from Jesus—"And wherever they do not receive you, when you leave that town shake off the dust from your feet as a testimony against them" (Lk 9:5). The dust is an icon of the worthlessness of the unwelcoming, and is a remembrance of our from-dust-to-dust existence, but I especially liked Jesus having them shake it off their feet, a non-aggressive rejection of the town's lack of Holy Spirit. The sand-demand gives the disciples some verve, but this soon fades when you use the disciples as witnesses to supernatural events—the appearance of Moses and Elijah—and then have them build booths for these apparitions and Jesus so that "a cloud came and overshadowed them; and [the disciples] were afraid as they entered the cloud" (Lk 9:34), topped off by the voice of God validating Jesus. Supernatural intervention erases the earthiness of your narratives. You don't need that intervention. I wondered again why you did not have more faith in a secular Jesus.

Once again, however, you capture my attention with the parables, such as the discourse between Jesus and the lawyer in Chapter 10. Regarding how to inherit eternal life, I admired your portrayal of Jesus's quick reaction, forcing the lawyer to answer his own question with, "You shall love the Lord your God with all your heart, and with all your soul, and with all your strength, and with all your mind; and your neighbor as yourself" (Lk 10:27), an amazing statement because, after the all-encompassing demands of commitment to the Lord, in the same breath, the statement climaxes by shifting to love of one's neighbor. The sequence is shocking, putting love of the Lord on the same level as love of neighbor. The lawyer immediately senses this equivalence, so he quickly asks Jesus, "And who is my neighbor?" (Lk 10:29). Instead of answering "your fellow worshiper" or "village resident" or "family member," Jesus answers with a parable about a traveler who is beaten, stripped, robbed, and left for dead. A priest sees him, but wishing no involvement, walks on the other side of the road. The same happens with a Levite (another temple functionary) who spots the person in need and avoids him. But a Samaritan (a believer in an off-brand Judaism, separated from those of the Babylonian deportation and left out of the Second Temple) "had compassion, and went to him and bound up his wounds, pouring on oil and wine; then he set him on his own beast and brought him to an inn, and took care of him" (Lk 10:33-34). The Samaritan even pays the inn's bill. Jesus redefines *neighbor*; it is not necessarily someone who is an expected part of one's familiar group, but one who unexpectedly helps a person in need, an outsider of good spirit, not always an insider of familiar spirit. The corollary is also true. The Samaritan has defined a neighbor as someone in need despite not being in his inner group. By cliché-busting the concept of neighbor, the parable widens one's scope of love but also requires one to discriminate. Your parable adds so much to Mark's storyline.

I also appreciate the Buddha-style mentality of your Jesus when he instructs how to maintain faith in the course life takes: Cast out anxiety. Keep expectations low. Avoid conflict. Stymie ambition. Be humble. "Of how much more value are you than the birds! And which of you by being anxious can add a cubit to his span of life? If then you are not able to do as small a thing as that, why are you anxious about the rest? Consider the lilies, how they grow; they neither toil nor spin; yet I tell you, even Solomon in all his glory was not arrayed like one of these. But if God so clothes the grass which is alive in the field today and tomorrow is thrown into the oven, how much more will he clothe you, O men of little faith!" (Lk 12:24-27). Anxiety about the fleetingness of life gets in the way of faith in life. Luke, your Jesus suggests that so much striving, writing, making, selling, and other doings of ambition are an attempt to hold on to life before it fades, but no activity defies the cycle of life. The birds and lilies exist without anxiety, exude their natural beauty, a beauty that exceeds human arts such as a king's clothing, and then burn away. I revere your having Jesus suggest that the stress-less witnessing and accepting of ephemeral natural beauty is the way to enter God's kingdom. Just writing this letter to you defies Jesus's attitude and gives me pause.

I wondered, though, why you didn't move some other passages closer to this one in Chapter 12, because they cleverly demonstrate that this non-toil-and-spin concept has social ramifications—such as Jesus asking why not cut your losses instead of going to court to win: "As you go with your accuser before the magistrate, make an effort to settle with him on the way, lest he drag you to the judge, and the judge hand you over to the officer, and the officer put you in prison. I tell you, you will never get out till you have paid the very last copper" (Lk 12:58-59). By going so far as to say even the last copper will be lost, the line suggests that we lose the last of many things when driven by our insistence to win or to be absolved of our positions or to be validated as the best, instead of compromising, giving up part—or even all—of what we feel is our due.

Later I connected your line, "But it is easier for heaven and earth to pass away, than for one dot of the law to become void" (Lk 16:17) to the above, a nice hyperbole that explains how entrenched laws can become in the face of new ways of looking at life and the world. Ironically, right after this, you write "Every one who divorces his wife and marries another commits adultery, and he who marries a woman divorced from her husband commits adultery" (Lk 16:18), and I was confused as to whether you believe this or are using this as an example of a stubborn, ingrown interpretation of the commandment "Thou shalt not commit adultery." Given Jesus's theme of rebirth and rejuvenation of spirit, I want to think you are presenting this divorce statement as an illustration of a stagnant law that is hard to void, but your writing does not make it clear. If the divorce is for trivial or unethical reasons, then this becomes a different matter, but again, I wish the passage was better contextualized.

Given these legal references, I reread the passage on lawyers from the previous chapter: "Woe to you lawyers also! for you load men with burdens hard to bear, and you yourselves do not touch the burdens with one of your fingers. Woe to you! for you build the tombs of the prophets whom your fathers killed. So you are witnesses and consent to the deeds of your fathers; for they killed them, and you build their tombs" (Lk 11:46-48). The Pharisees were lawyers, an eternal class of litigators who benefit from the conflict of others, who dismiss mediation, who profit from others' anxiety while the lawyer stands at a distance, outside the psychological and moral burdens of the case. Luke, you perceptively show Jesus going even further, knowing that the lawyers represent officialdom, responsible for monument-tombs in honor of prophets (including sculptures and churches for Jesus himself in the future), prophets who ironically were stymied or killed by past versions of those same official groups (here represented by their fathers) and their dogmatic traditions. Jesus addresses the disconnect between what was once fresh, innovative, free of dogma, and the present official group that—out of guilt or ignorance or formality—honors these past innovations that now have become stale, while they simultaneously and hypocritically dismiss the new prophets, with their fresh ideas, of their present time. When Jesus chastises, "Woe to you lawyers! for you have taken away the key of knowledge; you did not enter yourselves, and you hindered those who were entering" (Lk 11:52), he not only symbolically scolds establishments (religious, philosophical, cultural, governmental, educational) of all times for being of limited knowledge, but also for coveting learning and maintaining their status by muddying knowledge for those who thirst for it.

In connection with this view of knowledge, your Jesus becomes more enigmatic, hinting that genuine knowledge is obtained in the calmer waters of modesty, appropriately expressed in a line that is deceptively simple: "He who is faithful in a very little is faithful also in much; and he who is dishonest in a very little is dishonest also in much" (Lk 16:10). The first part has three meanings: caring much about something small, modest, seemingly inconsequential, yields the same satisfaction as caring about something large, important, consequential;

secondly, much is to be gained in being faithful to what is little; and finally suggesting that only someone who is faithful to little has the genuine faith and capacity needed for what is of greater value. The corollaries are also well expressed in the second part of the sentence: dishonesty about a little thing is the same as being dishonest about something bigger, or more importantly, dishonesty about something small leads to dishonesty about something bigger or more important. Then Jesus expands the parallels. One cannot be trusted to deal with material riches if the person is not faithful to mammon, the god of money, or spirit of indulgences, but "no servant can serve two masters; for either he will hate the one and love the other, or he will be devoted to the one and despise the other. You cannot serve God and mammon" (Lk 16:13). In this context, God represents integrity and humility and the lilies of the field, the antithesis of material indulgence.

In the lilies-of-the-field context, mammon is the force that demands anxiety and toil. So much of your gospel points to asking for less to gain more. I wonder if the earlier parable of the wedding guests would help define the passage about mammon if they were in closer proximity to each other? Jesus advises that "when you are invited by any one to a marriage feast, do not sit down in a place of honor, lest a more eminent man than you be invited by him; and he who invited you both will come and say to you, 'Give place to this man,' and then you will begin with shame to take the lowest place. But when you are invited, go and sit in the lowest place, so that when your host comes he may say to you, 'Friend, go up higher'; then you will be honored in the presence of all who sit at table with you. For every one who exalts himself will be humbled, and he who humbles himself will be exalted" (Lk 14:8-11). Several of your passages meld to give an almost Zen view of the world, suggesting that by asking for fewer indulgences and legal victories, and less status and wealth, in short, by voiding selfish ambition, one avoids shame and anxiety, instead merging with the dove of peace, love, and understanding. Humility engenders the Holy Spirit.

The anecdote about the prodigal son further demonstrates how the Holy Spirit depends on humility and forgiveness. In this parable, the younger of two sons journeys away from home, squanders all his money in loose living, has no resources to survive a famine, gets a job slopping pigs, envies the pods they feed on, and ends up with nothing (Lk 15:11-17). Only after losing everything does he appreciate the standing of his family's servants, who have bread enough to spare. Only now does he see the importance of "sitting in the lowest place," and imagines going to his father and saying "Father, I have sinned against heaven and before you; I am no longer worthy to be called your son; treat me as one of your hired servants" (Lk 15:18-19). When he returns and the father sees him, the father runs to embrace his son before he can deliver his conciliatory lines, the son instead delivering the lines of admission and forgiveness after he experiences his father's joy, a testament to his sincerity (Lk 15:20-21). His father lavishly clothes him and orders that a fatted calf be killed and grilled for a feast, the father claiming, "for this my son was dead, and is alive again; he was lost, and is found" (Lk 15:24), in essence celebrating a rebirth of the son's humility, his willingness to start low.

Luke, I thought you rightfully complicated the story by having the elder brother come in from the field, become baffled by the merrymaking, grow angry upon hearing the reason for it, and refuse to join the feast. When his father entreats him, the elder son answers "Lo, these many years I have served you, and I never disobeyed your command; yet you never gave a kid, that I might make merry with my friends. But when this son of yours came, who has devoured your living with harlots, you killed for him the fatted calf!" (Lk 15:29-30). The elder son is asking for something rightfully deserved, but his moral steadfastness already earns him a high place and indeed his father reassures him, "Son, you are always with me, and all that is mine is yours" (Lk 15:31). Through the father's joy, your Jesus implies that the journey of one's spirit from self-destruction to a renewed humility elicits more fulfillment than stasis, even if it is stasis in the form of positive devotion. When the father exclaims, "It was fitting to make merry and be glad, for this your brother was dead, and is alive; he was lost, and is found" (Lk 15:32), he reminds us that we have the potential to be rejuvenated by another's spiritual rebirth.

Your parable of the talents (or pounds of currency) further develops the importance of not taking one's gifts for granted, of nurturing an ability or aptitude so it grows into special assets. Jesus is motivated to tell the parable because the group who he is with, that includes Zacchaeus, a cheating tax collector who Jesus inspired to seek absolution, assumes the kingdom of God is close at hand. The parable includes a nobleman who the reader associates with Jesus because he goes to a far away kingdom to receive kingly power only to be despised by the people there. However, before he leaves home base to discover this rejection, he calls his servants together to give them currency to invest (Lk 19:12-15). The investment symbolically is tantamount to putting Jesus's teachings to work and also of taking one's gifts in life (artistic, moral, intellectual, mathematical, ministerial) and investing energy in them to generate even more self-worth and well being for others. Indeed, two of the servants do that, one turning one pound of currency into ten, the other turning one into five, and so the nobleman rewards them further, multiplying the fruits of the two servants' endeavors into gifts of authority over ten and five cities respectively (Lk 19:16-19). Nurturing and developing one's gifts yields even more rewards than one ever imagines. (I did wonder why the reward was authority over cities, because it is easy to equate that reward with the negative worldly power over cities that Satan tempts Jesus with in the wilderness. I tried to take the authority as symbolic of responsible leadership because the servants showed diligence. Am I close?)

In the parable, the third servant hides his single pound and does nothing with it, telling the nobleman, "I was afraid of you, because you are a severe man; you take up what you did not lay down, and reap what you did not sow" (Lk 19:21). The nobleman says he condemns the servant "out of [his] own mouth" (Lk 19:22) because he admits the nobleman is severe yet did nothing to earn interest on the funds he was given (Lk 19:23). I thought the nobleman to be Jesus's non-compromising double: he reaps the benefits from others' fruitfulness, not because he is a thief, but because when others do well through his teachings, Jesus reaps benefits. Those benefits can be in the form of others having faith in their own attributes to help themselves and others. In your gospel, Jesus triumphs through the empowerment of spirit.

The nobleman has been generous, but now takes the one pound from the "wicked" (Lk 19:22) servant who hid his gift, and gives it to the one with ten pounds because, despite Jesus's group being astounded that he would give to the person who already has ten, Jesus's noble double says "that to every one who has will more be given; but from him who has not, even what he has will be taken away" (Lk 19:26), implying that once someone fails to become creatively fruitful, or spiritually generous, or morally expansive, not only does that person gain nothing, but actually stagnates and becomes worse than the moment the person hoarded a gift. These implications make for a strong, challenging parable, but when I got to the last lines, I had a problem, because even as a metaphor it goes beyond the concept of a principled, severe man: "But as for these enemies of mine, who did not want me to reign over them, bring them here and slay them before me" (Lk 19:27). Did someone else give you advice on this line? I see your colleague Matthew does not use death in his rendition of this parable and instead ends the parable by "cast[ing] the worthless servant into the outer darkness; there men will weep and gnash their teeth" (Mt 25:30), capturing the frustration of those who refuse to make interest in life.

I noticed as you move to the end of your narrative, the solemnity of the events becomes enhanced by some of your additions and broken by others. For instance, the various dimensions of betrayal in Mark, mostly centered on the disciples who represent our vulnerabilities and also on the power structure that feels threatened, are changed in your gospel to include among the betrayers even those closer to us, a good move to make the tragedy even more universal: "You will be delivered up even by parents and brothers and kinsmen and friends, and some of you they will put to death; you will be hated by all for my name's sake" (Lk 21:16-17), although I would prefer this to read "hated by all for my teachings' sakes," to help move the concept away from Jesus as an icon. On the other hand, I hear Mark's voice for Jesus matched in your version when, knowing his crucifixion is eminent, he exclaims, "Father, forgive them; for they know not what they do" (Lk 23:34), the calm, somber tone capturing an understanding of the breadth of humanity's narrow vision, the world's violence committed out of so many impulses—banality, envy, greed, insecurity, and ignorance. I was deeply moved by Jesus's theme of forgiveness in this context.

On the other hand, with lines such as, "I tell you that this scripture must be fulfilled in me" (Lk 22:37), as well as Jesus confidently giving himself over to the crucifixion when he exclaims, "Father, into thy hands I commit my spirit!" (Lk 23:46), you shifted me away from the betrayal themes in Mark and pushed me into a hyped otherworldliness, a common problem I noticed with another manuscript by the apostle John, who centers almost entirely on Jesus as a shadow puppet in a prophesy script, emotionally distanced from the human tragedy I felt so strongly in Mark's gospel.

If I may add another quibble, your narrative also scrambles Mark's tragic tone through Herod's silly, adolescent mentality. Herod seems only interested in Jesus's magic tricks: "When Herod saw Jesus, he was very glad, for he had long desired to see him, because he had heard about him, and he was hoping to see some sign done by him" (Lk 23:8), an attempt, I realize, to show Herod's shallowness, but it snaps the tension leading to Jesus's death. The frivolity is extended by Herod's relationship with Pilate—you have them become good friends during the course of Jesus's trials, when before there was unexplained enmity between them. You also ruin Mark's view of Pilate's intelligence. Other touches seemed to me amateurish attempts to take us into a supernatural world and away from the secular tragedy of losing such a special prophet—instances such as the mysterious figure at Jesus's tomb being dressed in "dazzling apparel" (Lk 24:4) instead of white, a symbol of ostentation instead of purity; the resurrected Jesus racing through anything in scriptures related to himself "beginning with Moses and all the prophets" (Lk 24:27); or having Jesus go out of his way to prove his spirit is real, "for a spirit has not flesh and bones as you see that I have" (Lk 24:39) immediately followed by "Have you anything here to eat?" (Lk 24:41) and getting a broiled piece of fish to prove his ghost is "real." (A broiled fish? Come on, Luke.)

Also at the end of the gospel, you miss the importance of the women—here Mary Magdalene, Joanna, Mary the mother of James, and others—that Mark's special treatment turns into a symbol of our feminine selves. (I explain this in a piece I wrote, "From Hallow to Callow," that I could send you.) In your gospel, I had a difficult time deciphering which women are witnesses during and after the crucifixion. Your best passage with the women comes when they can finally recognize Jesus breaking bread with them, because you place the reader in a symbolic world where shared bread recalls Jesus's communal spirit and the sharing in the spirit of his teachings (Lk 24:30). The concreteness of the communal bread melds into the next line with an emphasis on shared memory, insight implied by the women's eyes and hearts opening, rather than their literal observation: "And their eyes were opened and they recognized him; and he vanished out of their sight. They said to each other 'Did not our hearts burn within us while he talked to us on the road, while he opened to us the scriptures?'" (Lk 24:31-32). I found the depiction of the women's spiritual experience credible and especially moving.

However, by the last verses, the women are simply an audience for Jesus reaffirming that everything written about him "in the law of Moses and the prophets and the psalms must be fulfilled" (Lk 24:44), reaffirming that "it is written, that the Christ should suffer and on the third day rise from the dead, and that the repentance and forgiveness of sins should be preached in his name to all nations" (Lk 24:46-47), reaffirming that he sends "the promise of my Father upon you" (Lk 24:49) (but tells them to stay in the city until they are clothed with power from on high, as if they need special protection before exposing themselves), and assuring that they will be left "continually in the temple blessing God" (Lk 24:53). This ending makes Jesus's fate antiseptic rather than painful, planned instead of tragic, grandiose instead of humble, neatly wrapped up instead of leaving the reader with eternal astonishment. Luke, I wish you had more faith in Mark's ending, where the women "fled from the tomb; for trembling and astonishment had come upon them; and they said nothing to any one, for they were afraid" (Mark 16:8). Mark leaves the reader with eyes wide open and the heart burning. In Mark's ending, less gives so much more.

Luke, for me your gospel is truly a mixed blessing and I cannot help but feel that sometimes your less-talented friends dropped into your narrative and messed with it. Nevertheless, I look forward to returning to the strongest parts of your gospel for the rest of my days.

May the grace of Jesus be with you,
and with all sincerity,
Gary Hoffman

HUMMUS IN EPHESUS
A Pagan Conversation

~ I don't know about you, but it seems to me that eating fresh sardines and hummus while looking out over the sparkling Aegean Sea after visiting Ephesus is the best.

~ This morning when you sandwiched my leg between your thighs was the best too.

~ What else did you like last night?

~ All of it. Let's role-play: you are a goddess like Athena, intellectual and sensual, who has decided to make me your mortal lover. Or did she have any?

~ I like the idea of mortal-immortal relationships. But the main goddess here at Ephesus was Artemis, right?

~ Well, yes; the ruins we just saw were the temple devoted to Artemis. That temple was the first made of all marble and larger than the Parthenon, one of the Seven Wonders of the World.

~ Why Artemis and not Athena?

~ She was the goddess of birth and the moon, wilderness and animals—the world of blood, passion, and violence, as well as natural beauty outside the reach of human-created beauty. She represented a fertility circle that included virginity of men and women, and the positive and negative results of birthing—successful labor as well as the killer of sick, suffering infants.

~ We saw a bronze sculpture of her Roman equivalent, *Diana*, by Augustus Saint-Gaudens in the Metropolitan Museum in New York. Remember her sleekness? You commented on her full athletic nudity, dancing up on one foot to draw her bow, pulling her perky breasts up and exposing the fullness of her firm, well-developed abdomen. We thought she was a body begging to be touched but too busy with her work. Let's pretend I'm her.

~ But the Artemis of Ephesus was not beautiful at all. More like an Eastern fertility goddess. She didn't even begin to have that special combination of softness and strength seen in more classical versions of her namesake such as *Diane de Versailles* at the Louvre, the second-century Roman copy of the Greek sculpture, with her wise, calm face, elegant but strong neck, soft but strong arms. Remember her hand controls a stag at her side; the other flexes, reaching to a quiver on her back for an arrow she delicately fingers despite its deadliness. *That* Artemis is a combination of femininity and masculinity that makes her human but too godly to get near.

~ So what was she at Ephesus?

~ You'll see at the Archaeology Museum. She's more like an Egyptian column than a human torso, her legs mostly nonexistent, tapering down to her feet, the whole body becoming a flat surface to hold rows and rows of fertility bombs—protruding balloon shapes that could be breasts, bull testicles, gourds. Hard to know. The rest of the flat surface is a background for a collection of bas-relief symbols—a ring of zodiac figures around her neck, and rows of cows and goats and some lions, domestic and wild life, adorning her surfaces. And bees. Big time fertility symbols. Here, at Ephesus, people paid homage to her for eight hundred years. Alexander the Great could have seen her around 300 BCE, and then the Romans at their prime here in the first century.

~ You said she was mentioned in the Acts of the Apostles. I guess that was the start of her downfall, after Paul's epistles? A shame that all those different gods and goddesses were written off as pagan.

~ I know. Maybe we should bring the Greco-Roman gods back: reintroduce the Church of the Ancient Greeks, where children learn that gods are men and women who deify different aspects of life—not just moral and political ones, but physical forces including oceans and seasons, the kinds of elements dropped after the Bible's creation stories. But to answer your question, in the Acts of the Apostles, often just called Acts, Paul confronts silversmiths in Ephesus for making figurines of Artemis, claiming, "that gods made with hands are not gods" (Acts 19:26). I wonder what he would say of all the badly painted plaster models of Jesus or Mary in so many churches around the world? The Reformation destroyed many European church statues as idols, wiping out beautiful works of art but also lots of kitsch.

~ People never see their own religious artists as idol-makers. Too bad Paul was in competition for people's allegiance to his God versus the pagan gods.

~ True, but the biggest competitor with the pagan gods was the writer of Revelation. The book is sometimes attributed to the gospel writer John and is usually titled the Revelation of John, but that authorship is unlikely since the first-person narration never claims apostolate authority nor makes any reference to the gospels. Many attribute it to another John, but in any case, it was written here in Ephesus around 90 CE. What amazes me is how much the Jesus of Revelation is a recreation of this Artemis of Ephesus, how John shuns any image of Jesus as being the flesh-and-blood person we see in the gospels, but instead a symbolic warrior statue, layered with symbols like Artemis of Ephesus, but moving and talking with "a loud voice like a trumpet" (Rev 1:10), asking the first-person narrator, John, to deliver a message to the key churches in Asia Minor, present-day Turkey, including Ephesus.

~ I don't hear Jesus sounding like a trumpet in any of the gospels. Too brassy. Well, maybe the Gospel of John. So what are the idol "bas-relief" designs on this Jesus of Revelation?

~ Okay, so on turning to see where the trumpeting voice is coming from in Chapter 1, the narrator sees "seven golden lampstands" (Rev 1:12), or candle holders, and here "in the midst of the lampstands one like a son of man, clothed with a long robe and with a golden girdle round his breast" (Rev 1:13). So Jesus is like a lampstand, representing light, faith, knowledge, not through wit or wisdom as in the gospels, but as a stiff sculpture, with military chest protection made out of gold, ready to do battle with Satan.

~ When I hear gold on a god, I think of the golden calf in Exodus, not of Jesus. And why is he ready to do physical battle? What happened to casting out demons by healing, keeping the emphasis on the human spirit and psychology?

~ I know. Many scholars think the Jesus of Revelation is antithetical to the gospel Jesus; others argue that Jesus can take on any role, including a warrior-killer if he's going after evil. I think the writer of Revelation is trying to rival pagan statues with his own Jesus statue. This Jesus has hair and a head that are as "white as snow" (Rev 1:14), giving him an ancient marble cast, but with eyes "like a flame of fire" (Rev 1:14) lest one think this is not a Jesus with passion; maybe John is also trying to catch the eye color in ancient Roman sculptures that has now faded away. Stronger sculptural elements are his feet, "like burnished bronze, refined as in a furnace" (Rev 1:15) and, in Kachina-doll symbolic design, "in his right hand he held seven stars, from his mouth issued a sharp two-edged sword, and his face was like the sun shining in full strength" (Rev 1:16).

~ Does this John realize the irony in the fact that, by reducing Jesus to a composite of symbolic objects, he's creating another idol?

~ Obviously not. This version of Jesus puts me off, lacking the strength and credibility he gained by being human in the Synoptic Gospels, where he equals my engagement with the flesh-and-blood Greek and Roman gods in story and in sculpture. I'm only intellectually curious when I see Artemis-of-Ephesus, objects-tacked-on-top-of object, collages that become purely symbolic figurines and the same thing happens when I visualize Revelation's rendition of Jesus.

~ Why do you think people are fascinated by Revelation's sculptured Jesus, or for that matter, Kachina dolls, totem poles, or any less anthropomorphic symbolic religious items?

~ I wonder if overtly symbolic objects capture our attention by reminding us of our dream world, but when they are done in a blunt manner, not carefully blended with concrete imagery (say the way ritual masks make facial features out of seashore items), these symbols only have intellectual appeal, and are not absorbed simultaneously by both the heart and mind, just the mind. By the way, even more annoying in Revelation is the fact that often the narrator interprets these blunt symbols for us, such as the Lamb (another rendition of Jesus) "with seven horns and with seven eyes, which are the seven spirits of God sent out into all the earth" (Rev 5:6). People get off on identifying stock symbols like the portents in "Revelation," ironically again reminiscent of heavy-handed pagan imagery, such as the woman who appears in the heavens, "clothed with the sun, with the moon under her feet, and on her head a crown of twelve stars" (Rev 12:1), here probably for the twelve tribes of Israel. Some symbols are put together with the gimmick of a child's flip book where one can line up different heads, torsos, and feet, such as the beast that represents Rome: it looks "like a leopard, its feet were like a bear's, and its mouth was like a lion's mouth" (Rev 13:2), "uttering haughty and blasphemous words" (Rev 13:5).

~ So then these images are not surreal enough. Not enough blending the bizarre with the mundane?

~ Right. On the other hand, there are a few images that do blend the two successfully to create the surreal, such as when the sixth seal is opened and "the sun became black as sackcloth, the full moon became like blood, and the stars of the sky fell to the earth as the fig tree sheds its winter fruit when shaken by a gale; the sky vanished like a scroll that is rolled up, and every mountain and island was removed from its place" (Rev 6:12-14). The destruction is magical because it links fantastic dissolution to everyday occurrences.

~ I love the sky rolling up. Reminds me of Dali's *The Disintegration of the Persistence of Memory*, where we see the sky has an unnoticed edge that could be used to roll it up. This seems like a symbol that readers would latch onto; mostly, when I hear fundamentalists talk about Revelation, since the book is about the apocalypse, they care more about symbols that are projections into the future, and since the images often lack defining contexts, it seems easy for anyone to imagine they represent any future threats or destruction.

~ Right. If enough time goes by, one can find a parallel in the modern world to many of the symbols in Revelation. For instance, locusts that arrive "arrayed for battle; on their heads were what looked like crowns of gold . . . and their teeth like lions' teeth" (Rev 9:7-8) are premonitions of modern drones, right?

~ Sure. Why not? So then, here's why I think I am also more attracted to the paganism of Greek and Roman myths and artwork, instead of the Artemis of Ephesus or the pagan-like symbols of Revelation—I like that mixing of flesh and intelligence, physical beauty and foolishness in the gods and goddesses, because that constantly reminds us how much those two pairs of attributes interact with fate or divine interventions. The Greeks and Romans don't just dismiss the sexuality as sinful. They merge the sacred and profane.

~ Right. The Bible has stories about sex, but they usually lack godly sponsorship.

~ It's weird how all that stuff about sex and the gods got lost and replaced. What if there was a gospel where Jesus had a girlfriend, like in Nikos Kazantzakis' novel *The Last Temptation of Christ?*

~ Yes. Modern Greeks never forgave Kazantzakis for retelling the gospel with details like that. Actually, the divide between spirit and anything having to do with flesh was an issue centuries after the gospels, especially right here at Ephesus, the site of big blowouts regarding to what extent Jesus was flesh and blood and to what extent he was God. Western Turkey is where Christianity, at the Council of Nicaea, could have gone one way and instead went the other, and neither Jesus nor his gospel writers nor Paul were around to have any say in the whole matter.

~ But even if he didn't have a girlfriend, Jesus is supposed to be a part of each, human and divine. What's the deal?

~ Not sure you want to know; the issue is a little unsexy. Have some more of these fresh sardines.

~ I like that you realize that these *mezzes* are making your baby happy.

~ I know. I could come here just for the food. So much of Turkey looks like central and northern agricultural California. I'm amazed that I am looking at the same terrain and farmland seen by Paul, and probably the writers who wrote the gospels in Greek, too.

~ And the same seafood. These sardines are nice and salty.

~ Hard to believe Paul could not connect the fecundity of this land with other sensual delights, being smack in the middle of the Greek and Roman world where their religions had the flesh–divine realms smoothly blended. In light of those cultures, from a secular point of view, it would have seemed unimportant that theologians in 431 CE were besides themselves with determining whether Jesus was an eternal god, consubstantial with the cosmic God during the creation and Old Testament world—in other words whether Jesus existed in eternal time before pushing through Mary's birth canal. In 325 CE, when Christianity was well on its way with churches all over the eastern Mediterranean, including the seven Asia Minor ones that get all the attention in Revelation, bishops came from all of them to Nicaea (now called Iznet, the place that produced all that great tile we saw in Istanbul) to make an official decision on whether there was ever a time and space in the universe when Jesus did not exist. Arius, a priest from Alexandria, argued that although Jesus was divine, he was created as a human who is born, walks the earth, and dies. The council decided that interpretation made Jesus less godly, too human, too capable of sin, so they decided he was divine, consubstantial with the Lord, eternal with the Lord and the Holy Spirit. Scholars refer to these arguments as having to do with "Christology," itself a spirit-killing term, no?

~ What an arduous, absurd journey for these men to take to argue about this. Why not argue about what Jesus said, the way Paul did in his epistles? Paul was here in Ephesus, a great reason for scholars to have a conference here today.

~ You sound like a conference organizer. Well, religion often insists on gods that are matchless, beyond human existence. And get this: Nicaea did not finish this business. Right here in this classical city, Ephesus became the scene of several other major councils on this issue, including a really dramatic one in 431 CE when Nestorius, the Archbishop of Constantinople, tried to make the distinction between Jesus's human and divine natures by calling Mary a Christ-bearer instead of a God-bearer.

~ Funny that he tried to build the issue by what Mary was forcing through the birth canal.

~ Well it didn't work. Cyril of Alexandria wanted Nestorius to recant or be excommunicated. Cyril was worried that if Christ were a man, then he would have been born into sin and mortality—hence, not divine. I have to wonder what Paul would have written about it all if he had been alive at the time. Nestorius thought he could reverse the accusations against him with the backing of the Christian Roman emperor, Theodosius II, and instead get Cyril to be the one to recant or be excommunicated. Ephesus was filled with Christians who already were big into the cult of the Virgin Mary, and the idea of *theotokos*, the birthing of one already divine, would have had great appeal to them. Anyway, around Easter in 431, as bishops began showing up in Ephesus—from Rome, Antioch, Palestine, Northern Africa—instead of forming camaraderie, each group worked over the newly arrived. When the council met and debated, Nestorius basically got his ass handed to him.

~ The disciple Mark would never have tolerated this kind of debate. He starts his gospel when Jesus is an adult. Why even talk about birthing?

~ True. And it's so amusing to me that when groups come together to decide anything—banking policy, university growth issues, answers to world poverty, protocol for autism at a children's hospital, or even the divinity of Jesus—everything comes down to haggling and winning. There is so little tolerance for flux when there is groupthink, and way too much desire to determine what is orthodoxy and what is heresy. Instead of the Lord's Prayer, I would have liked those councils to open with the passage from Matthew where Jesus comments on the reason for this prayer. He says when you pray you shouldn't be like the hypocrites who love to pray out loud in the synagogue and street corner where everyone can notice them, but that you should pray in secret, without show, and not run at the mouth (Mt 6:5-6).

~ Very anti-groupthink.

~ Yes, but the phrase I like the most is to "not heap up empty phrases as the Gentiles do" (Mt 6:7). The heaping up refers to wordy pretensions, but the "empty phrases" refer to those that have lost their meaning, reminding me of what has become of the "our-father-who-art-in-heaven" Lord's prayer, which Jesus initially offered as a new, fresh prayer but which, after centuries, ironically is now often mumbled mechanically, thoughtlessly, in a stale murmur. Jesus would now welcome its replacement with thoughtful, fresh prayers. He represents change, for God's sake. The councils wanted everything locked down as dogma. No changes. Reminds me of the narrator's mentality at the end of Revelation: he warns that anyone who adds to or takes away from his book will be bounced out of the new holy city of Jerusalem and cut off from a share of immortality represented by the tree of life.

~ I think the Jesus of Mark's gospel would have been sickened by all the Christology fuss; Jesus of John's gospel, on the other hand, would have loved it because the councils put Jesus outside of humanity.

~ You're probably right. By the way, the Gospel of John might also have been written here in Ephesus, and don't forget, John builds himself into his narrative, writing that he was favored by Jesus who, at the crucifixion, asked him to take care of his mom, so of course legend says she was buried near here. We could even visit that site.

~ Let's skip the legends. The Christology discussion, the question of the special divinity of Jesus, brings up Ralph Waldo Emerson. Didn't he blow the whole Jesus-mortality issue out of the water in the early 1800s at Harvard when he delivered his "Divinity School Address," essentially saying we can all be divine, that divinity has nothing to do with a particular person at a particular time in history, that in fact, Jesus only provided an example?

~ Well, sort of, but realize how many centuries you just jumped to get to that! Let's check quotes from Emerson on your laptop. Here: "If a man is at heart just, then in so far is he God; the safety of God, the immortality of God, the majesty of God do enter into that man," and regarding Jesus, "One man was true to what is in you and me. He saw that God incarnates himself in man, and evermore goes forth anew to take possession of his world. He said, in this jubilee of sublime emotion, 'I am divine. Through me, God acts; through me, speaks. Would you see God, see me; or, see thee, when thou also thinkest as I now think.'" [1] God, Jesus, all of us mortals can be divine.

~ I think of Whitman's praise of the divine, man, sex and everything. But the divinity of man and sex aside, too much for Paul, I wonder if he at least enjoyed the food here the way we are, or was he too much a man on a mission?

~ He wrote an epistle to the Ephesians, but many think it was more of a form letter because of some stock phrasing, such as addressing "God's Holy People" instead of, as he did more typically, "God's Holy People at Ephesus" or addressing people he remembered there after personally founding the church at Ephesus. However, he wrote his first epistle to the Corinthians here too, and I really love some key lines in it. For one thing—

~ Wait. You can tell me about it tomorrow after we visit the Roman terrace houses at Ephesus. After all this theology, I need a walk before we go to the archaeology museum and back to Sirence.

———

~ Pass me the red peppers. I'm going to order the *gozleme*, the big pancake with spinach the woman on the floor is making in that big pan over that burner. So, did you enjoy our outing today?

~ I really liked the terrace houses at Ephesus, stepped up so the unit above looks into the mosaic courtyards below. Or is that because the roofs have disappeared? Why can't we have condos designed like that where all the frescos and floor mosaics have the same aesthetic and everything runs smoothly together? So clean, and laid out like a modern building. Why have a hodgepodge of everyone expressing their individuality even though it clashes with all the others to no one's benefit?

~ And the sign said they were built in the first century BCE and were lived in for eight hundred years. Incredible. Maybe Paul visited someone here when those houses were new?

~ Yes, Paul. I really—

~ Wait. Did you call that cuddling this morning? Were you playing Zeus's swan to my Leda? What was that?

~ Which version are you talking about? Do you mean Peter Paul Reuben's painting where Leda pulls his whole soft, feathery body between her legs?

188

~ That's not cuddling; that's sex. You know, the swan is one of the only waterfowl with a penis.

~ I didn't know that. Okay, there's a painting by Louis Charles Bombled where the swan drifts like a dream along the side of Leda's sleeping body, more in the spirit of the myth, not about literal bestiality but a fantasy that combines what is innocent and soft with aggression. There is some of that same symbolism in the Roman sculpture by Timotheos done around Paul's time, where a swan is plastered against the side of Leda's body, its head resting on her chest while she holds the small body like a bagpipe or a lute.

~ Funny. Okay, so if Paul saw that here, would he appreciate this symbolism? Christian missionaries would sometimes incorporate pagan art and ritual into church liturgy, such as incorporating Christian symbols into indigenous Mexican dance masks, rather than always wiping the pagan images out.

~ Paul doesn't appear to move beyond Christian symbolism. In his first epistle to the Corinthians, he discusses bread as a symbol of the body of Christ when he says, "there is one bread, we who are many are one body, for we all partake of the one bread" (1 Cor 10:17), but any symbolism outside the Bible gets rough treatment, such as, "what pagans sacrifice they offer to demons and not to God . . . You cannot drink the cup of the LORD and the cup of demons" (1 Cor 10: 20-21). His reasons are often weak, though, not debating the intrinsic value of pagan art, but instead worrying about how God will respond: "Shall we provoke the LORD to jealousy? Are we stronger than he?" (1 Cor 10:22), flashing back to God's insistence not to have other gods before Him. I wish Paul thought more about Jesus's toleration than the Lord's jealousy. On the other hand, he is all for accepting other cultures if taking part in them is strategic for proselytizing. Earlier in the epistle he justifies becoming anything, presumably including joining pagans, in order to win a group over: "For though I am free from all men, I have made myself a slave to all, that I might win the more" (1 Cor 9:19), mentioning becoming a Jew to win the Jews over, going outside the law to win the lawless over, becoming weak to win over the weak. It's a good strategy, and does support what you were saying about missionaries incorporating pagan motifs into Christian ritual, but shouldn't entering the ethos of a group also build empathy? That's not the case with Roman pagans. Earlier in the epistle Paul fears if someone weak sees "a man of knowledge, at table in an idol's temple, might he not be encouraged, if his conscience is weak, to eat food offered to idols?" (1 Cor 8:10). He seems nervous about the sensual appeal of the Roman gods.

~ Right. His idea of joining a group to change them sounds like a strategy lesson for conniving and proselytizing, not compromising or building ethos.

~ There's a lot of desperation in Paul that I don't like. He links homosexuals with idolaters, the greedy, and drunkards, for instance. But scholars hear several voices in Paul's writing, and who knows which church officials inserted which lines into the various texts. That said, some of Paul is very subtle, poetic, or philosophical. Flannery O'Connor—whose self-righteous characters had revelations that forced them to reconsider their morality only when blindsided by an unexpected, grotesque character—must have found inspiration in the lines, "God chose what is weak in the world to shame the strong, God chose what is low and despised in the world, even things that are not, to bring to nothing things that are, so that no human being might boast in the presence of God" (1 Cor 1:27-29). A passage like this has me on Paul's side.

~ I see that in O'Connor, but let's get back to Leda and the swan. The Artemis of Ephesus aside, did Paul recognize a place for sex at all? What must he have thought gazing at all the lush Roman sexuality in sculptures and clothing?

~ He recognizes it, and seems threatened by it, trying to contain it by saying that "it is better to marry than to be aflame with passion" (1 Cor 7:9). And once he empathizes with the married state, he is surprisingly Whitmanesque in his democratic view of sexuality within a marriage, instructing that "the husband should give to his wife her conjugal rights, and likewise the wife to her husband. For the wife does not rule over her own body, but the husband does; likewise the husband does not rule over his own body, the wife does" (1 Cor 7:3-4).

~ That sounds surprisingly sexy.

~ Yes, but just as I'm feeling good about it, Paul's ambivalence causes him once again to reign in sexual passion, hoping maybe sexuality can go on respites, but not for too long, hinting that its absence in a marriage can lead to some form of betrayal: "Do not refuse one another except perhaps by agreement for a season, that you may devote yourselves to prayer; but then come together again, lest Satan tempt you through lack of self-control" (1 Cor 7:5). Paul thinks of one as a fisherman of passion, hooking passion, giving it line to swim off to firmly secure a moral hook, then slowly pulling the passion back in before letting it out some more, each time bringing it more and more under control. Then, lest we think he is overly concerned with sexual passion, he takes himself out of the need for sex, but is careful not to undo the importance of sex in marriage: "I wish that all were as I myself am. But each has his own special gift from God, one of one kind and one of another" (1 Cor 7:7). Later he confirms his belief that marriage can be good but that being unmarried and devoted to the Lord is better.

~ That's a pretty dim view of our sexual nature. But isn't the writer of Revelation even more down on sex?

~ You're probably thinking of Jezebel, the prophetess who some at the church of Thyatira are accused of tolerating despite the fact that the voice of the son of God claims she "is teaching and beguiling my servants to practice immorality and to eat food sacrificed to idols" (Rev 2:20) and adds that if she does not repent, she will be punished along with those who commit adultery with her.

~ You know adultery can be defined as adulterating love in any way. What about you? You know, having sex is a sin if you don't still love me.

~ I love you more than anything.

~ More than this book you are writing?

~ More than this book I am writing.

~ Why?

~ For lots of reasons. You know; I've made a list for you before. But I think it is harder to express love than give reasons.

~ Okay; express it.

~ That's funny. Can I use Paul in 1 Corinthians to help me? I know his lines are clichés at weddings, but when I stop to appreciate the love you give me or when I evaluate my own love for you, or other kinds of love for people in our lives, or love for life in general, I always think about one of Paul's best passages: "Love is patient and kind; love is not jealous or boastful; it is not arrogant or rude. Love does not insist in its own way; it is not irritable or resentful; it does not rejoice at wrong, but rejoices in the right. Love bears all things, believes all things, hopes all things, endures all things" (1 Cor 13:4-7). It's not easy to follow this advice, but I get depressed when I don't see these attributes between people, between countries, between ethnic and religious groups.

~ What about love of teaching or politics or carpentry, à la Jesus?

~ Yes, for those things too. All the time I think about people who have intelligence or charisma or knowledge but not love. When I see someone who does not love what he or she is doing, that person's worth goes flat. I get bored with the person or worried about their sanity or both. Paul saw that people could have the gift of healing, or the gift of speaking in tongues (which I take to mean a gift of using language, style, persuasion, maybe foreign languages), or the gift of interpretation, the ability to analyze and argue, but that without love, these mean nothing. Paul is at his most poetic when he writes, "If I speak in the tongues of men and of angels, but have not love, I am a noisy gong or a clanging cymbal. And if I have prophetic powers, and understand all mysteries and all knowledge, and if I have all faith, so as to remove mountains, but have not love, I am nothing. If I give away all I have, and if I deliver my body to be burned, but have not love, I gain nothing" (1 Cor 13:1-3). How many times have we seen colleagues, students, and administrators, people in our personal lives, all who sound like clanging symbols? Going through the motions, looking to climb to the next step, grabbing the next reward, degree, position, benefit, but who have no love of what they are doing? Sometimes they hate what they are doing, but mostly they are just inert, spiritless.

~ Of course. Much of the world seems like that. And it has nothing to do with social and economic status. I like that Paul's noisy gongs could include religious zealots who are sacrificing everything in their lives, but not out of love, so probably for something negative such as attention, pride, jealousy, anger, revenge, or some delusional reward. But how can Paul, who writes such a non-compromising passage about love, be so intolerant or uptight in other passages? What about his intolerant ideas, for instance that it is "shameful for a woman to speak in church" and his belief that women should get their knowledge from husbands (1 Cor 14:35)? Or what about his claim that if one does not believe in the resurrection of the dead, "then Christ has not been raised," causing all preaching to be in vain (1 Cor 15:12-14)? He gets so doctrinaire.

~ Yes. Amazing. Again, scholars who study the Greek style, organization, and cross-references in all the Pauline texts are not always in agreement, but most believe we are not always reading the same person when we read everything attributed to Paul. In any case, remember that this is a guy who had a strict upbringing in the law, becoming a Jewish zealot, "binding and delivering to prison both men and women" (Acts 22:4) for punishment in Jerusalem, and then one day on his journey, just outside Damascus, is struck by a blinding light where Jesus appears and declares that Paul, then called Saul, is prosecuting Jesus himself when Saul delivers these prisoners. The narration in Acts of the Apostles is formula travel writing, so no one should expect the subtle, more credible revelations that an author like Flannery O'Connor creates, but whatever Paul went through, it would make sense that he would become a conflicted person, understanding the value of tolerance and love which he expresses poetically, while at other times slipping back into prosaically expressed strict doctrinaire positions. Knowing his presumed background might explain some of the contradictions.

~ Too bad Flannery O'Connor didn't write historical fiction. Or maybe she recreates and updates Paul's revelation and conversion in all her stories?

~ That's a really good way of thinking about it. Actually I can never get Bruegel the Elder's painting of Paul's conversion out of my head. Bruegel forces the viewer's eye to pat a few big foreground horse rumps, as if to avoid getting kicked, in the viewer's attempt to maneuver from the foreground closer to the stunned Paul in the background, struck off his own horse, which is on its knees. Paul is perfectly caught in the moment of a revelation that blasts his misguided righteousness. Bruegel is an example of an artist who was not a noisy gong, a painter who loved his craft so much that he risked bringing commonplace images and everyday arrangements to Biblical incidents to show how Biblical events are not stuck in time but repeat themselves eternally. Here he goes out of his way to remind us we are in a world filled with animal buttholes, reminders of life's general baseness, as well as in a world of institutional rigidity represented by military precision in a line of soldiers winding from far below to high above in a gorge on the way to Damascus, a treacherous mountain pass where, despite baseness and rigidity, a momentous, private, and rare understanding happens in a flash, so dramatic but unrealized by everyone else traveling their arduous life journey.

~ Maybe we should have stopped in Vienna to see that painting instead of taking extra time to visit Cappadocia. But we would have missed those early primitive limestone-carved mini Christian sanctuaries. I wonder if Paul ever stayed in cave homes in that area.

~ It's a long way from Damascus, but he did travel through that area. It's certainly possible.

~ Then we are seeing a lot of what Paul saw—Turkey's fertile central areas and this coastline filled with native olive trees. He put out a lot of energy traveling here and to what is now Greece and Rome. It's things like that that draw me to Paul. I want to know him, but he seems hard to find.

~ Right. So much of his writing was an attempt to set up the universal church and get everything in order for eternity, and I think that responsibility sometimes made him panic, asserting religious notions that he knew would satisfy the vast majority for eternity. That's why we get ideas such as, "If for this life only we have hoped in Christ, we are of all men most to be pitied" (1 Cor 15:19), a line that Unamuno, the great Spanish writer, disintegrated in his novella *San Manuel, the Good Saint*, about a priest who knew the afterlife was a lie; therefore, his personal sacrifice would be the burden of keeping that secret from his small village so that they could maintain eternal hope in that afterlife. But ironically, it is Paul himself who validates that love is more important than hope. Sure, he believes that knowledge and prophesy are imperfect, that now we "see in a mirror dimly" (1 Cor 13:12), or "see through a glass darkly" in the King James version, and that the divine will clear everything up, and we will have full understanding of our place with a beneficent God, but then—

~ So sometimes he claims truth should be future-heaven oriented, maybe disturbed by us who believe only our living moments are the days of heaven and hell?

~ Yes. With these kinds of passages, Paul and I seem to part ways, but then he says "So faith, hope, love abide, these three; but the greatest of these is love" (1 Cor 13:13). I think he's implying that faith and hope steady one for positive endeavors at a future date, endeavors that may come to fruition or may not, but that love is alive in the moment and continues into the next moment because it "bears all things, believes all things, hopes all things, endures all things." When I think about Paul's prioritizing of love over faith and hope, Paul wins me back.

~ Unlike with a story or poem, I guess one must pick and choose when it comes to Paul.

~ Yes, I think so. Sometimes I think about Paul next to the gospel writer Matthew because—

~ Can we save that for the car tomorrow on the way to ruins at Aphrodisias?

~ This drive away from the coast and into the mountains reminds me of Bruegel's painting of Paul you talked about yesterday. Maybe we are going to slide off our spiritual horses for some kind of revelation. I wonder if Paul visited these mountain passes too. They look like the ones on the way to Damascus in the painting.

~ There's a record of a large Jewish population in Aphrodisias, so many had probably heard of Paul, but I don't think there is any written reference to Paul visiting here.

~ You know, I still cannot get over people feeling they have to choose between different religious concepts. Aphrodisias's main temple is devoted to Aphrodite, right? Didn't Paul see Aphrodite's hand in everything—a goddess who Zeus knew would create rivalries between the gods themselves, so he married her to a dullard in an attempt to defuse her, which only pushed her into affairs? It's sad that modern religions fight these realities by making them sinful and unnatural instead of inevitable and sometimes comic, sometimes tragic. A person is a lot wiser knowing Aphrodite's beauty won Paris's desire for her, resulting in Aphrodite's gift to him of the married Helen, the most beautiful woman in the world. Paris's rejection of Hera's gift of power or Athena's gift of wisdom for Aphrodite's power of beauty and love says so much about priorities.

~ I don't know that Paul appreciated Aphrodite's influence. He deals with sexuality very indirectly, referring more to love and marriage. There's a passage in 1 Corinthians where Paul says "those who marry will have worldly troubles, and I would spare you that" (1 Cor 7:28), as if he understands that even within marriage, emotional and sexual involvement takes one away from peace of mind, not just away from devotion to the Lord. Then he adds that the "time has grown very short" (1 Cor 7:29), implying that judgment day, or even the span of one's life, is not far off, so "let those who have wives live as though they had none, and those who mourn as though they were not mourning, and those who rejoice as though they were not rejoicing, and those who buy as though they had no goods, and those who deal with the world as though they had no dealings with it. For the form of this world is passing away" (7:29-31). This diverse list quickly covers all the essential forces of life and is a humble reminder that none of the forces lasts long. Paul implies that one should put faith in God, who is more eternal than life; however, from a secular point of view, it is interesting that love in marriage, and the problems that come with relationships, gets equal importance to general mourning and rejoicing and worldly goods. In Ecclesiastes, and even in Paul's earlier writings, love rises above everything, an end-all. By giving so much importance to intimate relationships, by understanding them as powerful, major forces of life in all its sadness and happiness, I cannot help but wonder if Paul desires intimacy but fears the loss of it and so refrains from it.

~ I sense that too. Because of his strong belief in love, his idea of the end seems much less apocalyptic than the one presented in Revelation. Paul's focus is still on the essentials of life even if they come to an end in one's personal life or even with the end of the world.

~ Absolutely. Paul seems more grounded in reality. The writer of Revelation tosses all the essentials in the fire with no respect for life, for "the city has no need of sun or moon to shine upon it, for the glory of God is its light" (Rev 21:23). The writer is an unrealistic idealist who believes that life can have *good* without *evil*, one no longer defining the other, a wiping out of all the nuances of the garden of Eden story. He even simplifies the complex personality of the serpent—who, by the way, was never referred to as Satan in Genesis—into pure evil: "that ancient serpent, who is called the Devil and Satan, the deceiver of the whole world—he was thrown down to the earth" (Rev 12:9), so at the end of the world "there shall no more be anything accursed" (Rev 22:3). Unlike Paul, the writer of Revelation has no sense that life must always involve the tragic, and instead fantasizes "a new heaven and a new earth" (Rev 21:1) where a new Jerusalem comes out of heaven "prepared as a bride adorned for her husband" (Rev 21:2), and hears a great voice say that God will live with men and "will wipe away every tear from their eyes, and death shall be no more, neither shall there be mourning nor crying nor pain any more, for the former things have passed away" (Rev 21:4).

~ Okay, let's give the whirlwind of Revelation a rest. The writer has too much faith in fantasy. Let's get back to Paul. Does Paul's attitude about the tragic nature of life jive with Jesus's? What would Jesus say to him if they could discuss priorities given a fleeting life? Wait—first let's delight in our own fleeting pleasure. Let's open that box of Turkish delight and special cookies.

~ I love these. Nothing at all like the overly gelatinous crap they call Turkish delight in America. And these pistachio and almond cookies are so nutty and buttery without being overly sweet.

197

~I know. We go through these comparisons whenever we travel. See—and you didn't want me to buy these yesterday for the car! But okay. Back to Jesus and Paul.

~ Most scholars believe Paul wrote his letters about thirty years before Mark's gospel was written. Who knows what Paul knew about the gospels and from whom? He never quotes the gospels. But if I could talk to Paul about Jesus, maybe I would start with some of the commands Jesus makes in his sermon on the mount, especially those that are unique to Matthew. For instance, "Enter by the narrow gate; for the gate is wide and the way is easy, that leads to destruction, and those who enter by it are many. For the gate is narrow and the way is hard, that leads to life, and those who find it are few" (Mt 7:13-14). I truly believe that these lines apply to everything in life: creating, raising, growing, destroying, rebuilding anything, anybody, any endeavor, including relationships, including love relationships. People who think everything—an artwork, a piece of writing, a crop, a design, a relationship—comes easily, through a wide gate without concern, care or effort, probably make a mess of their endeavors because they lack patience, discipline, persistence. If Paul had seen that the narrow gate was what gives meaning and principle to life, maybe he would put more spiritual value on that rather than afterlife. Jesus's poetic passages focus more on the richness of earthly life than the eternal.

~ Then in some ways Paul is really disappointed with living in the secular world. He's always turning away from a focus on living, thinking only the eternal is of ultimate value.

~ Yes, but sometimes not, as I mentioned regarding the definition of love. Maybe he would have identified with Matthew's paradoxes at the sermon's beginning: "Blessed are those who mourn, for they shall be comforted" (Mt 5:4). This blessing is changed in Luke, who replaces "for they shall be comforted" with "for you shall laugh" (Lk 6:21), putting the emphasis on realizing the fleeting nature of pain, suggesting a time will come for laughing again, but Matthew puts the emphasis on the specialness of being comforted that people can only know after they have mourned losing someone dear to them. Likewise Matthew tests the reader with the paradox, "Blessed are the meek, for they shall inherit the earth" (Mt 5:5), the reader having to dissolve all those layers of wealth, power, and station encountered with every human endeavor throughout history, in order to get closer to the meek who do the work of the world—child-rearing, teaching, building, crafting, cooking, farming. (This is in sync with the writer of Ecclesiastes, who sees all as vanity except love of a partner and work.) Sometimes Paul jump-cuts these secular complexities by focusing on rules and regulations and eternity.

~ You talk about heaven on earth, but Matthew's Jesus also talks about heaven outside the human experience on earth, right?

~ I can *verily* say to you, that Jesus uses the term "heaven" to mean something closer to Nirvana, the extinguishing of desires, aversions, and delusions, all the negative emotional elements that drive humans away from genuine interaction with the living. What else could heaven mean when used by such a grounded person as Jesus? A place where people sit on clouds and salute God the Father all day? A place where one indulges desires or is as numb as a rock? No, Jesus is defining heaven by what brings one to an existence outside of the gnashing of teeth. One thing that does is to prioritize mercy ahead of one's own desires. This dynamic is clear in a line such as, "Blessed are the merciful, for they shall obtain mercy" (Mt 5:7), where the act of being merciful is the only way to know the value of mercy, to obtain it through the inner strength of being able to offer it, experiencing the satisfaction of giving it, watching the unknotting of shame and anguish on the one it is bestowed upon. I'm not saying the one who receives mercy isn't grateful, but that person's need is great, their soul is vulnerable and desperate, so that person does not experience mercy the way the stronger one does who offers it. Then consider this: maybe the receiver will become a giver of mercy if that person now becomes strong. Or maybe that's Jesus's point: that once one has received mercy, one understands the consequence of giving mercy, so then is deserving of obtaining mercy again. Mercy becomes a cycle that brings heaven to earth.

~ You sound like a true believer. What pagan acceptance of sexuality is in Matthew compared to Paul's writings?

~ Matthew's Jesus sounds tough, saying that "every one who looks at a woman lustfully has already committed adultery with her in his heart" (Mt 5:28), but I think he is being overly dramatic because then he adds, "If your right eye causes you to sin, pluck it out and throw it away; it is better that you lose one of your members than that your whole body be thrown into hell" (Mt 5:29). It's all hyperbolic metaphor; only a fanatic would take it literally. We need to pluck out our bad shit and throw it away. Better that we have less physically or materially, if we are moral, principled, and emotionally healthy. Better to throw out our simple-minded, prejudiced ideas too. Promoting non-compromising positions in life needs all the metaphoric whack of a violent action.

~ The metaphor is so violent and angry.

~ But I think mostly delivered with passion. I've found myself thinking in hyperboles. Remember, in the same sermon, Matthew's Jesus says, "Blessed are the peacemakers, for they shall be called sons of God" (Mt 5:9), a quintessential praise of nonviolence and peace. In fact, he is seeing the old commandments as dealing only with extreme violations, not everyday realities, almost as if to say Moses's commandments are too easy for most decent people to fulfill, which leads to being too easy to feel all righteous. Matthew makes the commandments more applicable to everyone's everyday life. For instance, he takes the commandment "Thou Shall not Kill," and extends it to include, "every one who is angry with his brother shall be liable to judgment" (Mt 5:22), including insults and calling one a fool; then to make his point even more dramatic, he says if while making an offering at the altar one remembers that one's brother has something against one, to leave the altar immediately and correct the wrong before returning to offer altar-gifts (Mt 5:23-24). I like Matthew's Jesus's push-pull, peace-violence demands. It is one reason why "the crowds were astonished at his teaching, for he taught them as one who had authority, and not as their scribes" (Mt 7:28-29).

~ There is really no one like Jesus in Greek or Roman mythology, right? The gods and goddesses represent human impulses more than such complex moral positions.

~ The Greek pantheon can be tricky, but to get closer to something like Jesus, we would have to turn to Aristotle. That probably means discourse that appeals more to the mind rather than the heart, though. Jesus appeals to the emotions by being so dramatic, taking everything that seems sacrosanct and turning it on its head, such as pulling up the Old Testament "eye for eye, tooth for tooth . . . wound for wound" (Ex 21:24-25); he flips it and commands not to waste energy resisting evil forces, so that if one strikes you to turn the other cheek, to not run from violence nor perpetrate it, but to defuse it. Only insipid thinkers would interpret the metaphor as saying to get beat up. In fact, the next part of his sentence clears up this trope: "and if any one would sue you and take your coat, let him have your cloak as well; and if any one forces you to go one mile, go with him two miles" (Mt 5:40-41). These extensions clarify that the violent metaphor extends to coercion in general, and the non-violent images of the coat and miles clarify that the moral person rolls with the coercion, sometimes defusing it by folding one's cards, sometimes even extending the perpetrator's demand to demean and show lack of subservience to it by willfully taking the demand further.

~ I'm looking at how intimidating these mountains are and wondering if they provide a metaphor for absorbing what is intimidating. For instance, the Romans found tons of blue-gray marble in them, extracted it and brought it to Aphrodisias, making it the sculpture center of the ancient world, an artistic colony that supplied the Caesars of Rome. A macroscopic version of civilization saying to nature, "You overwhelm us but we will turn your inner stone muscle into art." Brute force turned into art, not just laying down to nature's destructive powers. So what about Matthew's Jesus commanding us to love our enemies?

~ Yes, for me, for most people, impossible. Forgiving? I can see that, especially if one has time for a gradual understanding of what brought on the wrongs. Loving? That seems like a stretch—but then Matthew's Jesus keeps us from thinking it is too big a stretch with lines such as, "For if you love those who love you, what reward have you?" (Mt 5:46), pulling us away from any notion of easy love. Regarding enemies—if I can take "love" to be a more dramatic version of "care," then I can sometimes buy into that. Several times, when someone has hated or disliked me, once I put aside my anger and reconsider my actions, I find myself sensing the wretch's personal anguish and disappointments that lead to that hate. I see nations hate nations and know it is out of disappointment or rejection and then out of a need for a scapegoat, and if it provokes a response out of vengeance, there is never a stopping point if we cannot defuse that fury by coming to understanding.

~ So one should always give of oneself to defuse?

~ Not totally. Jesus qualifies everything in the sermon. He asks that we be discriminating, careful what and to whom we give of ourselves—"do not throw your pearls before swine, lest they trample them under foot and turn to attack you" (Mt 7:6)—because many people are not only undeserving, but they will take the best you have to offer and try to ruin it or even use it against you. How many people do we know who take advantage of or try to undermine others' strengths? How many times do envious people want to belittle others' virtues and talents? Jesus extends the concern with "Beware of false prophets, who come to you in sheep's clothing but inwardly are ravenous wolves" (Mt 7:15), another fierce image that warns of all who come off as innocent, virtuous, well-intended, armed with popular catch phrases, but who are emotional, even physical, predators. Really, it takes so much experience to develop skills to see through sheep's clothing. Some never do. Jesus recognizes that many offerings are corrupt, insincere, and self-serving. Later he extends the metaphor, "Behold, I send you out as sheep in the midst of wolves; so be wise as serpents and innocent as doves" (Mt 10:16), giving homage to the serpent in Eden, the most insightful animal in the garden, misunderstood as the epitome of evil in Revelation. That writer ignores the fact that the serpent understands God's motivations—God will be jealous if His creations' eyes are opened to know what He exclusively knows about good and evil. Matthew, on the other hand, depicts Jesus calling for the serpent's insight lest one fall pray to people's bad motivations.

~ But often a person's own self-delusion makes them ripe prey.

~ Jesus recognizes this too. In the next line he adds, "Are grapes gathered from thorns, or figs from thistles? So, every sound tree bears good fruit, but the bad tree bears evil fruit. A sound tree cannot bear evil fruit, nor can a bad tree bear good fruit. Every tree that does not bear good fruit is cut down and thrown into the fire" (Mt 7:16-19). The obvious disconnect in the metaphors between knowing what is bad and good strongly conveys his frustration with people who want to pretend something or someone is not what or who is wished for, and I can feel Jesus's incredulity that people refuse to dump what is bad into the fire.

~ You know me. I'm dumping what's bad in the fire all the time. I think Mark's Jesus would be on board too. Or would he? We haven't really talked about whether Mark would have appreciated changes Matthew made to his gospel.

~ Matthew has some nice touches—I love the Sermon on the Mount—but as with much of Paul, one wonders if other writers contributed to different parts of Matthew's text. For instance, near the end when Pilate washes his hands of the mob's choice to crucify Jesus rather than Barabbas, the angry Jews are given the line, "His blood be on us and our children!" (Mt 27:25), as a way to blame Jews, who are outside of Jewish converts to the new idea called Christianity, making them collectively guilty of Jesus's death for generations to come. The line only exists in Matthew.

~ Interesting. Well, maybe we are done with Matthew. The sign says that the Aphrodisias site is in two kilometers, and I have been seeing more and more pomegranate trees. I know Jesus is making a point about not diluting the truth with his metaphor about a bad tree bearing bad fruit, a good one bearing good fruit, but the reality I am seeing here is that sometimes there are cracked pomegranates on the same tree with good pomegranates, so let's celebrate Matthew's good line and throw out his bad ones.

~ Generally speaking, I'd rather talk about Mark and Luke.

~ Believe me, I know. I edited the chapters in your book. Anyway, let's park and give Jesus a break and focus on this city of Aphrodite. Look! There's the Tetrapylon, the monumental gate of the city that is aligned on the distant mountains and starts the main axis of the city. Today this can be our "Damascus."

———— •-⊪-╼⊙●○●⊱╾•⊪• ————

~ The sculptures in the museum at Aphrodisias were amazing! I didn't realize the statue of Aphrodite would be so unsexy and more symbolic, though—like the Artemis of Ephesus. It wasn't Titian's Venus teasing a lute player by turning her head away while fingering her pubis, or Bronzino's Venus enjoying Eros playing with her nipple. It wasn't even the classical sculpture of Aphrodite of Cnidus, at ease with both her body and her powers—instead, it was an obelisk-like cylindrical sculpture, again with body encased in a column tunic, feet firmly planted with arms reaching out to receive and be accepted, her surface full of symbolic bas-reliefs of the Three Graces and Erotes, Helios, and Selene, the gods of the sun and moon (how many lovers came together in mythology under her Roman equivalent, Luna?). It's a bas-relief of what some consider to be the marriage of heaven and earth, Gaia and Uranus.

~ I take your point, but then look at the Three Graces at the Sebasteion. How sexy were those? Their missing body parts make them look modern, what's left out emphasizing the parts of the body that do exist so they become even more defining. I've seen Raphael's nude rendition of the Graces, disconnected, smiley-faced, prim and polite, not like these where they are so firmly connected to the earth, shifting their weight to one leg, exaggerating a hip so they all curve into each other, then gracefully entwining their arms, pulling themselves into a group. They are fleshy and strong and looking away from each other, a counter to their unity, making them appealing as individuals. Traditionally one represents splendor, one joy, and one fresh cheer. Something like that, an idealistic combination but each of the attributes symbolically appealing in its own right.

~ I think you like the nice ass of the middle one that gets as much attention, framed by the others with their full bodies and smooth crotches.

~ Right. No abstract symbols here.

~ Well, I thought the ass on the one Gigantes in the sculpture showing

Athena fighting them looked nice too, one body turned forward, the other back as with the Graces. Nice bodies even though their legs are serpents. What a tease between the sensual and the creepy. What about my ass?

~ You sure look good.

~ Tell the truth. It's all smoke and mirrors. Talking about ass, what about the heat from that dancer's movements the other night near the hotel? What about her ass? Amazing how her movements made up for her not really being very pretty, right?

~ I know. What gets to me is how Middle Eastern dancing is teasing, draped then undraped, still then moving, glancing, and then turning away. Actually, this is reminding me of one more scene in Matthew's and Mark's gospel, when Herodias's daughter danced for Herod the Tetrarch, probably doing this special teasing that makes all Middle Eastern dancers fun to watch. The young woman could never have guessed that her mother would turn the reward she would receive for dancing into something perverse. Legend always wants to blame the daughter's dance for the beheading of John the Baptist, but it was just the impetus for his being killed for a more insidious reason. Her mother, angry with John the Baptist for protesting her marriage to Herod since she was his brother Philip's wife, demands her daughter ask for something violent as a gift (Mt 14:3, Mk 6:17). Herod was an easy set-up, already spooked by Jesus's and John's following, already wanting to put John to death but fearing an uprising from his followers, already binding John up in prison. Now, pleased by her movements, Herod promises to give the daughter a reward she names, but when her mother prompts her to ask for the head of John, Herod "was sorry; but because of his oaths and his guests he commanded it to be given" (Mt 14:9), obviously a guy who cares more about not appearing weak than strong enough to hold to a moral perspective.

~ The episode doesn't seem to add much to John's character.

~ No, but it shows how quickly, and unjustifiably, a person with insight can be butchered.

~ What about the daughter? I think legend sometimes named

her Salome.

~ It's not her name in the gospel story, but whatever her name is, really she is nothing but a good dancer, and only in the context of the story does she become an early symbol of the banality of evil, mindlessly following her mom's order to serve up a prophet's head as if it were sliced roast on a platter. In Artemisia Gentileschi's *Salome with the Head of St. John the Baptist*, the executioner, his forehead slightly crinkled as if asking, "what the hell did you want this for?" grasps John's hair tightly in his hand and shoves the head at the daughter. She is shown backing up, unable to take her eyes off John's butchered face, but with her downcast lids her emotions blend fascination with only slight repulsion. She looks matronly, with a double chin and strong forearms, either the embodiment of her mother or perhaps she is the mother rather than a slithery dancer. Whereas in Caravaggio's *Salome with the Head of John the Baptist*, the daughter only nonchalantly tilts her head away from John's dead head, capturing her indifference, while her eyeballs strain to look away, knowing she does not want to see the crime she is being made an accomplice to: the conflict of mild head tilt and eye strain captures ambivalence that underscores the idea that evil thrives on amorality. Meanwhile, an older woman (Herodias?), deep in pleased thought, looks over the girl's shoulder and the executioner, a slightly ghoulish figure, looks at his work with a combination of pity and disgust. What comes across in the story and its paintings is that a great spirit can be done away with in flash, in a whim—the head, once a symbol of insight, reduced to a voiceless centerpiece.

~ Well, it will be hard to forget this story watching another Middle Eastern dancer. Anyway, we weren't talking about ass on the way up here. More about Matthew's use of hyperbole, not of hyperbolic ass. So much of Matthew seems antithetical to the writer of Revelation. But since they both use hyperbole, I was wondering if Matthew would appreciate anything at all in Revelation.

~ I do think Matthew's Jesus would like some of the passages in Revelation, such as when the narrator is told by a spiritual voice to take the scroll from an angel standing on the sea and the land, the angel saying "Take it and eat; it will be bitter to your stomach, but sweet

206

as honey to your mouth" (Rev 10:9). I can hear Jesus using this as a dramatic metaphor for the idea that knowledge will bring one pain, but it also brings charisma when one instructs with that knowledge.

~ But what you were saying about Matthew before makes me think Jesus of the Synoptic Gospels would throw up reading most of Revelation.

~ Yes, especially choking on the grotesque oxymoron of Jesus in Revelation being referred to as a warrior lamb. I don't get it. If Jesus is going to fight Satan, a silly idea from a Synoptic Gospel point of view, why not drop the innocent lamb bit and turn Jesus into an eagle or bull? But maybe more seriously, I think Jesus's tummy would turn if he knew the temptation he turned down from Satan in Luke—"And the devil took him up, and showed him all the kingdoms of the world in a moment in time, and said to him, 'To you I will give all this authority and their glory; for it has been delivered to me, and I give it to whom I will'" (Lk 4:5-6)—is reversed in Revelation to be a reward given by the Son of God to the followers of the Church of Thyatira, when he promises, "who conquers and who keeps my works until the end, I will give him power over the nations, and he shall rule them with a rod of iron, as when earthen pots are broken in pieces, even as I myself have received power from my Father" (Rev 2:26-27). Jesus of the Synoptic Gospels represents the opposite of giving earthly authority to anyone, even in his name. And again, as in much of Revelation, the pottery metaphor doesn't have enough of a context to give it meaning and doesn't work on its own. I think Matthew's Jesus would be bothered by other awards such as being made "a pillar in the temple of my God" (Rev 3:12), only because the temple is seen as a symbol of orthodox authority in the Synoptic Gospels.

~ Yes, and as a symbol of physical wealth and power. When he is accused of saying, "I am able to destroy the temple of God, and to build it in three days" (Matt 26:61), I always took that to be another metaphor expressing that the spirit has more to do with the heart than a physical space. Would he like anything in Revelation?

~ Maybe. I think Jesus would approve of the angel delivering the criticism to the Laodicea of being "neither cold nor hot" (Rev 3:15), cursing them for being "lukewarm" (Rev 3:16), a clear symbol for indifference, apathy, and being self-protective, but it is hard to imagine Jesus approving a gift of "gold refined by fire, that you may be rich" (Rev 3:18), a symbol of materialism and mammon. Nor does the synoptic Jesus seem so repressed or into physical purity as to be pleased with an award of "white garments to clothe you and to keep the shame of your nakedness from being seen" (Rev 3:18). I think about the disciples eating with defiled hands and Jesus redefining defilement as something that comes from bad values within, not dirt. In Mark, the disciples argue about sitting next to Jesus on his throne and he scolds them about the first being last and the last being first (Mk 10:31), but here in Revelation Jesus claims a reward is sitting "on my throne, as I myself conquered and sat down with my Father on his throne" (Rev 3:21). Overall, Jesus in Matthew would not identify the fire in Revelation with his gospel fire.

~ I see. What's strange is that one of your favorite films of all time is Ingmar Bergman's *The Seventh Seal*, and I remember near the end, the character of Death finally catches up with most of the other characters, all with such different ideas about God, love, and art, and the knight's wife reads from Revelation.

~ I know. She reads the passage, "When the Lamb opened the seventh seal, there was silence in heaven for about half an hour. Then I saw the seven angels who stand before God, and seven trumpets were given to them" (Rev 8:1-2), and then Death knocks at the door and the squire goes to answer, so the knight's wife, Karin, skips up a bit to the passage, "The first angel blew his trumpet, and there followed hail and fire, mixed with blood, which fell on the earth; and a third of the earth was burnt up, and a third of the trees were burnt up, and all green grass was burnt up" (Rev 8:7). The squire returns and refuses to admit Death has come for them all, and Karin continues with passages on the second and third angels, when "a great star fell from heaven, blazing like a torch" (Rev 8:10). In the context of Karin's soft voice, in the context of a diverse group of characters we have become intimate with and admired throughout the film but who have contacted the black plague, and outside the context of the other scolding and threatening passages we have discussed, the lines from Revelation here are both

208

magical and beautiful. That can happen with many passages in the Bible when pulled out of context, just as with lines from Shakespeare.

~ I think so too. Well, when we get back from Aphrodisias, we should get ready to go back to Istanbul. I want to revisit the Hagia Sophia.

~ I love that church-turned-mosque-turned-back-to-church. The voluminous spaces and carefully directed exterior light, the walls of mosaics and slabs of polished stone with intriguing veins of texture and color, all remind me that Christianity sometimes has very little to do with Jesus's or Paul's or the Revelation narrator's words and more to do with architecture, in this case, Roman architecture, power-arched and dome-driven architecture, surrounded by a large city with legions of armies and builders headed by a converted Roman emperor.

~ It is amazing. Although, that sounds like another book.

EXISTENTIAL MENU
ECCLESIASTES, JONAH, JOB

Dear reader,

So you wish to become an existentialist? The recipe is centuries old. You always begin with a big dollop of awareness that one's existence precedes essence—awareness that we are born into a void and then give our lives meaning rather than search for a preexisting meaning outside ourselves. Add a few tablespoons of perseverance to keep the recipe from suicidal souring. Crack eggs of facticity (concrete elements outside your control that limit your freedom, such as physical ability, birthplace, health, parents), but fold in only the values you want to give them, separating some items out, beating others in slowly or quickly. All is your choice. That's why good existentialism recipes always avoid the phrase "one should," indicative of a desperate attempt to have a completely rational process to follow. Of course, freedom to make these choices will give you angst, but a different anguish than fear of physical threats. Then—get ready for more angst—your recipe will face scrutiny from something called "the Other": other chefs, clientele, mentors, family, food critics who are watching you. How much will they objectify what you do? Will you let them limit your presentation? The presence of the Other can curtail your freedom. But wait. How much of their judgment is even real? How much imagined? Can you know? Should it matter? These questions give the recipe an aftertaste of absurdity, sometimes bitter, sometimes even humorous.

The Book of Ecclesiastes (which translates as "the preacher"), written after 400 BCE, probably closer to 180 BCE, is an early taste of existentialism. The writer never loses sight of the void, a space that is empty of ultimate values and ideal goals: (1) All our accomplishments melt into nothingness and we ultimately cannot shape reality into desirable forms—"I have seen everything that is done under the sun; and behold, all is vanity and a striving after wind. What is crooked cannot be made straight, and what is lacking cannot be numbered"

(Eccles 1:14-15); (2) Humanity's wisdom ultimately meets the same fate as humanity's foolishness—"The wise man has his eyes in his head, but the fool walks in darkness; and yet I perceived that one fate comes to all of them. . . . For of the wise man as of the fool there is no enduring remembrance, seeing that in the days to come all will have been long forgotten. How the wise man dies just like the fool!" (Eccles 2:14-16); (3) Humanity, despite any achievements, ultimately meets the same fate as animals—men and beasts "have the same breath, and man has no advantage over the beasts; for all is vanity . . . all are from the dust, and all turn to dust again" (Eccles 3:19-20); (4) Chance constantly undermines purpose—"Again I saw that under the sun the race is not to the swift, nor the battle to the strong, nor bread to the wise, nor riches to the intelligent, nor favor to the men of skill; but time and chance happen to them all" (Eccles 9:11). The writer has listed all the values that give meaning to life—wisdom, intelligence, prowess—and deflates all of them, leaving only an empty dish.

The void in Ecclesiastes ferments the absurd: there are teases of hope because everything falsely appears to have a beginning, a time of maturity, and an end—God "has made everything beautiful in its time; also he has put eternity into man's mind, yet so that he cannot find out what God has done from the beginning to the end" (Eccles 3:11); there are subversions—"a man to whom God gives wealth, possessions, and honor, so that he lacks nothing of all that he desires, yet God does not give him power to enjoy them, but a stranger enjoys them; this is vanity; it is a sore affliction. If a man begets a hundred children, and lives many years . . . but he does not enjoy life's good things, and has no burial, I say that an untimely birth is better off than he" (Eccles 6:2-3); there are unfair ironies—"there is a righteous man who perishes in his righteousness, and there is a wicked man who prolongs his life in his evil-doing" (Eccles 7:15); there are unattractive alternatives—"Again I saw all the oppressions that are practiced under the sun. And behold, the tears of the oppressed, and they had no one to comfort them! On the side of their oppressors there was power, and there was no one to comfort them. And I thought the dead who are already dead more fortunate than the living who are still alive" (Eccles 4:1-2). Much of life leaves a bad taste.

The writer does find a few things that give meaning or essence to an absurd existence. Undermining the Genesis God's idea of eventually making toil a punishment, in Ecclesiastes it can be a reward, especially when combined with well-being (when "God has given wealth and possessions and power to enjoy them, and to accept his lot and find enjoyment in his toil—this is the gift of God" [Eccles 5:19]), and a distraction from absurdities of the void ("For he will not much remember the days of his life because God keeps him occupied with joy in his heart"[Eccles 5:20]). In fact, passion for one's work overpowers cerebral ideals: "Whatever your hand finds to do, do it with your might; for there is no work or thought or knowledge or wisdom in Sheol [a place of darkness that all go to after death], to which you are going" (Eccles 9:10). Value also comes from close friendship, possibly in marriage, since "two are better than one, because they have a good reward for their toil. For if they fall, one will lift up his fellow; but woe to him who is alone when he falls and has not another to lift him up" (Eccles 4:9-10), and meaning or essence is found through intimacy when one can: "Enjoy life with the wife whom you love, all the days of your vain life" (Eccles 9:9). Life can offer an *amuse bouche*.

Then there is the sweet-salty, the milky-zesty, a balancing of flavors. There are moments in Ecclesiastes that suggest giving meaning to existence is dependent on one's depth of awareness, such as the appreciation of joy by knowing pain, something unattainable through a frivolous existence: "Sorrow is better than laughter, for by sadness of countenance the heart is made glad. The heart of the wise is in the house of mourning; but the heart of fools is in the house of mirth" (Eccles 7: 3-4). Also, despite being overwhelmed in life by "the hearts of men . . . full of evil, and madness" (Eccles 9:3), the writer offers "hope" as an intrinsic part of living, just breathing air itself being more substantial than fame because "he who is joined with all the living has hope, for a living dog is better than a dead lion" (Eccles 9:4).

However the most poetic expression of meaningfulness in Ecclesiastes is in the celebration of life's paradoxes and cycles, elements that keep existence stirred, dynamic, intriguing: "For everything there is a season" (Eccles 3:1), a time for birth and death, planting and plucking up, to kill and heal, break down and build up, weep and laugh, mourn and dance, "a time to cast away stones, and a time to gather stones together" (Eccles 3:5), embrace and refrain from embracing, seek and lose, keep and cast away, rend and sew, keep silent and speak, love and hate, war and peace. The awareness of these opposites offers a qualified purpose that is in keeping with one writer's awareness of the void expressed throughout the book. Indeed, it is much more in keeping than the mentality expressed in the last chapter, especially its last verses: "Fear God, and keep his commandments; for this is the whole duty of man. For God will bring every deed into judgment, with every secret thing, whether good or evil" (Eccles 12:13-14). This chapter was probably added by another writer, one who has bad faith in his or her ability to accept responsibility for creating a genuine meaning in a void where God gives no definitive answers.

The Book of Jonah, on the other hand, is a recipe for existential lite. In this book, the Lord is a major player, one who even has a sense of justice, an idea of fairness that normally would work to undermine an existential void. But the Lord plays the role of the Other, and therefore exerts limitations on Jonah, who is comically assigning his own meanings to events, never in sync with the Lord's sense of justice. The interaction of the two perspectives, the Lord's versus Jonah's, leaves Jonah with angst and the reader with a humorous sense of the void.

While Ecclesiastes had no traditional narrative or clear characters beyond the writer, Jonah has a fairly straightforward series of events. The narrative starts with the Lord choosing Jonah to go to the city of Nineveh, the great Assyrian city, and "cry against it; for their wickedness has come up before me" (Jon 1:2). The idea of taking on the role of a prophet and railing against a great city sounds like trouble to Jonah, who jumps on a ship "to flee to Tarshish [away] from the presence of the LORD" (Jon 1:3). The Lord punishes the ship by hurling strong winds. The mariners desperately pray to their god to no avail and then throw their wares overboard to lighten their load; meanwhile, Jonah sleeps away in the hull (an attempt to avoid the pressure of the Other). He is finally scolded by the captain for doing so, the captain incredulous that Jonah could be sleeping instead of taking responsibility by asking for help from his god: "What do you mean, you sleeper? Arise, call upon your god!" (Jon 1:6). The writer depicts the sailors in a world maneuvered by forces outside themselves, brought on by a stranger on the run, now found out through a drawing of lots and a barrage of who-the-hell-are-you, tell-us-on-whose-account-this-evil-has-come-upon-us? (Jon 1:8), what-is-this-that-you-have-done? (Jon 1:10) questions by the mariners, whose fears are increased as they realize Jonah is fleeing from his Lord.

The sense of the world as an absurd void is created in part by the Lord putting faith in a person whose complete lack of interest in the Lord's moral stance, especially against a powerful people the mortal does not even know, makes the situation unstable. For Jonah, this is not a genuine opportunity to give authenticity to his life. In serving as Jonah's Other, the Lord scares the hell out of Jonah and fills him with dread. The mariners also suffer even though they make no decision to harbor Jonah, and when Jonah's moral consciousness awakens, taking responsibility for the mariners' misery (although still not for the Lord's wishes), Jonah tells them to throw him overboard (Jon 1:12). After rowing harder to avoid this (they do have moral sensibility), they finally do toss him in the sea, at which point the seas instantaneously become still (Jon 1:13-15). Then, out of fear of a god who could click ocean turbulence on and off merely to punish His runaway prophet, just for insurance, the mariners start heaping on praises to the Lord, another desperate act of fear; rather than sacrificing in praise to a god who represents ideal values or a meaningful essence to them, this is a utilitarian act that adds no meaning to the void.

The Lord now serves a deconstructed fish platter: instead of Jonah eating a fish, a "great fish" (Jon 1:17) swallows Jonah for three days and three nights (not as a symbol of the trinity, a story far in the future, but three possibly representing in ancient cultures the mind, body, and spirit). In the great fish, Jonah presents a solemn psalm side dish about disappearing into the dark Pit, a place where he might have been denied the Lord's presence forever, before remembering the Lord "with the voice of thanksgiving" and coming to a realization that "deliverance belongs to the LORD!" (Jon 2:9). This image, Jonah in a whale-like fish giving thanks to the Lord, is the passage most familiar to Sunday schoolers but one that runs totally against the existential thrust of the story. After the whale barfs Jonah onto dry land, the Lord starts

His whole demand over. As per his confidence in the Lord expressed in his psalm, this time Jonah does go to Nineveh and rails against its people's evilness (Jon 3:3). Now, to Jonah and the reader's surprise, Nineveh's people actually take the message seriously (Jonah becomes their Other), believe in the Lord, repent—the king covering himself with sackcloth and ashes while proclaiming all others do the same (including the beasts)—and fast (including the beasts), and make a full repentance (Jon 3:5-9). The Lord forgives. The curse is over.

At this point, the writer seems to imply that if one forgoes personal fears and authentic judgments, the essentials for creating meaning in the void, and instead unquestioningly meets the Lord's requests no matter how frightful or seemingly superfluous, then all works out. But there is more to the recipe. This writer, who in the first chapter demonstrates an existential sensibility, knows that one's mind always snaps back to its own authentic, unpredictable view, not the Lord's. And a snap reaction comes now that is like no other. What does one expect will happen when a messenger runs from a forced, frightful endeavor, and then after a spiritual stomach-gurgle in the gut of a fish, has a change of heart, fulfills the fearful deed and, instead of negative blowback, has great success? Relief? Astonishment? No. Joy? Accomplishment? Think again. It "displeased Jonah exceedingly, and he was angry" (Jon 4:1). Yes, anger. Jonah has perverse expectations— never before revealed—that are not being fulfilled. To cover up his anger and his cowardice when the Lord made His first request to rail against Nineveh, Jonah pretends that he knew the Lord's plan from the beginning, for the first time uttering a reason for running from Tarshish: he knew the Lord is "a gracious God and merciful, slow to anger, and abounding in steadfast love, and repentest of evil" (Jon 4:2) and, he adds, it is better now that he should die (Jon 4:3). The reader knows this is a mixture of lying, flattery, and self-pity because it is delivered in anger, and disingenuous because the Lord had recently unleashed the fury of the seas upon Jonah and sent him into a fish's gut to rethink his allegiance to the Lord; these are not supernatural events Jonah would consider coming from a "slow-to-anger" god.

Seeing through Jonah's self-serving flattery, the Lord then asks Jonah if he does well by his anger. Jonah does not answer but scampers away to the outskirts of the city, building a booth to sit under "till he should see what would become of the city" (Jon 4:5). There is nothing to see. The Lord is done with Nineveh, but Jonah railed against the city and, goddamn it, wonders why it is not going up in smoke. Cooking in his own anger and in the heat of the sun, Jonah is relieved that the Lord appoints a plant to shoot up next to him for protection (Jon 4:6), but then the Lord appoints a "worm" (Jon 4:7) to chomp it down, followed by wind and sun to cook Jonah some more, leading Jonah to stew in a mixture of disappointment and pity, proclaiming, "It is better for me to die than to live" (Jon 4:8). God asks him if being angry about the plant does him any good and Jonah responds, "I do well to be angry, angry enough to die" (Jon 4:9). The Lord explains the meaning of his living parable of the plant: Jonah obtained a plant for shade without any effort of his own and then mourned its loss even though it came and went by what appeared to be fate, but certainly by God's will rather than Jonah's own (Jon 4:10); so the Lord asks why not pity the great town of Nineveh, implying that its fate can change just as easily as the plant's and, in this case, for the better.

At the end of the story, the writer never shows Jonah coming out of his funk, leaving him tormented by his perverse expectations (his attitude maybe even surprising himself) and unchanged by what ironically turns out to be the Lord's existential wisdom that in an absurd world, one's fate can be changed for unknown reasons, making it absurd to rejoice in one situation and then be angry in another (even though the reader might think such egocentrism is a natural condition of existence). Yet there is more. Almost as if to suggest that absurdities never cease to exist, the writer ends the story with the Lord exhibiting His seasoned sense of humor when He evaluates His action: "And should not I pity Nin'eveh, that great city, in which there are more than a hundred and twenty thousand persons who do not know their right hand from their left, and also much cattle?" (Jon 4:11). First of all, it is humorous to know that all the turmoil God has put Jonah through has been for a group who God considers dimwitted (not knowing their right hand from their left), so leaning more towards stupid than simply humble fools. (One wonders, how much can repenting be worth if the sinners are stooges and most likely only acting out of fear?) Secondly, by mentioning the actual population number, God adds just a touch of sarcasm, implying that when it comes to mindlessness, the city is without any exceptions; every single citizen is a fool. Then there are the cattle. Remember, they had to don sackcloth and ashes, too. Part of the city's silliness? Perhaps God remembers. In an existential void, any essence can find favor, including the absolution of cattle, God's special consideration of them bringing momentary humor to the void. This leaves the story with a pleasant final aftertaste of existential lite.

If the Book of Jonah is existential lite, a thicker stew is the Book of Job, probably written around 500 BCE, essentially an Ecclesiastes-stock base spiced with a dash of Jonah fickleness. The first two chapters are a folksy there-was-a-man-in-the-land-of-Uz narrative that immediately establishes that Job is "blameless and upright, one who feared God, and turned away from evil" (Job 1:1), even covering for his sons with sacrifices because they may "have sinned, and cursed God in their hearts" (Job 1:5). In an unusual turn of events that remind the reader of the folktales by the Brothers Grimm, Satan saunters into a meeting between God and the sons of God, surprising the Lord, who asks, "Whence have you come?" (Job 1:7). Satan casually answers that he has just been cruising around the earth, seemingly with no real purpose, to which God, with an attitude somewhere between a proud parent and a show-off athletic coach, abruptly calls attention to the innocent Job, as if Job's mere purpose is to come off the bench to challenge Satan: "Have you considered my servant Job, that there is none like him on the earth, a blameless and upright man, who fears God and turns away from evil?" (Job 1:8). Satan immediately jumps on the challenge, hustling God up with taunts of doubt that Job has no reason to be disloyal to God because He has "put a hedge around him" (Job 1:10), protecting Job and his possessions and blessing them to the point that they have even increased, but claiming that if God "touche[s]" (Job 1:11) Job in a negative way, Job would curse God to his face. God tells Satan to have a go at Job, allowing "all that he has is in your power; only upon himself do not put forth your hand" (Job 1:12).

Nothing can make the void more indigestible or unstable than the realization that, on a whim, God, who represents ultimate power and truth, can be tempted into a bet with Satan, the ultimate saboteur of truth. On one hand, God's being tempted helps make Him seem earthbound, human, almost comic in that His ego jumps to show off his star pupil, but the fact that His reactions are stimulated by Satan also makes Him even less reliable than He is in the Book of Jonah. With Satan in control, one messenger after another appears to Job announcing in order the destruction of his animals, servants, and finally sons and daughters. As in the Grimm Brothers' folktales, there is a repetition of a message, each one appearing in the same format, and each listing a unique destructive force, but always from a person who has escaped the slaughter. Remarkably, Job accepts his fate, knowing the gifts of life come with their losses, and that all comes from the Lord's wishes, that "the LORD gave, and the LORD has taken away; blessed be the name of the LORD" (Job 1:21), Job never sinning or charging God with wrong. Then, also in folktale repetition, once again Satan saunters into the Lord's meeting, the Lord wondering what has brought him by, and Satan claiming he is merely cruising up and down the world (Job 2:1-2). And once again the Lord asks Satan if he has considered his main servant Job, still holding fast to his integrity, with Satan taunting that if the Lord puts "forth thy hand now, and touch his bone and flesh, and he will curse thee to thy face" (Job 2:5). Once more the Lord tells Satan to have a go at Job but not to kill him.

When Job is afflicted from the soles of his feet to the crown of his head, his wife has had it and scolds him because she can see that somehow the Lord has ceased to foster a world with integrity at its essence. "Do you still hold fast your integrity? Curse God, and die" (Job 2:9), she exclaims. At least "with his lips" (Job 2:10), Job still insists one must accept both God's idea of good as well as evil. At this point Job's three friends hear of his plight, and "come to condole with him and comfort him" (Job 2:11), hardly recognizing him for all his tormented blistering, and sit with him for seven days without saying anything, "for they saw that his suffering was very great" (Job 2:13). The folktale structure creates an allegorical quality—despite the shrill tone of the wife's response—that universalizes the story so that it represents a core truth, a bleak view of unpredictability in a void that leaves Job's friends, and the reader, horrified and speechless. Job is left as a sacrificial piece of flesh, clinging Jesus-like to his faith, but essentially the victim of a dare between prideful God and loser Satan. And if God wins, so what? Life proves whimsical, unpredictable; attempts to create an essence in the existential void, such as integrity, are rendered fragile at best.

Then the writers (a different team?) shift gears from prose to verse, and instead of an allegorical folk tale, the story turns into a very long debate, the characters switching to new roles, with Job "curs[ing] the day of his birth" (Job 3:1) and his friends becoming unsympathetic, closing their eyes to the void, insisting there is a higher essence in the universe that implicates Job: he must have done something wrong, and furthermore, with all this railing, he is certainly asking for it. Job wishes the doors of his mother's womb had been shut, that he had died at birth so then he could "have been at rest, with kings and counselors of the earth who rebuilt ruins for themselves" (Job 3:13-14), escaping the vanity of power with its monuments that end in ruins while enjoying the same fate of these rulers and advisors, finding equity in death since "the small and the great are there, and the slave is free from his master" (Job 3:19).

Job's friend Eliphaz admonishes instead of comforts. His position is that Job can tell others who suffer to be patient but cannot himself; that the world is full of injustices (a lion starves when it cannot find prey and has its whelps scattered); that to claim righteousness is a bit absurd—"Can mortal man be righteous before God? Can a man be pure before his Maker?" (Job 4:17); that God is just, frustrating crafty people, helping the needy, giving hope, and shutting up injustice; that Job will get over fears of destruction, in fact, "at destruction and famine [he] shall laugh" (Job 5:22), inspecting his "fold and miss[ing] nothing" (Job 5:24); and finally admonishing "for [his own] good" (Job 5:27). This is all easy enough to say if one has not been turned into a grotesquerie; otherwise this is grotesquely patronizing advice.

Job slams back at Eliphaz's absurd assumption: "And what is my end, that I should be patient?" (Job 6:11); "Is my strength the strength of stones, or is my flesh bronze?" (Job 6:12); "In truth I have no help in me, and any resource is driven from me" (Job 6:13). In this time of injustice, he sees his friends becoming afraid and disappearing. Job asks Eliphaz if he has made any special demands or asked for help, requesting only for truthful observation: "Teach me, and I will be silent; make me understand how I have erred" (Job 6:24). He honestly expresses the bitterness of his soul, describing his days as becoming "swifter than a weaver's shuttle, and come to their end without hope" (Job 7:6). He asks for leniency and wonders why his friends are investing so much energy in avoiding his anguish or making him a scapegoat to explain cosmic evil: "I loathe my life; I would not live for ever. Let me alone, for my days are a breath. What is man, that thou dost make so much of him" (Job 7:16-17), and "Why dost thou not pardon my transgression and take away my iniquity? For now I shall lie in the earth; thou wilt seek me, but I shall not be" (Job 7:21). We know the answer: Job's friends need to believe there is a reason for his suffering and to believe they are exempt because of their own self-righteousness; otherwise they will be forced to confront the absurdity of their own existence in the existential void. What they thought was a gourmet feast would transform into scraps.

Job's next friend, Bildad, does not cut slack and scolds Job for his mouth being a "great wind" (Job 8:2). Bildad cannot believe God perverts justice, or rejects a blameless man, insisting on a dream that God "will yet fill your mouth with laughter . . . and the tent of the wicked will be no more" (Job 8:21-22). Maybe, but not now. Bildad closes his eyes to Job's misery as living proof that justice happens at random. Using a line similar to one that will be thrown back at him later by short-memory friends and a God insensitive to his plight and beliefs, Job asks if there actually is a way to prove himself just before a God "who does great things beyond understanding, and marvelous things without number" (Job 9:10) and the impossibility of questioning such an entity: "Who will say to him, 'What doest thou'?" (Job 9:12). A presumptuous and nervy question. The result is that God "will not let me get my breath, but fills me with bitterness" (Job 9:18), knowing "though I am blameless, he would prove me perverse" (Job 9:20) because "he destroys both the blameless and the wicked" (Job 9:22), something we noticed as *secondi piatti* on the Ecclesiastes menu.

Like Job's other friends, Zophar self-comforts by sublimating his angst of the void with self-righteous condemnation of Job: "Should your babble silence men, and when you mock, shall no one shame you?" (Job 11:3), and audaciously adds, "God exacts of you less than your guilt deserves" (Job 11:6). Then, to absolve his harshness, he presumptively inserts, "You will forget your misery" (Job 11:16). Not intimidated, Job fires back, "I have understanding as well as you; I am not inferior to you. Who does not know such things as these?" (Job 12:3), mocking Zophar's use of clichés: "Your maxims are proverbs of ashes, your defenses are defenses of clay" (Job 13:12). In fact, many of the lines hurled by the "comforters" are poetic clichés, the writer suggesting that truisms often provide false psychological comfort while simultaneously pumping up the speaker's self-importance. Job sarcastically strikes at the comforters' reliance on wisdom clichés: "Oh that you would keep silent, and it would be your wisdom!" (Job 13:5). In the spirit of William Blake's *The Marriage of Heaven and Hell* centuries later, Job creates his own proverbs to undermine Zophar, proverbs which echo the spirit of Ecclesiastes: "The tents of robbers are at peace, and those who provoke God are secure" (Job 12:6); God "deprives of speech those who are trusted, and takes away the discernment of the elders" (Job 12:20); God "makes nations great, and he destroys them" (Job 12:23); God "takes away understanding from the chiefs of the people of the earth, and makes them wander in a pathless waste . . . and he makes them stagger like a drunken man" (Job 12:24-25).

Eliphaz responds with more clichés, even seizing on words already hurled at the comforters of Job such as, "What do you know that we do not know?" (Job 15:9). Bildad likewise vomits forth a huge list of one cliché after another, such as, "Yea, the light of the wicked is put out, and the flame of his fire does not shine" (Job 18:5), all of which are totally irrelevant to Job's situation. In Chapter 19, Job again lists all his losses, including his friends alienating him, his becoming repulsive to his wife, and his children despising him, and simply asks for pity, but in Chapter 20, Zophar can only "hear censure which insults [him]" (Job 20:3), too self-involved to perceive Job's anguish. Job admits he is losing patience. Why not? Eliphaz insists that Job "agree with God, and be at peace; thereby good will come to you" (Job 22:21), ignoring that Job had already done this to no avail. Again, with friends more interested in self-protection than understanding, Job can only appear insane (and besieged by his own existential void) when he explains, "Behold, I go forward, but he is not there; and backward, but I cannot perceive him" (Job 23:8), or "God has made my heart faint; the Almighty has terrified me; for I am hemmed in by darkness, and thick darkness covers my face" (Job 23:16-17). Bildad responds by exalting imperfection, a sorry euphemism of Job's miserable condition, as normal: "How then can man be righteous before God? How can he who is born of woman be clean?" (Job 25:4).

Job finally gets to the bottom of his friends' values, requesting to know how many they have helped who have no power, reminding them how quickly fortunes change, wondering why—since they know all of this—they have "become altogether vain?" (Job 27:12). With what sounds like references to today's destruction of the planet, Job quickly overviews the ecological disaster humans have created by mining minerals and gems where a man "overturns mountains by the roots. He cuts out channels in the rocks, and his eye sees every precious thing. He binds up the streams so that they do not trickle, and the thing that is hid he brings forth to light." (Job 28:9-11). Then sounding Thoreau-like, turning away from material gain and "progress," he asks "But where shall wisdom be found? . . . Man does not know the way to it" (Job 28:12-13). "It cannot be gotten for gold, and silver cannot be weighed as its price" (Job 28:15). Job recalls days when God watched over him and righteousness clothed him; Job "was eyes to the blind, and feet to the lame. I was a father to the poor, and I searched out the cause of him whom I did not know. I broke the fangs of the unrighteous, and made him drop his prey from his teeth" (Job 29:15-17). But now God has weakened him and his vulnerability has unloosed evil men against him. In Chapter 31, Job makes a list of conditionals that would indict him if they were true—if he had walked with falsehood, if his heart had been enticed by a woman, if he had rejected the cause of his servants, if he had withheld from the poor, seen anyone lack for clothing, raised his hand against the fatherless, made gold by confidence, rejoiced at the ruin of a person that hated him, concealed transgressions, eaten the yield without payment, let thorn grow instead of wheat—then his suffering would make sense, but of course he is guiltless of all these things.

The writers of the Book of Job have devoted most of the narrative space towards arguments that justify Job's suffering, suggesting that the desperation of so-called friends to justify the horror they see becomes as painful as what Satan has inflicted on Job. Fear of cosmic injustice turns friends into creeps. There is no end to friend-pain. Elihu, who says he has been silent, only listening because of his youth, now gives himself credit for shunning flattery so he can tell Job he is angry with him for justifying himself instead of justifying God. He proclaims that God is greater than any man (not paying attention to Job having already said this) and then uses sophistry to acknowledge Job's misery and downplay it at the same time by claiming God "speaks in one way, and in two, though man does not perceive it" (Job 33:14). He seems to ridiculously equate God's terrifying messages in dreams with the terror Job has been through and finally believes "the Almighty will not pervert justice" (Job 34:12), ignoring the Lord's perversion of justice in allowing Satan to smack Job's righteousness out of him. He accuses Job of speaking without insight, "for he adds rebellion to his sin" (Job 34:37) and warns him, "Beware lest wrath entice you into scoffing" (36:18). Elihu seems delusional, burying the whole issue in the classic doubt-killer: God "does great things which we cannot comprehend" (Job 37:5). As if the friends' rationalizations are not enough, Job's having to defend himself creates its own static anguish reminiscent of the defenses in Kafka's *The Trial*.

Finally the Lord speaks to this idea: his decisions are beyond Job's understanding; but the writers have scripted a God whose articulation of this concept is nowhere near as affirmative as the Sanskrit line *Shantih, Shantih, Shantih*, (Peace, Peace, Peace) that appears in the Hindu Upanishad and begins and ends many Hindu prayers, and which T. S. Eliot translates as "the Peace which passeth understanding." The friends, sometimes ironically referred to as the "comforters" by other commentators, create a God well outside the spirit of the three values proclaimed by the thunder in the first line of the Upanishad, also used by Eliot, that booms *Datta, Dayadhvam, Damyata* (Give, Sympathize, Control). Instead when the Lord speaks He can only boast and taunt Job: "Where were you when I laid the foundation of the earth? Tell me, if you have understanding. Who determined its measurements," and then adds with a bit of smart-ass-ness, "surely you know!" (Job 38:4-5) There is no let up of bravado for three chapters: "Have you commanded the morning since your days began, and caused the dawn to know its place?" (Job 38:12); "Have the gates of death been revealed to you, or have you seen the gates of deep darkness?" (Job 38:17); "Can you lift up your voice to the clouds, that a flood of waters may cover you?" and "send forth lightnings?" (Job 38:34-35); "Can you hunt the prey for the lion, or satisfy the appetite of young lions?" (Job 38:39). The answer of course is no, no, no, and no, but then so what? Job never made any such claims and even had praised the magnificence of God.

In Chapter 39 the Lord gets more philosophical, but the result is still braggadocio. For instance, He has Job consider the ostrich with her proud feathers that are not feathers of love, for she abandons her eggs and lets the ground do the warming, "forgetting that a foot may crush them" (Job 39:15), then "deals cruelly with her young, as if they were not hers" (Job 39:16). Why all the abandonment? Because "God has made her forget wisdom, and given her no share in understanding" (39:17). God decides what is cruel and what ignores wisdom. Has Job ever doubted the cause of cruelty derives from somewhere else? And in any case, is this power something of which to be proud? The Lord is endless with lists of animal wildness He is responsible for, with a tremendous description of Leviathan's power, a creature who laughs at javelins, "counts iron as straw, and bronze as rotten wood" (Job 41:27) and counts clubs as "stubble" (Job 41:29), but there is never mention of His gamesmanship with Satan. Are new writers avoiding that uncomfortable beginning to the book?

Before the Lord is finished with this list, He briefly catches his breath, interrupting Himself to ask Job, "Shall a faultfinder contend with the Almighty? He who argues with God, let him answer it" (Job 40:2). Job answers that he is of small account, but the Lord, seemingly not even paying attention to Job's response, answers out of His whirlwind: "Will you even put me in the wrong? Will you condemn me that you may be justified?" (Job 40:8). The fury of the Lord sounds guilt-ridden, lashing out, like the comforters, crazily listing power plays and creations that are red herrings to avoid His own responsibility in

Job's misery, still never mentioning His game of brinkmanship with Satan. Before Job can get a word out, God is crashing in, like a braggart at a bar who wants to arm wrestle: "Have you an arm like God, and can you thunder with a voice like this?" (40:9). He challenges Job to bring down the proud and wicked, "bind their faces in the world below, Then will I also acknowledge to you, that your own right hand can give you victory" (Job 40:13-14). God's message is for the arrogant, not for someone who is shocked because he praised God only to be punished in a test run with Satan. The reader wonders, does God even know His servant Job?

Besieged by Satan, then by his friends, then by God himself, Job tosses everything to the wind. He refers back to God's entry into the debate when God asked, "Who is this that darkens counsel by words without knowledge?" (Job 38:2), or, who questions the ways of God without having His ultimate knowledge? Job quickly exalts God: "I know that thou canst do all things, and that no purpose of thine can be thwarted. 'Who is this that hides counsel without knowledge?' Therefore I have uttered what I did not understand" (42:2-3). Really? Job rightly complained about injustice, but never doubted God's power, only His injustice that cannot be denied, an injustice traced back to the folktale opening. After all the energy of the debate, Job takes a short breath and easily ditches the wrath of God by conceding his lack of understanding. Rather than implying that one should assume a calm acceptance of one's plight and never question God, the abruptness of the end seems to suggest that the spirit simply gets tired and that in the course of time, all the versions of the Other, tormenting the protagonist in the void, are ready to let go. After all, the Lord is ready to hear what Job knew and admitted to from the beginning and seems to have forgotten how all the torment started.

Adding to the absurdity, God abruptly turns His wrath towards Eliphaz and his two friends: "for you have not spoken of me what is right, as my servant Job has" (Job 42:7). What part of their debate did he miss? They were motivated subconsciously by fear that shut off their empathy, but their poetic attacks were often right on target with the Lord's point of view. Nonetheless, the Lord restores Job's losses and doubles what he had before; everyone now shows him sympathy; and the Lord blesses his days, including giving him the fairest daughters and enabling him to see his sons and his son's sons while living to 140 before he dies as "an old man, full of days" (Job 42:12-16). One wonders whether a less tired team of writers (righteous closers, perhaps?) wrote this mostly verse-back-to-prose, quick-turn-around, idealized ending composed of swift punishments for the comforters and rewards for Job that leave the reader artificially satiated, with all of the earlier energetic, poetic writing, depicting anguished souls in a long debate, put to rest. However, the folksy tale of camaraderie between God and Satan in the opening can never be forgotten. These last writers probably could not stand the existential weight of this most existential book, rushing back to the kitchen to put together a blander menu. Otherwise, the bulk of the Book of Job, along with Ecclesiastes and the Book of Jonah, form a menu that demonstrates existential tastes are "nothing new under the sun" (Eccles 1:9).

DAVID MR. BIG BALLS
An Icon Iced

M ichelangelo's iconic image of David, completed between 1501–1504, now in the Galleria dell'Accademia in Florence, sculpted with extra-large testicles, scaled up to fit his huge, heroic, marble body, is conceived as a statement about David's virility. In addition to virility, mentally David's profile looks self-assured and eagle-eyed from the front of the sculpture, but as one moves to the right side, a vantage point that offers a view of the entire brow and both eyes, one notices the brow is furrowed and the differently focused eyes register confusion. The lips look fuller, looser, less determined, less secure, glimpses of insecurity Michelangelo equivocates to a hidden humility that penetrates and balances David's stony nobility.

But when we meet him in the 1 Samuel, young David is neither noble nor humble. Most of us know the story of the Philistine Goliath, who challenged Israel and was met by the shepherd boy David, who rose admirably to the occasion, but that tidy little narrative leaves out much of what is actually in the text. Where, for instance, is the page in the Sunday school coloring book that shows the pile of riches and a king's daughter, offered as a wife, waiting for David as prizes for "tak[ing] away the reproach from Israel" after he slays the giant (1 Sam 17:26)? Where's the coloring book page showing David's older brother Eliab scolding David, asking his younger sibling why he left vulnerable sheep in the wilderness to come down for prize money—"I know your presumption, and the evil of your heart; for you have come down to see the battle" (1 Sam 17:28)? Where's the depiction of Saul, who tells an immature David that he is "not able to go against this Philistine to fight with him; for [he is] but a youth, and [the Philistine] has been a man of war from his youth" (1 Sam 17:33), and is dumbfounded when he receives David's braggadocio response, claiming that he has taken lambs from a bear's or lion's mouth, grabbing them "by [the] beard," just as he will do to Goliath (1 Sam 17:36)? Where's the coloring book page featuring David getting in everyone's faces? Prideful heroes do not make it to the Sunday school coloring book, let alone prayer books.

In the full account of the story as it appears in 1 Samuel, Saul, perhaps worrying that David is overestimating himself, tries to protect the young shepherd when he decides to take on Goliath by giving him protective armor, but David tosses it all. He does not do so because he says God is his spiritual armor, thereby creating the possibility that the tossing off of armor could be construed as an act of modesty, but because he is "not used to them" (1 Sam 17:39), implying they hinder the mobility that allows him to run "quickly towards the battle line" (1 Sam 17:48), and then, without hesitation (without any sense of being desperate or fumbling to protect himself), instantly sinks a sling-slotted stone into Goliath's forehead (1 Sam 17:49). Although the David and Goliath story survives as the penultimate myth of the archetypal underdog who becomes top dog, the writer of 1 Samuel is never actually depicting David as the underdog.

Once Goliath is on the ground, David finishes him off with a sword, and then, as a symbol of pride and arrogance, takes Goliath's head off, possessing it as a trophy for Jerusalem (but stashing Goliath's armor in his tent, perhaps for another battle where swiftness will not be enough, and bravura rejecting armor would be foolish) (1 Sam 17:54). How does one color "arrogance" in a Sunday school coloring book? Better to reproduce a dark outline of Caravaggio's *David with the Head of Goliath*. In his poem "David," George Garrett[1] (Poet Laureate of Virginia from 2004-2008) agrees that the painter "has seen it right," David, the "lean boy," staring at Goliath's head dangling by the hair from David's fist, David's "lips pursed to spit or kiss" and eyes, "if they show anything, reading / pity and contempt, hatred and love, / the look we keep for those we kill." Caravaggio has David rest the hard edge of his sword on his own thigh, close to his balls, a show of power and contempt. From Caravaggio's painting, Garrett also realizes "Never again a rock will do. / [The sword] fits his hand like a glove": David will use what is efficacious.

Donatello's depiction, a sleek bronze sculpture, finished around 1440 and which stands in the Bargello Museum in Florence, probes even deeper into an aspect of David's perverse psyche by depicting him as "sexually ambiguous." In *Sexual Personae* Camille Paglia[2] describes Donatello's David with his "hand on hip and cocked knee [to] create an air of sexual solicitation. From the side, one is struck by the peachy buttocks, bony shoulder blades, and petulantly protruding boy-belly" with "feminine locks of hair, tangled with ribbons, and a splendidly raffish wreathed hat" but "no traveller's cloak, only exquisitely etched leather buskins. A pornographic trope; the half-dressed is more erotic than the totally nude" (Paglia 146, 148). Paglia's analysis of Donatello's depiction of a homoerotic youth capturing an older man represents a seduce-and-destroy dynamic, David's foot crushing an older man's large skull, his toes creeping through his buskins enmeshing in Goliath's beard, while simultaneously David seems comfortable with the play of Goliath's helmet feather creeping up into his crotch. In another entirely different sculpture, David's "half-dressed" exposure might represent vulnerability, but here David's hard body (playing against his deceptive, seductive boyishness), what Paglia calls "armed nudity," is at ease with his massive sword, which he holds not in the palm of his hand like a dagger, but relaxed in his fingers like a conductor's baton (Paglia 149).

Sunday school assignment: study Caravaggio and Donatello to have a better idea of David as we look more carefully into his character in the next two chapters.

15:233

HOW TO BE KING DAVID
SAUL 101

I. Samuel Studies

David, before your rise to power, you need to be clear on your political lineage and think about past war-tribe dynamics under Samuel, a prophet and considered the last of the Hebrew judges. Realize that in 1 Samuel you are dealing with a hair-trigger decision-maker, the Lord, who backs a cranky Samuel, a ruler who is on edge after suffering major disappointments: first he makes his sons Joel and Abijah judges over Israel only to see they "did not walk in his ways, but turned aside after gain; they took bribes and perverted justice" (1 Sam 8:3); secondly, the Lord withholds any direct help to Samuel, dumping all responsibility on him to fulfill the people's desire for a monarchical leader (because Israel has treated the Lord like shit by believing in other gods since being delivered out of Egypt); thirdly, after Samuel tells the people that creating a king for them means they will have to turn over to the king, free of cost, their "daughters to be perfumers and cooks and bakers," plus give over percentages of their grains, servants, and flocks and that the people will essentially be the king's slaves and to expect disappointment so "you will cry out because of your king . . . but the LORD will not answer you" (1 Sam 8:13-18). The people, not surprisingly, refuse "to listen to the voice of Samuel" (1 Sam 8:19) because they only want a king who will "govern [them] and go out and fight [their] battles" (1 Sam 8:20); and finally, when "he repeated . . . in the ears of the LORD" (1 Sam 8:21) this guff that the people have given him, the Lord snubs Samuel, telling him to "Hearken to their voice" (1 Sam 8:22) and give them what they want anyway. These types of disappointments would make any ruler cynical. Take notice, David, that in the events to follow these kinds of interactions make Samuel neurotic, desperately seeking the stability of strict rules. Beware. This is not a good look for a king of Israel.

David, take note of Samuel's and the Lord's search for a king. Remember how the Lord and Samuel are impressed by what first appears to be Saul's good looks? You have those too. They count for something; however, looks can disguise poor self-image, Saul being a case in point. Look back to the immediate mess his poor self-esteem creates. When the Lord tells Samuel to anoint Saul as prince of His people in Israel, Saul is incredulous—"Am I not a Benjaminite, from the least of the tribes of Israel? And is not my family the humblest of all the families of the tribe of Benjamin? Why then have you spoken to me in this way?" (1 Sam 9:21)—and when Samuel brings all the tribes of Israel to witness Saul's inauguration, Saul panics and runs, hiding "himself among the baggage" (1 Sam 10:22). You probably notice that it does not help that Saul knows that there is a flaw to his good looks: even though he is "taller than any of the people from his shoulders upward" (1 Sam 10:23), this longneck, longhead shape is not a good look, rather one that is indicative of bobble-headed awkwardness.

Do not forget how all of Saul's spastic reactions make the people nervous and how their desperate demand for a king starts to dry up, some of them actually considering forming an alliance with the Ammonites despite having to comply with that tribe's hazing test to "gouge out all [their] right eyes, and thus put disgrace upon all Israel" (1 Sam 11:2). Only Saul could create an Israelite U-turn and stampede. Here's the lesson: build on your confidence; insecurity sickens constituents. When Saul hears that his people are considering leaving him, his humility turns from shame to fury: "He took a yoke of oxen, and cut them in pieces and sent them throughout all the territory of Israel" (1 Sam 11:7) as threats so that out of dread the people turn around and come back to him. And then, also out of dread, as a first show of allegiance, the people take his lead, slicing the Ammonites into meaty chunks. How stable is a kingdom based on fear?

Samuel, who worries that his own rep is vulnerable because he picked Saul, steps back in, asking the people to acknowledge his own ethical credentials: "Here I am; testify against me before the LORD and before his anointed" (1 Sam12: 3), to which Israel responds, "You have not defrauded us or oppressed us or taken anything from any man's hand" (1 Sam 12:4); and, in a desperate attempt to warn the people of Israel to keep allegiance to Saul, Samuel reminds everyone that he is the Lord's man—"Samuel called upon the LORD, and the LORD sent thunder and rain that day; and all the people greatly feared the LORD and Samuel" (1 Sam 12:18). David, take note of a past ruler's ability to create fear and trembling despite the instability of the present king.

However, never forget how, at the slightest breach of rules, main-man endorsements can be jerked away. For instance, when Saul takes on the Philistines, who regroup and retaliate, Israel's fear of the enemy trumps its dread of Saul, and the Israelites "hid themselves in caves and in holes and in rocks and in tombs and in cisterns" (1 Sam 13:6) and then scatter to other lands. Understand that once again Saul's need for Samuel's help is essential, but to get it, Samuel tells Saul to wait an allotted seven days, when their forces will rendezvous. When Samuel is tardy and Saul's armies scatter, Saul desperately fires up burnt peace offerings (sometimes thought of as praise offerings to God) only to piss the hell out of Samuel when he finally shows up late: "Saul went out to meet him and salute him. Samuel said, 'What have you done?' And Saul said, 'When I saw that the people were scattering from me, and that you did not come within the days appointed, and that the Philistines had mustered at Michmash . . . I forced myself, and offered the burnt offerings'" (1 Sam 13:10-12). Saul's disingenuous reference to "forcing" himself to desperately go ahead with burnt offerings (when he had actually done so without hesitation), instead of waiting for Samuel, gets him nowhere. David, watch what happens when someone like Samuel (who worships rules as if they are gods) sees the agreement to wait as a rule to follow no matter how dangerous the circumstances. Also, take note of the contradictory nature of rules: "wait seven days" could be a command to wait until Samuel arrives or to await exactly seven days—damned if you do, damned if you don't. In any case, desperately entreating the Lord is irrelevant. Samuel is done with Saul. Someone else needs to get the job.

However, David, pay attention to the reason Samuel changes his mind. (How many times do we make emotional investments in others, as if they are a reflection of ourselves, and, unwilling to admit we made a bad choice, desperately prop the weak person up so we do not look like a failure?) For one thing, Samuel sees that the popularity of Saul's son, Jonathan, has restored his father, so to make his God-given choice work out, Samuel is willing to give Saul yet another chance, anoint him king, and send him out on a hit-job to prove himself: command a full-course bloodbath of the Amalekites—man and woman, infants and animals (1 Sam 15:3). Saul almost obeys, butchering them all except their king Agag and the Amalekites' best animals. When the Lord and Samuel chastise Saul for again avoiding strict orders by holding back his sword, Saul uses flattering the Lord as his excuse, claiming that he "spared the best of the sheep and of the oxen, to sacrifice to the LORD your God" (1 Sam 15:15). Behold that again Samuel is shocked. Bloody orders have been ignored. Samuel uses chanted verse to underscore the Lord's priorities —"Has the LORD as great delight in burnt offerings and sacrifices, as in obeying the voice of the LORD?" (1 Sam 15:22)—attempting to create a hypnotic mantra that is actually a projection of Samuel's own neurosis for rules. He is incredulous that Saul chopped up babies but avoided slicing up oxen, showing a kind of "stubbornness" Samuel claims as tantamount to "idolatry" (1 Sam 15:23). Even though Saul desperately snatches at Samuel's clothes to make him stay near, Samuel stomps away from him and "hew[s]" (1 Sam 15:33) Agag himself, who "came to him cheerfully," thinking, "Surely the bitterness of death is past" (1 Sam 15:32). Samuel continues to stew in his anger, refusing to see Saul again until "the day of his death" (1 Sam 15:35); and pouts over his disappointment in Saul until he is lectured to by the Lord— "How long will you grieve over Saul, seeing I have rejected him" (1 Sam 16:1)—and ordered to see Jesse, who will provide a son to replace Saul. (You know now, David, that son is you).

Later when Saul torments you, explained below, you escape to Ramah to complain and tell Samuel all that has happened. While you and Samuel confer, Saul keeps sending waves of servants to find out what kind of prophesizing is going on; each time the servants show up, they are inspired to prophesy as if there is something special in Samuel's well water. When Saul decides he should go himself, he strips naked and lies around in the nude, day and night, as if making one crazily vulnerable is the key to joining the prophesy team, leaving everyone scratching their heads, "Is Saul also among the prophets?" (1 Sam 19:24). No answer. After this, references to Samuel seem to dry up. His death gets only a quick reference: "Now Samuel died; and all Israel assembled and mourned for him, and they buried him in his house at Ramah" (1 Sam 25:1). This inconsequential end should give you pause about the worth of ambition.

But behold, this is not quite the end of your Samuel Studies. After many interactions between you and Saul and Jonathan, discussed below, Saul, who, despite your anointment is amazingly still struggling to stay in the picture, is trembling over the strength of the Philistines and desperate for help since "the LORD did not answer him, either by dreams, or by Urim, or by prophets" (1 Sam 28:6). Saul has cut off the mediums and wizards of the land that might help him, but desperately disguises himself (knowing that any remaining medium will either be angry or see him as a threat) to ask the medium of Endor to bring up Samuel yet again to help him (1 Sam 28:7-8). The medium agrees to call from the dead the name that the disguised Saul gives her and then, at the mention of Samuel's name, the medium "crie[s] out with a loud voice" (1 Sam 28:12) on seeing Samuel appear from the dead, realizing at the same time Saul has deceived her.

The abruptly raised-from-the-dead Samuel is his cranky self, but who can blame him: "Why have you disturbed me by bringing me up?" (1 Sam 28:15). Watch how, when Saul whimpers and cries about the Philistines and about God not answering him and asks for Sammy to help him out yet again, Samuel smacks him down: "Why then do you ask me, since the LORD has turned from you and become your enemy?" (1 Sam 28:16). He lectures Saul that "the LORD has torn the kingdom out of [his] hand, and given it to [his] neighbor David" (1 Sam 28:17). The reason? Saul's not completing the Amalekite bloodbath! Yes, Samuel still cannot get over Saul's leaving an animal alive when a tribe's bloodbath is ordered. And to finish Saul off, Samuel tells him that, at the hand of the Philistines, he and his sons will be with him in the ground tomorrow. Beware, David. The havoc of the world does not always stem from the Lord; sometimes it comes from the neurotics who represent him—even though Samuel and the fickle-father Lord are on your side now.

II. Entrance Exams

David, how you will enter scenes, as well as new phases of life, will always be clever. However, how you come on the scene in the first place and are recognized as special in 1 Samuel is a matter of debate. The writers include three possible versions: a flattering account whereby Samuel picks you; a musical-talent adaptation where servants seek your musical abilities out to lessen Saul's dementia; or a not-so-holy version where Samuel is absent and, hearing about prize money for killing Goliath, your ambition drives you from your shepherd life with your brothers (1 Sam 17:12) to become a bounty hunter for Saul. In the flattering version, Samuel asks for all your brothers, Jesse's sons, to file in front of him, where the LORD delivers one of His most rational lines regarding the selection of a king: "Do not look on his appearance . . . because I have rejected him; for the LORD sees not as man sees; man looks on the outward appearance, but the LORD looks on the heart" (1 Sam 16:7). For a moment, His disillusionment with Saul seems to clear His head from His usual capriciousness. Nonetheless, ironically, tellingly, it is not your heart that is considered when the Lord tells Samuel to anoint you, but instead you are only admired in terms of your "appearance" as "ruddy," your having "beautiful eyes" and your being "handsome" (1 Sam 16:12). Within this context of your appearance, "the LORD said, 'Arise, anoint him; for this is he.' Then Samuel took the horn of oil, and anointed [you] in the midst of [your] brothers; and the Spirit of the LORD came mightily upon [you] from that day forward" (1 Sam 16:12-13). And behold, it is your looks that serve you well. In most of the episodes that follow this event, however, Saul is still the anointed king.

A second possibility for your entrance into the narrative follows immediately after this episode, when "the Spirit of the LORD departed from Saul, and an evil spirit from the LORD tormented him" (1 Sam 16:14). In this scenario, Saul's servants "seek out a man who is skillful in playing the lyre; and when the evil spirit from God is upon [Saul], he will play it, and [Saul] will be well" (1 Sam 16:16). One of Saul's men says he has seen a son of Jesse who "is skillful in playing, a man of valor, a man of war, prudent in speech, and a man of good presence;

and the LORD is with him" (1 Sam 16:18), and so Saul has you brought from Jesse and your flock of sheep. Indeed your music does refresh Saul so that the evil spirit departs; then Saul, loving you greatly, asks Jesse to allow you to remain in his service (1 Sam 16:23). In the third version, described above in "David Mr. Big Balls," it is only after you win prize money and one of Saul's daughters that Saul learns your whole background when his general Abner brings you to him.

Whatever your entrance into the narrative of 1 Samuel, Saul shifts from love of you to hate for you, because when you return from military victories, the women come out of all the cities of Israel singing and dancing and making merry in front of Saul with the lyrics "Saul has slain his thousands, and David his ten thousands" (1 Sam 18:7). The jealousy torments Saul, who "raved within his house" (1 Sam 18:10) and, fearing you, standing in awe of you, decides he will hurl spears to pin you to the wall. While cringing inside that all of Israel and Judah love you, he covers his hate by tossing his daughter Merab to you for marriage; you humbly dismiss her—"Who am I, and who are my kinsfolk, my father's family in Israel, that I should be son-in-law to the king?" (1 Sam 18:18)—and Saul pulls back the offer; then finding out that his other daughter Michal loves you, Saul gives her to you as a "snare" (1 Sam 18:21), you humbly refusing his offer again. But it is not women who seem to turn you on; instead, it is bloodlust. That lust is tickled when Saul sends a message to you that your wedding gift to him can be "a hundred foreskins of the Philistines" (1 Sam 18:25), Saul hoping the enemy will kill you instead of getting his own spear bloody. You are so turned on by the offer (you don't even think of Michal) that you immediately set out and kill enough Philistines to collect two hundred foreskins, a wedding gift that satisfies you more than any bride.

At this point your entrance to power starts to have more to do with getting close to and placating Saul, waiting for the right moment to replace him, trying to keep the approval of the one who, in most versions of your story, is still the anointed king. Even as Saul "sat in his house with his spear in his hand" (1 Sam 19:9), you continue to play the lyre, but when he tries to toss spears at you, you know it is time to flee. Your wife Michal serves you well; she is clever like you. When

Saul's spies watch you, Michal helps you escape and creates a goat-hair surrogate to lie in your bed. When Saul discovers her complicity, she fabricates dialogue: "He said to me, 'Let me go; why should I kill you?'" (1 Sam 19:17). Often tricksters are drawn to each other. They make good teams.

Saul is not to be placated; however, you know Saul is losing his mind and it is only a matter of time before you will replace him. I wish you could look at yourself in Rembrandt's painting finished between 1655 and 1660 that hangs in the Royal Picture Gallery at the Hague of you playing the lyre, your head centered on the instrument, leaning slightly into it as if your attention is only focused on your skillfully outstretched fingers plucking out music that enters one's spirit, forcefully driving out all our own torments, let alone Saul's. But your eyes give away your priorities. They are shifting away from the strings, pulling your thoughts forcefully from the music, acting like ears that listen for Saul's mind to crack. You do not have long to wait. Saul's unfocused eye is getting ready to loosen from his head, his large, rich cloak incapable of hiding his dementia, whereas you can hide out, tucked into the corner of the painting. Saul is exposed. His layered turban of rich, colorful fabric is tucked tight, a hopeless gesture of royalty on a head whose mind is ready to unravel. His hand relaxes on his javelin-scepter, ready for you to snatch. The frame of your lyre, catching the full light, is the only shape of strength. Rembrandt shows you that Saul will never keep up with you.

On the run, you continue to use clever entry skills. When you run into Ahimelech the priest, he wonders why you are strangely alone and you cleverly whip up a lie: Saul has charged you with a secret matter that involves a rendezvous with unnamed young men in a secret place, and you will need a supply of five loaves of bread (1 Sam 21:3). The priest has bread reserved only for holy occasions but justifies giving the bread to you only if the men "ke[ep] themselves from women" (1 Sam 21:4). You know to use an elaborate explanation of half-truths that will please the priest, and to employ circular logic by suggesting the holy bread itself will keep your group holy: "Of a truth women have been kept from us as always when I go on an expedition; the vessels of the young men are holy, even when it is a common journey; how much more today will their vessels be holy?" (1 Sam 21:5). You explain that you had to leave in haste (of course not mentioning that you were running from Saul) and so are in need of a spear or sword, and conveniently the priest has kept Goliath's sword wrapped behind the ephod. So, naturally, you take it.

Your next entry point is with Achish, the Philistine king of Gath, whose servants spook the crap out of you because they remind Achish that you are the David of the legendary song about killing more Philistines than Saul (1 Sam 21:12). You fear an unfavorable welcome at best, a treacherous one at worst. To bail out, you have no problem feigning a disguise, using your confidence and chutzpah, making yourself "mad in their hands," slashing "marks on the doors of the gate, and let[ting] [your] spittle run down [your] beard" (1 Sam 21:13). The ploy not only works, it brings forth Achish's sarcasm: "Lo, you see the man is mad; why then have you brought him to me? Do I lack madmen . . . ?" (1 Sam 21:14-15). When you leave and later enter the cave of Adulam, and all your father's house hear about it and think that you can solve all problems, you are flooded by "every one who was in distress, and every one who was in debt, and every one who was discontented" (1 Sam 22:2), until you are surrounded by about four hundred needy men. Hanging with this group (including your father and mother) is not the way to kingship, so you take your parents to the king of Moab, asking him to watch over them until you "know what God will do" (1 Sam 21:3) for you. The prophet Gad pushes you on to the land of Judah with a few men.

Meanwhile Saul pouts, desperately promising the Benjaminites the world in return for allegiance to him over David: "will the son of Jesse give every one of you fields and vineyards, will he make you all commanders of thousands . . . that all of you have conspired against me?" (1 Sam 22:7-8), and then scolds them for not ratting out liaisons between Jonathan and David (1 Sam 22:8). This encourages Doeg, one of your herdsmen, to come forth as witness to the fact that Ahimelech provided for you. Watch out. Nothing works as well as a combination of guilt and desperate need for attention when it comes to being able to rat someone out. When Saul accuses Ahimelech for conspiring with you as a traitor, you are on the run so you miss his defense of himself, which is essentially a defense of you: "And who among all your servants is so faithful as David, who is the king's son-in-law, and captain over your bodyguard, and honored in your house? Is today the first time that I have inquired of God for him? No! Let not the king impute anything to his servant or to all the house of my father; for your servant has known nothing of all this, much or little" (1 Sam 22:14-15).

Saul's dementia leads the way, and he orders his servants to kill Ahimelech and his whole house, and also the priests of the Lord because "their hand also is with David" (1 Sam 22:17), but the servants refuse to kill them. You have learned to beware of opportunists like Doeg who will do anything for the acceptance of a king, even a demented one, and who indeed butchers eighty-five of the priests and destroys their city by killing all the other men, women, children, and animals of Nod. Only one son of Ahimelech, Abiathar, escapes to report the killings; you must admit that when you saw Doeg while you asked Ahimelech for provisions, you knew Doeg would be trouble, and now you can only protect Ahimelech's last living son, Doeg having massacred the rest to satisfy Saul.

One of your next dramatic entrances is behind Saul's open rectum. Yes, complete with fumes. For a while, after the Ahimelech situation, you have forays against the Philistines, reconnect briefly with Jonathan (discussed below), and avoid Saul, who is also distracted by the Philistines. But now, back in pursuit of you, Saul finds a cave to relieve his bowels of a turd, not realizing that you will even put up with cave stink (a symbol of Saul's innermost, foul confusions) to demonstrate to him how easily you can take his life, you and your men "sitting in the innermost parts of the cave. And [your] men said to [you], 'Here is the day of which the LORD said to you, "Behold, I will give your enemy into your hand, and you shall do to him as it shall seem good to you"'" (1 Sam 24:3-4). You, however, hope that by sparing Saul you might gain the constituency of the Lord's anointed, so you "arose and stealthily cut off this skirt of Saul's robe" (1 Sam 24:4), even feeling a little spooked for doing that to a king, reminding your men that Saul is the Lord's anointed, and to spare him. Saul leaves.

Then you leave, following Saul, forcing him to turn around to notice you giving a dramatic bow while you chastise him for listening to those who say you will hurt him, exclaiming how easily your men could have killed Saul in the cave (waving a piece of his robe as proof), righteously proclaiming "May the LORD judge between me and you, may the LORD avenge me upon you; but my hand shall not be against you" (1 Sam: 24:12), and cleverly downplaying your strength: "After whom do you pursue? After a dead dog! After a flea!" (1 Sam 24:14). Saul caves, weeps, repents, admits you will one day be king, and begs you not to cut off the house of his descendants. Only a Medieval artist, such as the one commissioned by Louis IX in 1240 for a picture Bible (Folio 33, now at the Pierpont Morgan Library), would have dared depict the nastiness of the toilet scene; the Renaissance will be too idealistic, only interested in Biblical scenes that can be romanticized.

You know that, as with his relieved bowels, Saul's relief from his angry jealousy will not last for long. In fact, only two episodes later you and your men make a similar entrance, this time while Saul is chasing you with thousands of men through the wilderness of Ziph. During the night, you take Ahimelech and Abishai, Joab's brother, sneak past Saul's encamped soldiers, and charge right into the tent where Saul sleeps with his commander, Abner. Noticing Saul's spear (probably the one you recognize from all the tosses he has taken at you when you played your lyre) stuck in the ground near his head, your men, namely Abishai, see this as a sign once again for you to kill Saul: "God has given your enemy into your hand this day; now therefore let me pin him to the earth with one stroke of the spear" (1 Sam 26:8). But again you hold murder off, proclaiming, "Who can put forth his hand against the LORD'S anointed, and be guiltless?" (1 Sam 26:9). Partly you fear repercussions from God if you kill Saul, your anxiety manifest in the list of consequences you spin with: "As the LORD lives, the LORD will smite him; or his day shall come to die; or he shall go down into battle and perish" (1 Sam 26:10). Again, you probably also worry about losing Saul's constituency, typically inherent in protecting an anointed king. Every ruler craves big numbers.

Yet you are not so rattled as to not take advantage of your entrance to the anointed king's private quarter; take his spear and his jar of water, then standing on a mountain at a great distance from the encampment, try to have Abner destroyed by yelling out a question as to why he did not keep better watch over the quarters of the anointed king, "for one of the people came in to destroy the king your lord. This thing you have done is not good. As the LORD lives, you deserve to die, because you have not kept watch over your lord, the LORD'S anointed" (1 Sam 26:15-16). As proof of your knowledge, you ask the king to search for the spear and jar. When Saul recognizes your voice, you again beg to know if it is the Lord or other men who have driven you out of the good grace of Saul, who now hunts you like a partridge, you knowing full well it is Saul's jealousy for you that fuels his violence. Again Saul feels guilt, calls you his son, asks for your return, believing that his life was precious in your eyes, admitting that he has "played the fool, and [that he has] erred exceedingly" (1 Sam 26:21). You produce the spear, using it now as a weapon of threat, proof again that you could have killed Saul and that you did not. Despite Saul's blubbering, you "say in [your] heart, 'I shall now perish one day by the hand of Saul'" (1 Sam 27:1), so you move on to make an even more surprising entries.

However, before that entry, and between Saul's two private places of poop and sleep, you make a manipulative entrance elsewhere, right after Samuel's death (which you have no personal reaction to, your focus resting entirely on Saul), on hearing that a man named Nabal was sheep shearing in the wilderness near Carmel. To precede your entrance, you send ten young men with a specific, overwrought greeting of peace to Nabal, asking for whatever he has at hand. You cleverly veil a threat in the greeting of peace: "Your shepherds have been with us, and we did them no harm, and they missed nothing" (1 Sam 25:7). Why would you? Nabal is a "churlish man and ill-behaved" (1 Sam 25:3), ignorant of your existence, and your veiled threat agitates him, he thus responding, "Who is David? Who is the son of Jesse? There are many servants nowadays who are breaking away from their masters. Shall I take my bread and my water and my meat that I have killed for my shearers, and give it to men who come from I do not know where?" (1 Sam 25:10-11). The response is cranky but not unreasonable, yet insulting enough to give you and your men an excuse to gird your swords and move on Nabal. Why are you insulted? You are the guest.

You have put up with more personal insults from those who wish you harm and who are closer to you—like Saul.

When Nabal's wife, Abigail who is "of good understanding and beautiful" (1 Sam 25:3), gets wind of both Nabal's railing and your plan, and also hears that your men so far have treated Nabal's men well, without telling Nabal she saddles up a mass of supplies on asses and takes them to you, falls before you, presents herself to you as your handmaid, admits to Nabal's bad behavior and asks forgiveness for him and herself. Abigail's mush goes on and on with classic phrases such as, "evil shall not be found in you as long as you live" (1 Sam 25:28). You lap it up and bless her because she has "kept [you] this day from bloodguilt and from avenging [yourself] with [your] own hand" (1 Sam 25:33). When she returns to Nabal, who is drunk, Abigail does not tell him of any of her long-winded, groveling pleas to you until he is sober in the morning. When she does tell him every detail of how she begged to be your handmaiden, Nabal's "heart died within him, and he became as a stone" (1 Sam 25:37); the Lord smites him, and ten days later he dies. If someone betrayed you, would your heart die? Would you turn to stone? Perhaps Nabal suffers in deep, undetected ways that make him act so churlishly. Your insensitivity to these emotional nuances in people moves you to only praise the Lord for avenging the person who insulted you after you threatened him. You woo and take Abigail as your wife. This time you gain so much with just the threat of entry. Your other entries have been, and will be, much riskier.

An example is your dramatic entrance into the tribe of the Philistines, becoming one with a group that was always Israel's enemy. You figure that by joining them, "Saul will despair of seeking [you] any longer within the borders of Israel" (1 Sam 27:1), and indeed he stops. Perhaps to put memories of your defeat of the Philistine Goliath aside, you assure Achish king of the Philistines (who does not appear to recognize you as the madman who visited him earlier), that he has your loyalty, and you prove it through your and your men's start now of yearlong gang raids, killing scores of men, women, and animals, sparing nothing of many different tribes. Achish puts so much trust in you that he is willing to "make you [his] bodyguard for life" (1 Sam 28:2). One day the Philistines amass near the encampments of

Israel and the Philistines ask Achish why you and your Hebrews are riding with them; to which Achish points out that you have "been with [him] now for days and years," and since you deserted Saul to be with Achish, he has "found no fault in [you] to this day" (1 Sam 29:3).

As often happens in life, one's past catches up with the present. The commanders grow angry because they fear your loyalty will change in upcoming battles with Israel and you will become an adversary, and they remind Achish that you are *the* David praised for killing ten thousands for Saul's thousands. Achish respects and reveres you, but he can not ignore their fears, so when he tells you to go he says, "I have found nothing wrong in you from the day of your coming to me to this day. Nevertheless the lords do not approve of you. So go back now; and go peaceably, that you may not displease the lords of the Philistines" (1 Sam 29:6-7). You greatly protest, wondering what you have done wrong that you "may not go and fight against the enemies of my lord the king?" (1 Sam 29:8). Your ability to sincerely immerse yourself in the culture of an ancient enemy of Israel—for there is never any indication that there is doubt in your mind that you belong here with the Philistines—attests to your ability to become anything that serves your own interests.

Perhaps there is some retribution for your disloyalty to Israel, for when you return to Ziklag where you have left your wives and daughters, the Amalekites have burned the city to the ground and taken all the women, including your family, and the people remaining take their anger out on you, even considering "stoning [you], because all the people were bitter in soul, each for his sons and daughters" (30:6). You strengthen yourself and set out with even more men in pursuit of the Amalekites, intercepting a young Egyptian who was a servant of the Amalekites but was left behind for being sick and now, on the promise that you will spare him, pinpoints the tribe's location and leads you to their encampment. In your surprise attack you recover your wives, defeat the enemy, and take spoils. You had left two hundred exhausted men encamped away from the battle, and now those that went with you demand that those who rested only get their families back, none of the loot, but you are politically astute and insist that all serve, even those who stand and wait, so that the loot must be divided equally between all your men. You even wisely take some bounty to the elders of Judah (1 Sam 30:26). You know what you have to do to start switching your loyalties back to Israel.

III. Jonathan Studies

Before you grow close to Jonathan, Saul's son, there are episodes with him that you would find instructive. Consider the time Jonathan and his young armor bearer decide that the Lord will work favorably in their behalf because "nothing can hinder the LORD from saving by many or by few" (1 Sam 14:6). True enough, but on what terms does the Lord save a few? Jonathan never considers what these terms might be, so seems almost playfully reckless, rationalizing acting on a whim. This attitude is reinforced by making up a frivolous "sign" for whether the Lord will favor him against the Philistines or not: "If they say to us, 'Wait until we come to you,' then we will stand still in our place, and we will not go up to them. But if they say, 'Come up to us,' then we will go up; for the LORD has given them into our hand" (1 Sam 14:9-10). Notice that Jonathan's charisma, devoid in Saul, commands attention—it is evident by Jonathan's enamored armor bearer, who tells him, "Do all that your mind inclines to; behold, I am with you, as is your mind so is mine" (1 Sam 14:7). The tables will turn when you enamor Jonathan; so pay attention to Jonathan's strength brought forth by the armor bearer's sentiments. He works with Jonathan to slaughter all the "uncircumcised" (1 Sam 14:6) Philistines. Notice how their bravado pays off when the men of Israel, who before joined the Philistines, now come to Jonathan because the Lord is on his side.

Later Saul creates a crazy oath—until he is avenged, nobody gets to eat, including abstaining from eating the honey dropping on the forest ground (1 Sam 14:24-25). Jonathan, not having heard about this oath, tastes the honey, and his eyes turn "bright" (1 Sam 14:27) as if the honey is a version of the fruit of good and evil. Behold the result, how Jonathan draws a line between himself and his father. When everyone warns Jonathan of his father's oath, Jonathan responds, "My father has troubled the land; see how my eyes have become bright, because I tasted a little of this honey" (1 Sam 14:29), displaying an independence reminiscent of Eve's, rebelliously energizing himself to the point of encouraging others to go even further on the tasting menu, breaking dietary laws and eating all the enemy's animals with their blood. The embarrassed Saul then must messily correct this non-kosher feast, allowing only for the consumption of animals drained of blood (1 Sam 14:34). When Saul's prayers are not answered in his next fight with the Philistines, and Saul asks for lots to be drawn between him and Jonathan to establish blame for those failed prayers, Saul believes justice prevails when Jonathan gets taken, or chosen by the lot, because of breaking Saul's honey-tasting oath. Notice Saul's mistake in believing this means Jonathan will die, and his mistake in not anticipating the people will prioritize Jonathan's previous military victory over Saul's oaths and even over the breaking of dietary laws. Contrary to Saul's expectations, the people ransom Jonathan—"there shall not one hair of his head fall to the ground" (1 Sam 14:45). David, observe the power charismatic youth holds in trumping tradition and oaths.

David, remember when Jonathan first becomes the enchanted rather than the object of enchantment? It is when he first sees you. You had just killed Goliath and gone up against the Philistines, feats that offered a sexual high for a warrior such as Jonathan, so Saul asks his commander Abner to bring you to him, and when you "had finished speaking to Saul, the soul of Jonathan was knit to [your] soul . . . and Jonathan loved [you] as his own soul. . . . Then Jonathan made a covenant with [you], because he loved [you] as his own soul" (1 Sam 18:1-3). But you give no indication that you love him. Even when he "stripped himself of the robe that was upon him, and gave it to [you], and his armor, and even his sword and his bow and his girdle" (1 Sam 18:4), you give him nothing. Not even an earing keepsake. You immediately leave and enjoy more military success, pissing off Saul. Maybe you are enjoying the charisma that rubs off on you from your association with Jonathan, because now your military campaigns are "good in the sight of all the people and also in the sight of Saul's servants" (1 Sam 18:5).

You learn that your bloodlust grants you fame and acceptance. You sense that Jonathan's love for you will serve you well. When Saul tells Jonathan and his servants to kill you, Jonathan tells you of his father's desires for your death, has you hide, speaks well of you to his father, and warns him, "Let not the king sin against his servant David; because he has not sinned against you, and because his deeds have been of good service to you" (1 Sam 19:4). When you and Jonathan meet up again, you express your fears and Jonathan tells you not to worry because "[his] father does nothing either great or small without disclosing it to [him]; and why should [his] father hide this from [him]?" (1 Sam 20:2). You, so aware of Jonathan's feeling for you, are forced to remind him, "Your father knows well that I have found favor in your eyes; and he thinks, 'Let not Jonathan know this, lest he be grieved'" (1 Sam 20:3). There is no mention of Saul's concern regarding your feelings for Jonathan. Do you have any? Jonathan has enough to go around, as he adds, "Whatever you say, I will do for you" (1 Sam 20:4), words reminiscent of the young armor bearer's line to Jonathan earlier.

When you plan to be absent from Saul's table, you have Jonathan study Saul's response to determine whether he is out to get you again, and then you make the type of preposterous, disingenuous demand on Jonathan that you know only a lover would take seriously, that he "deal kindly with your servant [you, David], for you have brought your servant into a sacred covenant with you. But if there is guilt in me, slay me yourself; for why should you bring me to your father?" (1 Sam 20:8) Of course, you get the response of devotion you expect is forthcoming from Jonathan: "Far be it from you! If I knew that it was determined by my father that evil should come upon you, would I not tell you?" (1 Sam 20:9).

Jonathan not only swears to signal his father's disposition to you (an elaborate scheme with shot arrows) (1 Sam 20:18-22), but adds that if he does not warn you and the Lord visits harm on you, that he, Jonathan, will suffer as well. Jonathan wishes the Lord be with you as much as his father and that the Lord takes vengeance on your enemies, but he does so with a premonition that, with a father like Saul, all will end tragically for him as Saul's son. Jonathan touchingly declares his faith and hope in you: "If I am still alive, show me the loyal love of the LORD, that I may not die; and do not cut off your loyalty from my house for ever. When the LORD cuts off every one of the enemies of

David from the face of the earth, let not the name of Jonathan be cut off from the house of David" (1 Sam 20:14-16). David, will you let the name of Jonathan be cut off from you? Do you secretly wish Saul to die but not Jonathan? Are you waiting for fate to decide?

When your place at Saul's table is empty, at first Saul thinks his fantasy that something had befallen you has come true, but on the second day you are absent he turns to Jonathan and asks about you, denying your name by referring to you as "the son of Jesse," to which Jonathan lies by claiming you had asked him if you could return to your family for a sacrifice at the command of your brother. Saul senses a fabrication and his "anger is kindled against Jonathan, and he said to him, 'You son of a perverse, rebellious woman, do I not know that you have chosen the son of Jesse to your own shame, and to the shame of your mother's nakedness? For as long as the son of Jesse lives upon the earth, neither you nor your kingdom shall be established'" (1 Sam 20:30-31). Saul now is not only fueled by Jonathan's allegiance to you, but also by homophobia, implied by Saul's curse that Jonathan's sexual attraction to you could only be generated by a mother, never a father, and only a mother who flouts sexual norms; but Saul works his insult both ways, also suggesting that Jonathan's sexual attraction to you undermines his mother's sexuality, her nakedness. Behold that even a crazed king can turn up a truth: as Jonathan tried to address before when he begged to be linked with you and not his father, Saul senses that your desire to maintain power by distancing yourself from his dynasty, his sons, is more important than your relationship with Jonathan.

But for the present, the fact that your ambition comes before personal relationships is not apparent to Jonathan, who challenges his father, asking what you have done. In turn, his father casts a spear at you, sickening Jonathan who "rose from the table in fierce anger and ate no food the second day of the month, for he was grieved for [you], because his father had disgraced him" (1 Sam 20:34). After the arrow signal, Jonathan meets you; you fall on your face and bow to the earth three times before you kiss one another and weep with one another until you "recover" (1 Sam 20:41) yourself and Jonathan tells you to "go in peace, forasmuch as we have sworn both of us in the name of the LORD, saying, 'The LORD shall be between me and you, and between my descendants and your descendants, for ever'" (1 Sam 20:42), but you offer no words of agreement or condolence, your heart not committed to anyone but your own house. You sense what it takes to be king.

After military encounters discussed above with the Philistines, you see Jonathan one more time in the Wilderness of Ziph at Horesh, where you are trying to avoid Saul who is seeking your life. Jonathan, still full of love for you, tells you to "fear not; for the hand of Saul my father shall not find you; you shall be king over Israel, and I shall be next to you; Saul my father also knows this" (1 Sam 23:17), and even though the two of you make a covenant before the Lord, there is no indication that it has anything to do with Jonathan existing with you in a combined house. You always let him have the fantasy; his love for you is "far greater" than your love for him. Your mind is now preoccupied with many events discussed above, and Jonathan never comes into your thoughts. Over time, the Philistines fight against Israel and overtake Saul and his sons, slaughtering Jonathan. Saul is badly wounded and asks his armor bearer to finish him off "lest these uncircumcised come and thrust me through, and make sport of me" (1 Sam 31:4), but the armor bearer is afraid to, so Saul takes his own sword and falls upon it, and his armor bearer follows suit. The next day the Philistines strip him and cut his head off, and finally the inhabitants of Jabesh-glead cremate him, Jonathan, and his brothers.

In the opening of 2 Samuel, you hear about their deaths from a young man who escapes from the camp of Israel, who tells you he witnessed Saul leaning on his spear (2 Sam 1:6). Is this a different writer's version of Saul's death, or is there confusion about the weapon Saul used? Does it matter? However, the young man tells you that Saul did not die from this self-piercing; and so he picked the young man, demanding that he "stand beside [him] and slay [him]; for anguish has seized [him], and yet [his] life still lingers" (2 Sam 1:9), and so the young man slayed Saul because he was sure he could not live after he had fallen; and "I took the crown which was on his head and the armlet which was on his arm, and I have brought them here to my lord" (2 Sam 1:10). Then, despite the young man showing the honor you have been waiting for, and despite the fact that you have evaded

Saul's countless attempts to murder you, and despite Saul's degrading treatment of Jonathan who loved you, you put on a dramatic show of mourning for Saul and Jonathan, rending your clothes, weeping and fasting (2 Sam 1:12) until evening. And then, instead of commending the young man, you scold him: "How is it you were not afraid to put forth your hand to destroy the LORD'S anointed?" (2 Sam 1:14); and proceed to have him slain, and then, leaving out the circumstances, proclaim that by his own mouth he testified that he slayed the Lord's anointed. This is your way of cleverly keeping Saul's constituency and acting as his defender, by taking advantage of an innocent youth who aids Saul in a mercy killing. You lament Jonathan's death, but where is the same outrage you had for Saul's "killer" when it comes to the Philistines who killed Jonathan? Is it absent because his death did not provide a messenger scapegoat? Because there is no one for a political blood spectacle?

You offer a lamentation hymn that "should be taught to the people of Judah" (2 Sam 1:18) where Saul and Jonathan are treated as one, both "beloved and lovely!" (2 Sam 1:23). This is a lie. You know Jonathan's lifelong wish was to stand with you, not his father, yet you insist, "In life and in death they were not divided; they were swifter than eagles, they were stronger than lions" (2 Sam 1:23). In the hymn, you refer to Jonathan as your brother and end with, "very pleasant have you been to me; your love to me was wonderful, passing the love of women" (2 Sam 1:26). Your admission that Jonathan loved you more than the women in your life is demeaned by your admission of what he meant to you: not a love you reciprocated but a love that was merely "very pleasant." Your hard heart makes you a soldier king and political king. You will not be a king one can depend on as a friend, lover, or a symbol of justice.

I SPY DAVID
DETECTING JOAB, DOPPELGANGER

After working through the protracted passages of 1 and 2 Samuel and the first part of 1 Kings, it is evident that these parts of the Bible compose one of the first psychological novels of the ancient world, perhaps written and developed between 700 and 550 BCE, and based on events between 1000 and 950 BCE. Because these passages would normally be tightened in the modern novel to highlight their meaningful Henry-Jamesian details, I can understand how one might fail to detect the story's rich psychological revelations. Now in 2 Samuel, I am even more intrigued that an ancient writer abandons folktale format, instead developing a complex narrative whereby David's soul is revealed through carefully rendered actions (or avoidance of actions) and dialogue, instead of articulating his thoughts through an omniscient narrator.

This storytelling style shows much respect for King David's conscious, and sometimes unconscious, ability to hide himself. A writer penetrating David's mind through an omniscient narrator who spells out all of David's thoughts would have distracted from experiencing the powerful outward appearance of David's manipulative spirit. The narrator's devices instead tease me, make me want to put on Biblical robes and enter the scene. Because I understand that watching David will reveal his interior psychology, I am conflicted: I want to distance myself from David's vileness but also want to draw close to him to know why he hides and protects himself. I also am realizing that Joab, David's cousin and commander, becomes David's alter ego, his dark shadow creating a psychological dimension that leaves me awestruck as events unfold.

Entering the novel, I notice that after Saul's and Jonathan's deaths (covered in the previous chapter), the Lord gives David permission to move into the cities of Judah, where he receives his anointment as king, praises the men of Jabesh-glead for burying Saul (2 Sam 2:1-7), and slyly confronts a new problem: Abner, the commander of the house of Saul's army, has given Saul's son, Ishobesheth, rule over several tribes, including Israel, a constituency David wants (2 Sam 2:8-9). Ishobesheth and Abner stand off Joab, David's personal commander who is looking out for David's interest by supplanting the house of Saul. Each side has twelve men (2 Sam 2:12-15). Abner suggests sportive games between the teams, although both sides are skeptical that sport is truly on the agenda. And, indeed, both sets of twelve simultaneously catch "his opponent by the head, and thrust his sword in his opponent's side; so they fell down together" (2 Sam 2:16). All stand up; all fall down. The rest of the day, Joab slays even more of Abner's army. David, however, is sly. He stays away from the slaughter. He has been in competition with the house of Saul since his Goliath days and wants that house defeated, but he has always wanted the house of Saul as part of his constituency. So he allows Joab to slice off one part at a time.

Joab has two brothers, Abishai and Asahel. The latter takes off after Abner and catches up with him, but this is not just a chase-and-kill story—rather, it is a story about psychological gamesmanship. Abner squares around and tells Asahel to take one of his own young men as spoils, and to stop following him. (2 Sam 21-22). Why, Abner asks, "should I smite you to the ground? How then could I lift up my face to your brother Jo'ab?" (2 Sam 2:22), unabashedly admitting that politics govern whom he guts and to whom he gives a reprieve. Asahel, swift as a cheetah, only knows how to dash forward, so Abner only needs to hold onto his spear as Asahel drives into it, the tip skewering from his front through his back (2 Sam 2:23).

To revenge their brother, Joab and Abishai pursue Abner, who temporarily stops their pursuit with a "shall-the-sword-devour-forever?" (2 Sam 2:26) plea. Joab seems to demur, but I wonder if he is turning back only temporarily, knowing he will reset the time for revenge later? At this point, I still do not see David. In the meantime, other battles rage between the house of David and the house of Saul, with David growing stronger; and at his home base in Hebron, six of his wives have offspring, including his firstborn Amnon and later

Absalom and Solomon (2 Sam 3:1-5).

In a perverse parallel to David getting stronger, within the house of Saul, Abner makes himself appear bolder by going into the vagina of Saul's concubine, Rizpah. Saul's son Ishbosheth promptly questions Abner's lack of respect for his dead father (2 Sam 3:6-7), which in turn incurs Abner's wrath whereby he reveals his derision of women: "Am I a dog's head of Judah? This day I keep showing loyalty to the house of Saul your father, to his brothers, and to his friends, and have not given you into the hand of David; and yet you charge me today with a fault concerning a woman" (2 Sam 3:8). I find Abner sickening, but wonder if David and his shadow self, Joab, are any more upstanding or if they are simply more cunning. Abner completes his squashing of Ishbosheth when he reminds him that, if Abner was playing by the Lord's rules, he should be turning Saul's whole kingdom over to David (2 Sam 3:9-10). Ishbosheth shuts up.

I soon find out that the warning to Ishbosheth is empty rhetoric because Abner wastes no time sending messengers to David anyway, asking for a covenant and, in return, Abner says, he will turn over Israel to him. David responds, "Good; I will make a covenant with you; but one thing I require of you; that is, you shall not see my face, unless you first bring Michal, Saul's daughter" (2 Sam 3:13). David may be remembering that he once won Michal by delivering a hundred Philistine foreskins to Saul, only to have an angry Saul renege on the daughter-for-foreskins deal (1 Sam 18:25-27). David, who collects women as if they are blankets, smells when one is missing. He is so impatient to get Michal that he demands her from Saul's son Ishbosheth, who, still shaken from Abner's threats, drags her from her weeping husband (2 Sam 3:15-16). Meanwhile, conferring with Israel and the whole house of Benjamin, Abner reminds them of the Lord's promise that David would eventually be king (2 Sam 3:17), Abner quickly arriving with a small contingent at David's headquarters to let him know the deal to combine all with the house of David is sealed, after which he enjoys a feast hosted by David. Just as Abner leaves in peace, I notice Joab and his looting gang arrive in Hebron (2 Sam 3:19-20).

When Joab hears that David allowed Abner to go in peace, he is incensed. He scolds David for allowing Abner to leave, and reinterprets

Abner's mission: "What have you done? . . . You know that Abner the son of Ner came to deceive you, and to know your going out and your coming in, and to know all that you are doing" (2 Sam 3:24-25). I intuit that David takes this tongue-lashing because he knows Joab is his sword hand. I watch for proof. I remember that Joab has recently won Abner's trust by turning away from him when he pleaded for peace after Joab tracked him down. Joab has the patience of a cat. He can sit quietly and then spring. Keeping David out of the picture, Joab sends messengers to tell Abner to return to David's fort (2 Sam 3:26), and on his arrival, pulls him into "the midst of the gate" (2 Sam 3:27) for a private conversation, then rips out his blood-filled guts for having killed his brother (2 Sam 3:27). David benefits from this death of the house of Saul's main killer-general. But when he hears about it, I notice he says nothing to Joab, who more and more embodies what David does not want to see in himself, what he would hate in himself—an ambitious killer. I wonder if David will ever understand that Joab is his shadow.

As I watch David now, I learn more about his politics. He can play the righteous king. After first saying nothing, he now quickly distances himself from Joab, although I predict he will depend on him over and over again. Despite it being clear that Abner was a cynic who despised women and who always acted out of self-interest, David curses Joab's family, wishing them oozing sores, poverty, and bloody deaths (2 Sam 3:29), and then tells Joab to rend his clothes and mourn for Abner (which he never does). David himself follows the bier, lamenting Abner as having fallen before the wicked (the people weep) (2 Sam 3:34), refusing bread from the people until the sun goes down (the crowd loves this devotion) (2 Sam 3:35-36), and going so far as to glamorize Abner as a core component of his own spirit: "Do you not know that a prince and a great man has fallen this day in Israel? And I am this day weak, though anointed king. . . . The LORD requite the evildoer according to his wickedness!" (2 Sam 3:38-39). David is a Hebrew thespian: he will pretend anything for Saul's constituency. Especially when their principles are dead.

When Saul's son Ishbosheth hears of Abner's death, he is so fearful that he has little time to lament: "his courage failed, and all Israel was dismayed" (2 Sam 4:1). Ishbosheth must wonder if he is next. And indeed he is next, but not in a way he could have predicted. His own two captains, Baanah and Rechab, slay him in his bed (2 Sam 4:7) and take his head to David, expecting praise. Instead, David reminds them that he previously slew the person who brought him news of Saul's death (2 Sam 4:8-10)—and in fact, he continues the tradition, slaying Ishbosheth's captains and then displaying their hands and feet at the pool in Hebron (2 Sam 4:12). I am surprised how violently David reacts in one situation; how quickly he withdraws in others. Like his shadow, he stays still and then unexpectedly springs like a crocodile. However, unlike his shadow, he has the uncanny ability to send conflicting signals, allowing many to believe he wants the house of Saul diminished, only to curse or butcher those who bring him pieces of the house of Saul on a platter.

At thirty years old, David receives the power to reign from the tribes of Israel (2 Sam 5:4). He then goes after the land and water sites of the Jebusites, who crazily (kiddingly? gloatingly? symbolically?) claim, "the blind and the lame will ward [him] off" (2 Sam 5:6), and instead of attacking, David, blowing this threat off, invites others to "attack the lame and the blind, who are hated by David's soul" (2 Sam 5:8). I think the blind and lame represent weakness and vulnerability, attributes that disgust David. Watching carefully, I never find that David is any kind of Jesus figure (who will forgive the lame and the blind, even when their afflictions birth psychic demons), as future scribes and theologians sometime suggest; instead, this aggressiveness is startling. David insultingly uses the Jebusites' stronghold as his "city of David" (2 Sam 5:9) and grows greater, "for the LORD, the God of hosts, was with him" (2 Sam 5:10). His treatment of the Jebusites will add to David's future shame.

David takes more wives and concubines, breeding like an alpha wolf (2 Sam 5:13-16). As in old times when David worked for Saul, the Philistines challenge David, but he checks in with God, who tells him not to worry and to pursue with victory (2 Sam 5:17-19). The Philistines blitz David, but God tells him to hit their rear guard, and victory comes easily as in years past (2 Sam 5:23-25). However, then God gets tweaked and stings like a scorpion. It starts when David, with all his soldiers and people, decides to relocate the ark of God with a new cart: "And David and all the house of Israel were making merry before the LORD with all their might, with songs and lyres and harps and tambourines and castanets and cymbals" (2 Sam 6:5). It is a jubilee all for the Lord. What more could He want? Yet when the oxen that are pulling the cart stumble, Uzzah, who is helping drive the cart, puts out his hand to keep the ark from tumbling, and suddenly "the anger of the LORD was kindled against Uzzah; and God smote him there because he put forth his hand to the ark" (2 Sam 6:7). So much for a helping hand. God makes me nervous, let alone David, whose gut must be churning. God is a smoldering hot spot, flaming into an unexpected crank, enforcing a literal, no-touch command of the Holy Ark.

David witnesses it all, bristles, and panics about taking this touch-sensitive ark into his city, so he nervously dumps it at the house of Obededom the Hittite (2 Sam 6:8-10). Later David hears the Lord has blessed that house for maintaining the ark, so now of course he wants it back. He hustles over and gets it, but he is still a wreck and unsure what God will do next, so before the ark can move six paces, he starts piling up a mountain of sacrificed animals (2 Sam 6:13). Still feeling insecure, he "danced before the LORD with all his might; and David was girded with a linen ephod. So David and all the house of Israel brought up the ark of the LORD with shouting, and with the sound of the horn" (2 Sam 6:14-15). I am embarrassed watching all these ark-fanatics desperately sweating out their praises.

I learn from arguing priests that there is debate about what an ephod is, ranging from special curtains for the ark to two-piece tunics for priests, and that much of it depends on context. At this point, the reaction of David's desperately acquired wife, Michal, gives the best clue for what an ephod is in the current scene. Glimpsing out the window, she sees "King David leaping and dancing before the LORD; and she despised him in her heart" (2 Sam 6:16)—I do not think she ever saw him so delirious before—and scolds him for "uncovering himself today before the eyes of his servants' maids, as one of the vulgar fellows shamelessly uncovers himself!" (2 Sam 6:20). In this context, I can see the ephod as a bulky butt thong. David makes a sweaty mess of himself hoping to get the army-slaughtering Lord back on track. He adds peace and burnt offerings and stuffs the crowd with raisin cakes before they go home. (An all-you-can-eat buffet is always good for politicking.)

What shocks me the most, though, is how insecure and foolish Michal has made David feel, and in turn, how David's hatred is aroused by this shame. I notice that the touchiest issue, the one at the top of his mind so quickly leaping from his snarling, insecure soul, is about his supplanting the house of Saul. He manages to twist this topic into his reasons for stripping down and jumping around like a gibbon before the Lord, "who chose [him] above [Michal's] father, and above all his house, to appoint [David] as prince over Israel, the people of the LORD—and [he] will make merry before the LORD" (2 Sam 6:21). Then, still blistered with humiliation, David tries to destroy Michal with a spiteful, crotch-clutching, adolescent threat: "I will make myself yet more contemptible than this, and I will be abased in your eyes; but by the maids of whom you have spoken, by them I shall be held in honor" (2 Sam 6:22). Michal, who had been the reminder of Saul's rejection for so long that David had insisted Abner yank her from a marriage to another for himself, is now dumped: "the daughter of Saul had no child to the day of her death" (2 Sam 6:23). I am nervous watching David become an adolescent husband.

After shedding his wife, David, who I deduce is still a wreck about not having done the ark justice, mentions to the prophet Nathan that he feels an imbalance because he lives "in a house of cedar, but the ark of God dwells in a tent" (2 Sam 7:2). God piggy-backs on the same speech, telling Nathan, "Go and tell my servant David, 'Thus says the LORD: Would you build me a house to dwell in? I have not dwelt in a house since the day I brought up the people of Israel from Egypt to this day, but I have been moving about in a tent for my dwelling'" (2 Sam 7:5-6). A space-restricting request from an omnipotent, omnipresent deity amuses me, but lest anyone not take the Lord's request seriously, He lists all the crucial victories He has been responsible for and the generations of the people He will stand behind and how the house will become a throne for the kingdom and how He will be a father to David (2 Sam 7:7-14), and yet He "will chasten him with the rod of men, with the stripes of the sons of men; but [the Lord] will not take

[His] steadfast love from him, as [He] took it from Saul" (2 Sam 7:14-15). Four cedar walls give David a lot of "house of David," but yes, the Lord finally includes rod-chastening morality as part of the power package. It makes me wonder why the Lord has never come down on David's immorality before. I cannot help but think that finally having the comforts of home makes the Lord feel like He can chasten others like the father of a household.

David responds by obliging the Lord with piles of flattery: "Therefore thou art great, O LORD God; for there is none like thee, and there is no God besides thee, according to all that we have heard with our ears. What other nation on earth is like thy people Israel, whom God went to redeem to be his people, making himself a name, and doing for them great and terrible things, by driving out before his people a nation and its gods?" (2 Sam 7:22-23). And the Lord soon responds to the flattery big time, standing behind David, who knocks out one group after another, killing tens of thousands of soldiers to seize their lands: the Philistines, the Moabites (ironically the tribe of Ruth, the beginning of David's lineage), the Syrians, the Edomites (2 Sam 8:1-13).

I start speculating who will now be David's main man in command—but it turns out to still be Joab, his alter ego. I never see David patch up his relationship with this man he so reviled at Abner's death. Maybe there was no need. Joab is his own shadow. I begin to figure out David's show of disgust was simply theater. Soon David performs again, still contemplating the constituency of the house of Saul: "Is there still any one left of the house of Saul, that I may show him kindness for Jonathan's sake?" (2 Sam 9:1). David finds Mephibosheth, Jonathan's son, Saul's grandson, who was five at the time of Jonathan and Saul's deaths, and crippled by his nurse when she was forced to flee with him so the house of Saul would not be entirely wiped off the face of the earth. So now David has Mephibosheth always eat at his table, where David can satiate both guilt and political expediency with progeny that symbolizes the hobbled house of Saul (2 Sam 9:7).

I find out David's next target for power and land is the Ammonites, and since their ruler Nahash always dealt loyally with David (2 Sam 10:2), after he dies, David feels he can deal fairly with Nahash's son, Hanun. However, the Ammonite princes are distrustful, echoing both the past skepticism Achish the Philistine's commanders had for David when he joined Achish to torment Saul and his armies (1 Sam 27:1-12), and the past doubt of Joab's recent concern for Abner when David allowed him to go in peace. Hanun's princes ask, "Do you think, because David has sent comforters to you, that he is honoring your father? Has not David sent his servants to you to search the city, and to spy it out, and to overthrow it?" (2 Sam 10:3). The lines stoke Hanun's paranoia, so he shaves off half of David's men's beards and cuts out the middle of their clothing, probably exposing their genitals, turning them into surrealistic clowns (2 Sam 10:4). When the Ammonites figure out how furious this makes David, they enlist the help of the Syrians (2 Sam 10:6) to protect them from his coming wrath. Neither group is a match for Joab, who teams with his brother Abishai to split the tribal forces. Then, in the final seconds, David enters the fray to seal the victory (2 Sam 10:7-17). No doubt about it; Joab rides with David. David does not want to face his dark side, so the two selves are inseparable. I wonder if David can ever acknowledge and confront his shadow, thereby becoming a man of understanding, or whether his resentment for Joab will fester and result in more blood.

With a rare reference to seasons, the storyteller pricks up my ears: "In the spring of the year, the time when kings go forth to battle, David sent Jo'ab, and his servants with him, and all Israel" (2 Sam 11:1). Suddenly, I am caught off guard by a storyteller who enters David's life with an upbeat, bouncy-stepped description of spring reminiscent of Chaucer's "When in April the sweet showers fall / And pierce the drought of March to the root . . . Then people long to go on pilgrimages." But instead of this being a jaunty pilgrimage to a holy shrine, with travelers full of creative tales to while away the time, the spring-fevered soldiers "ravaged the Ammonites, and besieged Rabbah" (2 Sam 11:1). The upbeat tone plunges my spirits even further on the next detail: "But David remained in Jerusalem" (2 Sam 11:1). This blunt statement of inertia dampens the energy of Joab's military parade. Even worse, David's inertia quickly morphs into the perverse. He is walking on his roof, spies a beautiful woman bathing, makes inquiries of her to find out she is the wife of Uriah the Hittite, named Bathsheba, sends for her, goes into her vagina, and soon after going into her learns she is with child (2 Sam 11:2-5).

It is unclear to me why Bathsheba gives in to David's original request. There are no clues. Instead, I look at Rembrandt's *Bathsheba at Her Bath*, painted in 1654, hanging in the Louvre. Bathsheba's servant wears a ritualistic, heavily tasseled cap, her face devoid of femininity, as if Rembrandt wants the viewer to focus only on the servant's solemn, non-judgmental features, such as her downcast eyes and relaxed mouth, all hinting that she intuits she is cleaning the feet of a woman being prepared for a sacrifice. Bathsheba's bejeweled hair and droplet earring give her an air of confidence that conflicts with her vulnerable nudity. She holds the note from David, the emotional weight of its contents forcing her to drop her hand, clasping the note on her knee, while her other arm and splayed hand brace her body. Fate is pushing her off balance. Her mouth is carefully depicted: relaxed with the corner only slightly curved upward, indicating she is only slightly pleased or flattered, nowhere near gloating, while her large eyelids drop in contemplation, capturing her sense of the sorrowful consequences of a married woman going to an admiring king.

In denial of the Lord's recent moral agenda, David continues a series of actions that become increasingly grotesque. Bathsheba has no idea how vicious David is when she allows him to go into her, because hidden from her is his killer instinct, which is now directed at her husband. David has Joab order her husband Uriah, who is in Joab's battling army, to come to him (2 Sam 11:6). On arrival, David makes false conversation so Uriah thinks he has been brought home as a messenger for a debriefing of the battle. David asks Uriah how Joab is doing and other news from the front, but then he sends him home with a gift, seemingly to have Uriah sleep with his wife so that he will appear responsible for her offspring (2 Sam 11:7-8). Ironically, unlike David, Uriah has a sense of morality and loyalty, and will not go home; instead he sleeps at the king's door with David's servants. When David asks him why, after such a journey, he will not go home, Uriah answers "The ark and Israel and Judah dwell in booths; and my lord Jo'ab and the servants of my lord are camping in the open field; shall I then go to my house to eat and to drink, and to lie with my wife? As you live, and as your soul lives, I will not do this thing" (2 Sam 11:11).

David continues to feign friendliness, inviting Uriah to rest at the king's residence for a few days and eat and drink in his presence before returning to battle. Uriah loyally obeys, still denying himself the pleasure of his home and wife (2 Sam 11:12-13). Meanwhile, David writes to Joab, "Set Uri'ah in the forefront of the hardest fighting, and then draw back from him, that he may be struck down, and die" (2 Sam 11:15). Indeed when Uriah returns, Joab puts him in the front lines, and Uriah is slain (2 Sam 11:17). This episode is filled with sadness, but I start to pick up hints that the sadistic fun has just begun for Joab. He knows nothing of David's situation with Bathsheba, but knows David desperately wants Uriah killed, and Joab feels he knows David so well that he can predict his reaction to Uriah's death. Therefore he sends a messenger back to David, with details about attacking a city's walls that he knows will make David furious, telling the messenger to expect to hear David's favorite lecture about Abimelech being killed by a woman throwing a millstone from a wall, and to expect an unrelenting berating about how foolish Joab was to attack the walls, and tells the messenger that when David is at his highest emotional pitch, to calmly puncture his fury with the line "Your servant Uri'ah the Hittite is dead also" (2 Sam 11:21). Joab's teasing equals David's brutality. I can already imagine David's sudden, miffed silence.

The courier delivers Joab's message and tells David that Uriah is dead. Ironically, this time David does not get flustered (he stays in sync with his alter ego Joab) and instead taunts Joab by sending a teasing statement formatted in a philosophical statement about fate, telling the messenger to say, "Do not let this matter trouble you, for the sword devours now one and now another; strengthen your attack upon the city, and overthrow it" (2 Sam 11:25). In fact, since David knows Joab has no problem with which way the sword devours, the remark comes off as more of a smart-ass response, David attacking Joab to assuage his own guilt, a shift from the cold reality that he ordered a killing to make room for his own lust.

After Bathsheba laments the death of her husband Uriah, I am now not surprised how quickly David marries her and they have a son. However, the Lord is "displeased" (2 Sam 11:27) with David's behavior (finally, but one never knows when the Lord will wax moral) and sends the prophet Nathan to deliver David a parable: There is a rich man with plenty of livestock living near a poor man with only a sweet lamb he cherishes, brings it up with his children, feeds it from his cup and cuddles it. When a traveler visits the rich man, instead of using his own stock, he kills the poor man's lamb for his guest (2 Sam 12:1-6).

I wince as David flares with indignation at the rich man's actions, insisting he should die because he "had no pity" (2 Sam 12:6). Nathan slams David—"You are the man. Thus says the LORD, the God of Israel, 'I anointed you king over Israel, and I delivered you out of the hand of Saul; and I gave you your master's house, and your master's wives into your bosom, and gave you the house of Israel and of Judah; and if this were too little, I would add to you as much more. Why have you despised the word of the LORD, to do what is evil in his sight? You have smitten Uri'ah the Hittite with the sword, and have taken his wife to be your wife, and have slain him with the sword of the Ammonites'" (2 Sam 12:7-9). Through Nathan's challenge, David's blindness is made clear and I realize that if David has trouble perceiving his double in this story, I can only have a dim hope for his understanding that Joab is his double that embodies David's own hideous self.

When it comes to chastening, the Lord knows how to yank on a misogynist where it hurts, letting David know that He will take his "wives before [his] eyes, and give them to [his] neighbor, and he shall lie with [his] wives in the sight of this sun" (2 Sam 12:11). This is a well-lit, punch-out punishment, antithetical to David's lack of transparency. Furthermore, he is told his child with Bathsheba will die (2 Sam 12:14), and in what appears to be a more sincere, yet still dramatic appeal to the Lord, David fasts and lays on the ground all night, pleading for the child's life, but to no avail (2 Sam 12:16). The servants are afraid to tell David the news of the infant's death lest he harm himself out of grief, but the opposite happens (2 Sam 12:18). When he learns of the infant's death, David quickly cleans up, changes his clothes, calmly prays to God, and sits down to a delicious meal (2 Sam 12:19-21). The servants are shocked. They ask David how he could have grieved before the child's death but eats without grief when the child dies. David cannot help but reveal that expediency drives his actions, telling the servants that he fasted and wept while the child was alive because he thought, "'Who knows whether the LORD will be gracious to me, that the child may live?' But now he is dead; why should I fast? Can I bring him back again?" (2 Sam 12:22-23). I am nonplussed that in a flash, David's heart can turn from spring fever to winter frost.

I know I should be shocked that David wastes no further time in mourning; but I am not surprised when, after comforting Bathsheba, he puts his penis into her again and she bears another son, Solomon (2 Sam 12:24). David's actions are of no surprise to me, but the Lord's are: quickly and unexpectedly He puts his anger for the house of David aside and loves Solomon, calling him Jedidiah, meaning "beloved by the LORD" (2 Sam 12:24-25). I suspect, however, that this reprieve will not last long. In the meantime, Joab takes the royal city of the Ammonites and tells David to get off his ass and use his people to encamp at the outskirts of the city so they take credit for the victory, Joab warning, "lest I take the city, and it be called by my name" (2 Sam 12:28). David can now easily finish off the city and remove the crown from the king, which is then placed on his head (2 Sam 12:30). Again, Joab is David's sword and owns stock in his soul. David puts all the cities of the Ammonites under heavy labor and returns to Jerusalem (2 Sam 12:31).

Bigger problems for David are yet to come. I find out that his son Amnon falls in love with Tamar, the sister of David's other son, Absalom (different mother). Amnon frustrates the hell out of himself knowing she is a virgin and that he cannot have her (2 Sam 13:1-2). Amnon's friend Jonadab, a nasty spider, sees his bud looking glum, probes to find out that he furiously wants to go into Tamar's vagina, and advises Amnon to start a web by feigning illness. When David shows concern and wants to help with what appears to be his son's sickness, Jonadab tells Amnon to have David request that Tamar prepare him food and "eat it from her hand" (2 Sam 13:5), a camouflaged baby-step of foreplay. Tamar bakes cakes for Amnon, emptying them on his lap (unintentional baby-step foreplay?), but he refuses to eat until everyone is sent away except her, and when he asks if he can eat cakes from her hand, grabs her and asks her to lie with him (2 Sam 13:10-11). Tamar responds, "No, my brother, do not force me; for such a thing is not done in Israel; do not do this wanton folly. As for me, where could I carry my shame? And as for you, you would be as one of the wanton fools in Israel" (2 Sam 13:12-13). She tells Amnon to "speak to the king; for he will not withhold [her] from [him] (2 Sam 13:13). But Amnon does not listen and, "being stronger than she" (2 Sam 13:14), rapes Tamar.

Then Amnon gets especially ugly. Because of his shame and love-defeated lust, he shifts his self-hatred onto Tamar, despising "her with very great hatred; so that the hatred with which he hated her was greater than the love with which he had loved her" (2 Sam 13:15). Finding out about this makes me sick to my stomach. And things keep getting worse. Amnon bolts the door on Tamar (2 Sam 13:16-17); she protests that this rejection is even a greater sin than the rape, and, ironically still wearing the long-sleeved robes of virgins, rends them and smears ashes on her head (2 Sam 13:18-19). Her grief draws the attention of her brother Absalom, who guesses she has been with Amnon and takes her into his house where she lives in desolation (2 Sam 13:20). The violation piques David's anger. Of course, this time I cannot help but sympathize with David.

Absalom is furious; he hates Amnon for raping Tamar, but carefully speaks with him "neither good nor bad" (2 Sam 13:22), revealing neither positive nor negative feelings, hiding out until an opportune time, using the same cat-like patience I see used by both Joab and David over and over again. But I am surprised how long he keeps his anger under his robes. In fact, Absalom waits two years; then during a sheep-shearing endeavor, he convinces David to let him take all his brothers along and then commands his servants to kill Amnon, which they do. The other brothers immediately scatter (2 Sam 13:23-29); however, David receives a rumor that Absalom killed all his sons (2 Sam 13:30). Then, out of nowhere, sleazy Jonadab appears again, the nasty spider who had encouraged Amnon to violate Tamar in the first place, but this time he takes delight in being the one to correct the rumor of the death of all the sons, letting David know that only Amnon was skewered for Tamar's sake (2 Sam 13:32). From what I have learned about Jonadab, I see he slyly uses his message-bringing status to help cover his own threads in the sordid affair.

When the sons reappear, David is emotionally undone. Absalom flees (2 Sam 13:37). David longs for Absalom, who disappears for three years, not realizing that David is "comforted about Amnon, seeing he was dead" (2 Sam 13:39). I need to investigate as to whether Absalom might feel he cannot come home without facing repercussions, although no one ever suggests he should, and in fact, David's private reaction implies that he thinks Amnon's death is justified—although I know David can be one person in private and another in public. Maybe Absalom knows too. In any case, Joab soon steps in, after perceiving "that the king's heart went out to Ab'salom" (2 Sam 14:1). Joab stages an elaborate performance that, based on previous plots, I doubt comes from any good intent. He wants Absalom to come home, not out of love for David (the shadow does not empathize with his master), but because he senses that rebellious outsiders are dangerous and must be watched. He fetches a wise woman from Tekoa, whom he disguises as a mourner, and instructs her to act like a grief-stricken person, then gives her a script, putting "the words in her mouth" (2 Sam 14:3). She delivers to David what appears to be a parable about having lost her husband, then having her two sons quarrel, one killing the other, necessitating her fending off family that wants revenge for the killing, but whom she fears would, by killing her only son, "quench my coal which is left, and leave to my husband neither name nor remnant upon the face of the earth" (2 Sam 14:7).

Again I am both impressed and sickened at how skillful Joab is at staging a performance. Once he sets it in motion and the woman knows she has David's sympathy, Joab has her in position to persuade David to make an effort to bring Absalom home. The woman plays humble, claiming any guilt for giving her living son a reprieve can be on her and to "let the king and his throne be guiltless" (2 Sam 14:9), thereby securing assurances from David that if anyone bothers her about revenging her dead son by killing her live son, to bring that person to him because "as the LORD lives, not one hair of your son shall fall to the ground" (2 Sam 14:11). Knowing David is committed to her, she asks for an honest word with him whereby she points out that "in giving this decision the king convicts himself, inasmuch as the king does not bring his banished one home again" (2 Sam 14:13), and then waxes philosophical, "We must all die, we are like water spilt on the ground, which cannot be gathered up again" (an appeal to his fear of fleeting time), but adds, "God will not take away the life of him who devises means not to keep his banished one an outcast" (2 Sam 14:14) (an appeal to David's guilt), and then finishes off with a heavy dose of flattery—"My lord the king is like the angel of God to discern good and evil" (2 Sam 14:17).

I know David and Joab are mirrors: even if David cannot articulate Joab's reasons for wanting Absalom back into the fold, he subconsciously knows that Joab has driven the whole performance; so I am not caught off guard when suddenly David point-blank asks the wise woman if Joab put her up to her morality play. The woman immediately confesses (2 Sam 14:19) and, as a kindred David-Joab falsifier, even uses her exposure as another excuse to flatter David, praising his ability to perceive a deception (2 Sam 14:20). When David asks Joab to bring Absalom back, Joab enters center stage and plays his part, falling on his face to the ground and blessing the king (2 Sam 14:22). David, in concert with his shadow, says nothing to Joab about his deception.

Despite years of absence, Joab brings Absalom back immediately (2 Sam 14:23). I expect David to grasp his son to his bosom; instead the public David plays the disciplinarian to show he is in command, ordering Absalom to stay in his own house and "not to come into [his] presence" (2 Sam 14:24); and Absalom obeys. Absalom, now described as a paragon of beauty, has three sons and a beautiful daughter who he names after his abused sister, Tamar (2 Sam 14:25-27). He lives with his family for two years in Jerusalem without seeing David (2 Sam 14:28).

After two years, Absalom has a harsh reality check with Joab after the latter ignores two requests to come to Absalom. Absalom, I ascertain, then has the hutzpah to set Joab's barley fields on fire to get his attention (2 Sam 14:29-30). This gives Joab even more reason to be inflamed, but he dampers his anger for now and goes to Absalom, who asks why Joab made him return to David if he was not going to be with his father. He requests that Joab deliver his wishes to see David (2 Sam 14:31-32), and seems willing to pay any cost: "If there is any guilt in me, let him kill me" (2 Sam 14:32). The message delivered, Absalom comes before David, who kisses him (2 Sam 14:33). Absalom's acceptance results in his prosperity, underscored by "a chariot and horses, and fifty men to run before him" (2 Sam 15:1). This seems to be an attempt to make up for lost prince-time.

Still Absalom is not satisfied. I am startled by his newly aggressive actions: early every morning he rushes to the city gate and sets up shop, grabbing anyone coming to see David to settle a suit, seducing them with, "your claims are good and right" (2 Sam 15:3), but warning them there will be "no man deputed by the king to hear [them]" (2 Sam 15:3), adding that if he were the judge, "then every man with a suit or cause might come to me, and I would give him justice" (2 Sam 15:4); then, really laying the gush on, he takes the person's hand and kisses it (2 Sam 15:5). Political sleaze at his fingertips, Absalom "stole the hearts of the men of Israel" (2 Sam 15:6). I need to investigate to see if all this desperation to win acceptance from the kingdom is compensation for having been out of his father's graces for so long. David's kiss obviously does not make up for that rejection. In fact, just as Absalom grabs David's attention, he punishes David by stealing his subjects' hearts.

I discover that after four years the treachery escalates. Absalom is a power-desperate David yet without David's sly caution, resulting in child-sloppy moves. After asking David's permission to return to Jerusalem to worship the Lord, and David telling him to go in peace, Absalom "sent secret messengers throughout all the tribes of Israel, saying, 'As soon as you hear the sound of the trumpet, then say, 'Ab'salom is king at Hebron!'" (2 Sam 15:10). He even sends for Ahithophel, David's counselor, to strengthen the façade that Absalom is now in charge (2 Sam 15:12). The conspiracy grows stronger. David, hearing of Absalom's trick, knows how quickly power-lust can shift to the sword, even within families, and so he flees, leaving ten of his concubines to keep his household (2 Sam 15:14-16).

Like the captain of a ship, David allows all the tribes of Israel to flee in safety before him, although many, such as the loyal Ittai the Gittite, refuse to do this (2 Sam 15:18-19). This support keeps David in humble mode. He tells his priests to carry the ark back to Jerusalem, claiming that if God is still with him, the Lord will have

David see the ark and the city again, and if not, then he will accept the Lord's pleasure in dumping him (2 Sam 15:25-26). In another large gesture of humility, David waits in the wilderness for word of God's acceptance; then he walks barefoot and weeping up the Mount of Olives (2 Sam 15:30). However, on hearing of Ahithophel's desertion, ever the tactician, David's spunk returns as he begs the Lord to "turn the counsel of Ahith'ophel into foolishness" (2 Sam 15:31). I discover that David has enough fire to convince Hushai the Archite to pretend to be a defector and go to Absalom promising the same counsel he gave David as a pretext to spy on him (2 Sam 15:32-36).

I begin to perceive that the psychic torments get more complicated. A remnant of Saul's kingdom becomes a new splinter. David runs into Ziba, the servant of Jonathan's son Mephibosheth, who unexpectedly freshens David's supplies (2 Sam 16:1). David, always apprehensive when it comes to the house of Saul, asks Ziba why all the concern and wonders where Mephibosheth is, to which Ziba leaks out that "he remains in Jerusalem; for he said, 'Today the house of Israel will give me back the kingdom of my father'" (2 Sam 16:3). David immediately undermines this hope by offering Ziba all that belongs to Mephibosheth (2 Sam 16:4). Soon after, Shimei, from the house of Saul, who is not so hospitable, obviously intuiting David's hidden antipathies, curses and throws stones at David, calling him a worthless man of blood, and taunting him: "The LORD has avenged upon you all the blood of the house of Saul, in whose place you have reigned; and the LORD has given the kingdom into the hand of your son Ab'salom" (2 Sam 16:8).

Joab's brother Abishai calls Shimei a "dead dog" (2 Sam 16:9) and is willing to lop his head off, so David immediately distances himself from the two brothers (still not wanting to be perceived as anti-the-house-of-Saul), exclaiming, "What have I to do with you, you sons of Zeru'iah?" (2 Sam 16:10), and claiming if he is being cursed because the Lord has directed it, then who are they to say he does not deserve it, especially since his own son seeks his life, so how much more a Benjaminite would want it. David the humble. The unimpressed Shimei, looking down at David's party, continues his frantic tossing of stones and cursing all along the ridge (2 Sam 16:13). I have seen

David kill for lesser reasons, so his humility seems disingenuous. I find it hard to imagine, based on David's past aggressiveness, that he will allow these insults, which he pretends to blow off, fade any more than Joab or Abishai would, and the fact that both those killers are on his mind, even though only one is present, tells me his Joab-alter-ego is never far from influencing his decisions.

I detect that David's humility withers further. In the next scene, I witness Hushai greeting and flattering Absalom as part of his espionage work, but when he is asked why he has left his friend David and responds with a phony response about wanting to help David's son (2 Sam 16:16-19), Absalom abruptly turns away from him. Instead Absalom asks advice from Ahithophel, a sleazy hired sword, looked up to by both David and Absalom, whose advises Absalom to strengthen his men's commitment by proving his disloyalty to his father (like a gang member proving loyalty to a new group by shanking a past confident). The plan is meant to hit David, who collects women like rugs, in the testicles. A tent is pitched on a roof for a pornographic show where "Ab'salom [goes] in to his father's concubines in sight of all of Israel" (2 Sam 16:22). (I bet Hushai must be wondering what kind of act he could possibly come up with that would have appealed as much to Absalom's ego.)

Pumped up from seeing his roof production come off, Ahithophel requests to go after David while he is weary and discouraged, strike him down, and bring all the people back to Absalom "as a bride comes home to her husband" (2 Sam 17:3). It's a distasteful metaphor that nonetheless captures all the love and acceptance I think Ahithophel senses Absalom so desperately desires from his father. At the same time, I observe that Absalom unexpectedly bites David's bait and calls in undercover Hushai for advice, who in turn undermines Ahithophel's advice, suggesting David and his men are not weary but rather enraged "like a bear robbed of her cubs in the field" (2 Sam 17:8), his own counter-metaphor implying David's fierceness is solely aimed at getting his son back. To sabotage Ahithophel's plans, Hushai reminds Absalom that David is a military expert who will hide out and use the first fallen as a sign of Absalom's weakness, scaring off further rebellion, and advises that the best counter to David is for Absalom to go into battle himself.

If David goes into a city, Hushai suggests, then he and Absalom with all of Israel will drag that whole city into the valley (2 Sam 17:13). I find out that Absalom's war counsel picks Hushai's advice over Ahithophel's counsel, thus ensuring Absalom's defeat. Hushai sends word to David of Absalom's plans and warns that Ahithophel is counseling against David (2 Sam 17:15-16). I speculate that because Ahithophel knows Absalom will not follow his counsel (and understands he has burned his bridges with David), his purpose in life based on a symbiotic relationship with powerful leaders dries to desert dust. Nevertheless, I am stunned when Ahithophel hangs himself (2 Sam 17:23), but not surprised when, without any commemoration of Ahithophel's death, Absalom picks a new general, Amasa (2 Sam 17:25).

I watch David gather up thousands of soldiers and divide them in thirds, equal parts to Joab, Abishai, and Ittai (2 Sam 18:1-2). He tells them he will march with them, but these warriors order him, "You shall not go out. For if we flee, they will not care about us. If half of us die, they will not care about us. But you are worth ten thousand of us; therefore it is better that you send us help from the city" (2 Sam 18:3). David does not argue, agreeing to do what they think best, and stands by the side of the gate while the armies, in thousands and hundreds, pass by him (2 Sam 18:4). I have seen this before: David in a stand-back position while others do his miserable work. Also, I wonder if the commanders realize that this time, especially with his son the object of attack, David would be likely to compromise their military aggression. I bet deep down David knows it too. He has to be torn. A mixture of guilt, political expediency, fear, and love must wrack his soul when he orders the three commanders to "deal gently for my sake with the young man Ab'salom" (2 Sam 18:5). However, I conjecture that political expediency, so much in David's blood, underlies the impulse to give those orders so loudly that all the people hear them, insuring they know his heart is with his son who he needs to capture.

Deep in the forests of Ephraim, David's armies attack Absalom's armies of Israel, where twenty thousand men are slaughtered (2 Sam 18:6-7), the battles spreading out over the country, but "the forest devoured more people that day than the sword" (2 Sam 18:8), as if nature has lashed back at the indecency of a power struggle that originated with Absalom's terrible sense of rejection and David's need to persevere against his son at any cost. This disjointed misery, the world out of order when an estranged adult child cannot find a parent, let alone that same child does battle with that parent, is accentuated by Absalom "left hanging between heaven and earth" (2 Sam 18:9) because his mule passes under heavy branches, leaving Absalom wedged in the tree by the neck during a chance encounter with David's servants.

When Joab gets this news from a witness, he tells the messenger he would have paid him in silver if he had struck Absalom to the ground (2 Sam 18:11). As David's shadow, Joab has no guilt, no empathy, no indecisiveness, and focuses only on military advantage. The witness answers, "Even if I felt in my hand the weight of a thousand pieces of silver, I would not put forth my hand against the king's son" (2 Sam 18:12), reminding Joab that all heard David's request to not harm Absalom. Then the witness strikes at Joab's infidelity: "On the other hand, if I had dealt treacherously against [Absalom's] life (and there is nothing hidden from the king), then you yourself would have stood aloof" (2 Sam18:13). Joab tells the man he "will not waste time like this" (2 Sam 18:14), and then takes action into his own hand, slamming three darts into Absalom's heart as he dangles, still alive, from the branch. Ten of Joab's armor-bearers then alleviate Joab's culpability by striking and killing Absalom themselves, throwing his body into a pit, and covering it with boulders (2 Sam 18:14-17). Joab calls off the pursuit of the forces of Israel and, with their leader dead, Absalom's supporters all flee for their homes (2 Sam 18:17).

When Ahimaaz wants to send tidings to David that the Lord has delivered him (2 Sam 18:19), Joab flips to decency mode, ordering, "You may carry tidings another day, but today you shall carry no tidings, because the king's son is dead" (2 Sam 18:20). Joab sends a Cushite with news to David instead, but Ahimaaz outruns him. Seeing Ahimaaz, who is a man of good reputation, David assumes good tidings (2 Sam 18:23-27); however, when David asks about Absalom, Ahimaaz pretends the fighting was too obscure to know what actually happened (2 Sam 18:29). When the Cushite arrives with the same message, and is asked the same question, he tries to answer indirectly with what he thinks is a more appropriate text: "May the enemies of my lord the king, and all who rise up against you for evil, be like that young man" (2 Sam 18:32). David quickly sees through the euphemisms and is moved to tears: "O my son Ab'salom, my son, my son Ab'salom! Would I had died instead of you, O Ab'salom, my son, my son" (2 Sam 18:33). I can feel that David is pained more than ever before, now at his most sincere, his love of his lost son trumping any considerations for political perseverance. The people are told of David's grief, "so the victory that day was turned into mourning for all the people" (2 Sam 19:2), which in turn sparks communal guilt so that "the people stole into the city that day as people steal in who are ashamed when they flee in battle" (2 Sam 19:3).

Joab suffers no such shame, and in fact delivers the most insightful, albeit disturbing, passage I hear in David's story. With the full dark force of David's own aggressiveness, Joab marches into the grief-stricken David's house and scolds him:

> You have today covered with shame the faces of all your servants, who have this day saved your life, and the lives of your sons and your daughters, and the lives of your wives and your concubines, because you love those who hate you and hate those who love you. For you have made clear today that commanders and servants are nothing to you; for today I perceive that if Ab'salom were alive and all of us were dead today, then you would be pleased. Now therefore arise, go out and speak kindly to your servants; for I swear by the LORD, if you do not go, not a man will stay with you this night; and this will be worse for you than all the evil that has come upon you from your youth until now (2 Sam 19:5-7).

Joab tries to guilt David by turning his grief into poison that shames those who serve him ("You have today covered with shame the faces of your servants"), by raising the evilness of Absalom's ambitions above David's grief for him ("love those who hate you"), by acknowledging David's contempt for his Joab-shadow and by recasting Joab's own devotion as love ("hate those who love you"), by acknowledging David's use and manipulation of people ("commanders and servants are nothing to you"), and by referencing all the deceptions David commits throughout his life ("all the evil that has come upon you from your youth until now"). I am sure David must feel disgusted with Joab, but there is too much truth in the statement for David to ignore him; therefore, he takes his seat at the gate where he must dry up his grief and make himself presentable to his people (2 Sam 19:8). Watching David depend on Joab's sword and verbal muscle, I can sense David's growing resentment. Is this disguised disgust of himself, his own shadow? If David could acknowledge that Joab was his dark alter ego and confront him, David could become immune to Joab's affronts, and rise in heroic stature.

With Absalom dead and Joab shaking David back into action, political pieces that David lost begin to meld. All of Israel forgets Absalom and instead remembers David delivering them from the Philistines (2 Sam 19:9-10). David reminds the tribes of Judah that they are his "bone and [his] flesh" (2 Sam 19:12) and so should not be the last to accept him. With resentment for Joab festering his soul, David makes Absalom's commander, Amasa, his own commander, also calling him his "bone and [his] flesh" (2 Sam 19:13). David accepts Shimei's apologies for cursing and rock-throwing (despite Abishai still offering to lop his head off [2 Sam 19:20-21]) and greets Saul's grandson Mephibosheth, who calls David an angel of God and tries to diminish any guilt David has about replacing the house of Saul by saying it was doomed before David was king (and when David in turn tries to throw him a bone by dividing up land between Mephibosheth and Saul's servant Ziba, Mephibosheth demurs, saying to give it all to Ziba since the only important thing is for David to return safely home [2 Sam 19:26-30]). Yet I find it difficult to have any faith in David's "good will." His spiritual well-being has bled out more and more to Joab's will. I need to discover his hidden agenda.

Getting ready to cross the Jordan, David runs into Barzillai the Gileadite, who gave David provisions in the past and is now eighty years old. Despite David's generous offer to provide for Barzillai in Jerusalem, Barzillai claims he is only dead weight, and gives away his servant Chimham to David instead (who graciously offers to do whatever is a benefit to him and his master) (2 Sam 19:32-37). David also benefits from a competition between the men of Israel and the men of Judah, regarding who came over to David first and thus has first rights to him (2 Sam 19:41-43). It's one big love fest. I am startled by how quickly David benefits from his son's death, how quickly a tragedy turns to political advantage, and how much this success is dependent on Joab dragging David's psyche back into the public arena.

I can see the niceties do not last for long. Out of the blue, nastiness sweeps the scene. A Benjaminite named Sheba, craving a following, pulls the men of Israel, a fickle group, out of allegiance with David (2 Sam 20:1-2). Next David, the collector of women as if blankets, visits his ten concubines, whom Absalom had put his penis into, and proceeds to transfer his anger for Absalom onto them and resolve his guilt for doing so all in one process: he makes sure they have provisions but never again goes into their vaginas and shuts them up under guard until the day they die (2 Sam 20:3). Next he orders Amasa to go after Sheba, who "will do us more harm than Ab'salom" (2 Sam 20:6), with Joab and Abishai joining pursuit. I know that Joab has not bothered grabbing David by his pubic hairs only to concede his own command to someone else; therefore, when he meets up with Amasa, Joab trips forward, his sword seeming to mistakenly slide out, so that as he greets Amasa, asking, "Is it well with you, my brother?" (2 Sam 20:9)—Joab grabbing him by his beard to kiss him—the sword has already slid into Joab's other hand, and he "shed [Amasa's] bowels to the ground, without striking a second blow; and he died" (2 Sam 20:10).

Then I witness another nauseating, violent Joab performance. As Joab and Abishai continue to pursue Sheba, one of Joab's puerile-humored thugs gloatingly stands next to Amasa, who is "wallowing in his own blood" (2 Sam 20:12), the thug mockingly pretending Amasa is still an alternative leader to line up behind and asking all those who are instead for Joab and David to move on and follow Joab instead, but the soldiers are so literal that they stop where Amasa lies until his body is finally dragged off the main road and buried under a garment (2 Sam 20:12). I doubt I am witnessing the same army that went forth in spring with a snap to its step. When Joab's army finally gets to Abel of Bethmaacah, where Sheba is holed up, they mound up earth to the walls and get ready to take out the whole city until a wise woman inhabitant calls out to Joab, reminding him that in the good old days people would take counsel to settle such matters, and that she is "one of those who are peaceable and faithful in Israel" and wonders why Joab would "seek to destroy a city which is a mother in Israel; why will you swallow up the heritage of the LORD?" (2 Sam 20:19). I wince when Joab responds, "Far be it, that I should swallow up or destroy! That is not true" (2 Sam 20:20-21). He explains what Sheba has done, but the wise woman of peace is already on Joab's page, yelling, "Behold, his head shall be thrown to you over the wall" (2 Sam 20:21), and in the next second the noggin comes flying over the embankments (2 Sam 20:22). Joab returns to David and I notice not a word is said about either Sheba or Amasa. David and his shadow have no need to talk. I behold David silently depending on Joab once more and wonder how much longer David can secretly grind his teeth.

In the quirky world of power, the Lord suddenly antes in with a long-forgotten thorn. The Lord starts a famine, remembering, "There is bloodguilt on Saul and on this house, because he put the Gib'eonites to death" (2 Sam 21:1). The people of Israel had sworn to protect the Gibeonites but "Saul had sought to slay them in his zeal for the people of Israel and Judah" (2 Sam 21:2). Zeal is a universal poison, a deadly, self-righteous fervor. David wants a quick fix. The Gibeonites do not want treasure or Israel's blood as retribution (2 Sam 21:4); instead they demand vengeance closer to the source—the hanging of seven of Saul's sons (2 Sam 21:6). The pragmatic David moves quickly. David hangs two sons of Ripzah, Saul's concubine, and five sons of Merab (2 Sam 21:8), Saul's daughter, but Jonathan's son Mephibosheth gets a pass because of David's oath with Jonathan before the Lord (2 Sam 21:7).

When David hears of Ripzah's grief, driving all birds and animals away, he is inspired to take Saul's and Jonathan's bones away from the men of Jabeshgilead, who had stolen them after the Philistines hung the two men (2 Sam 21:12-13). I wonder if David feels this makes up for Ripzah's interference with nature, which appears to be preventing famine-ending rains because, as soon as David takes the bones away, the Lord revives the land (2 Sam 21:14). I have learned how natural it is for David to shift from being a killer to using compassion for pragmatic solutions.

Then a second thorn sticks David: the Philistines decide to try another go at him. Abishai needs to step in to put them down, because "David grew weary" (2 Sam 21:15), and David's men become protective: "You shall no more go out with us to battle, lest you quench the lamp of Israel" (2 Sam 21:17). After more encounters and wins over the Philistines, David sings to the Lord in appreciation of his victory over both the hand of his enemies and the hand of Saul (2 Sam 22:1). I think a publicist is writing his material, someone who wants to glamorize the David I have been spying. The song is full of braggadocio that David has learned to hide: the Lord "delivered me, because he delighted in me" (2 Sam 22:20), "by thee I can crush a troop, and by my God I can leap over a wall" (2 Sam 22:30), "my arms can bend a bow of bronze" (2 Sam 22:35), "thou didst deliver me from men of violence" (2 Sam 22:49). I wonder, what makes David different from those violent men? Different because Joab wields his sword for him? Different because David seethes silently with resentment and guilt and hides his hand?

David is not someone who would exclaim his destiny has been a clean sweep or without torment or without dependency on someone who is disgusting; however, the phrases in the song suggest the opposite: the "LORD rewarded me according to my righteousness" (2 Sam 22:21), "I was blameless before him, and I kept myself from guilt" (2 Sam 22:24), "Thou didst make my enemies turn their backs to me, those who hated me" (2 Sam 22:41). The lyrics are supposed to be "the last words of David" (2 Sam 23:1), but when the lyrics include such lines as "the Spirit of the LORD speaks by me, his word is upon my tongue" (2 Sam 23:2), or "but godless men are all like thorns that are thrown away; for they cannot be taken with the hand" (2 Sam 23:6), I think now I understand why there is no mention of Joab, neither for credit or blame—the person who wrote these lyrics is a paid sloganeer who, even if he had insights about David and his doppelganger, is paid to bite his tongue.

Now I am concerned that someone is deliberately trying to rebrand David, because suddenly his life is surrounded by new lists of commanders and of victories, written without the revelation of the psychological relationships I have glimpsed up to this point. My vision begins to clear when the writer describes the Lord getting irritable and incites David against Israel by asking David to number the people of Israel and Judah, a task that is generally looked down upon because large numbers make a group seem arrogant. David passes the job on to Joab, who wonders, "Why does my lord the king delight in this thing?" (2 Sam 24:3). I do, too. Is God testing David? How? After more than nine months, Joab comes back with a count of "men who drew the sword" (2 Sam 24:9) of eight hundred thousand in Israel and five hundred thousand in Judah. The whole affair makes David feel sick and sinful (2 Sam 24:10).

Whether intended or not, the Lord has tested David, whose queasiness might come from his understanding that the pride he feels knowing the strength of his army is a sin, and he asks the Lord to "take away the iniquity of thy servant; for I have done very foolishly" (2 Sam 24:10). The Lord obliges and tells David's seer Gad to present three alternative punishments for David to pick from: three years of famine over all his lands, flight for three months from a pursuing enemy, or three days of pestilence (2 Sam 24:13). David's humility does not last long. His choice should not surprise me. He turns away from the least harmful punishment to his people, having an enemy chase him—it would only be for three months and there is no mention of ultimate defeat—but David's ego will not suffer from looking like a loser. Instead he gives the go-ahead with either of the punishments that will hurt his people the most, plague or pestilence.

David rationalizes not picking the curse of being pursued—"let us fall into the hand of the LORD, for his mercy is great; but let me not fall into the hand of man" (2 Sam 24:14)—pretending only pestilence and famine come from the Lord (they are natural occurrences), ignoring that the Lord is responsible for all three punishments. When the angel of death starts by wiping out seventy thousand with the pestilence and is on a roll to take out more, the Lord finally stops him (2 Sam 24:15-16). David sees the horror of his choice, now asking the Lord to raise his hand only against him and not his innocent tribes (2 Sam 24:17). (This is not the first time I observe David face the consequences of his decisions too late.) Although Araunah, a person who the angel stands next to, offers up his threshing floor for an altar place and his oxen to sacrifice, David insists he pay in silver as part of his penitence (2 Sam 24:21-24). This has the look of humility, but really David gets off cheap. The plague stops.

I notice 2 Samuel melds seamlessly into 1 Kings, where I find David, now old, incapable of getting warm. He is given a beautiful maiden, Abishag, to cuddle and nurse him (1 Kings 1:1-3), although he never goes into her (1 Kings 1:4). Before he gets too comfortable, Adonijah, another of David's handsome sons, pulls an "Absalom" and declares himself king, again complete with fifty runners announcing his arrival (1 Kings 1:5). Joab and David's priest Abiathar reach out to join Adonijah, but not Nathan the prophet, nor Shimei, the reformed rock-thrower, nor other strong men who stay with David (1 Kings 7-8). To mobilize against Adonijah, Nathan, in cahoots with Bathsheba, Solomon's mother, plans for a one-two punch whereby first Bathsheba bee-lines to David in disbelief that Adonijah is replacing Solomon as the promised heir to his throne, and then, before David can absorb her words, Nathan scampers into the room uttering the same disbelief (1 Kings 1:11-14). Their teamed-up incredulity pressures David to immediately signal Solomon's rightful place by having him ride David's mule, ordering the priests to blow the horn, and announcing Solomon as king (1 Kings 1:30-33).

Joab, meanwhile, is caught off guard and wonders, "What does this uproar in the city mean?" (1 Kings 1:41). He finds out that Nathan the prophet has anointed Solomon, and furthermore, that the crowd noise is from people rejoicing that David has set Solomon up to be even more famous than himself (1 Kings 1:42-48). Adonijah's supporters quickly check out (1 Kings 1:49). Adonijah fears Solomon will kill him (1 Kings 1:50). Solomon, who crushes like a millstone, has no bones about it: "If [Adonijah] prove to be a worthy man, not one of his hairs shall fall to the earth; but if wickedness is found in him, he shall die" (1 Kings 1:52).

I realize that David is getting closer to death. As the end of his life approaches, he starts acting on years of buried resentments. At long last, it seems, he no longer needs his shadow Joab for his dirty work. Only now does he voice indignation of Joab's killing of Amasa and, from much earlier, his killing of the scoundrel Abner, both commanders who never were the muscle that built David's success but also—because they never embodied David's guilt-ridden ambitions or shamed him into action—are now easily idealized (1 Kings 2:5). Of course, he takes no responsibility at all for Joab's violence. He still cannot face his shadow. David tells Solomon to act on his own wisdom regarding Joab, but his message is clear: "You know also what Jo'ab the son of Zeru'iah did to me" (I Kings 2:5). David also terminates disguising his resentment for the house of Saul, taking back the forgiveness he gave to rock-throwing Shimei, who has been loyal to David since he repented (1 Kings 2:8). Again David disingenuously tells Solomon to act on his wisdom, but reminds Solomon of Shimei's rock-throwing curses, making it clear that even though he told Shimei he would not kill him, he didn't mean it, as he tells Solomon to "hold him not guiltless, for you are a wise man; you will know what you ought to do to him, and you shall bring his gray head down with blood to Sheol" (I Kings 2:9). Solomon is not being asked to make wise decisions. I can hear David's bitterness in these last requests before death.

Watching David makes me wonder what in one's soul determines whether that person leaves life, if not forgiving those one resents, at least allowing those resentments to dissipate? What determines if one dies unclenching the fist that holds the sword? How much is determined by the soul one is born with, how much by experience? How much was impossible for David to learn—about others, about himself, about his love-hate relationship with his shadow Joab—after a forty-five year rule, because of his hardened soul?

After David dies, Adonijah has the nerve to ask Solomon's mother, Bathsheba, for help with one last request: to grant him, for his wife, David's cuddling maiden, Abishag (1 Kings 2:17). Solomon's response to his mother reveals an unexpected sarcastic side to his personality: "And why do you ask Ab'ishag the Shu'nammite for Adoni'jah? Ask for him the kingdom also; for he is my elder brother, and on his side are Abi'athar the priest and Joab" (I Kings 2:22). Then, however, he gets very unfunny—he immediately has Adonijah slaughtered (1 Kings 2:25). I watch Solomon, who crushes like a millstone again, act less cautiously than his father. He tells Abiathar, the priest, that he also should be killed for allying with Adonijah but he will spare him for bearing the ark on David's behalf; however, he expels him and strips him of his priesthood (1 Kings 2:26-27).

Joab, now in a panic, runs to the tent of the lord, and demands that if he must die, he will die there (1 Kings 2:29-30); so Solomon orders his hit man, Benaiah, to oblige and kill Joab in the tent of the Lord "and thus take away from [him] and from [his] father's house the guilt for the blood which Jo'ab shed without cause . . . because, without the knowledge of my father David, he attacked and slew with the sword two men more righteous and better than himself" (I Kings 2:31-32). I watched Abner turn against David, and I saw that David never wanted to know of Abner's and Amasa's killings, and I perceived why he remained silent when he did know—because so much of his power was dependent on Joab. Solomon is not wise yet. He does not understand that to acknowledge one's shadow is to join humanity, let alone that his father never acknowledged his own. He has no idea that Joab, who he now kills (1 Kings 2:34), is David's shadow. I understand that Solomon is too innocent to see David the way I have been allowed to spy him. Are we not all too innocent to know all our parents' impure fantasies and ambitions?

Now Benaiah becomes Solomon's commander (1 Kings 2:35), and I suspect he will become his shadow, a rebirth of Joab. To ease his own conscience, Solomon works out a nonsensical compromise with Shimei, a remnant from the house of Saul, telling him to stay in Jerusalem and that if he ventures out, he will bring about his own death (1 Kings 2:36-37). Three years later, Shimei crosses city boundaries to track down runaway slaves (1 Kings 2:39-40) and is reported to Solomon, who brings Shimei before him and reminds him of the restrictions and of his curses and rock throwing at David, and then, without further hesitation, orders Benaiah to smash him to death (1 Kings 2:43-46). So much for remembrances.

Solomon marries the Pharaoh's daughter, thereby forming an allegiance with Egypt (1 Kings 3:1). With the kingdom calm, he has a dream in which the Lord appears and asks him what He could give him (1 Kings 3:5). Solomon thanks the Lord for standing with his father, who walked before the Lord in righteousness (again, not the David I have watched), and then Solomon admits to his own ignorance—"I am but a little child; I do not know how to go out or come in. And thy servant is in the midst of thy people whom thou hast chosen. . . . Give thy servant therefore an understanding mind to govern thy people, that I may discern between good and evil" (I Kings 3:7-9). Since Solomon does not ask for riches or the deaths of enemies, the Lord is so pleased He says, "Behold, I give you a wise and discerning mind, so that none like you has been before you and none like you shall arise after you" (I Kings 3:12), and then He throws in riches and honor too and promises, "If you will walk in my ways, keeping my statutes and my commandments, as your father David walked, then I will lengthen your days" (I Kings 3:14). Again I am puzzled why the Lord remembers David as so righteous, but then realize that Solomon hears the Lord's message in one of his own dreams, where hopeful thinking can make anything positive. I know Solomon will be rewarded, but I also wonder how much the Lord's words are part of Solomon's wish fulfillment. I speculate that Solomon's change in attitude, his becoming wiser, is his own self-fulfilling prophecy. In any case, even if the Lord has spoken to Solomon, I have seen the Lord's views of David change with the winds.

Solomon's first intelligence test comes in a form reminiscent of a parable. Two harlots come to Solomon, both having delivered babies, the first claiming that the second woman slept on her own baby and killed it, then switched her dead baby with the first woman's live baby (1 Kings 3:16-20). When the first woman starts to nurse the baby at her side, she sees it is dead but on closer inspection can see that it is the second woman's infant (1 Kings 3:21). The second woman insists the live baby is hers (1 Kings 3:22). Solomon cleverly mixes drama with psychological insight to bring justice. He asks for his sword and says, "Divide the living child in two, and give half to the one, and half to the other" (I Kings 3:25). The true mother whose child is alive interrupts and says, "Oh, my lord, give her the living child, and by no means slay it" (1 Kings 3:26), so Solomon immediately commands, "Give the living child to the first woman, and by no means slay it; she is its mother" (I Kings 3:27), knowing that a true mother would rather keep her child alive even if it meant having to give the child to another. His decision leaves all of Israel awestruck, convinced that Solomon has the wisdom of God (1 Kings 3:28). I'm impressed too. I like Solomon's boldness, having the security to test plaintiffs and audiences with a moral performance that reminds me of Jesus's render-unto-Caesar encounters with the Pharisees and Herodians.

Yet I know Solomon's magic and wisdom will not last: his kingdom will become divided; his foreign wives and concubines (collected, as with his father, like rugs) will lead him away from God and to idolatry of foreign gods; his relationship with the Queen of Sheba will collapse into Ethiopian legends; his legacy will be desperately kept alive by ancient editors assigning him as the author of the Book of Proverbs, Ecclesiastes, and Song of Songs, even though none of these books have his voice or mentality that I experience in the first book of Kings. Wisdom has different voices, and they are not all Solomon's. He is a human being, part of the house of David, and I can see he will be complex like David; however, I cannot be a further witness to that complexity because those who write about him in the book of Kings take on a different voice that does not reveal an inner self through responses and silences. Now I am only allowed to witness exterior accounts as an outsider, without the writer giving me hints of the hidden. I am grateful that a different voice revealed the story of David. I feel privileged to read a narrative from a writer from so very long ago who took so much care to reveal the hidden nuances and intimacies of power. For me, the story of the Davidic Dynasty comes to a close.

EPISTLE TO *GRAPHINK*
THE ILLUSTRATED JUDGES

Dear *Graphink*,

I hope, by the grace of God, that I will be helpful in assisting you, a cutting-edge publisher of graphic novels, in your desire to illustrate the Book of Judges. Because the book is loaded with battles, ambushes, and grisly scenes, you will be tempted to illustrate the book in a graphic novel format, which always depends on some version of Marvel-DC-based stylistics: radical shifts of visual point of view between frames (i.e. quickly moving from a facial close-up to a distant bird's-eye view of the same character to a worm's-eye-view of the scene from the character's foot); hot lighting that defines everything with dark shadows (from forehead furrows to landscapes); unexpected frame arrangements and changes of frame sizes to focus on action details; 3-D, exaggerated perspective to pull the viewer into the action; images and dialogue balloons occasionally allowed to unexpectedly spill across frame gutters, sharpening frenzied actions.

However, because your marketing plan is to sell this edition through modern art museums, I will suggest to you a method for complementing the narrative with illustrations that appeal to a modern art sensibility. First, you must realize the stories in Judges are surreal narrations: they have panoramic actions that unexpectedly zoom in and focus on nightmarish details; bizarre leaders, often with spotty, undeveloped character traits, arising out of nowhere; plots with large jumps in time; recurring evil incidents that link the strange mini-plots. So, instead of a graphic novel, why not use surreal illustrations that capture one of the most surreal books in the Bible? If you agree, I suggest modeling on René Magritte, who, unlike other surrealists such as Salvador Dali, primarily uses non-action still-life scenes that invite quiet contemplation, an ironic counterpoint to the frenetic activity and bloody horrors of Judges.

Using this method, the illustrations can be repeated with subtle changes as the narrative text moves forward, much as images do in an animated film. In fact, you might want to consider expanding the project to include an animated film of Judges, using these images with narrative voiceovers. As per our contract, I will explain some of the book's important refrains, vignettes, and stories (some of the stories are more complex and longer than others), which I refer to as "Contexts"; then describe a key illustration for each one. I will also mention the Magritte painting that is my recommendation as each illustration's prototype, helping you to understand the colors, spaces, lighting, shapes, and other elements of style to use for your own Judges image.

CONTEXT 1: The unique unifying device of the Book of Judges, repeated almost comically *ad nauseam* as a transition to open virtually every story, is the phrase "And the people of Israel did what was evil in the sight of the LORD" (Judg 2:11). Sometimes they do evil by explicitly worshipping other gods, but in every case they commit the evil of diminishing God's importance, the Israelites taking their well-being for granted, often as a result of having "another generation after them, who did not know the LORD or the work which he had done for Israel" (Judg 2:10). These transitional motifs are the writer's poignant acknowledgement that not only does everybody or every group lose sight of dearly held values, but that this emotional amnesia is unfortunately part of a surreal, repetitive cycle throughout any person's life or any group's history. Human beings slack off.

And within every cycle in Judges, God zaps back by delivering the Israelites into the hands of an enemy who makes Israel utterly miserable, always followed by Israel clamoring for forgiveness, pleading to God to deliver a leader. The Lord is always "moved to pity by their groaning" (Judg 2:18) and empowers a leader in the role of a judge (never elected or part of a monarchist or family dynasty typical in other Old Testament books), and the quirky judge inevitably leads the Israelites to victory (although never with Moses's and Joshua's piety from earlier books nor with the psychological depth of Samuel, Saul, or David who come in later books). Then always, over decades of well-being, the Lord is gradually forgotten, the Israelites behaving "worse than their fathers" (Judg 2:19), and so the cycle starts all over, an endlessly recurring historical nightmare.

ILLUSTRATION FOR CONTEXT 1: The prototypes for these illustrations are Magritte's *La Peine Perdue* (*Wasted Effort*), 1962; *Le Chateau des Pyrenees* (*The Castle of the Pyrenees*), 1959; and *L'échelle de Feu* (*The Ladder of Fire*), 1939. The illustrations should appear every time the line "And the people of Israel did what was evil in the sight of the Lord" appears in the text (Judg 2:11, 3:7, 3:12, 4:1, 6:1, 10:6, 13:1), to represent the disrespect to God. In the illustrations, God will be represented by a stone box that sits on the ground in front of curtains drawn to the sides like curtains of an ark. The box takes on a sense of mystery and importance because there are no other items on the ground, but behind the open curtains there is a bright blue sky full of white clouds, creating an air of everyday normality that is out of sync with the mysterious box. Every time the text about doing evil appears, this box will be defaced differently: one time a soft brown puddle on top of it (reminiscent of cow manure); one time a larger box placed over it; one time with a chiseled crack and a hammer next to it; one time with a boulder on top that has cracked the box; one time with a soft liquid puddle (reminiscent of a pool of urine) surrounding it; one time with part of the box melted; one time with the side of the box pried open, exposing dowels that hold it together. However, every time the Lord punishes the Israelites for their evil, there can be a new illustration where the box is not defaced, but floating off the ground in defiance of gravity, a parallel to the surprise felt by the Israelites when God reminds them of His displeasure and His might. In these scenes, there will be a sword, consumed by flames, lying on the floor in the box's place, an image that will represent God's retribution achieved through the destruction of Israel's power, reminiscent of the flaming sword guarding the tree of life in Genesis (Gen 2:24).

CONTEXT 2: The remaining contexts relate only to particular stories. After the judge Othniel has been given the spirit of the Lord to defeat the king of Mesopotamia, the Israelites do evil in sight of the Lord, so the Lord "strengthened Eglon the king of Moab against Israel" (Judg 3:12) as punishment, and after the Israelites groan and gripe with regret, the Lord raises up Ehud to deliver them (Judg 3:15).

Ehud tricks Eglon, who "was a very fat man" (Judg 3:17), by telling Eglon he has a secret message for him from God. Eglon sends everyone out of the room and then, the two men alone, Ehud thrusts his sword into Eglon's belly and "the hilt also went in after the blade, and the fat closed over the blade, for he did not draw the sword out of his belly; and the dirt came out" (Judg 3:22). As with other parts of Judges, the writer tends to scan a larger plot and then zero in on bizarre, grotesque, darkly humorous details such as all Eglon's abdominal blubber with the intestinal gore that was in the process of making more blubber until it is spilled out. (The name Eglon itself sounds blubbery.) Even Eglon's servants are focused on the blubber-making waste product: when they return to find the door locked by Ehud, they assume Eglon "is only relieving himself in the closet of the cool chamber" (Judg 3:24). The people of Israel slay thousands of Moabites and praise the Lord, but over the course of the next eighty years gradually put Him out of mind, and then a new generation does evil in sight of the Lord and the cycle starts over again.

ILLUSTRATION FOR CONTEXT 2: This story will be illustrated using Magritte's *La Chambre d'Écoute* (*The Listening Room*), 1952-1958, as a template. A stone blocked-wall fortress room is depicted in one-point perspective, the sidewalls running out of the frame, and a locked wooden door is built into one of these sidewalls. There appears to be no other way out. The room has a large bunch of polished grapes, symbols of life, fertility, and well-being, but here they are shockingly out of scale, so large that they unexpectedly dominate the room thereby undermining their own positive symbolism because the cluster, touching the ceiling and sidewalls, leaves no room for other objects or people, thus turning the room into a claustrophobic nightmare. The image captures Eglon's blubbery overindulgence, but also the nightmare created by the Israelites taking their fertile years for granted.

CONTEXT 3: After Ehud dies, the Israelites again do evil in the sight of the Lord (Judg 4:1), so the Lord delivers the Israelites into the hands of Jabin, king of Canaan, and his general Sisera, who beat the crap out of the Israelites for twenty years until they once again groan for forgiveness. This time the Lord emboldens Deborah, a prophetess of Israel, who teams up with her general, Barak, to strike back (Judg 4:3-6). They rise up to defeat Jabin and Sisera's nine hundred chariots but, as in the previous story with Ehud, the sweeping action comes to an abrupt halt and focuses on grisly details. In this case, Sisera flees to the tent of Jael that appears to be a safe haven because Jael's husband, Heber, has a treaty with Jabin. But Jael, implicitly taking over the female power inherent in Deborah, tricks Sisera, asking him to let her comfort him, to "turn aside, my lord, turn aside to me; have no fear" (Judg 4:18), to let her cover him with a rug and give him drink, while she keeps watch for him. When Sisera is all comfy, Jael then "took a tent peg, and took a hammer in her hand, and went softly to him and drove the peg into his temple, till it went down into the ground, as he was lying fast asleep from weariness" (Judg 4:21), the peg cracking through both sides of the skull before staking the head onto terra firma. When Barak arrives, Jael shows off her peg work. Deborah and Jael are celebrated in a lengthy song that some scholars think was written earlier than Judges. The Israelites get another forty years of recycling the recurring nightmare of praise, then becoming complacent and doing evil, only to be punished once again.

ILLUSTRATION FOR CONTEXT 3: Look at Magritte's *La Philosophie dans le Boudoir* (*Philosophy in the Boudoir*), 1947, for a prototype of this description. A frontal view of full ancient Hebrew battle armor hangs on a hook in front of a slightly pockmarked, mud-plastered wall. Two round, full female breasts grow out of the armor, momentarily making the viewer see the armor as the clothing of a person with breasts exposed, Minoan style, but then, in the next moment, the hanging armor snaps the viewer back to seeing the breasts as an illusion. The viewer is left with the final impression of being caught between the two illusions. In front of the armor there is part of a table cut by the picture frame with a pair of war sandals sitting on the table, the toe parts of the sandals having turned into actual toes, making the viewer question whether feet are symbolically demanding the sandals to exist or the sandals are trying to dominate feet asserting their own independence. Scattered around the table surface are several wooden stakes and an ancient mallet. The image captures the ambiguity of female softness and vulnerability being coupled with courage, power, and unhesitant violence.

CONTEXT 4: After forty years to become spiritually cavalier, again the Israelites do what is "evil in the sight of the Lord" (Judg 6:1), get pounded and starved out by the Lord-empowered "Mid'ianites and the Amal'ekites and the people of the East" (Judg 6:3), cry out for forgiveness, and are given Gideon to lead them out of misery. Much of the next three chapters are devoted to Gideon's comical neurosis and lack of faith, not believing the Lord would stand behind his clan, the weakest in Israel, nor behind the weakest guy in the clan, himself, so he demands, "If now I have found favor with thee, then show me a sign that it is thou who speakest with me" (Judg 6:15). In a surreal image, the angel of God has Gideon put "the meat and the unleavened cakes" (Judg 6:20) on a rock, touches the rock with a staff, and burns the items to a crisp. This act is convincing enough for Gideon to feel confident about pulling down an altar devoted to Baal, but not confident enough to do it in the light of day, only at night (Judg 6:27). Still lacking faith, Gideon then sets up another bizarre test for God: he lays out a fleece of wool and demands God show He can create dew on the fleece but not on the ground (Judg 6:37). Even though the next morning Gideon "wrung enough dew from the fleece to fill a bowl with water" (Judg 6:38), Gideon's faith in himself and God is so shaky that he asks God to reverse the order the next day, leaving the fleece dry and the ground wet (Judg 6:39). The Lord obliges.

Now it is the Lord's turn to be skeptical, not about Gideon, who He has empowered, but about whether He, the Lord Himself, will get enough credit for any victories. He cautions Gideon, "The people with you are too many for me to give the Mid'ianites into their hand, lest Israel vaunt themselves against me, saying, 'My own hand has delivered me'" (Judg 7:2), and so asks Gideon to diminish his army by sending home whomever is "fearful and trembling" (Judg 7:3), just to make it clear to everyone that any wins are because of God, not the army's size. The army size shrinks. But God, still insecure about getting a weak press release, thinks Gideon's still-sizable army might get the credit for any victory, so He makes one of the most comical demands in the Bible: He tells Gideon to take his men down to the water and separate out "every one that laps the water with his tongue, as a dog laps" (Judg 7:5) from those who kneel down to drink. When the dog lappers prove to be only three hundred men, God approves that number for an underdog win that will imply God's backing with the requisite praise He will receive (Judg 7:7).

Then the plot turns into a splatter of bizarre actions typical in dreams, flipping between scenes where Gideon displays confidence to ones where he is morally derelict. For instance, Gideon dreams of "a cake of barley bread tumbl[ing] into the camp of Mid'ian" (Judg 7:13), interpreting this dream as a symbol of his victory over the Mid'ians, and so routes them with trumpets and jars of fire (early Molotov cocktails) (Judg 7:18). He then abates the anger of the men of Epharim, who feel left out of the battle until Gideon points out that they were the ones who beheaded the two Mid'ian princes (more than Gideon feels he has done) (Judg 8:1-3), threatens the men of Succoth and of Penuel for not feeding his faint army because they think the weak army should first deliver the Mid'ian kings (Judg 8:5-6), fulfills his physical threats to the men of Succoth and Penuel, catches up with the Mid'ian kings and asks his firstborn to slay them. The firstborn's youthfulness makes him fearful of killing them (Judg 8:20), so the kings ask Gideon to slice their heads off (a surer hand?) and he obliges (Judg 8:21). The men of Israel then ask Gideon to start a dynastic rule over them, but he refuses, worried this could distract from focusing on the Lord (perhaps still thinking about God's earlier skepticism about appropriate praise for wins) (Judg 8:23). Then, out of nowhere, Gideon goes gold crazy, collecting all the gold earrings of the Ishmaelites, the crescents off the Mid'ian's camels, and the Mid'ian kings' jewelry, to make a gold "ephod" so "all Israel played the harlot after it there, and it became a snare to Gideon and to his family" (Judg 8:27), but the reader is never given details on the gold-whoring or why the land enjoys forty years of peace (Judg 8:28) until the cycle starts over again.

ILLUSTRATION FOR CONTEXT 4: The prototype for this illustration idea is Magritte's *Le Blanc-Seing* (*Carte Blanche*), 1965. A camel crosses the desert, his saddle and breastplate shining with gold and gold jewelry dripping off the camel's cavalryman. However, the camel and rider divide into strips interrupted by strips of the desert background, normally hidden by the camel and rider; instead those background strips come forward to replace strips of the camel and rider. In other words, sometimes the background becomes foreground; sometimes the foreground disappears into the background. The uncanny cutting back and forth paradoxically makes each reality unstable, so there is now little trust in either one representing reality. The viewer is jolted into realizing that if the concreteness of one's physical perceptions can become unreliable and never entirely trusted, then how easily one's moral or psychological point of view can become unstable—one point of view pushing forward into another point of view and vice versa—one of them never allowed to be a moral or psychological guide. This captures not only Gideon's erratic behavior but also the Lord's discontent in deciding how best to represent himself during Gideon's travails.

CONTEXT 5: Possibly as punishment for the gold worship under Gideon, in Chapter 10 the Israelites for the first time get a judge with an evil spirit, Abimelech. After Abimelech's reign comes to an end, first by an unspecified woman dropping a millstone to crush his skull and then a request to be finished off by a swordsman lest men say of him, "A woman killed him" (Judg 9:54). The people of Israel again do "evil in the sight of the Lord" (Judg 10:6), and so must suffer at the hands of the Ammonites. As always they cry out to the Lord, who this time gets testy, sarcastically claiming He will deliver them no more and telling the people to "go and cry to the gods whom [they] have chosen; let them deliver you in the time of your distress" (Judg 10:14), to which the Israelites respond by admitting sin and insisting God "do to us whatever seems good to thee" (Judg 10:15). The Lord gives them Jephthah, who had earlier been scorned for being "the son of a harlot" (Judg 11:1), but because he is a great warrior, the elders beg him to come back and lead. Jephthah makes a fateful vow to the Lord that "if thou wilt give the Ammonites into my hand, then whoever comes forth from the doors of my house to meet me, when I return victorious . . . shall be the LORD's, and I will offer him up for a burnt offering" (Judg 11:30-31). This first visitor to Jephthah's door turns out not to be a "him," but his daughter, his only child, who, with horrible irony, unknowingly greets his victory "with timbrels and with dances" (Judg 11:34). Jephthah's ambition has created his own nightmare, blinding him from any thought of who might celebrate his victory, and leading him to promise the Lord anything for a victory. Yet when he sees the mess he has created, he is not humbled; instead he becomes the personification of self-centeredness, projecting his guilt on his own daughter: "Alas, my daughter! You have brought me very low, and you have become the cause of great trouble to me; for I have opened my mouth to the LORD, and I cannot take back my vow" (Judg 11:35). Who caused *who* trouble?

The daughter accepts her plight (and her dad's blame) in reverence to any vow made to the Lord but asks for two months alone with female companions in the mountains to "bewail [her] virginity" (Judg 11:37). After doing so she returns and is promptly sacrificed by her father, her death starting a custom whereby the daughters of Israel take four days every year to "lament the daughter of Jephtah" (Judg 11:40). The fact that the text points out she had never known a man and is sacrificed for her father's ambition subtly implies some perverse fathers' latent jealousies of suitors, or, at the very least, symbolizes a refusal of fathers to recognize their daughters' independence manifest by their unions with other men.

As with the response Gideon received, when the men of Ephraim are "called to arms" (Judg 12:1) against the Ammonites, they have an angry grudge with Jephthah because they were not called on before. Jephthah disagrees, claiming the men of Ephraim had left him on his own before so he could not wait and had to take immediate action to win (Judg 12:2), and now, because the men of Ephraim have worked themselves into a lather against him, he is forced to go up against them with the help of the Gileadites, and lo and behold, in a quick turn around, together they route and defeat the men of Ephraim (Judg 12:4). Allegiances burst with every mood swing. As in many of the stories in Judges, this panorama of back-and-forth battle scenes abruptly halts when the narration zeros in on an unexpected, dreamlike detail. Here when the men of Gilead encounter fugitives from Ephraim who claim they are not the enemy, the Gileadites create a pronunciation test: capturing one, "the men of Gilead said to him, 'Are you an E'phraimite?' When he said, 'No," they said to him, 'Then say Shibboleth,' and he said, 'Sibboleth' [leaving out the first "h"], for he could not pronounce it right; then they seized him and slew him" (Judg 12:5-6). A dark sensibility emerges through this archetypal test-taker's anxiety dream.

ILLUSTRATION FOR CONTEXT 5: See Magritte's *Homme avec le y Chapeau Feutre* (*Man in a Bowler Hat*), 1964, and *Le Fils de l'Homme* (*The Son of Man*), 1964, to better imagine this description. A Hebrew warrior stands at full attention, a frontal position to the viewer with a war helmet and relaxed arms at his side, one hand holding a shield against his body. The sky behind is ominous, cloudy gray with only limited light breaking through. The warrior seems to be posing in anticipation of full military honors or recognition; but instead a pomegranate floats in the air, lined up perfectly with his head so the viewer sees the warrior's body at attention but none of the face, only the top of the war helmet. The gravity-defying pomegranate's assertion implies that the fruit, with all its associations—fertility, myriad seeds for myriad truths, the plant world—makes for a more forceful, authentic reality than the warrior's ego. In fact, despite all the pomp and circumstance, the warrior will never be completely recognized because his actions resulted in tragedy. Since the pomegranate is so unexpected, hovering improbably in the air and appearing for no apparent reason, it has the shock of an unexpected fate, a reminder that the success of our ambitions, here begging for the simple recognition that a portrait typically offers, are really out of our control or unimportant or even something that should never have occurred.

CONTEXT 6: Regarding the most widely known judge, Samson, the first detail the writer focuses on is Samson zooming his desire on one of "the daughters of the Philistines" (Judg 14:1). With caveman abruptness and the attitude of a self-centered adolescent, he demands that his parents "get her for me as my wife" (Judg 14:2), but they cannot understand why he would not want some nice Hebrew girl instead of a wife from "uncircumcised Philistines" (Judg 14:3). Their expectations cannot catch up with Samson's demands: "Get her for me; for she pleases me well" (Judg 14:3). In this story, there are none of the panoramic battle sketches of the others; rather, this story relies on a combination of dreamlike images and folktale repetitions of plot. For instance, Samson goes to Timnah to get his Philistine wife, encounters a lion who roars at him so he rips "the lion asunder as one tears a kid; and he had nothing in his hand" (Judg 14:6), keeps this killing secret from his parents (instinctively hiding his great strength), returns to get his lady but notices the lion's carcass is now swarming with bees and honey, scrapes up globs of honey, "eating as he went" (Judg 14:9) as one does when eating ice cream cones, shares the honey with his parents (perhaps a transparent tactic to make up for not fulfilling his parents nice-Israelite-girl aspirations), but does not mention where the honey came from.

When his father makes a feast for Samson's new wife, Samson offers a riddle for the young male Philistine guests to bet fine clothes on: "Out of the eater came something to eat. Out of the strong came something sweet" (Judg 14:14). By the fourth day of the feast, when they are not able to imagine an answer, they are so frustrated they threaten to burn the bride and her father's house down and ask the bride if she has "invited [them] here to impoverish [them]?" (Judg 4:15). Treating Samson like a riddle shark is an amusing idea given his lion-ripping, physical orientation.

Next begins what will be a recurring betrayal nightmare, a pouting female trying to guilt her husband into revealing information to relay to her hostile countrymen, a blood-is-thicker-than-water scenario totally opposite from what is found in, for instance, the Book of Ruth. Samson's bride of Timnah "pressed him hard" (Judg 14:17), claiming he must not love her (Judg 14:16), and weeping before him for seven days until Samson caves in and tells her the riddle. The bride immediately passes the answer on to the "uncircumcised" males who in turn repeat it back to win the fine-clothes bet. At first Samson displays great metaphoric wit, telling the wife's countrymen, "If you had not plowed with my heifer, you would not have found out my riddle" (Judg 14:18), humorously insulting the wife's heft with the reference to a heifer while also referring to her betrayal of loyalty by subtly suggesting that what her male countrymen have done is equivalent to a sexual (plowing) betrayal.

But then his wit quickly dries up, and when "the Spirit of the LORD came mightily upon him" (Judg 14:15), Samson becomes his own nightmare, slaughtering men in one Philistine town to grab "festal garments" (Judg 14:19) for the other Philistines who won the riddle. Since he is "in hot anger" (Judg 14:19), his wife is given to his best man as a wife (Judg 14:20), and when Samson returns during the harvest and declares that he will "go in to [his] wife in the chamber" (Judg 15:1), he is turned away by her father. Samson, enraged, and sexually frustrated, immediately proclaims, "This time I shall be blameless in regard to the Philistines, when I do them mischief" (Judg 15:3) and he commences to wreak havoc in a way that only could occur in a dream: he catches three hundred foxes, puts them "tail to tail" (Judg 15:4) to somehow hold torches between those tails, creating a vulpine menorah, and then releases them to torch all the Philistine's fields and orchards. When word gets out that he did it because his wife was taken from him, the Philistines, ignoring that earlier the wife had been a traitor on their behalf, mindlessly retaliate by killing her and her father (Judg 15:6). Ironically, this angers Samson, who now, ignoring how treacherous his wife was, slaughters even more Philistines. The nightmare appears to have no end. As with the Gideon story, the Samson scenes flip between those where Samson displays confidence to those where he is morally derelict, a jolting juxtaposition familiar in dreams.

The Philistines lash back by going after the men of Judah, who in turn immediately scold Samson, reminding him that at this time the Philistines are the rulers (Judg 15:9-10). As a compromise and instead of killing him for the trouble he has brought, the men of Judah tell Samson they will need to bind his hands (Judg 15:13). Making the men of Judah promise not to kill him, Samson goes along with the plan, but as soon as he does, the "Spirit of the LORD [comes] mightily upon him" (Judg 15:14) and melts off the bindings. As in a dream, an unexpected item takes on a surprise use, and here it is the "jawbone of an ass" (Judg 15:15) that Samson picks up to whack to death thousands of men. As you might expect, Samson gets terribly thirsty from this bone-swinging workout. As in the other Judges dreamlike narratives, the large, blurry actions of battle abruptly shift to a very defined detail, here in the form of an unexpected, out-of-scale, non-sequitur question to God, Samson wondering, "Shall I now die of thirst, and fall into the hands of the uncircumcised?" (Judg 15:18). The Lord splits open the earth for water and Samson leads the Israelites for twenty years (Judg 15:19-20).

The story picks up new steam when Samson uses his penis to go "in to" (Judg 16:1) a harlot (he seems done with wives for a while); then in the dark of night, he sneaks past the Philistines who still want to kill him and who are waiting outside the prostitute's dwelling, and pulls up the city gates as he escapes (Judg 16:3). Soon afterwards, Samson finally falls in love again with a woman, Delilah, who, in a plot reminiscent of the earlier wedding story, is seduced with silver by the Philistines to "entice" (Judge 16:5) Samson to reveal the source of his strength. Using a plot device typical in folktales, Delilah's attempts to break Samson for his secrets come in a set of three. Each time Samson gives false answers about how he can be bound to remove the source of his strength, and each time the Philistines try the made-up binding method only to have Samson bust it. Delilah has the nerve in all three cases to claim that by not telling the truth, Samson has mocked her, crazily making the moral issue her embarrassment at getting it wrong for her countrymen— "Behold, you have mocked me, and told me lies" (Judg 16:10)—rather than the immorality of her treachery and her being an unloving bitch. To top it off, as with the Philistine woman from Timnah, Delilah has the nerve to say, "How can you say, 'I love you,' when your heart is not with me?" (Judg 16:15). The reader might assume Samson had set up the lies as decoys (after all, he does it three times) to test Delilah's loyalty, but he never comments on her repeated offenses.

In fact, as happened before in his earlier marriage, when Delilah "pressed him hard with her words day after day, and urged him, his soul was vexed to death" (Judg 16:16); so Samson folds, telling her his strength has to do with the growth of his hair. She makes him sleep with his head on her lap while she shaves it (Judg 16:19), at which point the Lord immediately leaves him (Judg 16:20). (No hair, no God? Another typical emasculation nightmare.) The Philistines now can seize Samson and gouge out his eyes, claiming their god has delivered them from this crazy, bone-bashing killer (Judg 16:23-24). The striking aspect of the story is that Samson is so passive throughout these actions, apparently having learned nothing about treacherous women, not even after setting up decoy lies three times to test Delilah's loyalty, or after watching her countrymen make fools of themselves three times, or after Delilah employs such obvious, manipulative logic to flip her guilt. The removal of any rational response from Samson during any of the action further enhances the story as a dream narrative, revealing subconscious anxieties Samson is internalizing but not acting upon.

But when the blind Samson is brought out of prison so the Philistines can make "sport" (Judg 16:25) of him, he does finally become an active agent in his own story. He requests to be placed next to the pillars of a structure so that he might lean against them. The structure is covering thousands of Philistines, so when Samson puts his considerable strength against the pillars, the structure collapses, and kills both them and him. The result is that "he slew at his death . . . more than those whom he had slain during his life" (Judg 16:30). Justice is reduced to a numbers game. By dying with his enemies, however, the character of Samson, who earlier was depicted as an adolescent, or out of control, or a witness in a dream, is quickly forgotten and the reader is left only with the image of Samson as a martyr.

ILLUSTRATION FOR CONTEXT 6: For prototypes see Magritte's *Les Jours Gigantesques* (*The Titanic Days*), 1928, and *Les Amants I* (*The Lovers I*), 1928. These paintings will provide a great model for capturing how women's entanglements with Samson, and his struggle to perceive their motives, define his personality and fate. A strong, bulky nude man bends his head to the side as if staring down at the ground to check his balance, but a loosely wrapped cloth covers his entire head so he sees nothing, rendering the balancing act futile. The man is lifting one leg slightly off the ground as if trying to avoid an obstacle, but the viewer soon notices that the "obstacle" is actually another person, part of a female who also defines part of the man's shadow on his right side. Only the back of her dark hair, rear of one ear and jaw, and one shoulder and elbow are revealed as a female blending into the man's torso. However, the partial female figure does have two items that are definitely not part of a shadow: two hands, one grasping the man's inner thigh near his genitals, in position to control his actions, and the other curled around his waist. The man uses one of his hands in a futile attempt to push away the woman-shadow's shoulder, and he lifts his other arm in the air to balance. The overall symbolic image depicts a male struggling with his feminine self, but the female is incomplete and out of balance with his larger proportioned masculine self. His covered head symbolizes his inability to understand the ambiguity of his existence: the treacherous nature of his female self and the violence of his male self; his need to have his female and male selves join in harmony; and confusion as to why they have disconnected. There are no other objects or people in the scene, only an opaque gray-blue background, brown, earthy floor surface, and a dark structure partially visible on one side, all underscoring the private loneliness of this struggle.

The Samson story is the last of the significant contexts that should be included without question in your illustrated version of Judges; others are more negotiable. After the Samson story, there are no more stories about judges in the book, although there are a few strange tales that are especially demeaning to women. One is about a Levite, traveling with his concubine, who finds a host in a foreign land, but annoyed by the town's Sodomesque rapists, the Levite and host toss the concubine to the men of the town to ravage her all night. When she crawls to their threshold in the morning, the Levite chops her into twelve pieces and sends them out parcel post throughout the territory of Israel (Judg 19:1-29). When questioned by others about the evil, the Levite shifts all the blame to the men of Gibeah where he sojourned (Judg 20:4). End of story.

Another tale has to do with the men of Israel agreeing at Mizpah that no one give their daughters in marriage to the tribe of Benjamin, but then, feeling sorry about this solo rejection of a tribe of Israel, decide to get virgins for the Benjamites from another tribe. They can do so, however, only after wiping out all other men, women, and children to steal those virgins (Judg 21:1-12). When there are still not enough virgins, again out of "compassion on Benjamin" (Judg 21:15) (of whom the other people of Israel "had sworn, 'Cursed be he who gives a wife to Benjamin'") (Judg 21:18), they now decide to rob the tribe of Shiloh of their virgin daughters, thus topping off the Benjamite males remaining without virgin wives. If such stories are examples of doing evil in sight of the Lord, the narrator never proclaims it; but he does mention that "in those days there was no king in Israel; every man did what was right in his own eyes" (Judg 21:25). I suspect the "Judges stories" gave other writers an excuse to create these epilogues of gratuitous violence. We need to discuss whether these stories are worthy of illustrations.

Hopefully this concept of using a modern surrealist as a model for illustrating one of the most surreal books in the Bible will spark your interest. Thank you for your generous advance for my appraisal and illustration concept. After you have time to give them consideration let me know if you would like my help in developing more images. In the meantime, the grace of God be with you, and

with all sincerity,
Gary Hoffman

BRAINS-AND-BREASTS POETRY
PROVERBS, PSALMS,
SONG OF SOLOMON

W hen a layperson thinks of Biblical poetry, the first three books that come to mind are most likely the Book of Psalms, the Book of Proverbs, and the Song of Solomon. Of course there are proverbial lines throughout the Bible, many in Ecclesiastes and the Gospel of Matthew; and some books are written in lengthy narrative verse, such as the Book of Job and the books of the prophets; but for most contemporary laypeople, the defining quality of poetry is a text of compressed length, composed of rhythmic lines and a density of figurative language.

A close reading of Biblical poetry's word choice and structure can allow for greater appreciation of these texts. Yet an additional helpful device for understanding their strengths and limitations is to pair the books of poetry with more recent poems that derive some of their own bouquet from their Biblical antecedents, but also whose newer poetic vigor clarifies the Biblical poetry's qualities of depth. Thus we find a William Blake work adding fire to Proverbs, an Emily Dickinson poem infusing air into Psalms, a John Donne poem bringing wit to the religious sex in the Song of Solomon. The order of the books to be considered below begins with the most apparently simple, the Proverbs; then the slightly more extended in length, the Psalms; and then the longest piece, the Song of Solomon.

(1) Proverbs meet William Blake

The Proverbs are compact wisdom pills: easily swallowed, but if read by the handful (as relentlessly listed in the book), one could easily gag on the platitudes. Some are extended for several lines, but most are made up of two lines (referred to as versets), whereby the second line either parallels, affirms, elaborates on, or clarifies a puzzling statement in the first line; or is antithetical or reverses the first line. Consider Proverb 14:

"There is a way which seems right to a man, / but its end is the way to death" (Prov 14:12).

This proverb contains a reversal that knocks the wind out of the reader: the first line has wide application, referring to any physical, moral, or intellectual endeavor that we take comfort in as being "correct," but the last line quickly undoes that confidence, reminding us that there is never an ultimate positive ending—that no matter what we do correctly, death will trump those good deeds.

In contrast, an example of a second line confirming the first is the proverb, "Iron sharpens iron, / and one man sharpens another" (Prov 27:17), reminding us that people of equal strength—physical, emotional, intellectual—who interact with each other can bring out the best of or improve each other. Even more layered is the second line in Proverbs 12:

"Whoever loves discipline loves knowledge, / but he who hates reproof is stupid" (Prov 12:1)

The proverb supports its statement about wisdom with its own cleverness, first by using the verb "loves" twice to stress that discipline, not only knowledge, deserves and demands love, while simultaneously suggesting they are interdependent. The cleverness continues by using love's antonym "hate," to not only set up a contrast to love, but to define the opposite of knowledge, "stupid," as the inability to accept criticism, a killer of knowledge.

With some proverbs, such as Proverb 10, the second line's verb jolts the reader into revelation because it breaks from the simplicity of the verb in the first line:

"The mouth of the righteous is a fountain of life, / but the mouth of the wicked conceals violence" (Prov 10:11).

The "fountain of life," a hyperbolic metaphor with associations of pleasant sounds, delightful sculptural artistry, and rejuvenation associated with water, expresses the positive potential offered by the truly righteous. The verb "is" could not be simpler, quickly binding "mouth" with "fountain," but the verb in the second line, "conceals," is a shock. When we are presented with "the mouth of the wicked," we are not only startled by the wickedness coming in the form of "violence," but by the idea that we cannot be forewarned of it since the mouth, ironically despite its flapping open, "conceals" violence, a threatening verb that makes violence especially insidious. In addition, the second line makes the reader wonder how one can discern what is righteous from what is wicked, if the violence that is symptomatic of wickedness is concealed.

Instead of a surprising verb as in the last example, in Proverb 11 a stunning simile holds off on the object it is describing until the second line.

"Like a gold ring in a swine's snout / is a beautiful woman without discretion" (Prov 11:22).

In the first line, the reader's attention is quickly caught by the grotesque juxtaposition of a shiny, valuable object wasted on a non-kosher animal, and certainly not one to be cuddled like a woman. Then the reader is shocked by the unexpected comparison of a bejeweled swine to a "beautiful woman." For a split second, the reader wonders if the simile is about a link of the pig's bulk to the woman, but then "without discretion" becomes her defining characteristic, her carelessness in all matters (sexual, moral, social) wiping away her beauty the way a swine deflates the worth of the golden ring.

Sometimes, rather than employing a delayed simile to shock, a proverb will use two similes to fuse the lines, demonstrated here in Proverb 18:

"A brother helped is like a strong city, / but quarreling is like the bars of a castle" (Prov 18:19).

Both lines have images that represent strength—a "strong city" and "bars of a castle"—but of very different sorts: the city signifies unified purpose, production, and protection, while the second space, an inescapable dungeon in a castle, itself a structure that usually would be a place of unified purpose and protection, is now limited to a space that is stifling, unproductive, and entrapping. The mirrored similes hold the two ideas together like intertwined brothers, but the metaphors capture the different emotional or spiritual mentalities that result from "helping" versus "quarreling."

Not all proverbs are so satisfying to the secularist; some lack concrete imagery and depend more on faith than secular knowledge. Consider "Trust in the LORD with all your heart, / and do not rely on your own insight" (Prov 3:5). The proverb does not offer advice as to what aspects of the Lord to trust in (the more one knows the Old Testament stories, the more volatile and irrational one knows the Lord can be), nor does it give any clue as to which specific insights we are supposed to dispose ourselves of. And, one might argue, are not the proverbs themselves instruments for having insights? Consider, "A tranquil mind gives life to the flesh, / but passion makes the bones rot" (Prov 14:30), which requires the reader to take several steps outside the verset to think about how tranquility might give life to the flesh. Is the reader supposed to think that when one does not act on passion, but instead remains "tranquil" in order to discern with whom to be passionate with, sex is more positive? Or does the proverb mean that when one is tranquil, one safely fantasizes by bringing life to flesh as a substitute for evil passion? The proverb also assumes a very negative view about passion in general, without hinting at the nature of that passion, which is often a positive force. One could just as well imagine a proverb that says, "tranquility makes the bones rot," making passion an essential life spirit and depicting tranquility as spirit deadening.

In fact, centuries later, the great British romantic poet William Blake wrote exactly that. Consider his proverb, "Expect poison from standing water," poetically implying that tranquility—lacking energy, movement, change—equates to deadening stagnation. This idea is extended through another of Blake's proverbs, "He who desires but acts not, breeds pestilence," a metaphoric warning that repressing and internalizing desires instead of channeling them into action where they can be tested—regardless of whether they lead to failure or success— leads to frustrations and ultimately hidden rage or violence.

These proverbs are from "Proverbs of Hell," a section in Blake's *The Marriage of Heaven and Hell*,[1] published in 1793, when the French revolution was exploding and the British were worried about revolutionary fire in their own country. The work is multifaceted, using different writing strategies to satirize Biblical orthodoxy while simultaneously offering new spiritual enlightenment. In the opening argument of the work, Blake writes, "Without Contraries is no progression. Attraction and Repulsion, Reason and Energy, Love and Hate, are necessary to Human existence." The contraries might be called dialectical in the sense that one of the contraries does not win out over the other: love does not conquer hate, good does not conquer evil. The forces of the world do not polarize, Blake suggests, but are locked in eternal dialogue or tension. From a secular point of view, then, they can offer a more realistic view of life.

Reading Blake's proverbs, which demonstrate the need for dialectical contraries, shines a different light on many of the Biblical proverbs, calling attention to their biases and foregroundings, and by comparison, their sometimes smug tone: a simple-minded optimism— "The righteousness of the blameless keeps his way straight, / but the wicked falls by his own wickedness" (Prov 11:5); an anti-rebellious streak—"Drive out a scoffer, and strife will go out" (Prov 22:10); an anti-self-reflection sensibility—"He who trusts in his own mind is a fool" (Prov 28:26); a controlling feeling—"The fear of the LORD is instruction in wisdom" (Prov 15:33); an anti-nonconformist stance— "Do not swerve to the right or to the left" (Prov 4:27); anxiety about female sexuality—"A foolish woman is noisy; / she is wanton and knows no shame" (Prov 9:13). Despite many wise proverbs, there is an overall anti-energetic thread throughout the Book of Proverbs that undermines the passion Blake wishes to promote and that he wishes to respond to. With several exceptions, many are a call for what is prudent—which, in light of Blake's proverbs, fosters spiritual death.

Blake's "Proverbs of Hell" attacks prudence, bias against foolishness, and anti-risk head on: "Prudence is a rich, ugly old maid courted by Incapacity," and "If the fool would persist in his folly he would become wise." These proverbs highlight the downside of prudence, in that it can bring about a self-indulgent ("rich"), sluggish ("old maid"), grotesque ("ugly") mindset that becomes an excuse for being inert or stagnant ("Incapacity"). On the other hand, Blake implies that only through the folly of foolishness—a big negative in the Old Testament proverbs—can one really learn. When we are fearful of making a fool of ourselves, we avoid taking chances that might enable us to grow—we might refrain from trying to talk in a newly learned foreign language; worry about sounding stupid trying out a new political position; fret about offending guests with a new recipe. We stymie our own growth, never becoming wise. Blake, in contrast to the Old Testament proverbs, argues that we benefit also from those fools who went before us: "If others had not been foolish, we should be so."

Blake also attacks the Biblical proverbs' generally negative views of rebelliousness, independence, self-reliance, and nonconformity. His proverb "No bird soars too high, if he soars with his own wings," encourages expansive thinking, going outside of traditional boundaries, rules, and assumptions ("soars"), as long as the thinking is the result of one's own understanding ("his own wings"), rather than ballooning into the air by mindlessly mimicking others, a sure way to crash-land. Soaring can only come through a genuine attempt to have a genuine liftoff through one's own learning experiences and by carefully understanding the thoughts of others.

On the other hand, Blake promotes experimenting or taking risks: "Improvement makes straight roads; but the crooked roads without Improvement are roads of Genius." Blake's proverb makes a distinction between refinement and discipline ("Improvement makes straight roads") and working outside of precise patterns ("crooked roads without improvement") to discover the new, the unique, and the amazing, all impossible gains when adhering to the Biblical proverbial concern for not "swerving to the right or left."

In contradiction to the Proverbs' stance that "he who restrains his words has knowledge" (Prov 17:27), Blake's proverb advises, "Always be ready to speak your mind, and a base man will avoid you." Where the Bible warns, "Pride goes before destruction" (16:18), Blake counters with, "The pride of the peacock is the glory of God," favoring the energetic display of bravado over fear of indulgence, which does in fact have its place in becoming wise, as Blake adds, "You never know what is enough unless you know what is more than enough." The inability to revel in the energy of pride, Blake suggests, leads to shame: "Shame is Pride's cloak." Blake's proverbs will have nothing to do with shame, especially that of human sexuality: "The lust of the goat is the bounty of God" and "the nakedness of woman is the work of God."

In general, for Blake, passion runs riot over the prudence and constraint of the Biblical proverbs. When we see Blake's proverbs paired with those from the Bible, the Bible's stunted, less nuanced vision of life comes more into focus. We begin to see that the Bible's proverbs generally deny our passionate, trial-and-error, foolish, chancier human impulses so necessary for maturity and living a creative, healthy life. As Blake dramatically articulates it: "The tigers of wrath are wiser than the horses of instruction."

(2) Psalms meet Emily Dickinson

In many congregations, worship services center on singing the Bible's psalms. When hearing them, one cannot help but think the way Huckleberry Finn does about much church music. In Twain's *Adventures of Huckleberry Finn*,[2] the king and the duke, a pair of frauds, pretend to be British relatives of Peter Wilks, who they know has just died, the duke going so far as to pretend to be a deaf relative making use of fake sign language, fake tears, fake accents, fake hugs; and the king giving a "pious goody-goody Amen" (124) to everything. The two ultimately manipulate Peter's hometown villagers, who are anxious to exercise their virtuousness with tears of sentimentality and unctuous hospitality. Watching it all go down, Huck exclaims, "It was enough to make a body ashamed of the human race." But in the midst of all the "rot and slush," someone strikes up a doxolojer and people start singing with all their might, and Huck momentarily loosens his disgust, noting that "it just warmed you up and made you feel as good as church letting out. Music is a good thing; and after all the soul-butter and hogwash, I never see it freshen things so, and sound so honest and bully."

The Book of Psalms contains 150 lyrical poems, and when they are put to music, regardless of their "soul-butter" lyrics, they can make everything sound "so honest and bully." Yet they need that music. When studied as written poetry, without melodies to carry them to the heavens, with the exception of surprisingly few psalms, most lack depth, repeating the same motifs over and over again without specifics. They are mostly general expressions of joy, fear, anguish, and hope—so general, indeed, that the listener and singer feel they have permission to mentally substitute their personal thoughts to validate the lyrics. The psalms do not provide much poetic insight on their own. Consider the first lines of the first psalm:

> Blessed is the man
> who walks not in the counsel of the wicked,
> nor stands in the way of sinners;
> nor sits in the seat of scoffers;
> but his delight is in the law of the LORD,
> and on his law he meditates day and night.
> He is like a tree planted by streams of water,
> that yields its fruit in its season, and its leaf does not wither.
> In all that he does, he prospers.
> The wicked are not so,
> but are like chaff which the wind drives away (Ps 1:1-4).

Neither the attributes of the blessed man that keep him from withering, the counsel of the wicked, the sins of the sinners, the blasphemies of the scoffers, nor the deeds of the wicked are ever defined. Yet specifics are essential if we are to accept the psalm's optimism—how many of us willingly accept that the wicked are so easily blown away?

However, when our voices and feelings rise up on defiant major chords, a singer can believe in anything. Kim Hill's 1995 album *Testimony*[3] opens with a rendition of Psalm 1, a brooding-to-triumphal piece that contrasts greatly with Stephen Pearson's bright, silvery, C-to-G-to-C-again chord progression that would make for effortless singing in church. According to professional musician and English instructor Andy Stuart,[4] Hill's track stands out against Pearson's because the chord progressions open up melodic possibilities beyond expectations in most church settings. The bridge of Psalm 1 makes this most apparent with a succession of chords stacked over a suspended F. These chords help Hill's smoky croon waft over the lines "The Lord holds the plans and the paths of all who follow Him, / The righteous will stand secure and last forever," a sentiment, by the way, that is subtly different from the Bible's: "for the LORD knows the way of the righteous, / but the way of the wicked will perish" (Ps 1:6). The psalm chides the wicked repeatedly, brushing them aside as though they somehow undo themselves, since the Lord attends only to the righteous and ignores the wicked—this is already an overly optimistic view based on what is written in the other books of the Bible, where we have seen the morally bankrupt too often perpetuate cycles of cowardice, arrogance, and selfishness. But paraphrasing of the psalm's optimistic view of evil in this song goes even further to emphasize glory and protection given to those following the Lord, assurance more readily bought into by singer and audience alike when beefed up by an upbeat, syncopated melody with notes that soar over and in between dancing chords.

In fact, optimism is a major thread in the psalms, leaving one to wonder if the writers read much of the Old Testament stories, the well-known ones being so chock-full of tragic consequences, not to mention the success of boastful, violent rulers and the damage wrecked by a fickle God. For instance, one wonders if the psalmist has read Job when he offers the following lyrics: "I have been young, and now am old; / yet I have not seen the righteous forsaken / or his children begging bread" (Ps 37:25). Or has he studied the cyclical strife of siblings in Genesis or considered the selfishness of the judges of Israel in the Book of Judges when he sings, "Fret not yourself because of the wicked, / be not envious of wrongdoers! / For they will soon fade like the grass" (Ps 37:1-2)? At any time in history we might wish to have been so lucky that "the wicked man sees [the Lord's righteousness] and is angry; / he gnashes his teeth and melts away; / the desire of the wicked man comes to nought" (Ps 112:10). And when a psalmist does remember that justice is sometimes erratic and the Lord seems unnecessarily vengeful or out of control, the Lord gets excused: "For his anger is but for a moment, / and his favor is for a lifetime. / Weeping may tarry in the night, / but joy comes with the morning" (Ps 30:5).

Despite claims that many of the psalms are by David, anyone who has studied 1 and 2 Samuel will question David's authorship of any loving or sentimental psalms. David does come to mind, however, with those many psalms that brim with egotism and confidence. Consider the bravado of "I am not afraid of ten thousands of people" (Ps 3:6), reminiscent of David's collecting hundreds of enemy foreskins for

Saul; or "The LORD is the stronghold of my life; / of whom shall I be afraid?" (Ps 27:1), David's attitude even when he joins the Philistines against Israel; or the self-congratulation of "Clap your hands, all peoples! / Shout to God with loud songs of joy! / For the LORD, the Most High, is terrible, / a great king over all the earth. / He subdued peoples under us, / and nations under our feet. / He chose our heritage for us, / the pride of Jacob whom he loves" (Ps 47:1-4), reminding us of how David desperately compensates for God's touchiness during the shocking moment when God zaps Uzzah for touching the ark. One can also hear David, and other judges and kings, singing that the Lord "said to me, 'You are my son, / today I have begotten you. / Ask of me, and I will make the nations your heritage, / and the ends of the earth your possession. / You shall break them with a rod of iron / and dash them in pieces like a potter's vessel'" (Ps 2:7-9). "Possession" seems guaranteed to rulers who "serve the LORD with fear, / with trembling / kiss his feet, / lest he be angry, and you perish in the way" (Ps 2:11-12).

Uncharacteristic of David, a focus on self-deprecation permeates many psalms: "My wounds grow foul and fester / because of my foolishness, / I am utterly bowed down and prostrate" (Ps 38:5-6), as does a sense of fearfulness about others taking advantage when one sins, "For I pray, 'Only let them not rejoice over me, / who boast against me when my foot slips!'" (Ps 38:16). Some psalms include more aggressive attacks on those who take advantage of our mess-ups: "let them be turned back and brought to dishonor / who desire my hurt! / Let them be appalled because of their shame / who say to me, 'Aha, Aha!'" (Ps 40:14-15). Other psalms are humble, praising a level playing field with lines that seem right out of Ecclesiastes: "Yea, he shall see that even the wise die, / the fool and the stupid alike must perish / and leave their wealth to others. / Their graves are their homes for ever, / their dwelling places to all generations, / though they named lands their own. / Man cannot abide in his pomp, / he is like the beasts that perish" (Ps 49:10-12), and even humble in the face of a fleeting life— "For my days pass away like smoke" (Ps 102:3) and that "for thou hast taken me up and thrown me away. / My days are like an evening shadow; / I wither away like grass" (Ps 102:10-11).

The times the psalms do get specific about injustices, they often have to do with deceit: "I do not sit with false men, / nor do I consort with dissemblers" (Ps 26:4); "No man who utters lies / shall continue in my presence" (Ps 101:7); "For they do not speak peace, / but against those who are quiet in the land / they conceive words of deceit" (Ps 35:19-20); "His speech was smoother than butter, / yet war was in his heart; / his words were softer than oil, / yet they were drawn swords (Ps 55:21). As is central to the betrayal in the gospels, deceit from those intimate with us is the most painful: "It is not an enemy who taunts me— / then I could bear it; / it is not an adversary who deals insolently with me— / then I could hide from him. / But it is you, my equal, / my companion, my familiar friend. / We used to hold sweet converse together; / within God's house we walked in fellowship" (55:12-14). Instead of philosophical acceptance that such betrayals are the way of the world, however, the psalmist calls for revenge: "Let death come upon them;/ let them go down to She'ol alive; let them go away in terror into their graves (55:15).

Indeed, a major theme in the Psalms is desire for violent revenge: "Break thou the arm of the wicked and evildoer" (Ps 10:15); and for accusers "speaking against me with lying tongues" (Ps 109:2), "let his prayer be counted as sin! / May his days be few; / may another seize his goods! / May his children be fatherless, / and his wife a widow! / May his children wander about and beg" (Ps 109:7-10), and "let there be none to extend kindness to him, / nor any to pity his fatherless children!" (Ps 109:12). This is strong poison, hard to soften with music, all for unspecified wrongs. The least objectionable retributions are calls for nonviolent judgment: "they flatter with their tongue. / Make them bear their guilt, O God; / let them fall by their own counsels" (Ps 5:9-10). The most noble and rare reaction to injustice in the Psalms takes the form of nonviolent protest—after suffering in a foreign land, the psalmist is weeping by the waters of Babylon, remembering Zion, so "we hung up our lyres. / For there our captors / required of us songs, / and our tormentors, mirth, saying, / 'Sing us one of the songs of Zion!'" (Ps 137:2-3). However, in the next stanza, during a quick moment of self-reflection, the psalmist directs the punishment on himself: "If I forget you, O Jerusalem,/ let my right hand wither! / Let my tongue cleave to the roof of my mouth" (Ps 137:5-6); and by the end of psalm, all self-doubt has evaporated, and, remembering of the destruction by the Edomites, the psalmist hoots a perverse war cry—"Happy shall he be who takes your little ones / and dashes them against the rock!" (Ps 137:9). What musical note should we hit to exalt that line?

Given all the shrill praise, brash bravado, and jarring revenge, when God does not come through, the psalmists are unexpectedly shocked with disappointment: "Why dost thou stand afar off, O LORD? / Why dost thou hide thyself in times of trouble? / In arrogance the wicked hotly pursue the poor" (Ps 10:1-2); or "How long, O LORD? Wilt thou forget me for ever? . . . How long shall my enemy be exalted over me?" (Ps 13:1-2); or "My God, my God, why hast thou forsaken me? / Why art thou so far from helping me, from the words of my groaning?" (Ps 22:1). The first part of this line is later echoed by Jesus on the Cross in Mark's gospel; either Jesus or Mark could have remembered Psalm 22 because it has crucifixion imagery: "a company of evildoers encircle me; / they have pierced my hands and feet— / I can count all my bones— / they stare and gloat over me; / they divide my garments among them, / and for my raiment they cast lots" (Ps 22:16-18).

These lamentations about the Lord not being there in time of need pop up throughout the Book of Psalms. For instance, "Thou hast made us like sheep for slaughter, / and hast scattered us among the nations. / Thou hast sold thy people for a trifle, / demanding no high price for them" (Ps: 44:11-12); the psalmist even challenges God for his double standards: "If we had forgotten the name of our God, / or spread forth our hands to a strange god, / would not God discover this? / For he knows the secrets of the heart. / Nay, for thy sake we are slain all the day long, / and accounted as sheep for the slaughter" (Ps 44:20-22). Other psalmists goad God: "Are his promises at an end for all time? / Has God forgotten to be gracious? / Has he in anger shut up his compassion?" (Ps 77:8-9) or "They crush thy people, O LORD, / and afflict thy heritage. / They slay the widow and the sojourner, / and murder the fatherless; / and they say 'The LORD does not see; / the God of Jacob does not perceive'" (Ps 94:5-7). Andy Stuart, mentioned above, wonders if, as a church psalm, these lines ought to be sung in complete dissonance, with leaps in the melody that veer outside the key of the song? Or perhaps an artful composer could pass out two different melodic versions of the psalm, each line only one note apart, creating discord between singers in the pews. A more church-friendly and completely absurd interpretation would be to joyously chant these psalms over airy chords, the piety of crystalline music juxtaposed against the sorrows of the wailing psalmists represented here. How many congregations would ever be so creative and daring?

To understand the limitations of many psalms, it is interesting to compare one of the most famous, about darkness and death, to one of Emily Dickinson's poems on the same subject. The most famous Psalm is number 23: "The LORD is my shepherd, / I shall not want; / he makes me lie down in green pastures" (Ps 23:1). Surely it is one of the most comforting, the psalmist certain that the Lord protects like a "shepherd," a metaphor also implying that we are essentially gentle sheep, that all our "wants" will be taken care by the Lord, including having us lay "down in green pastures." In the next stanza, however, the psalmist imagines the journey leaving the tranquility of the first stanza, and now the first-person persona walks "through the valley of the shadow of death" (Ps 23:4), fearing no evil. Since death is a natural part of the life cycle, the idea that it is evil seems strange; one might prefer another common translation of the Hebrew, mentioned in a footnote in the Revised Standard Bible, that it is "the shadow of deep darkness," a better metaphor for negative forces within or outside of the soul. Fear of evil or death or deep darkness is dissipated not because the psalmist has voiced a way to understand the nature of darkness or death, but because of continued faith that the Lord's "rod and staff" will "comfort" (Ps 23:4) the psalmist.

The psalm is designed to ensure our well-being in the face of death and darkness, but to understand the psalm's limitations, compare it to Emily Dickinson's comforting poem,[5] here a close transcription from 1863 without a title (later it was titled "The Chariot," and published posthumously in 1890). Instead of assuming there is a benevolent Lord who will shepherd us through darkness, Dickinson gives us a new way to conceive of the ultimate darkness:

Because I could not stop for Death—
He kindly stopped for me—

> The Carriage held but just Ourselves—
> And Immortality.

First, the frightening arrival of death is softened by being made partially our responsibility; death looks assertive only because we are too busy living: "Because I could not stop for Death / He kindly stopped for me." Dickinson also uses personification to capture the nonchalance of death, which "kindly" takes the time to stop for us—death takes us without malice of forethought. The fear of death is further eased by the personification of "Immortality," a fantastical concept we desperately wish for while living a healthy life, but one that ironically fades the closer we get to the inevitability of our death, so here Immortality, capitalized like a person's name, comfortably joins the persona on the way to death.

The journeys of both the psalm and poem are calming. Psalm 23 assumes a soothing atmosphere of "still waters," through which the Lord "restores" (Ps 23:3) one's soul (without the persona having to do anything) and leads the persona onto paths of righteousness (with no hint as to what the righteousness is about), all for the Lord's sake. As with the other psalms, the reader does not obtain new insight (as one does, for instance, by understanding parables) but rather is allowed to indulge the imagination as to what a restored soul and righteousness might be. The carriage with Dickinson's narrator creates some of the same calm of the psalm:

> We slowly drove—He knew no haste
> And I had put away
> My labor and my leisure too,
> For His Civility—

Calm exists because the carriage "slowly drove," Death knowing "no haste"; however, the persona puts both "labor" and "leisure too" away, a reminder that in death or dark times, one does not easily escape to "still waters" and "green pastures" of the Psalm 23; rather, the pleasures of life also dissipate. Labor and leisure are a package deal. Calm acceptance of this loss is maintained by having both "put away"— not ripped away as we often imagine or see depicted in literature and art—a suggestion that we have the potential to accept death by giving up all parts of life, uncomfortable and comfortable, whereas Psalm 23 promises everlasting comfort, "dwell[ing] in the house of the LORD / for ever" (Ps 23:6).

Before that ending, the psalm continues in a self-serving fantasy, believing the Lord "preparest a table before me / in the presence of my enemies; / thou anointest my head with oil, / my cup overflows" (Ps 23:5). The necessity to flaunt a bountiful table in front of "enemies," instead of simply relishing in the good fortune of the Lord's blessing, seems primitive and indulgent despite the calm tone. In the Dickinson poem, the focus moves off the self and onto a greater circle of life, including the beginnings of childhood, here not idealized but seen to be one of striving, even when at game (recess and rings); and then onto the indifferent fields of grain—where as adults we strive to maintain our lives—that passively "gaze" at us as our lives end.

> We passed the School, where Children strove
> At Recess—in the Ring—
> We passed the Fields of Gazing Grain—
> We passed the Setting Sun—

The setting sun is a reminder that every day has death built into it and any feeling of well-being or control, being in position to pass the sun, is immediately taken away by the opening of the next stanza:

> Or rather—He passed Us—
> The Dews drew quivering and Chill—
> For only Gossamer, my Gown—
> My Tippet—only Tulle—

Whereas at first the speaker perceived she was passing the setting sun, the life force, the shepherd of the grain, now she realizes the sun passes the carriage group, leaving the speaker in the cold. The persona felt in control of movement and now feels overwhelmed as the sun moves on and darkness does in fact permeate the world. Death begins to overtake the persona, forcing the persona, with stuttered voice, to notice the frailness of "gossamer" clothing (our bodies?), its inability to ward off chill with a tippet, or a shawl, and tulle, very lightweight material. In contrast, the psalm bypasses remembrances of the cycles of light and darkness, heat and cold, the essence of life, and instead is sure that the good and merciful (once again presented as general notions that can be defined as one wishes) will continue to death, maybe beyond death: "Surely goodness and mercy [sometimes translated "kindness"] shall follow me / all the days of my life; / and I shall dwell in the house of the LORD/ for ever" (Ps 23:6).

The Lord's house is a metaphor that can refer to any abstract well-being the listener or singer wants to imagine, while Dickinson, trying to build the same acceptance of the eternal as comforting and simultaneously remind us we become dust again, combines both notions of loss and security, in a powerful image of the grave as the house:

> We paused before a House that seemed
> A Swelling of the Ground—
> The Roof was scarcely visible—
> The Cornice—in the Ground—
>
> Since then—'tis Centuries—and yet
> Feels shorter than the Day
> I first surmised the Horses' Heads
> Were toward Eternity—

The grave itself, by "swelling," also suggests productivity and fertility, and is melded with the permanent comforts suggested by the sheltered house metaphor, complete with roof and cornice.

Then Dickinson, discouraging faith in an eternal life with the Lord as in Psalm 23, reminds us that the centuries of eternity replace fantasies of immortality, because those centuries shrink the actual time of our lives (becoming "shorter than the Day"). In light of centuries, too, only the split-second we first realize that death is imminent becomes an anxiety-filled time that seems to last an eternity, whereas the centuries of death are no longer a threat. Dickinson is able to take us out of the shadow of death and into an eternal optimism without the fantasy of faith-based hope.

(3) Song of Solomon meet John Donne

The Song of Solomon is the only book in the Bible to praise luscious female breasts and the wetness of sex. The imagery is doled out in dialogues alternating between a man (sometimes referred to as a king, perhaps Solomon) and a woman (a few times referred to as a Shulammite, or daughter of Jerusalem), both of whom are often encouraged, sometimes cautioned, by an undesignated chorus. High priests sorting through the canon probably let the juices flow because the poem flies under the banner of Solomon's authorship, but modern scholars believe the work most likely was put together out of Egyptian love poetry or other Eastern wedding ceremonies and then attributed to Solomon. The juiciest parts of the love poem might also have escaped notice because they are disguised or softened by suggestive metaphors. However, this poem is not just about potently sexual encounters; indeed, it goes in many different directions, almost as if several poems about love have been interwoven. For instance, parts of the poem are sexually charged, others having more to do with nonsexual affection. Furthermore, there are two kinds of metaphors, one that enhances the sexual relationship of the lovers and another that chills it enough so that at times the poem seems more about love of a land than between two people. This dichotomy will be considered last.

Sometimes the highly sexual metaphors in Song of Solomon are self-conscious, and sometimes they are uttered in exuberant innocence, where the risqué implications seem unconscious and unintentional. For instance, consider these images from the woman: "While the king was on his couch, / my nard gave forth its fragrance. / My beloved is to me a bag of myrrh, / that lies between my breasts" (Song 1:12-13). Nard is exotic oil from far away India or the Himalayans, and the verb "gave forth" makes it especially aggressive and fetching to a royal male waiting on a couch. Its immediate effect brings the male lover—perceived as a bag of myrrh, another intoxicating scent—to a place "between [the woman's] breasts" (Song 1:13). It is hard not to imagine the woman's desire is for her naked lover to hover above her with his "bag" resting on her chest. Sound farfetched? Any more than speculating that myrrh might have been worn in a necklace bag? (And even so this is the male as a bag, not a necklace, between breasts.) Or is it any more farfetched than understanding the poem as an allegory of the love between God and Israel or between Christ and the Church, standard interpretations by many Judeo-Christian theologians?

On the cliché but sweeter side, the woman claims, "I am a rose of Sharon, / a lily of the valleys" (Song 2:1) to which the male confirms and praises, "As a lily among brambles, / so is my love among maidens" (Song 2:2). Then the metaphors swell up again, the woman eventually shifting the emphasis to oral delights: "As an apple tree among the trees of the wood, / so is my beloved among young men. / With great delight I sat in his shadow, / and his fruit was sweet to my taste" (Song 2:3), the apples refreshing her because she is "sick with love" (Song 2:5). Fruit trees are symbols of fertility and nourishment, but here the woman links the tree directly to the male's sexuality, so perhaps she is in his shadow not just for protection by placing herself under him but also where she can best taste his fruit and in the next second wish "that his left hand were under [her] head, / and that his right hand embraced [her]!" (Song 2:6).

The female using moistening metaphors in the first lines establishes the delights of oral, lubricated sexuality early in the poem: "O that you would kiss me with the kisses of your mouth! / For your love is better than wine, / your anointing oils are fragrant, / your name is oil poured out" (Song 1:2-3). Later the male matches this dewy desire with his own: "How much better is your love than wine, / and the fragrance of your oils than any spice! / Your lips distil nectar, my bride; / honey and milk are under your tongue" (Song 4:10-11), as well as tasting her female fruits: "How fair and pleasant you are, / O loved one, delectable maiden! / You are stately as a palm tree, / and your breasts are like its clusters. / I say I will climb the palm tree / and lay hold of its branches. / Oh, may your breasts be like clusters of the vine, / and the scent of your breath like apples, / and your kisses like the best wine / that goes down smoothly, / gliding over lips and teeth" (Song 7:6-9). The date-grape-wine nectar captures his anticipation at finding the juices flowing, and indeed she signals her readiness, asking to "go out early to the vineyards, / and see whether the vines have budded, / whether the grape blossoms have opened / and the pomegranates are in bloom. / There I will give you my love" (Song 7:12). The garden is so juicy—the female's "shoots are an orchard of pomegranates/ with all choicest fruits" (Song 4:13)—one cannot help but wonder if the poem is consciously recreating the sex Adam and Eve had before they knew shame and wore fig leaf crotch-covers.

In fact, other aspects of the poem likewise dissolve the shame that crept into Eden. Early in the poem, the female calls attention to what is conceivably a criticism to her beauty but for which she is shameless: "I am very dark, but comely, / O daughters of Jerusalem, / like the tents of Kedar, / like the curtains of Solomon. / Do not gaze at me because I am swarthy, / because the sun has scorched me" (Song 1:5-6). Most historians mention that over centuries people who are suntanned from field work have always been marked as lower class in contrast to untoasted royalty, sun-protected inside their residences, and indeed, in the next lines the female adds that the work in the sun was a punishment: "My mother's sons were angry with me, / they made me keeper of the vineyards" (Song 1:6). However, she also has no shame deflating the punishment, pointing to her beauty despite her dark skin and, as we saw above, transforming her vineyard work into luscious metaphors. We have no idea why her brothers are down on her, but sibling jealousy or jealousy of male lovers comes to mind when brothers boss sisters. In any case, she pays no heed to the brothers, and has given up on the work they demand, mentioning that her "own vineyard [she has] not kept!" (Song 1:6), allowing it to go to ruins.

In the next lines she asks the person "whom my soul loves" (Song 1:7) where he takes his flock, presumably so she can meet him and not wander into other males' territory. She wants him, only him, and there is no shame in her desire, further supporting the idea that this is an Eve redo, sans fig leaves, and in this Eden redux she is a bold female, focused on the person from whom she wants loving sex, probably a king—maybe even Solomon, since later in the poem a wedding procession with king Solomon breaks into the text out of nowhere, perhaps a dream, "coming up from the wilderness / like a column of smoke" (Song 3:6).

On the other hand, though shame is not a hindrance to sex, the sexual joy is never promiscuous; instead the sexiness grows out of a committed love that is the basis of marriage. For one thing, throughout the poem the female desires to have the mother's approval of the lover. At one point, when she is looking for her lover, the female affirms, "When I found him whom my soul loves, / I held him, and would not let him go / until I had brought him into my mother's house, / and into the chamber of her that conceived me" (Song 3:4), lines especially empathetic to her mother's emotional connection and her need for her lover to join in that family dynamic. Later the male connects with the female's mother by recognizing, "My dove, my perfect one, is only one, / the darling of her mother, / flawless to her that bore her" (Song 6:9) and then later proclaims, "Under the apple tree I awakened you. / There your mother was in travail with you, / there she who bore you was in travail" (Song 8:5). The male's identification with his female lover's conception and her mother is highly unusual in any love poem, which makes the reader wonder if, among other things, the poem is an allegory celebrating the universal female spirit that gives birth to passion and beauty in everything. In any case, the poem is partially about love of being part of a family, and the mother-birthing praise tempers the sexuality in the poem.

There is also a second theme that tempers the passion; one that confirms the love is a force outside of sexual gratification. Either the male or the chorus—impossible to be definitive since there are no dialogue labels—interrupts the female's desire to be loved up ("O that his left hand were under my head, / and that his right hand embraced me!" [Song 2:6]) to caution that love can neither be forced nor denied, but has a life of its own: "I adjure you, O daughters of Jerusalem, / by the gazelles or the hinds of the field, / that you stir not up nor awaken love / until it please" (Song 2:7)—these lines repeating again in 3:5 and near the end of the poem in 8:4. That such a solemn request is made in the name of gazelles reinforces a specific concept of love. Gazelles are extremely swift—sometimes bursting at sixty miles an hour—a delicate, sleek, quick-pivoting herd animals, at times airborne, outmaneuvering large cats such as cheetahs, usually evading them until the gazelles let their guard down, thinking they have lost their predator. In the context of this poem about passion, they are a symbol of love's mixture of ethereal beauty and energy that moves in unpredictable directions, maintaining its pulse as long as lovers' interest in each other does not rest in apathy or indifference. Gazelles glide through the whole poem, an embroidered motif: repeated three times in the "abjuring" statement; when the female says, "My beloved is like a gazelle, / or a young stag" (Song 2:9 and paraphrased again at 2:17); when the male tells her, "Your two breasts are like two fawns, / twins of a gazelle" (Song 4:5 and verbatim at 7:3); and when the poem ends with the female's demand to "make haste, my beloved, / and be like a gazelle / or a young stag / upon the mountains of spices" (Song 8:14). Gazelles are jumping everywhere.

A third element that expands the poem's content beyond the mere sexual has to do with the garden's depiction as a symbol not only for a place of luscious fruits, but also of a protected union under threat. Earlier the female had not tended her garden as demanded by her brothers, partially an act of rebellion but also perhaps a symbol for despair and not caring about herself. Later in the poem, the lover encourages renewed participation in the garden and thus care for herself, when he asks her to participate in protecting it: "Catch us the foxes, / the little foxes, / that spoil the vineyards, / for our vineyards are in blossom" (Song 2:15). The foxes could be symbolic of outside nuisances that often distract from tending a garden, nuisances or obligations whose demands sneak into a relationship and have the potential to ruin it. The garden is further defined as a metaphor for the lovers' relationship when the male proclaims, "A garden locked is my sister, my bride, / a garden locked, a fountain sealed" (Song 4:12), suggesting that their union is a commitment, protected and closed. Here and other places, the lovers refer to each other as a sister or brother, common references in Egyptian love poetry, also putting the relationship on a level of platonic love and not exclusively on sexual affection. The brother-sister motif is also seen as a protection from a world that frowns on sexual unions (and especially this one which could be between a king and a dark-skinned laborer), the female later wishing, "O that you were like a brother to me, / that nursed at my mother's breast! / If I met you outside, I would kiss you, / and none would despise me" (Song 8:1).

The concept of a locked garden is developed further by the male when he addresses the power of the commitment: "Set me as a seal upon your heart, / as a seal upon your arm; / for love is strong as death, / jealousy is cruel as the grave. / Its flashes are flashes of fire, a most vehement flame. / Many waters cannot quench love, / neither can floods drown it" (Song 8:6-7). The lock is a seal upon the heart, with perhaps a symbol of that union worn on the arm. By comparing the emotional strength of love to the overpowering finality of death, the male emphasizes the importance of the seal in keeping that love alive— and in protecting it from jealousy, something that can make love as hurtful or as sad as death. However, despite jealousy's vehement flame, the upside to the emotional intensity that can fire up that jealousy is that it is not easily distinguished. Love is a fertile garden that is always vulnerable to the cutworm, but it stays fertile.

A fourth element that complicates both the sexual and nonsexual love in the poem is the insecurity felt in the woman's sex nightmare. The woman sleeps but her "heart was awake" (Song 5:2), and she hears her lover knocking, calling out for his "sister, [his] love, / [his] dove, [his] perfect one" (Song 5:2) to open up. The woman mentions she is undressed, bathed, and "thrilled" when her lover puts "his hand to the latch" (Song 5:4), her fingers dripping with myrrh as she arises to let him in. The image reads as a wet dream, the dwelling a metaphor for the female's body, her wetness fueled by the emotions of the heart. The dream turns nightmarish, however, when she opens her door to find that her "beloved had turned and gone" (Song 5:6). In the next line, when she says, "My soul failed me when he spoke" (Song 5:6), one cannot wonder if this is a dream about her insecurity in responding to her lover effectively, expressing her feelings so that her lover will find her love credible, not reject her, not find her sexual openness solely tied to their appetites. She calls out for her lover, gets no response, and goes to look for him but is stripped and beaten by the town's watchmen (Song 5:7), a nightmare image that captures her sense of vulnerability from a failed attempt to connect with her lover. The dream ends with the woman or the chorus calling out to the daughters of Jerusalem to tell her lover that she is "sick with love" (Song 5:8).

While all the above dimensions reinforce the poem's emphasis on the sexual and spiritual connection between a man and woman, two strange metaphorical lists praising the lovers appear in the poem, which could be used as evidence that the poem is just as much about the love between people with their land, produce, and power. For instance, the male compares his lover's hair to "a flock of goats,

/ moving down the slopes of Gilead" (Song 4:1)—an image of vast distance and busyness, not just luster and flow; her teeth to "a flock of shorn ewes / that have come up from the washing, / all of which bear twins, / and not one among them is bereaved" (Song 4:2)—an even more elaborate image of busyness and successful production, grotesque when visualized as a mouth full of teeth; her cheeks to "halves of a pomegranate" (Song 4:3)—the inside slices sexual but the hard, red rounded outside suggests cheeks that are hard shells, not soft; her neck to the "tower of David, / built for an arsenal, / whereon hang a thousand bucklers, / all of them shields of warriors" (Song 4:4)—a praise more of a threatening, unapproachable fort than an elegant neck to be nuzzled; and her breasts to "two fawns, / twins of a gazelle" (Song 4:5)— metaphoric possibilities for gazelles listed above aside, fawns are images of bony restlessness, symbolic of a productive herd, soft only on their surface, not embodying the curves associated with breasts. Later in Chapter 7, the male continues giving compliments so that round thighs are compared to crafted jewels (Song 7:1), a navel to a rounded bowl (Song 7:2), belly to wheat (Song 7:2), a neck to an ivory tower (Song 7:4), a head to the city Carmel (Song 7:5), hair locks to the color purple (Song 7:5)—the color capturing exuberance and royalty rather than actual hair color—all body images disconnected from sensual metaphors but connected instead to the staples and products of a culture.

In further support for this being a poem about love of a specific culture, near the end of the poem, apropos of the stanza discussed above on the power of love and jealousy, the chorus chimes in with, "We have a little sister, / and she has no breasts. / What shall we do for our sister, / on the day when she is spoken for? / If she is a wall, / we will build upon her a battlement of silver; / but if she is a door, / we will enclose her with boards of cedar" (Song 8:8-9). The little sister has no connection with the full-breasted, courageous, questioning female of the poem up to this point, but instead to a new city. This is a new, chaste female city, not developed, one in need of a male workforce to turn her into a city of strength. This female takes part in the city or fortress metaphor, and takes credit for her developed power bringing positive results of peace, the archetypal function of everyone's feminine side: "I was a wall, / and my breasts were like towers; / then I was in his eyes / as one who brings peace" (Song 8:10). At the end of the poem, the female imagery shifts away from this city paradigm and instead we hear the voice of the previous, mature woman of the vineyards who feels comfortable with herself because of her love relationship with the male of the poem. She refers to Solomon having a vineyard that he leased out to workers who are to bring in a thousand pieces of silver, but as for her, she insists her vineyard is "my very own, is for myself; / you, O Solomon, may have the thousand, / and the keepers of the fruit two hundred" (Song 8:12), determining her own rules whereby the keepers get fair pay and she wants none of Solomon's wealth. The lines imply that she is an independent soul, not part of a wall system, further substantiated as she ends the poem by asking her beloved to make haste with their union.

Needless to say, this is a hectic poem that sends the reader in different directions, most likely because it is a blend of elements found in Greek, Mesopotamian, and Egyptian love poetry, dating anywhere from the tenth to second centuries BCE (although not part of the canon until the second century CE). Perhaps unintentionally, it became one of the seeds of a new tradition of multi-directional poetry that bounces between the sexual, religious, and political. However, the more conscious concept of smoothly combining sexual enticement with both loving affection and religious overtones did not come until centuries later, with poets such as John Donne (1572-1631). Donne, who had an assortment of mistresses but was also the dean of St. Paul's of London, found a poetic way of merging his praise of sexuality with his religious traditions. The element that made the merger more seamless than in Song of Solomon, however, was wit.

A good short example is his poem "The Flea,"[6] first published in 1633. The title humorously calls attention to the worth of a lowly insect whose bite will, as we shall see, diminish both the sinfulness of sexual appetite as well as the cost of satisfying sexual cravings, and yet still maintains the importance of the whole affair by recalling the importance of marriage as a holy sacrament, as it is still often referred to in the Anglican Church, with several other important associations. Here are the first six lines of the first stanza:

Mark but this flea, and mark in this,
How little that which thou deniest me is;
Me it sucked first, and now sucks thee,
And in this flea our two bloods mingled be;
Thou knowest that this cannot be said
A sin, or shame, or loss of maidenhood.

The mingling of blood carries a host of associations. In the Book of Leviticus, blood is viewed as such a strong energy force—"For the life of the flesh is in the blood; and I have given it for you upon the altar to make atonement for your souls" (Lev 17:11)—that to eat animals whose blood has not be drained is tantamount to eating them alive and not allowed. Centuries later the Christian Church mixed water and blood to create the "precious blood" in communion, a remembrance of Jesus's death and sacrifice. Marriage is sometimes viewed as the comingling of bloodlines or, more mythically, the completion of the circle of man and woman after their bodily separation when Adam's rib is torn from him to create woman, a new entity in Genesis. The mingling of blood is not a small deal.

Blood is also sexy. During sexual encounters the male phallus swells with blood entering inside the female, whose clitoral arteries fill with blood, together creating a special synergy between the couple. With tongue in cheek, the poet persona of Donne's poem takes any reservations or gravity of the comingling away for the female by saying this comingling has already happened before she has given it any thought. The humor comes from the idea that a flea can act as a sexual intermediary, fucking both the male and female before they settle on doing it. The word in the poem is "suck," but in the facsimile of the poem, the long "s" used by printers in the seventeenth and eighteenth centuries, which is neither like the normal "s'" or "f" used in the rest of the poem, looks much more like an "f." (Of course "suck" is even sexual compared to "bite.")

Unlike the female in the Song of Solomon, who is as sexually forceful as the male, the persona of Donne's poem assumes the female is coy—or is he pretending she is coy? Or is she pretending to be coy? If her coyness is only a ploy, she likely finds the blend of blood, sex, and fleas amusing. Humor adds a dimension to the love poem that is missing in Song of Solomon, and Donne's poem suggests a relationship based not only on sex but appreciation of humor, of the ability to see everything in the world—including such serious endeavors as marriage and other religious ceremonies—as amusingly faulty, a more irreverent worldview that highlights this special attribute not shared by all couples. The last three playful rhyming lines of the first stanza even take the female to task for being party to the flea getting more satisfaction than the two lovers (and without social courtship or foreplay), his swelling with blood reminiscent of an erection: "Yet this enjoys before it woo, / And pampered swells with one blood made of two, / And this alas is more than we would do."

Almost a parody of Jesus explaining a parable, in the second stanza the male persona develops the significance of killing the flea, raising the importance of the consequences. The stanza begins with a dramatic demand on the female, "Oh stay"—meaning refrain or stop:

> Oh stay, three lives in one flea spare,
> Where we almost, nay more than married are.
> The flea is you and I, and this
> Our marriage bed and marriage temple is;
> Though parents grudge, and you, we are met,
> And cloistered in these living walls of jet.
>   Though use make you apt to kill me
>   Let not to that, self-murder added be,
>   And sacrilege, three sins in killing three.

The lowly, pesky flea consecrates the marriage, the comingling of fluids taking place inside its body, which becomes a mock "marriage bed and marriage temple" and a holy "cloistered" space pulsing with pure black (jet) ceremonial walls, a protection from disapproving parents. The male, with humorous self-deprecation, points to his habitual rejection by his lover—"Though use make you apt to kill me"—alarming with the hyperbolic command to not commit sacrilege: the sin of killing the her-him-flea trinity, the holy of holies, the holy spirit of "you and I." "Kill me," moreover, was often a metaphor for orgasm (again adding to the idea that the persona is pretending his lady friend is coy). Donne creates just the right balance of seriousness and humor. A lover with a sense of humor has to be amused by the holy flea fuck; a lover without a sense of humor would have left. Again, it is wit that solves the problem found in Song of Solomon as it tries to blend care for another person with themes that are outside the lovers' realm: in Donne, sex outside of marriage successfully blends with religious sanctity; in Song of Solomon, sexual attraction clashes with metaphors that point to love of the land and culture. Now, in the last stanza of "The Flea," the action takes place out of our view—the female kills the flea, and the male persona takes her to task:

> Cruel and sudden, hast thou since
> Purpled thy nail in blood of innocence?
> Wherein could this flea guilty be,
> Except in that drop which it sucked from thee?
> Yet thou triumph'st, and say'st that thou
> Find'st not thy self nor me the weaker now;
>   'Tis true; then learn how false fears be:
>   Just so much honor, when thou yield'st to me,
>   Will waste, as this flea's death took life from thee.

The humor here derives from an incredulous question: why, despite hearing all the rationales for sanctified sex already having taken place thanks to the holy flea, does the lover, without compunction, kill the innocent flea with her nail (the female's nail size again reminding the reader of the flea's tininess and insignificance)? "Purple," instead of "red," suggests royal robes, an arrogant ruler who kills the innocent, and some critics have suggested it recalls Herod's killing of the innocents in the Gospel of Matthew. When the female lover points out that nothing seems lost by the flea's death in terms of both lovers' well-being, she provides the male persona with another excuse to reference their fucking directly instead of through the flea, as involving no more lost honor as this dead flea took from her to begin with: "Just so much honor, when thou yield'st to me, / Will waste, as this flea's death took life from thee."

It is true that Song of Solomon is more sensual, gives more homage to a parent, defines the energy of love through the gazelle, at times suggests love of the land and culture, but aside from these elements being forced together erratically, the poem's lack of a sense of humor about them all, as with many love poems, leaves out a crucial element that makes relationships strong. Many intuitively recognize this importance and will say they want a partner with a sense of humor, but often they mean someone who is not serious or dour. Indeed, we do not always clearly define what we mean when listing this quality as a desired trait in a mate. Cutesy? Smart-ass? Cliché? John Donne's humor is dark and clever. One should only wish to have a partner who puts such energy into a relationship. The inability to laugh, or even sincerely smile, at both the sacred and profane puts one on the road to disappointment, delusion, fanaticism, and failed relationships.

Through close reading of metaphor, diction and syntax, Song of Solomon, as with Psalms and Proverbs, has much to offer. However, when all three books are compared, based on common themes, with poetry that comes later, one is struck by the complexity or depth missing in the Biblical poetry. The pairings leave one wondering how much would have been gained if Proverbs had incorporated more rebel cries from Blake's hell or parts of the Song of Solomon had the wit brought by Donne's flea. How amazed would we be if the uniform visions and rhythms of the Psalms had been interrupted by Dickinson's carriage jolts as the psalmists described our runs past the setting sun?

AFTERWORD

T he characters in the Bible live. They are brought to life as soon as we enter their stories. They are a blend of reality and myth, but because of the work of many writers, most of whom we will never know, melding their observations of other people with their own personal experiences to breathe life into creations from centuries ago, they are nonetheless fully alive. Why fret about whether David or Jesus existed in the flesh? As we have witnessed, they could not be more vibrantly present. Yes, they are constructs, but on some level we all are—especially after we die and our story is told, if not written, carried in the minds of those who bereave us until they also die. Even as we live and breathe, we are all constructs of inner thoughts and outer actions, of what we learn through personal experience and what we learn from others, of what outsiders think of us, sometimes getting close to how we see ourselves, sometimes seeing parts of us to which we are blind, but contributing to an idea of who we are nonetheless.

Whether David, Jesus, or anyone else in the Bible really existed in the flesh is of no more consequence than if Hamlet or Huck Finn lived in the flesh. In some ways, the characters in literature are more alive to us than some in the physical world because their storyteller has allowed us to enter their inner lives, to understand their thoughts and emotions and basest desires. In real life, we only get limited glimpses of others' internal worlds. Storytellers create from careful observations, partially from their imagination, partially from past stories told by others, and partially from personal experiences. A truly effective storyteller knows that details have to be carefully selected, edited to interest a reader or listener, but also presented with the belief that the character's story is worth telling to anyone, including strangers, offering something universal that others can learn from.

Resurrecting lives by creating stories is nothing short of a miraculous feat, a miracle that rests on the storyteller's belief that a specific life is worthy of being kept alive for personal reasons; then on the storyteller's desire to show that life to others; and finally on the storyteller's ability to craft that story so others can step into it and at the same time perceive the significance of it. I praise Mark (perhaps a pseudonym, the writer's own construct) for resurrecting Jesus, even though we can never know how much of the resurrection is based on direct observation of Jesus himself, or on others serving as a model for Jesus, or on Mark's own imagination. We can never know, yet Jesus lives!

The Lord also lives. However, I have heard two conflicting clichés all my life: that everyone's idea of God is a personal matter; and yet that all the great religions worship the same God. I have also heard the cliché that the Old Testament God is a jealous God and the New Testament God is a loving god. However, *Pomegranate Gospel* makes clear that the character of the Lord varies per writer and is a function of how that writer sees fate, love and hate, power and strife. The satisfied God who creates the world in seven days is not the same emotionally-bent God of the Garden of Eden, and neither God is the one with a sense of humor in Jonah, or with neuroses in Exodus, or the nerviness to gamble with Satan in Job, or the God who makes ridiculous demands to get more personal credit in Judges, or the God who stands back so that love can operate in Ruth. We have seen why the God contemplated by Mark's Jesus is not the same God imagined by the Apostle John. God has many faces in the Bible, and we owe his creators credit for dramatizing how our cosmos could be controlled by any one of them at any time.

The many faces of God only become clear, however, when one pushes back against the simplified understanding of the Bible prevalent in our culture today. As *Pomegranate Gospel* makes evident, the books of the Bible all need revivals, retellings mixed with literary interpretation, because secondary storytellers often obscured the core stories. The books also need revivals because for centuries the stories have been thought of primarily as sacred texts, an approach that distracts both the faithful and the atheist from perceiving many of the Bible's secular literary values. My hope is that *Pomegranate Gospel* has knocked down some of the barriers that have prevented many from reading the Bible as literature and that this book serves as a model for others to join the interpretive dialogue started by so many great thinkers, writers, and painters over the centuries. My desire is to provoke a new interest in readers to notice details I point out and ones I leave aside, and then build enthusiasm for contemplating those details' significances, many having become devalued or lost over time. Tasting these seeds of interpretations can add so much to our lives. After all, like all great literature, the Bible is a cautionary tale, revealing the pitfalls of life before we blindly step into them, and at the same time, dramatizing morals and values for us to believe in for our emotional, political, intellectual, and spiritual health.

SOURCES

Chapter 2

1. Op-Ed. "Book Burning that Worked," *The New York Times*. April 25, 1997. Web. http://www.nytimes.com/1997/04/25/opinion/book-burning-that-worked.html 13 July, 2015.

Chapter 6

1. Mayo Clinic Staff. "Sibling Rivalry: Helping your children get along." *Healthy Lifestyle, Children's Health*. MAYO CLINIC. 20 February 2015. Web. 5 June 2015.

2. Kramer, Dr. Laurie. "Supporting Sibling Relationships." *Sibling Development: Implications for Mental Health Practitioners*. Ed. Dr. Jonathan Caspi. New York: Spring Publishing Company, 2011, 41-58. Print.

3. Melville, Herman. "Billy Budd, Sailor." *Billy Budd and Other Stories*. New York: Penguin Group, 1986. Print.

4. Hoffman, Dr. Casey, child psychologist. Personal Interview. 23 June 2015.

5. Pernoff, J., Ruffman T., & Leekam, S. R. (1994). "Theory of mind is contagious: You catch it from your sibs." *Child Development*, 65, 1228-1238. Print.

6. Caspi, Dr. Jonathan, ed. "Preface." *Sibling Development: Implications for Mental Health Practitioners*. New York: Spring Publishing Company, 2011, xiii-xvii. Print.

Chapter 7

1. Eshman, Rob "Wolpe's Hurricane," *Jewish Journal of Greater Los Angeles*. April 19, 2001. http://www.jewishjournal.com/rob_eshman/article/wolpes_hurricane_20010420

2. *Decalogue* (*Dekalog*). Director: Krzysztof Kieslowski. Performers: Olgierd Lukaszewicz. Facets Video, 1989. Film.

Chapter 12
1. Emerson, Ralph Waldo. "The Divinity School Address." *Ralph Waldo Emerson Texts. The American Scholar*, 3 Sept. 2009. Web. 10 July, 2015.

Chapter 14
1. Garrett, George, "David." Editor D.G. Kehl. *Poetry and the Visual Arts*. Belmont, California: Wadsworth Publishing Company, Inc., 1975. Print.

2. Paglia, Camille. *Sexual Personae*. New York: Vintage Books: 1991. Print.

Chapter 18
1. Blake, William. "Proverbs of Hell." *The Marriage of Heaven and Hell*. General Editor M. H. Abrams. *The Norton Anthology of English Literature*, Vol. II. 5th edition. New York: W.W. Norton & Co., 1986. Print.

2. Twain, Mark. *Adventures of Huckleberry Finn*. Mineola, New York: Dover Publications Inc., 1994. Print.

3. Hill, Kim. "Psalm 1." *Testimony*. Comp. Michele Wagner. Reunion Records, 1995. CD.

4. Stuart, Andy. Personal interview. 19 July 2015.

5. Dickinson, Emily. "Because I could not stop for Death—" General Editor Nina Baym. *The Norton Anthology of American Literature*, Volume C. 6th edition. New York: W. W. Norton & Co., 2003. Print.

6. Donne, John. "The Flea." General Editor M. H. Abrams. *The Norton Anthology of English Literature*. Vol. I. 5th edition. New York: W. W. Norton & Co., 1986. Print.

INDEX